AUSTRALIAN COMMEMORATIVE POSTMARKS

4th Edition
2024

PETER JAMES BOND, PUBLISHER

Australian Commemorative Postmarks
4th edition, 2024

Editor: Peter Bond

ISBN 978-0-6487713-6-4

First edition published in Australia in 2014

Cover background image courtesy photos-public-domain.com

Peter James Bond, Publisher

COPYRIGHT NOTICE
All rights reserved. No part of this publication may be reproduced, stored in a retrieval system, or transmitted, in any form or by any means, electronic, mechanical, photocopying, recording or otherwise (except under the statutory exceptions provisions of the *Australian Copyright Act 1968*) without the prior written permission of the publisher.

Contents

Introduction
   Scope 4
   Definitions 4
   Numbering 5
   Rarity 5
   Values 6
   Entries in this Guide 6
   Images 6

Part 1 – The Pre-decimal Years
1879 – 1900 7
• *1879 Sydney International Exhibition* 9
1901 – 1929 11
1930 – 1939 16
   1932 17
   1933 18
   1934 19
   1935 21
   1936 21
   1937 23
   1938 25
   1939 28
• *A Cinderella Story* 29
1940 – 1949 30
   1940 31
   1945 33
   1946 33
   1947 33
   1948 35
   1949 37
• *Australian Philatelic Exhibition Postmarks* . . 39
1950 – 1954 42
   1950 43
   1951 45
   1952 45
   1953 47
   1954 49

1955 – 1959 51
   1955 51
   1956 53
   1957 59
   1958 59
   1959 61
• *Commemorative Postmarks on Registered Covers* 64
   1960 66
   1961 71
   1962 75
   1963 80
   1964 84
   1965 96

Part 2 – The Decimal Years
1966 91
1967 95
1968 103
1969 106
1970 111
1971 120
1972 130
1973 137
1974 143
1975 150
1976 155
1977 162
1978 171
• *1980 and All That* 181
1979 184
1980 198
1981 – 2023 212

Outro 249
Bibliography 250
Also Published by Peter James Bond 251

INTRODUCTION

Several books have been published on the subject of Australian postmarks. Before the first edition of this title in 2014, none dedicated solely to postmarks used for special events were in print.

Research is always in progress, and the editor invites readers to contribute data for an improved future edition. One area, in particular, can benefit from collector assistance. Where official statistics are lacking, the number of Registered covers bearing a specific postmark can only be estimated. If you own a Registered cover with a higher numbered R6 label than identified in this guide, you are invited to contact the editor:

Peter Bond
PO Box 964
ROSNY PARK   TAS   7018
Australia

SCOPE

This guide covers the following Australian commemorative postmarks:
- short-term hand-applied postmarks used for specific events and anniversaries, including postmarks such as showground cancels used for any event where a temporary post office was provided
- as above but machine-printed postmarks where a hand-cancel equivalent was also used or was designed to appear to be a hand-applied postmark.

Postmarks not included are:
- long-term or permanent pictorial postmarks (e.g. Ayres Rock)
- seasonal usage postmarks which do not mark a recurring event (e.g. Mt Kosciusko)
- relief postmarks
- Australian Antarctic Territory postmarks
- FDI (first day of issue) postmarks.

Collectors often used FDCs when a commemorative postmark coincided with a related or other stamp issue. Such instances are recorded in this guide, but listing the various publishers of such covers is outside its scope.

Entries in the guide include event-specific illustrated, generic (i.e. other) illustrated, and plain covers. Where examples are unlikely to exist or have not been verified, they are omitted.

DEFINITIONS

Ordinary Covers:

Non-Registered and non-Certified covers, including postcards, postal cards, aerogrammes, and other postal stationery. The category is divided into:

Event-specific illustrated covers:

Event-specific illustrated covers are those printed expressly for the event a postmark relates to. They may be printed with text only, without any illustration. Entries in this guide will identify the particular cover, except where the editor has not yet sighted an example. In this case, it will be described as 'event-specific illustrated cover'. Plain covers with promotional stickers or labels (i.e. Cinderellas) affixed are not taken to be illustrated.

Other illustrated covers:

These are usually envelopes illustrated with a generic design. Commonly encountered examples are:
- Australian Post Office Communications 'Hermes' first day cover
- Australian Post Office 'shield' first day cover
- Australian Post Office 'map and wattle' philatelic cover (from 10 August 1972)
- Australia Post Wildlife series 1 (i.e. kangaroo, koala, kookaburra) souvenir cover (from April 1977)
- First day and souvenir covers from private publishers such as Seven Seas Stamps, Wesley Cover Service, Royal and Excelsior.

This category includes covers printed for a stamp issued close to or during the currency of the postmark but not directly related to the postmark event. An example is the 1953 Young Farmers' Clubs stamp issued on 3 September 1953, which was also the first day of the Brighton Philatelic Exhibition (BRIPEX).

Plain covers:

A plain cover is a blank envelope or one that shows only a printed business address and/or logo but not one related to the postmark event. This category may also include pre-paid and post-paid postal cards. Most collectors prefer an illustrated cover over a plain envelope, though an apparently non-philatelic cover will hold more appeal to some.

Registered and Certified Covers:

This refers to items sent by Registered or Certified mail.

NUMBERING

Each entry in this guide is allocated an identifying number commencing with the event number. For events where more than one postmark was provided, the event number has an alphabetical suffix.

The secondary numbering system has been changed from previous editions of this publication to simplify entries. The secondary number previously identified an entry as event-specific, other illustrated, plain covers, etc. It is now a simple sequence.

Registered and Certified covers have the letter 'R' or 'C' suffixed to the entry number. Modern postmarks are found on these covers in very low numbers, and most entries have the secondary number as a wild card (#), which can be replaced with '1' or '2', etc., as appropriate.

RARITY

A postmark's availability plays the most significant part in determining its value. From 1953, with only a few exceptions, statistics were kept on the number of articles processed with each postmark. Any modern postmark with which more than 4,000 mail items were processed can be regarded as common, but only relatively. Australian stamps in such low numbers are highly valued and fetch more than similarly quantified postmarks.

The jewel of any event is usually a Registered cover, particularly if a dedicated R6 label was made available. These can exist in tiny numbers, often fewer than 50 and sometimes only in single figures.

VALUES

In the first edition of this guide, many items were listed without an indication of value. For this edition, all items are valued, but it is stressed that the value is notional for many. Scarcer items come on the market only infrequently, and establishing a realistic value is difficult.

There are many factors that collectors should consider when deciding what an item is worth to them.
- **Supply** – a combination of the number produced, survival rate and how often they come on the market.
- **Demand** – the market competition for an item.
- **Condition** – the older the item, the more likely its condition will have deteriorated; defects may include creasing, scuffing, edge knocks and tears, general grubbiness and 'rust'. Modern covers are generally over-the-counter products and rarely pass through the postal system. For these, you may rightly demand pristine condition. Except when very scarce, defective items should be considered spacefillers only.

Modern, relatively common material can realistically be valued at only a couple of dollars. Thematic considerations come into play with popular subjects increasing demand. Of course, it's just as likely that more examples exist anyway because of that popularity.

The values listed in this guide are drawn from dealers' regular channels, including online and published price lists and private sales online. Where sales activity is minimal or effectively non-existent, values have been extrapolated from theoretical availability.

With a few exceptions, the lowest value assigned to the more common (usually modern) items is two dollars.

All values are quoted in Australian dollars.

ENTRIES IN THIS GUIDE

Items are included in this guide 'as appropriate'. For example, no event-specific covers are listed where none has been sighted and/or is unlikely to exist. It seems that, in Australia at least, the concept of generic illustrated covers is relatively modern. For events before 1950, 'other illustrated covers' will not be listed until their existence can be verified.

Other illustrated covers may not be listed for modern postmarks, where event-specific covers are commonly encountered. These are generally, though not always, valued at half to three-quarters of the event-specific equivalent.

From 1970, plain covers may not be included in this guide, though they certainly exist. Should a market eventuate for such items, all will be included in a future edition. However, plain cover entries are now included for postmarks of fewer than 1,000 recorded impressions. Values would typically be less than an illustrated cover.

Entries for recurring events, such as Sydney's Royal Easter Show, are now included chronologically, whereas, in the first edition of this guide, they were all listed under the earliest instance. To identify events as recurring, occurrences after the first event are indicated in *italics*.

IMAGES

Postmarks are illustrated using scans of genuine examples, where clear examples could be sourced. Others, particularly early postmarks, have been digitally reconstructed for clarity. These are stylistically as close as possible to the original design.

This guide illustrates covers from the editor's collection and several collectors who have generously allowed them to be reproduced. Most prefer to remain anonymous. The editor gratefully acknowledges these contributors.

Part 1
The Pre-decimal Years

1879 - 1900

EVENTS

001	1879	Sydney International Exhibition
002	1880	Melbourne International Exhibition
003	1887	Jubilee Exhibition
004	1887	Geelong Jubilee Juvenile and Industrial Exhibition
005	1888	Melbourne Centennial International Exhibition
006	1894	Tasmanian International Exhibition

001   001.2

001   **1879 SYDNEY INTERNATIONAL EXHIBITION**
Garden Palace, Sydney, NSW
17 Sep 1879 – 20 Apr 1880

Qty: 26,536
001.1	plain cover	$1000
001.2	on stamp	$200

003   003.2

003   **1887 JUBILEE EXHIBITION**
Adelaide, SA
21 Jun 1887 – 7 Jan 1888

003.1	plain cover	$300
003.2	on stamp	$150

002A   002B

002   **1880 MELBOURNE INTERNATIONAL EXHIBITION**
Melbourne, Vic
1 Oct 1880 – 31 Mar 1881

002A-B.1	International Exhibition cover	$600
002A-B.2	plain cover	$300
002A.3	on stamp	50.00
002B.4	on stamp	50.00

004

004   **1887 GEELONG JUBILEE JUVENILE AND INDUSTRIAL EXHIBITION**
Geelong, Vic
22 Nov 1887 – 17 Feb 1888

004.1	plain cover	$400
004.2	on stamp	$200

005A 005B 005B1 006

005	**1888 MELBOURNE CENTENNIAL INTERNATIONAL EXHIBITION**		006	**1894 TASMANIAN INTERNATIONAL EXHIBITION**	
	Melbourne, Vic			Hobart, Tas	
	1 Aug 1888 – 31 Jan 1889			15 Nov 1894 – 15 May 1895	
005A-B.1	plain cover	$500	006.1	plain cover	$500
005A.1	on stamp	$100	006.2	on stamp	$200
005B.1	on stamp	$100			

Note: In this group (001-006), values quoted are indicative only.

006.1 | 1894 Tasmanian International Exhibition

For many early postmarks, a fantasy cover is the best most collectors could aspire to. This example exists only digitally and is a rendition of the postmark on a scan of a genuine 1½d Exhibition postcard. The real thing would be a remarkable find.

1879 Sydney International Exhibition

The Allure of Number 1

Number 1.

It has a certain cachet. It's special. A number one result in a race or election means a win. In most pursuits, to be number one is a triumph. But being first is sometimes just an accident of history. Had circumstances been different, the first man to walk on the moon could have been a Soviet cosmonaut.

The first circumnavigation of the world in a single voyage might not have been the expedition attributed to Ferdinand Magellan. If other countries' governments had been more enlightened, the world's first postage stamp might not have been Great Britain's Penny Black in 1840. Number one is a memorable thing. Few people would remember which horse ran second in last year's Melbourne Cup. It was just the first of the losers.

Not many people could name a single event in Australia in 1879. Yet the Sydney International Exhibition, which opened in September of that year, holds a place in the minds of at least some collectors of Australian postmarks.

With a little foresight, the first commemorative postmark may have been for the first government railway in Western Australia, which opened for traffic in July 1879. Even earlier, in March, a wrought-iron bridge crossing the Murray River in South Australia was opened, but without any celebration. In a case of historical curiosity, the artist and writer Norman Lindsay was born in 1879. He was afforded a commemorative postmark in 1979 to mark the centenary of his birth.

So it is that the 1879 Sydney International Exhibition is number one, and not only for its claim in producing the first Australian commemorative postmark. It was the first such exhibition held in the southern hemisphere, though its international

001.1 | 1879 Sydney International Exhibition

One of only two covers known showing the 991 barred numeral canceller (in this instance inverted), used at Garden Palace, the site of the exhibition.

Collection: Powerhouse Museum, Sydney.

claim is tenuous, as only seven other countries were invited to participate. Never intended to be global in reach, and despite claims to the contrary, it was not a World Expo. However, let us not allow semantics to detract from a remarkable event. Several earlier exhibitions had already been held in Melbourne and Sydney, dating back to 1854, but the 1879 event was noteworthy in several respects.

To begin, what was to be called the Garden Palace was built specifically to house the exhibition. Named for its proximity to Sydney's Botanic Gardens, it was sited on the Domain, though the grounds are now incorporated into the Gardens. The designer was Colonial Architect James Barnet. This urban visionary had already designed many courthouses and post offices in New South Wales, including the then incomplete General Post Office.

A post office was established at the main entrance of the exhibition grounds. Open for the duration, it operated from 17 September 1879 till 20 April 1880. Barred numeral canceller 991 was provided to postmark mail. Some 26,536 items are recorded as having been lodged at the post office. Remarkably, only two covers are known to have survived. One of these is held in the Powerhouse Museum, Sydney. Presumably, it will remain in the collection permanently.

Another item held at the Museum, of interest to philatelists, is a cover which would have been ideal for securing an example of BN 991. Posted five weeks before the exhibition's opening, it is the Sydney International Exhibition 'business' envelope. Sadly, as far as this writer knows, no such covers have come to light.

Values assigned to this postmark are purely notional, at $1000 for a plain cover and $200 for the postmark 'on stamp'. However, a collector would be very fortunate to find examples for less. Indeed, to locate a cover at all, at any price, would be astonishing.

None of the 19th-century Australian postmarks considered commemorative are easy to find. Most collectors content themselves by beginning their album with the 1905 five-pence diadem stamp jubilee postmark. The digital creation of phantom covers can include earlier cancels, though this is somewhat cheating. The card illustrated is such an example and, while only a Photoshop-created pretence, at least shows what might have been.

But isn't that the allure of number one?

001.1 | 1879 Sydney International Exhibition

A digital fantasy cover.

1901 – 1929

EVENTS

007	1905	Jubilee of 5d Diadem Stamp
008	1907	Australian Exhibtion of Women's Work
009	1914	First Australian Aerial Mail – Melbourne to Sydney
010	1917	Australian Aerial Mail – Mt Gambier to Melbourne
011	1920	First Aerial Mail – Great Britain to Australia
012	1920	National Rifle Association of NSW Annual Prize Meeting
013	1921	First Regular Aerial Mail – Perth to Derby
014	1928	4th International Philatelic Exhibition (ANPEX)

007

008

007 1905 JUBILEE OF 5D DIADEM STAMP

Sydney, NSW
1 – 2 Dec 1905

007.1	Sydney Philatelic Club souvenir postcard	$150
007.2	plain cover	$100
007.3	on stamp	50.00

Extract from *The Australian Philatelist*, 1 July 1905:

'… as the leading philatelic institution in New South Wales, the Sydney Philatelic Club should take the form of celebration in its own hand. Were it not that the postal administration of this state is now a Federal concern, something might be suggested to the postal authorities. But in the interest of collectors we are against the issue of a special stamp for the occasion. It is very likely that the matter will be broached at the annual meeting in July of the Sydney Philatelic Club, and some definite steps taken to mark the jubilee.'

Extract from the *Sydney Morning Herald*, Monday, 4 December 1905:

The New South Wales five-penny stamp enjoys the distinction of being the oldest postage stamp in use in the world. The occasion of its jubilee was celebrated by philatelists on Saturday evening by a conversazione held at St James's Hall, Phillip Street, which was attended by a large number of enthusiastic stamp collectors, devotees of this hobby, which was referred to by Mr H Montgomery Hamilton during the evening as "a harmless species of insanity." The venerable five-pence, surrounded by its contemporaries of former years, long since cancelled and defunct, received due homage from those worshippers. "They don't print stamps like that now," signed one of them, indicating the delicate lines of the steel plate engraving. "Such stamps as live in these degenerate days" evidently have not the merit of their ancestors, in the opinion of the discriminating philatelist.

008 1907 AUSTRALIAN EXHIBITION OF WOMEN'S WORK

Melbourne, Vic
23 Oct – 30 Nov 1907

008/005B.1	pictorial postcard	$200
008/005B.2	plain cover	$125
008.3	on stamp	75.00

This exhibition of over 16,000 exhibits from Australia and around the world demonstrated the advancement of women in various fields. It included displays of arts and crafts, including painting, drawing, sculpture, photography, pottery, needlework, leatherwork, woodwork, spinning, and weaving. There were also demonstrations of shorthand, typewriting, music, elocution, games and sports. An onsite crèche allowed mothers to view the exhibition while their children were cared for. Entries were open to all women and girls resident in Australia, including Aboriginal women, when indigenous people were not recognised equally in Australia. The exhibition was instigated by Lady Northcote, wife of the governor-general.

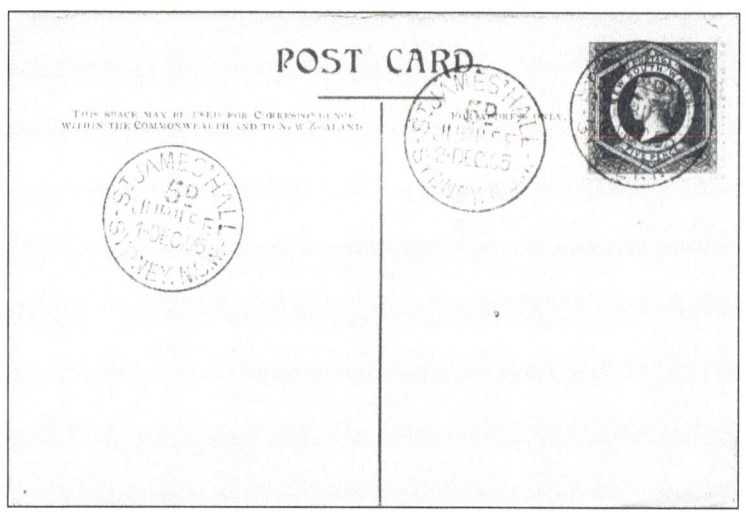

007.1 | 1 and 2 December 1905

Jubilee of 5d Diadem Stamp postcard

An example with two strikes of the postmark, showing both dates.

The Sydney Philatelic Club held an exhibition to coincide with the 50th anniversary of the 5d Diadem stamp.

Four types of postcard were produced to commemorate the two day event.

010.1 | 27 February 1917

Australian Aerial Mail - Mt Gambier to Melbourne

This mail was carried by Basil Watson in an aeroplane he built himself. The flight left Mt. Gambier on 15 February 1917 and, with four intermediate stops, arrived in Melbourne on 27 February where the postmark was applied to the 1,331 items carried.

Tragically, Watson died in a plane crash a month later, on 28 March 1917.

009 **1914 FIRST AUSTRALIAN AERIAL MAIL – MELBOURNE TO SYDNEY**

Melbourne, Vic
16 Jul 1914

Qty: 1,785

009.1	Souvenir Australian Aerial Mail postcard	$500
009.2	plain cover	$2,500
009.3	on stamp	$250

From Melbourne to Sydney, Australia's first official airmail was carried in a Bleriot XI monoplane by Ernest François (Maurice) Guillaux. Souvenir cards were issued and sold at one shilling each, and the post office prepared a special oval cachet for the mail carried. These cards required the standard one-penny postage. Correspondence was cancelled in Melbourne with the cachet in violet ink and backstamped on arrival in Sydney.

All mail carried was then forwarded to the address by ordinary mail. Newspapers of the time reported that several letters were carried in addition to the souvenir postcards. In *The Australian Air Mail Catalogue*, Nelson Eustis reports that two such covers remain extant. The total mail weighing 40 pounds (18kg) comprised 1,785 items, most of which were postcards. Guillaux also had the honour of carrying Australia's first air freight, Lipton tea and some O.T. lemon squash.

Gullaux was in Australia for seven months. His July 1914 airmail flight was then the longest such route in the world. The fiftieth anniversary of this event was commemorated by two Australian postage stamps issued in 1964.

While testing a prototype Morane-Saulnier aircraft, Guillaux was killed when it crashed at Villacoublay, France, on 21 May 1917.

010 **1917 AUSTRALIAN AERIAL MAIL – MT GAMBIER TO MELBOURNE**

Melbourne, Vic
27 Feb 1917

Qty: 1,331

010.1	Souvenir Australian Aerial Mail postcard	$350
010.2	on stamp	$200

This 12-day journey was made by the aviator Basil Watson, flying a home-built biplane. He left Mt Gambier, South Australia, on 15 February and made four intermediate stops before reaching Melbourne on 27 February. Souvenir postcards, costing one shilling each (plus one-penny postage), were carried and postmarked on arrival. Tragically, Watson was killed when his plane crashed a month later.

011 **1920 FIRST AERIAL MAIL – GREAT BRITAIN TO AUSTRALIA**

Melbourne, Vic
26 Feb 1920

Qty: 364

011.1	plain cover	$5,000
011.2	on Aerial Mail label	$3,000

On 12 November 1919, a Vickers Vimy aircraft (registration G-EAOU) took off from London, competing in the England-Australia Air Race. It landed in Darwin on 10 December, piloted by Captain Ross Smith, winning the £10,000 prize.

On arrival, the flight became the first to carry airmail from Great Britain to Australia. This, the most famous Australian airmail, was a minimal cargo. Reaching Melbourne on 25 February 1920, commemorative First Aerial Post labels were affixed to 364 items.

The three-line cachet, Per / Vickers "Vimy" Aeroplane / to Australia, was applied to (it is estimated) less than half the mail carried. This cachet adds to the value of covers, especially if a clear impression.

The First Aerial Post label was printed by the Australian Government stamp printer in Melbourne. Of the 576 labels printed, 364 were affixed to mail items. This label and the aerial mail covers represent the gold standard of an Australian airmail collection.

012 **1920 NATIONAL RIFLE ASSOCIATION OF NSW ANNUAL PRIZE MEETING**

ANZAC Rifle Range, NSW
15 Oct 1920

012.1.20	plain cover	$100

This postmark is reported to have been used annually at the ANZAC Rifle Range (near Liverpool) till 1938, then from 1948 to 1967. Use of the ANZAC Rifle Range postmark was discontinued when the National Rifle Association of NSW moved to Malabar. The range was closed at the end of 1967. Shooting activities were transferred to the Long Bay Rifle Range, renamed the ANZAC Rifle Range in 1973.

The Malabar (postcode 2036) Licensed Post Office is nearby, negating the need for a temporary post office during Annual Prize Meetings.

Only years of usage sighted by the editor are listed. As other instances are verified, they will be added with the relevant year suffix.

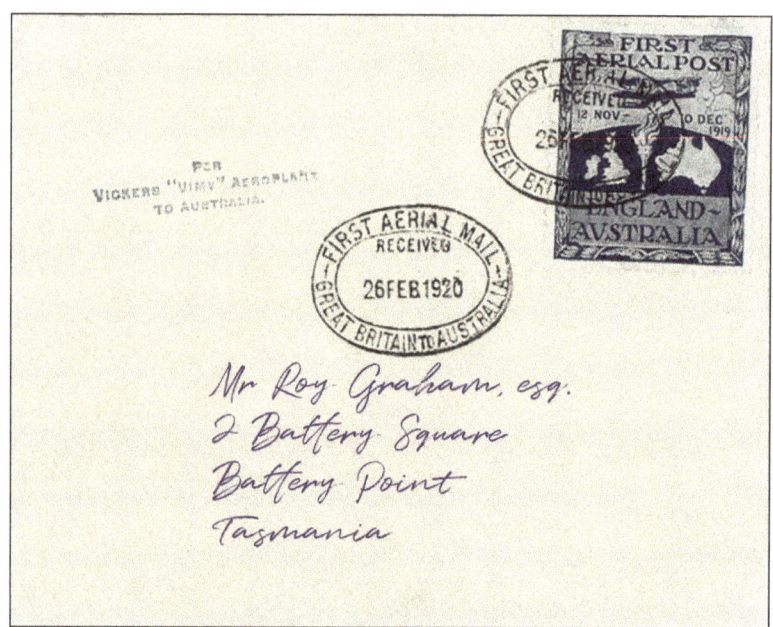

011.1 | 27 February 1917

First Aerial Mail - Great Britain to Australia

A genuine envelope digitally enhanced.

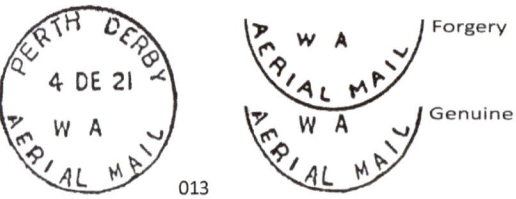

013 1921 FIRST REGULAR AERIAL MAIL – PERTH TO DERBY

Perth / Derby, WA
4 Dec 1921

Qty: 2,288

013.1	plain cover	$800
013.1R	plain cover Registered	$2,000
013.2	on stamp	$200

Forgeries of this postmark exist but are easily identified. In particular, on the genuine postmark, the second 'A' of AERIAL is narrow, on the forgery it is wider.

Ordinary cover

014.1	International Philatelic Exhibition cover	$175
014.2	'Ackland' souvenir card	50.00
014.3	plain cover	25.00
014.4	plain cover with 3d Kookaburra miniature sheet	$400
014.5	on 3d Kookaburra stamp	10.00
014.6	on 3d Kookaburra miniature sheet	$350

Registered cover Qty: est. 700*

014.1R	International Philatelic Exhibition cover	$200
014.3R	plain cover	$150

* Highest R6 number sighted: 627 (31 Oct 1928).

Related stamp issue:
29 Oct 1928 – 3d and 4 x 3d miniature sheet, 4th Australian International Philatelic Exhibition (SG106, MS106a)

This postmark was applied in red, green and blue inks, apparently at random. Red is the most commonly found. The postmark images presented here are digital reconstructions.

014 red   014 green   014 blue

014 1928 4TH INTERNATIONAL PHILATELIC EXHIBITION (ANPEX)

Melbourne, Vic
29 Oct – 1 Nov 1928

Philatelic exhibitions have been held in Australia since at least 1894, when the Philatelic Society of Victoria hosted an event in Melbourne. Not to be outdone, the Sydney Philatelic Club also presented exhibitions in 1900 and 1905. In 1911 – still before the first regular Australian stamps – the 1st Australasian Philatelic Congress and Exhibition was held over two days in Sydney.

Commemorative postmarks were used in 1905 and consistently from the 1928 ANPEX, but other exhibitions from those early years leave a historical gap. Cinderella labels, however, were produced to promote the 1911 Congress and Exhibition.

014.2 | 30 October 1928

4th International Philatelic Exhibition (ANPEX)

A popular exhibition souvenir card was this one, published by Melbourne stamp dealer William Ackland.

014.3R | 31 October 1928

4th International Philatelic Exhibition (ANPEX)

In this Guide the earliest event for which Registered covers are recorded is, appropriately for philatelists, the International Philatelic Exhibition of 1928, held in Melbourne. Approximately 700 such covers are thought to have been processed over the four days of the exhibition.

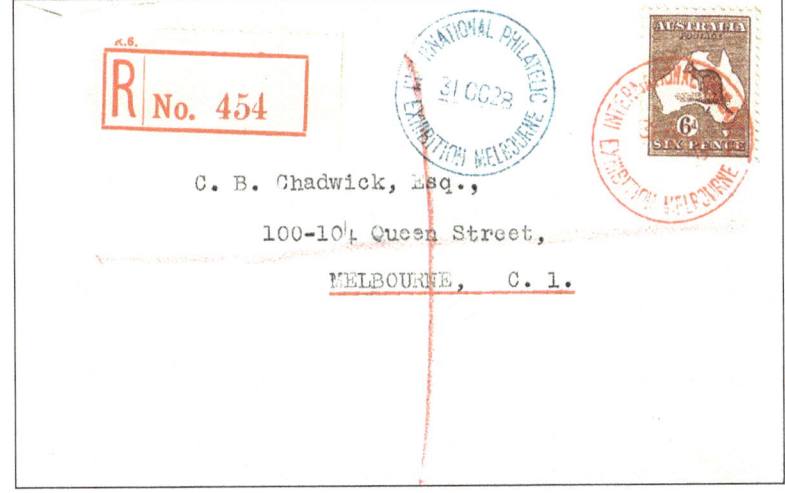

1930 – 1939

EVENTS

015	19 Mar 1932	Opening of Sydney Harbour Bridge
016	22 Mar 1932	5th Australian Philatelic Exhibition (ANPEX)
017	Sep 1932	Royal Melbourne Show
018	6 Oct 1932	Government House Garden Fete
019	Mar 1933	Wesley Church Synod Sessions
020	Apr 1933	[reserved]
021	25 Aug 1933	Royal Show Hobart
022	11 Aug 1934	Brisbane Exhibition
023	4 Oct 1934	Victorian Centenary Celebrations
024	7 Nov 1934	Bendigo Show
025	8 Nov 1934	6th Australasian Philatelic Exhibition (ANPEX)
026	24 Dec 1934	1st Australian Pan-Pacific Jamboree
027	Apr 1935	Royal Easter Show
028	16 Mar 1936	Centennial Exhibition
029	24 Sep 1936	1st Queensland Philatelic Society's Exhibition
030	20 Oct 1936	South Australian Centenary and 7th Australasian Philatelic Exhibition (ANPEX)
031	24 Dec 1936	Scouts Centenary Corroboree
032	30 Sep 1937	A.I.F. and Victorian Golf Tournament
033	5 Oct 1937	Air Mail Exhibition
034	3 Jan 1938	British Empire Games
035	14 Feb 1938	Newcastle Philatelic Exhibition
036	4 Apr 1938	Australia's 150th Anniversary / 8th Australian Philatelic Exhibition (ANPEX)
037	19 May 1938	International Motor Show
038	2 Aug 1938	Christian Endeavour Convention
039	28 Sep 1938	2nd Queensland Philatelic Society's Exhibition
040	26 Dec 1938	2nd Australasian Scouts Jamboree
041	1 Oct 1939	Returned Servicemen's Golf Tournament

Recurring events.
See the original event number entry for the first occurrence.

012	15 Oct 1934	*National Rifle Association of NSW Annual Prize Meeting*
021	17 Oct 1934	*Royal Show Hobart*
017	Oct 1934	*Royal Melbourne Show*
019	8 Mar 1935	*Wesley Church Synod Sessions*
019	7 Mar 1936	*Wesley Church Synod Sessions*
027	Apr 1936	*Royal Easter Show*
012	Oct 1936	*National Rifle Association of NSW Annual Prize Meeting*
027	Mar 1937	*Royal Easter Show*
021	20 Oct 1937	*Royal Show Hobart*
012	Feb 1938	*National Rifle Association of NSW Annual Prize Meeting*
027	Apr 1938	*Royal Easter Show*
022	15 Aug 1938	*Brisbane Exhibition*
032	Sep 1938	*A.I.F. and Victorian Golf Tournament*
021	19 Oct 1938	*Royal Show Hobart*
019	2 Mar 1939	*Wesley Church Synod Sessions*
027	10 Apr 1939	*Royal Easter Show*
032	28 Sep 1939	*A.I.F. and Victorian Golf Tournament*
021	28 Oct 1939	*Royal Show Hobart*

1932

015A N.E. Pylon | 015B S.E. Pylon | 015C −1−

015   1932 OPENING OF SYDNEY HARBOUR BRIDGE
Sydney, NSW
19 Mar – 1 Apr 1932

Type 015A | N.E. PYLON
Registered cover

015A.1R	Opening of Sydney Harbour Bridge cover	$100
015A.2R	5th ANPEX cover	$100
015A.3R	plain cover	80.00

Type 015B | S.E. PYLON
Registered cover

015B.1R	Opening of Sydney Harbour Bridge cover	$100
015B.2R	5th ANPEX cover	$100
015B.3R	plain cover	70.00

Type 015C | −1−
ordinary cover

015C.1	Opening of Sydney Harbour Bridge cover	20.00
015C.2	5th ANPEX cover	15.00
015C.3	plain cover	10.00
015C.4	souvenir telegram	$500

Related stamp issue:
14 Mar 1932 – 2d, 3d and 5s, Opening of Sydney Harbour Bridge (SG141-144).

Quantities:
Letters.............43,995   Registered items..........2,177
Other articles.........13,440   Telegrams.................12,327

015B.3R | 19 March 1932

Opening of Sydney Harbour Bridge

The ultimate cover for the 'opening' postmarks must be one franked with the 5/- Harbour Bridge stamp.

Image courtesy James Prosser.

016A/B.1R | 1 April 1932

5th Australian Philatelic Exhibition (ANPEX)

Coinciding with the Opening of Sydney Harbour Bridge, most ANPEX covers are franked with one or more Bridge stamps. Note that both postmarks appear on this cover. Green ink impressions are usually faded.

 016A  016B

 018

016 **1932 5TH AUSTRALIAN PHILATELIC EXHIBITION (ANPEX)**

Sydney, NSW
22 Mar – 1 Apr 1932

Type 016A
ordinary cover
016A.1   5th ANPEX cover – green ink.................................25.00
016A.2   5th ANPEX cover – red ink...................................25.00
016A.3   plain cover – green ink...20.00
016A.4   plain cover – red ink 20.00
016A.#R   Registered cover............ Qty: est. 2,000*...........50.00

Type 016B
ordinary cover
016B.1   5th ANPEX cover – green ink.................................25.00
016B.2   5th ANPEX cover – red ink...................................25.00
016B.3   plain cover – green ink...20.00
016B.4   plain cover – red ink 20.00
016B.#R   Registered cover .... Qty: est. 2,000*...........50.00

* Quantity is for both postmarks combined.
Highest R6 number sighted: 1820 (1 Apr 1932).

 Cinderella label

Interest in the 1932 ANPEX was buoyed by the opening, on 19 March, of the Sydney Harbour Bridge, and the 300 displays were viewed by an estimated 10,000 people. The exhibition was held in the Blaxland Galleries, George Street, Sydney. A temporary post office sold the Bridge stamps for collectors to affix to souvenir envelopes for cancelling with the special postmarks provided

 017A

017 **1932 ROYAL MELBOURNE SHOW**

Show Grounds, Melbourne, Vic
Sep 1932

017A.1.32   plain cover...50.00
017A.1.32R   plain cover Registered..$150

018 **1932 GOVERNMENT HOUSE GARDEN FETE**

Sydney, NSW
6 – 7 Oct 1932

Ordinary cover
018.1   souvenir cover..$150
018.2   plain cover..$120
018.#R   Registered cover..$500

1933

 019

019 **1933 WESLEY CHURCH SYNOD SESSIONS**

Melbourne, Vic
Mar 1933

019.1.33   plain cover..$300

Registered mail facilities were provided at the Wesley Church post office. Handwritten R6 labels have been sighted for the 1935 Synod and it is possible a generic R6 label was also used, rubber stamped with the WESLEY CHURCH / MELBOURNE C1 location.

1933 FIRST AUSTRALIAN EXHIBITION SHIP TO THE EAST
Apr/May 1933

A postal service was available on board the KPM Line's TSS Nieuw Holland on its April/May 1933 Australia to south-east Asia return voyage. A cachet was applied to mail, and it is reported that some impressions actually cancelled stamps, rendering it a de facto postmark. Until its status can be confirmed, the postmark is not listed in this guide. However, event number 020 has been reserved.

The cachet inscription Royal Packet Navigation Co. is the anglicised Koninklijke Paketvaart Maatschappij, i.e. the KPM company.

021A

021   1933 ROYAL SHOW HOBART
Hobart, Tas
25 Aug 1933

021A.1.33   plain cover $300

The annual Royal Hobart Show originated in 1822. It was cancelled from 1915 to 1918, and from 1940 to 1944, due to the world wars. It was also cancelled in 2020 due to COVID-19 restrictions.

1934

022A

022   1934 BRISBANE EXHIBITION
Brisbane, Qld
11 Aug 1934

022A.1.34   plain cover...$100
022A.1.34R   plain cover Registered .... Qty: min. 79 ....$375

023A | Royal Train

023   1934 VICTORIAN CENTENARY CELEBRATIONS
ROYAL VISIT – Prince Henry, Duke of Gloucester
Royal Train
4 Oct – 10 Dec 1934

023A.1   plain cover $150

Prince Henry, Duke of Gloucester, visited Australia for a 67-day tour from October to December 1934. The main purpose was to open Victoria's centenary celebrations on 18 October. He arrived on HMS *Sussex* at Fremantle, then travelled on the Royal Train to Adelaide and ship to Melbourne. In November, the Duke also visited the Shrine of Remembrance in Melbourne and opened the ANZAC War Memorial in Sydney. He sailed to New Zealand before returning to England.

The Duke again visited Australia in 1945 to serve as Governor-General for two years.

023B | Victoria Dock, Melbourne C3

023   1934 VICTORIAN CENTENARY CELEBRATIONS
VISIT OF NAVAL SHIPS
Victoria Dock, Melbourne, Vic
9 Oct – 13 Nov 1934

     ordinary cover
023B.1   Souvenir cover $250
023B.2   plain cover...$150
023B.#R   Registered cover................ Qty: est. 100* $525

* Highest R6 number sighted:
76 (9 Nov 1934) – label handwritten 'Victoria Dock / C3'

023C | All Aust. Exhbtn, Melbne N3

023   1934 VICTORIAN CENTENARY CELEBRATIONS
ALL AUSTRALIAN EXHIBITION
Melbourne N3, Vic
13 Oct – 10 Nov 1934

     ordinary cover
023C.1   Exhibition souvenir cover $250
023C.2   plain cover...$150
023C.#R   Registered cover.................. Qty: est. 450 ....$525

Highest R6 number sighted: 431 (10 Nov 1934)

Extract from *The Argus*, 13 October 1934:
'Today at the Centenary All-Australian Exhibition, the manufacturers of Australia will show proudly to the world the range of their products and the degree of skill which they have attained in a comparatively small number of years. The exhibition... will be opened by the Premier (Sir Stanley Argyle) at 3 p.m. today. Next Saturday, His Royal Highness, the Duke of Gloucester, will make an official visit.'

023D | Princes Pier, Port Melb SC7

023   1934 VICTORIAN CENTENARY CELEBRATIONS
ROYAL VISIT – Prince Henry, Duke of Gloucester
Princes Pier, Port Melbourne, Vic
18 Oct – 16 Nov 1934

023D.1	plain cover	$150
023D.1R	plain cover Registered	$600

R6 numbers sighted:
411 (1 Nov 1934) – label 'Princes Pier, / Port Melbourne, Victoria'
3 (9 Nov 1934) – label handwritten 'Princes Pier / SC7'

012 1934 NATIONAL RIFLE ASSOCIATION OF NSW ANNUAL PRIZE MEETING

ANZAC Rifle Range, NSW
15 Oct 1934

Type 012
(see illustration under 1920)

012.1.34	plain cover	$100

021 1934 ROYAL SHOW HOBART

Hobart, Tas
17 Oct 1934

Type 021A
(see illustration under 1933)

021A.1.34	plain cover	$250

017 1934 ROYAL MELBOURNE SHOW

Show Grounds, Melbourne, Vic
Oct 1934

Type 017A
(see illustration under 1932)

017A.1.34	plain cover	50.00
017A.1.34R	plain cover Registered	$150

024

024 1934 BENDIGO SHOW

Bendigo, Vic
7 Nov 1934

024.1	plain cover	$100
024.1R	plain cover Registered	$200

Highest R6 number sighted:
101 (7 Nov 1934) – label handwritten 'BENDIGO SHOWGROUNDS'

025

025 1934 6TH AUSTRALASIAN PHILATELIC EXHIBITION (ANPEX)

Melbourne Vic
8 - 17 Nov 1934

	ordinary cover	
025.1	Victorian Centenary and 6th ANPEX cover	15.00
025.2	Airmail Society of Australia Pigeongram cover	45.00
025.3	plain cover	10.00
	Registered cover Qty: est. 2,200*	
025.1R	Centenary / 6th ANPEX cover (R6 black text)	35.00
025.2R	Centenary / 6th ANPEX cover (R6 red text)	75.00
025.3R	plain cover (R6 black text)	25.00
025.4R	plain cover (R6 red text)	60.00

025.1R | 8 November 1934

6th Australasian Philatelic Exhibition (ANPEX)

* Highest R6 numbers sighted:
1914 (17 Nov 1934) – label with black text
104 (17 Nov 1934) – label with red text

It seems 2000 Registration labels were used, with the text in black. Labels with the text in red exist, dated the last day of the exhibition, 17 November 1934.

026A | Date only   026B | Time and date

026   1934-35 1ST AUSTRALIAN PAN-PACIFIC JAMBOREE
Frankston, Vic
24 Dec 1934 – 10 Jan 1935

ordinary cover
026A.1	Australian Jamboree postcard	$100
026A.2	plain cover	50.00
026A.#R	Registered cover....... Qty: est 200*	$325

ordinary cover
026B.1	Australian Jamboree cover	$100
026B.2	plain cover	50.00
026B.#R	Registered cover....... Qty: est 200*	$325

* Quantity is for both postmarks combined.

1935

019   1935 WESLEY CHURCH SYNOD SESSIONS
Melbourne, Vic
8 Mar 1935

Type 019
(see illustration under 1933)

019.1.35	plain cover	$200
019.1.35R	plain cover Registered	$300

027A

027   1935 ROYAL EASTER SHOW
Sydney, NSW
Apr 1935

027A.1.35	plain cover	50.00
027A.1.35R	plain cover Registered	$150

1936

019   1936 WESLEY CHURCH SYNOD SESSIONS
Melbourne, Vic
7 Mar 1936

Type 019
(see illustration under 1933)

019.1.36	plain cover	$200
019.1.36R	plain cover Registered	$300

028A | Date only   028B | Time and date

028   1936 CENTENNIAL EXHIBITION
(Adelaide) SA
16 Mar – 16 May 1936

ordinary cover
028A.1	souvenir cover	$100
028A.2	Submarine Telephone Link FDC (1 Apr)	75.00
028A.3	plain cover	50.00
028B.1	Souvenir cover	$100
028B.2	Submarine Telephone Link FDC (1 Apr)	75.00
028B.3	plain cover	50.00

Registered cover
028#.#R	any cover	$200

Coincidental stamp issue:
1 Apr 1936 – 2d and 3d Opening of Submarine Telephone Link to Tasmania (SG159-160)

027   1936 ROYAL EASTER SHOW
Sydney, NSW
Apr 1936

Type 027A
(see illustration under 1935)

027A.1.36	plain cover	50.00
027A.1.36R	plain cover Registered	$150

029

029   1936 1ST QUEENSLAND PHILATELIC SOCIETY'S EXHIBITION
Brisbane, Qld
24 – 26 Sep 1936

029.1R | 25 September 1936

1st Queensland Philatelic Society's Exhibition

029.2R | 24 September 1936

1st Queensland Philatelic Society's Exhibition

An unknown number of Registered covers were prepared by the Australian Rocket Society in conjunction with an experimental flight on 24 September 1936.

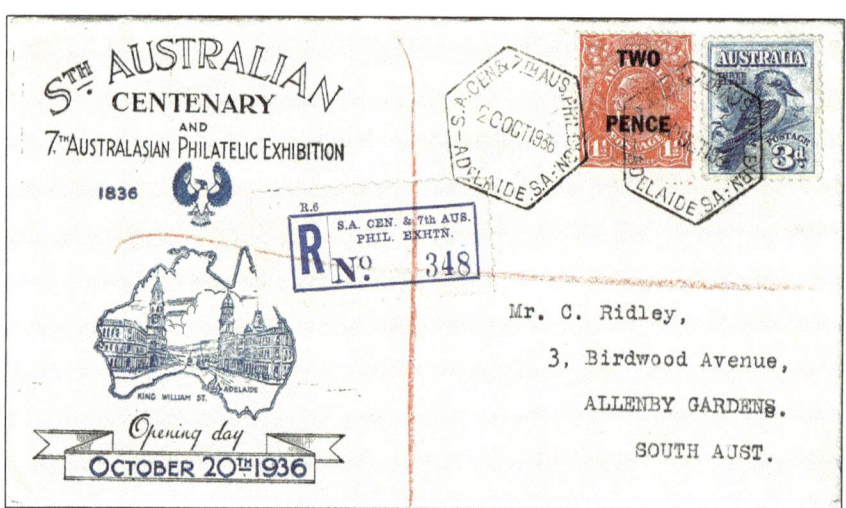

030.1R | 20 October 1936

South Australian Centenary and 7th ANPEX

The Opening Day cover exists in at least three variations. They can be found with the map of Australian in green, blue and dull orange with different illustrations within the map.

1937

	ordinary cover	
029.1	Queensland Philatelic Society cover	15.00
029.2	Australian Rocket Society cover	$125
029.3	plain cover	10.00

Registered cover   Qty: est. 800*

029.1R	Queensland Philatelic Society cover	40.00
029.2R	Australian Rocket Society cover	$250
029.3R	plain cover	25.00

* 328 Registered items were processed on the first day; the highest R6 label sighted is 783 (8:45pm, 26 September 1936).

030

030 1936 SOUTH AUSTRALIAN CENTENARY AND 7TH AUSTRALASIAN PHILATELIC EXHIBITION

Adelaide, SA
20 – 23 Oct 1936

ordinary cover   Qty: 6,277

030.1	Centenary / Exhibition Opening Day cover	20.00
030.2	Centenary / Exhibition cover	20.00
030.3	plain cover	10.00

Registered cover   Qty: 2,187

030.1R	Centenary / Exhibition Opening Day cover	45.00
030.2R	Centenary / Exhibition cover	45.00
030.3R	plain cover	30.00

012 1936 NATIONAL RIFLE ASSOCIATION OF NSW ANNUAL PRIZE MEETING

ANZAC Rifle Range, NSW
Oct 1936

Type 012 (see illustration under 1920)

| 012.1.36 | plain cover | $100 |
| 012.1.36R | plain cover Registered | $250 |

031

031 1936-37 SCOUTS CENTENARY CORROBOREE

Belair, SA
24 Dec 1936 – 4 Jan 1937

ordinary cover

| 031.1 | souvenir cover | 50.00 |
| 031.2 | plain cover | 25.00 |

Registered cover

| 031.1R | souvenir cover | $200 |
| 031.2R | plain cover | $150 |

027 1937 ROYAL EASTER SHOW

Sydney, NSW
Mar 1937

Type 027A
(see illustration under 1935)

| 027A.1.37 | plain cover | 50.00 |
| 027A.1.37R | plain cover Registered | $150 |

032A

032 1937 A.I.F. AND VICTORIAN GOLF TOURNAMENT

Doncaster, Vic
30 Sep 1937

ordinary cover

032A.1	Australia's First Field PO souvenir postcard	75.00
032A.2	10th Australian A.I.F. Cup souvenir postcard	$100
032A.3	plain cover	25.00
032A.#R	Registered cover or card Qty: 140	$200

A similar postmark was used at the 1938 and 1939 tournaments.

033

033 1937 AIR MAIL EXHIBITION

Melbourne, Vic
5 – 7 Oct 1937

ordinary cover

033.1	Airmail Exhibition cover	50.00
033.2	plain cover	30.00
033.#R	Registered cover Qty: est. 1,500*	75.00

* Highest R6 number sighted: 1493 (7 Oct 1937)

021 1937 ROYAL SHOW HOBART

Hobart, Tas
20 Oct 1937

Type 021A
(see illustration under 1933)

| 021A.1.37 | plain cover | $250 |

030.2R | 20 October 1936

South Australian Centenary and 7th ANPEX

This cover has been embellished with the ANPEX Cinderella label printed in red and dark blue. It is the highest R6 label number sighted for the first day of the exhibition.

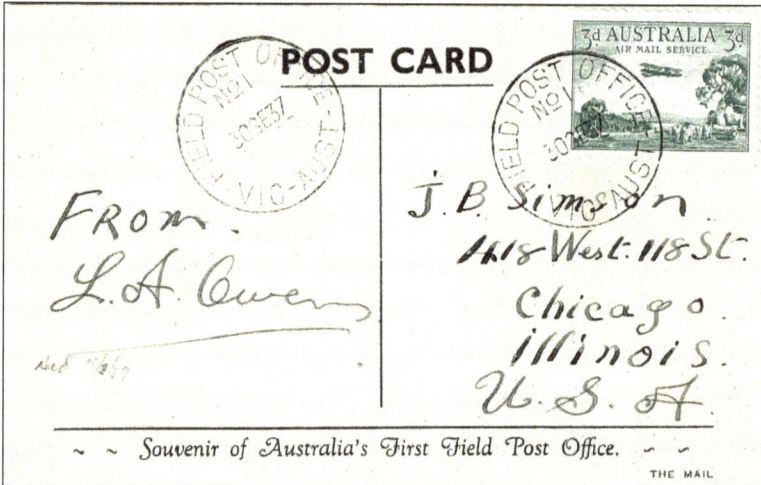

032A.1 | 30 September 1937

A.I.F. and Victorian Golf Tournament

033.1R | 5 October 1937

Airmail Exhibition

About half the Registered covers done for this three day exhibition were processed on the first day, 5 October.

1938

034

034 1938 BRITISH EMPIRE GAMES
Sydney, NSW
3 Jan – 19 Feb 1938

ordinary cover
034.1	any illustrated cover	$120
034.2	plain cover	$120
034.#R	Registered cover .... Qty: est. 80*	$200

* Highest R6 label sighted: 75 (on last day, 19 Feb 1938)

Coincidental stamp issue:
1 Feb 1938 – 4d definitive depicting a koala (SG170)

035

035 1938 NEWCASTLE PHILATELIC EXHIBITION
Newcastle, NSW
14 – 23 Feb 1938

ordinary cover
035.1	any illustrated cover	30.00
035.2	plain cover	20.00
035.#R	Registered cover ......Qty: 500-1000	50.00

012 1938 NATIONAL RIFLE ASSOCIATION OF NSW ANNUAL PRIZE MEETING
ANZAC Rifle Range, NSW
Feb 1938

Type 012 (see illustration under 1920)
012.1.38	plain cover	$100
012.1.38R	plain cover Registered	$250

036

036 1938 AUSTRALIA'S 150TH ANNIVERSARY / 8TH AUSTRALIAN PHILATELIC EXHIBITION
Sydney, NSW
4 – 16 Apr 1938

ordinary cover
036.1	Exhibition souvenir cover	20.00
036.2	plain cover	10.00
036.#R	Registered cover .... Qty: est. 3,500	40.00

Related stamp issue:
1 Oct 1937 – 2d, 3d and 9d, 150th Anniversary of Foundation of New South Wales (SG193-195).

027 1938 ROYAL EASTER SHOW
Sydney, NSW
9 – 23 Apr 1938

Type 027A (see illustration under 1935)
027A.1.38	plain cover	50.00
027A.1.38R	plain cover Registered	$150

034.1R | 1 February 1938

British Empire Games

The Empire Games and use of this postmark coincided, on 1 February 1938, with the issue of the 4d koala definitive stamp.

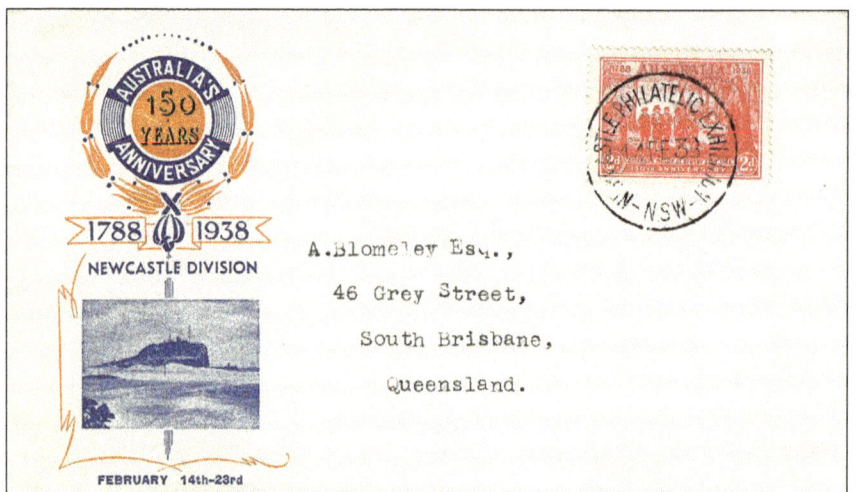

035.1 | 14 February 1938

Newcastle Philatelic Exhibition

036.1R | 8 April 1938

Australia's 150th Anniversary and 8th ANPEX

038.1R | 8 August 1938

Christian Endeavour Convention

037

037 1938 INTERNATIONAL MOTOR SHOW
Melbourne, Vic
19 – 30 May 1938

    ordinary cover
037.1   any illustrated cover 75.00
037.2   plain cover 50.00
037.2R   plain cover Registered $150

038

038 1938 CHRISTIAN ENDEAVOUR CONVENTION
Melbourne, Vic
2 – 9 Aug 1938

038.1   plain cover 50.00
038.1R   plain cover Registered .... Qty: est. 130 .... $150

022 1938 BRISBANE EXHIBITION
Brisbane, Qld
15 Aug 1938

    Type 022A (see illustration under 1934)
022A.1.38   plain cover $100
022A.1.38R   plain cover Registered $300

039

039 1938 2ND QUEENSLAND PHILATELIC SOCIETY'S EXHIBITION
Brisbane, Qld
28 – 30 Sep 1938

    ordinary cover
039.1   Queensland Philatelic Society Exhibition cover ... 20.00
039.2   plain cover 10.00
039.#R   Registered cover .... Qty: est. <600* 50.00

* Highest R6 number sighted: 551 (30 Sep 1938, 8:45pm)

032B | FIELD POST OFFICE No. 2

032 1938 A.I.F. AND VICTORIAN GOLF TOURNAMENT
Doncaster, Vic
29 Sep 1938

    ordinary cover
032B.1   Australia's First Field PO souvenir postcard 75.00
032B.2   11th Australian A.I.F. Cup souvenir postcard $100
032B.3   plain cover 25.00
032B.#R   Registered cover or card .... Qty: 240 .... $225

A similar postmark was used at the 1937 and 1939 tournaments.

039.1R | 28 September 1938

2nd Queensland Philatelic Society's Exhibition

021   *1938 ROYAL SHOW HOBART*

        Hobart, Tas
        19 Oct 1938

        Type 021A
        (see illustration under 1933)

021A.1.38   plain cover $250

040A   040B

040   *1938-39 2ND AUSTRALASIAN SCOUTS JAMBOREE*

        Bradfield, NSW
        26 Dec 1938 – 11 Jan 1939

        ordinary cover
040A.1   Australasian Jamboree postcard $175
040A.2   plain cover $100
040B.1   Australasian Jamboree postcard $200
040B.2   plain cover $100

        Registered cover
040A.2R   plain cover $300
040B.2R   plain cover $400

Postmarks exist in black, magenta and purple. Black was used for regular mail and the colours were intended for internal post office markings and some registered mail.

Highest R6 number sighted: 155 (3 Jan 1939 – Type A black)

1939

019   *1939 WESLEY CHURCH SYNOD SESSIONS*

        Melbourne, Vic
        2 Mar 1939

        Type 019
        (see illustration under 1933)

019.1.39   plain cover $200
019.1.39R   plain cover Registered $300

027   *1939 ROYAL EASTER SHOW*

        Sydney, NSW
        10 Apr 1939

        Type 027A
        (see illustration under 1935)

027A.1.39   plain cover 50.00
027A.1.39R   plain cover Registered $150

032C | FIELD POST OFFICE No. 3

032   *1939 A.I.F. AND VICTORIAN GOLF TOURNAMENT*

        Doncaster, Vic
        28 Sep 1939

        ordinary cover
032C.1   Australia's First Field PO souvenir postcard $100
032C.2   any other illustrated cover 75.00
032C.3   plain cover 25.00
032C.#R   Registered cover or card .... Qty: 28 .... $550

A similar postmark was used at the 1937 and 1938 tournaments.

041

041   *1939 RETURNED SERVICEMEN'S GOLF TOURNAMENT*

        Field P.O. Mt Yokine, WA
        1 Oct 1939

041.1   plain cover 40.00
041.1R   plain cover Registered $125

021   *1939 ROYAL SHOW HOBART*

        Hobart, Tas
        28 Oct 1939

        Type 021A
        (see illustration under 1933)

021A.1.39   plain cover $250

In a case of historical irony, the first two events afforded commemorative postmarks during the Second World War were the 1939 A.I.F. and Victorian Golf Tournament (28 Sep) and the 1939 Returned Servicemen's Golf Tournament (1 Oct).

Both postmarks are scarce, particularly on Registered covers, but make a suitable starting point for enthusiasts wanting to start their collections during this turbulent time.

More readily available is the 1940 Opening of Story Bridge (Brisbane) postmark. The addition of censor markings on covers addressed overseas adds a sense of drama to an otherwise purely peaceful event. Again, Registered covers are scarce but can be found at prices that fail (fortunately) to reflect that scarcity.

Three recurring events in 1939 and 1940 complete the brief catalogue of commemorative postmarks used during the war.

A CINDERELLA STORY

More than a label

A Cinderella is a small piece of printed paper resembling a postage stamp but without any postal value. Such is the bland, clinical definition you might find in a philatelic dictionary. The reality of these labels 'without any postal value' is that they often provide a delightful embellishment to what would otherwise be a less attractive cover. A Cinderella may also be described as a thing whose merit, value or beauty is, for a time, unrecognised.

Usually intended as promotional tools, some Cinderellas are more functional than decorative. Others are excellent examples of graphic design and the printers' craft and worthy of their pseudo-stamp status. Some cover collectors love them.

Collectors of first day, first flight and commemorative postmark covers have usually acquired some examples of Cinderellas without even trying. Often found affixed to the back of envelopes, they may also adorn the front. This can sometimes produce a cluttered item, especially if there are multiple stamps

and the cover was sent by Registered post. Such a cover might also be autographed by an appropriate personality, creating an almost 'ultimate' version. If it's an autographed, Registered cover with a Cinderella affixed, you pretty well have it all.

Cinderella labels inspire collectors who are not necessarily interested in the covers they adorn, but early productions are more likely to be found on covers. So it is that cover collectors will have the competition of pure Cinderella collectors to contend with to secure items for their albums. For this reason, otherwise identical items, with and without an associated Cinderella label, are rightly valued differently.

This book illustrates a tantalising handful of Cinderellas, on and off cover, amid the nearly 200 covers depicted. The editor suggests that, as a rule of thumb, a Cinderella-adorned envelope is worth 25% more than its naked counterpart.

Early labels are rarely encountered off-cover, particularly unused examples, though the 1934 Melbourne Centenary is a notable exception. Still in the inter-war years is the ornate Souvenir Stamp provided for the 1932 ANPEX. This production combines the exhibition and the opening of the Sydney Harbour Bridge.

The 1920s were halcyon years for the new-fangled airmail services, and flight cover collectors will know of the Herald and Pals labels used from 1920. In the 1930s, new airmail routes burgeoned and in 1937 – happily for collectors – an Airmail Exhibition was treated to a commemorative postmark and a Cinderella label. The previous year, the Australian Rocket Society produced a triangular label for the Young Rocket Experiment, which can be found affixed to covers commemorating the first Queensland Philatelic Society Exhibition of September 1936.

Another bridge opening, Brisbane's Story Bridge, was afforded a one-day commemorative postmark in 1940. The opportunity was taken to promote the Joint War Fund Appeal, with a Cinderella label, in combination with bridge opening celebrations. Being a wartime event, commemorative covers posted to overseas addresses may show censor markings, adding another dimension to a collection.

Post-1950, Cinderellas were often considered to be collectible as stand-alone productions.

Notably, several labels were produced for the 1950 ANPEX event and are still readily available through online sales sites. The large *On To Melbourne* promotional labels are very attractive items replicating a series of cover designs. Another label promoting this exhibition was printed in sheets of 12, with the lower-left example intentionally inverted to shamelessly create a demand for the whole sheet.

Philatelic exhibitions appear to be the most commonly encountered subject for which Cinderella labels were printed. Later events produced many, which were, it seems, intended as souvenirs rather than promotional devices. A specialist collection of non-exhibition covers with commemorative postmarks and related Cinderellas would make an interesting display.

In these modern times, Cinderellas as promotional devices and, more generally, seem to have fallen out of favour. This is undoubtedly a result of a decrease in the use of postal services for communication. There are more efficient, though less attractive, means of publicity these days.

As with many aspects of stamp collecting, one thing leads to another, and I trust this very brief exposé may have inspired you to look at your own first day, first flight, and commemorative postmark covers again.

1940 – 1949

EVENTS

042	6 Jul 1940	Opening of Story Bridge, Brisbane
043	17 Dec 1945	Ludwig Leichhardt Centenary
044	23 Apr 1946	Sir Thomas Mitchell Centenary
045	3 Feb 1947	PICAO Conference
046	21 Mar 1947	Royal Adelaide Exhibition
047	6 Sep 1947	Newcastle Industrial Fair
048	8 Sep 1947	Newcastle's 150th Anniversary Philatelic Exhibition
049	3 Nov 1947	Edmund Kennedy Centenary (Charleville, Qld)
050	15 Nov 1948	ECAFE Conference
051	29 Dec 1948	Pan-Pacific Scout Jamboree
052	5 Mar 1949	SS *Fortitude* Centenary
053	26 Apr 1949	Queensland Industries Fair
054	17 Jul 1949	150th Anniversary Matthew Flinders Voyage
055	8 Sep 1949	Royal Adelaide Show

Recurring events.
See the original event number entry for the first occurrence.

019	6 Mar 1940	*Wesley Church Synod Sessions*
022	17 Aug 1940	*Brisbane Exhibition*
022	9 Aug 1947	*Brisbane Exhibition*
017	Sep 1947	*Royal Melbourne Show*
027	Mar 1948	*Royal Easter Show*
049	26 Jun 1948	*Edmund Kennedy Centenary (Kennedy, Qld)*
017	Sep 1948	*Royal Melbourne Show*
017	19 Sep 1949	*Royal Melbourne Show*

1940

019	**1940 WESLEY CHURCH SYNOD SESSIONS**

Melbourne, Vic
6 Mar 1940

Type 019 (see illustration under 1933)

019.1.40	plain cover	$150
019.1.40R	plain cover Registered	$200

	Registered cover	Qty: est. 200*
042.1R	Story Bridge / Miss Post Office cover	60.00
042.2R	plain cover	50.00

* Highest R6 number sighted: A158

As this event occurred during the Second World War, covers addressed to overseas recipients may show censor markings.

042

022B

042	**1940 OPENING OF STORY BRIDGE**

Brisbane, Qld
6 Jul 1940

	ordinary cover	
042.1	Story Bridge / Miss Post Office cover	40.00
042.2	plain cover	30.00

022	**1940 BRISBANE EXHIBITION**

Brisbane, Qld
17 Aug 1940

022B.1.40	R.N.A. 1st World War Exhibition cover	$100
022B.2.40	plain cover	75.00
022B.2.40R	plain cover Registered	$200

042.1R | 6 July 1940

Opening of Story Bridge, Brisbane

Some covers show the JOINT WAR FUND APPEAL Cinderella label issued in connection with the opening of the bridge. As this event occurred during the Second World War, covers addressed to overseas recipients may show censor markings.

022B.1.40 | 17 August 1940

Brisbane Exhibition

The July 1940 Story Bridge first day cover design was modified the following month for the Royal National Association 1st World War Exhibition. This coincided with the 1940 Brisbane Exhibition.

043.1R | 17 December 1945

Ludwig Leichhardt Centenary

044B.1R | 7 May 1946

Thomas Mitchell Centenary, Roma

045.1R | 12 February 1947

PICAO Conference.

1945

043

043 **1945 LUDWIG LEICHHARDT CENTENARY**
Brisbane, Qld
17 Dec 1945

    ordinary cover
043.1   Ludwig Leichhardt Centenary cover 25.00
043.2   plain cover 10.00

043.1R   Ludwig Leichhardt Centenary cover Registered ... 55.00

1946

044A   044B   044C

044 **1946 SIR THOMAS MITCHELL CENTENARY**
St. George, Qld
23 Apr 1946

044A.1   Royal Geographic Society cover 15.00
044A.1R   Royal Geographic Society cover Registered 25.00

Roma, Qld
7 May 1946

044B.1   Royal Geographic Society cover 15.00
044B.1R   Royal Geographic Society cover Registered 25.00

Blackall, Qld
19 Sep 1946

044C.1   Royal Geographic Society cover 15.00
044C.1R   Royal Geographic Society cover Registered 25.00

Related stamp issue:
14 Oct 1946 – 2½d, 3½d and 1s, Centenary of Mitchell's Exploration of Central Queensland. The three postmarks predate the stamp issue.

Extract from *Warwick Daily News*, 1 April 1946
The Postal Department will strike a special cancellation postmark for the Royal Geographical Society's centenary of the explorer Sir Thomas Mitchell. The society secretary (Mr D.A. O'Brien) said last night that the stamp would be used at St George, Roma and Blackall on April 23, May 7, and September 19, respectively. Postage stamps bearing this cancellation would be of tremendous value to philatelists, he said.

1947

045

045 **1947 PICAO CONFERENCE**
Melbourne, Vic
3 – 17 Feb 1947

045.1   plain cover 30.00
045.1R   plain cover Registered .... Qty: est. 250 .... $100

PICAO = Provisional International Civil Aviation Organisation.

046

046 **1947 ROYAL ADELAIDE EXHIBITION**
Adelaide, SA
21 Mar – 1 May 1947

    ordinary cover
046.1.47   Exhibition souvenir cover 40.00
046.2.47   plain cover 20.00
046.#.47R   Registered cover 60.00

022 **1947 BRISBANE EXHIBITION**
Brisbane, Qld
9 Aug 1947

Type 022B
(see illustration under 1940)

    ordinary cover
022B.1.47   Brisbane R.N.A. Exhibition Opening Day cover 40.00
022B.2.47   plain cover 20.00

022B.#.47R   Registered cover 75.00

047

047 **1947 NEWCASTLE INDUSTRIAL FAIR**
Newcastle, NSW
6 – 13 Sep 1947

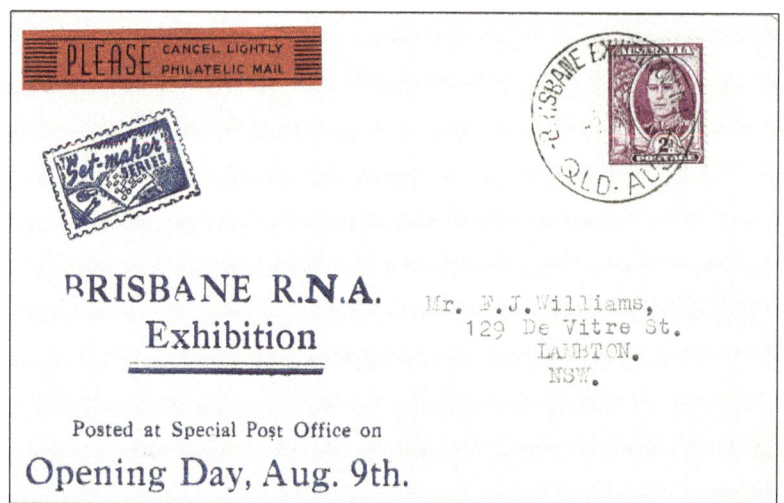

022B.1.47 | 9 August 1947

Brisbane Exhibition

On these covers, the date of the postmark is usually unclear.

047.2R | 13 September 1947

Newcastle Industrial Fair

An example of a plain envelope affixed with an event's promotional Cinderella.

048.1R | 8 September 1947

Newcastle's 150th Anniversary Philatelic Exhibition

	ordinary cover	
047.1	any illustrated cover	15.00
047.2	plain cover	10.00
	Registered cover Qty: est. 350*	
047.1R	any illustrated cover	75.00
047.2R	plain cover	50.00

* Highest R6 number sighted: 322 (13 Sep 1947)

Related stamp issue:
8 Sep 1947 – 2½d, 3½d and 5½d, 150th Anniversary of the City of Newcastle (SG219-222)

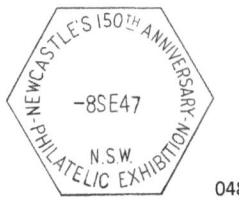

048 1947 NEWCASTLE'S 150TH ANNIVERSARY PHILATELIC EXHIBITION

Newcastle, NSW
8 – 18 Sep 1947

	ordinary cover	
048.1	Newcastle Philatelic Exhibition souvenir cover	10.00
048.2	any other illustrated cover	10.00
	Registered cover	
048.1R	Newcastle Philatelic Exhibition souvenir cover	25.00
048.2R	any other illustrated cover	25.00

Related stamp issue:
8 Sep 1947 – 2½d, 3½d and 5½d, 150th Anniversary of the City of Newcastle (SG219-222)

Highest R6 numbers sighted:

Label printed **Newcastle's 150th / Anniversary Philatelic / Exhibition, N.S.W.** on three lines:
1999 (8 Sep 1947)

Blank label rubber stamped **NEWCASTLE'S 150TH ANNIVERSARY / PHILATELIC EXHIBITION, N.S.W.** on two lines:
492 (12 Sep 1947)

Label printed **NEWCASTLE / NEW SOUTH WALES** on two lines, additionally rubber stamped **NEWCASTLE'S 150TH ANNIVERSARY / PHILATELIC EXHIBITION, N.S.W.** on two lines:
5428 (8 Sep 1947)

Label printed **NEWCASTLE / NEW SOUTH WALES** on two lines, with no exhibition identification:
8692 (18 Sep 1947)

017 1947 ROYAL MELBOURNE SHOW

Show Grounds, Melbourne, Vic
Sep 1947

Type 017A
(see illustration under 1932)

017A.1.47	plain cover	35.00
017A.1.47R	plain cover Registered	75.00

049 1947 EDMUND KENNEDY CENTENARY

Charleville, Qld
3 Nov 1947

049A.1	Royal Geographic Society cover	15.00
049A.1R	Royal Geographic Society Registered cover	40.00

1948

027 1948 ROYAL EASTER SHOW

Sydney, NSW
Mar 1948

Type 027A (see illustration under 1935)

027A.1.48	plain cover	40.00
027A.1.48R	plain cover Registered	$125

049 1948 EDMUND KENNEDY CENTENARY

Kennedy, Qld
26 Jun 1948

049B.1	Royal Geographic Society cover	15.00

017 1948 ROYAL MELBOURNE SHOW

Show Grounds, Melbourne, Vic
Sep 1948

Type 017A (see illustration under 1932)

017A.1.48	plain cover	35.00
017A.1.48R	plain cover Registered	75.00

050 1948 ECAFE CONFERENCE

Sydney, NSW
15 Nov – c14 Dec 1948

017A.1.48R | 20 September 1948

Royal Melbourne Show

051B.1R | 29 December 1948

3rd Pan-Pacific Scout Jamboree

052.1R | 5 March 1949

SS *Fortitude* Centenary

050.1	plain cover	40.00
050.1R	plain cover Registered....... Qty: est. 150*	$100

* Highest R6 number sighted: 072 (1 Dec 1948)

051A
YARRA-BRAE
(with hyphen)

051B
YARRA BRAE
(no hyphen)

051 1948-49 3RD PAN-PACIFIC SCOUT JAMBOREE
Yarra Brae, Vic
29 Dec 1948 – 9 Jan 1949

ordinary cover
051A.1	Pan-Pacific Scout Jamboree cover	15.00
051A.2	plain cover	10.00

Registered cover   Qty: est. 500*
051A.1R	Pan-Pacific Scout Jamboree cover	25.00
051A.2R	plain cover	20.00

ordinary cover
051B.1	Pan-Pacific Scout Jamboree cover	15.00
051B.2	plain cover	10.00

Registered cover   Qty: est. 500*
051B.1R	Pan-Pacific Scout Jamboree cover	25.00
051B.2R	plain cover	20.00

* Quantity is for both postmarks combined.
* Highest R6 number sighted: 376 (29 Dec 1948)

Related stamp issue:
15 Nov 1948 – 2½d, Pan-Pacific Jamboree, Wonga Park (SG227)

1949

052 1949 SS *FORTITUDE* CENTENARY
Fortitude Valley, Qld
5 Mar 1949

052.1	Royal Geographical Society cover	10.00
052.1R	Royal Geographical Society Registered cover	30.00

053 1949 QUEENSLAND INDUSTRIES FAIR
Brisbane, Qld
26 Apr – May 1949

053.1.49	plain cover	40.00

054 1949 150TH ANNIVERSARY MATTHEW FLINDERS VOYAGE
Redcliffe, Qld
17 Jul 1949

054.1	Royal Geographical Society cover	15.00

055 1949 ROYAL ADELAIDE SHOW
Wayville Showgrounds, SA
5 – 15 Sep 1949

055A.1.49	Royal Adelaide Show cover	50.00

017 1949 ROYAL MELBOURNE SHOW
Show Grounds, Melbourne, Vic
19 Sep – 1 Oct 1949

ordinary cover
017B.1.49	Royal Melbourne Show cover	75.00
017B.2.49	plain cover	50.00

Registered cover
017B.2.49R	plain cover	$150

054.1 | 17 July 1949

150th Anniversary Matthew Flinders Voyage

055A.1.49 | 5 September 1949

Royal Adelaide Show

017B.1.49 | 19 September 1949

Royal Melbourne Show

Australian Philatelic Exhibition Postmarks

A specialist option

It would be a rare collector who visited a stamp show and didn't buy a souvenir. So it is that many, who don't necessarily collect them, own covers bearing a philatelic exhibition commemorative postmark. Some such items are available only at the show in question, which, of course, was once always the case. Acquiring such items by mail order was once 'not done.'

Exhibitions are not the only philatelic events for which special postmarks have been provided. Stamp anniversaries, Stamp Weeks and less formal Stamp Fairs also feature. It is the 'PEX' events, however, that most specialists in this area concentrate on.

In the early days of organised stamp collecting in Australia, the Philatelic Society of Victoria and the Sydney Philatelic Club organised several exhibitions. Indeed, since 1894, probably earlier, collectors could display their prized possessions for the benefit of like-minded enthusiasts. It wasn't till 1905, however, that a special postmark was produced to mark such an event. This was the jubilee of the 1855 five-pence diadem stamp of New South Wales. The Sydney Philatelic Club created an attractive souvenir card, and this, with the postmark cancelling a diadem stamp, makes an ideal first page to a collection.

In 1928, the 4th Australian International Philatelic Exhibition (ANPEX) was treated to a special postmark. This event provided several collecting opportunities, thanks to the three-pence kookaburra stamp issued to mark the exhibition. With the single stamp and a miniature sheet, impressions of the postmark in the three colours used can make for a fascinating collection in its own right. Hunting down one of the estimated 700 Registered covers adds to the complexity.

In the 1930s, exhibition postmarks came of age with no fewer than eight events commemorated, including the 5th, 6th, 7th and 8th ANPEXs. In a departure from the regular circular cancels, the 1932 ANPEX was afforded a square postmark, as well as the round variety. Both are listed as having been applied in red and green inks, with the latter challenging to find in unfaded condition. Another innovation, which was to find lasting popularity, was the hexagonal postmark of the 1934 ANPEX. This one was applied only in black ink, but to make life interesting, collectors of Registered covers will find the R6 label with the event title printed in black or red.

Perhaps the most novel design amongst these early postmarks was for the 1937 Air Mail Exhibition. The regular circular design was adorned with stylised wings – curiously, feathered wings – to indicate air transport. This postmark is also in demand by aero philatelists. As with most 1930s events, registered covers are readily available, although in limited numbers. For the Air Mail Exhibition, about 1,500 Registered items were processed, which makes it relatively scarce.

By the time the final 1930s exhibition postmark was used, in September of 1938, Australia and the world were just a year away from the Second World War. Collectors attending the 2nd Queensland Philatelic Exhibition could not have known that it would be almost nine years before a similar would be afforded a special postmark.

Based solely on the number of registered covers mailed at the 1947 Newcastle Philatelic Exhibition, it was an exceptionally popular event. Possibly, following the trauma and hardships of a lengthy war, the opportunity to resume one's hobbies brought out a degree of activity not considered appropriate during hostilities.

Post-war, particularly in the 50s and 60s, Australia entered a phase of what has been popularly described as thrusting development. This is reflected in the proliferation of events demanding commemorative postmarks. Philatelic exhibitions feature prominently in the catalogue of events so celebrated. Fortunately for collectors of today, their popularity at the time has led to relatively plentiful supplies. This makes putting together an extensive collection an undemanding exercise.

Two later pre-decimal events are worthy of mention. The 1956 Olympic Games spawned no fewer than 52 commemorative postmarks and another two for the Olympic Philatelic Exhibition (OLYMPEX). These two postmarks show a runner, usually described as running to the left or right, but does this mean from the runner's perspective or the viewers? Describing the runner as holding the Olympic torch in his left or right hand removes this ambiguity.

The 1963 Melbourne International Exhibition (MIPEX) also was treated to two postmarks. Applied in green, black, purple or green ink, even a simplified collection demands eight covers. To complicate the issue, Registered and Certified Mail covers exist, but the scarcest item is the First Hovercraft Mail Certified cover. For MIPEX, only 47 Certified items were 'done,' making the Hovercraft cover a true rarity.

The decimal era was only months old when Perth hosted the 1966 WAPEX – Western Australian Philatelic Exhibition – a six-day event. Day one, 24 October 1966, coincided with the release of the 4c Dirk Hartog Anniversary stamp (SG 408). Most exhibition covers of this date are also FDCs, all with the postmark in red ink. The postmark was applied in black ink for the following five days and is scarcer than the red. Some enterprising collectors used spare souvenir cards of the 1954 WAPEX to secure their postmarks. Only 406 registered covers were processed, of which approximately three-quarters were done on the first day. Notably, the 1966 WAPEX was the last philatelic exhibition postmark before the introduction of postcodes in Australia in 1967.

No exhibition for the rest of the 60s was blessed with a commemorative postmark, though the 1967 Melbourne and Adelaide GPO Centenaries were so honoured.

ANPEX 70, in April and May, saw just one postmark, though like the 1966 WAPEX, it was applied in red and black ink. The canceller was a duplex style, similar to that used in 1967 for the 50th Anniversary of the First Air Mail within South Australia. Replicated in later years, this format proved popular and over 155,000 impressions were made. It is, therefore, an easily located postmark.

With the associated Cook Bicentenary stamps (SG 459-464) and miniature sheet (SG MS465),

there are many variations of cover to collect. Impressions in red ink were intended to have been made on the first day only, but examples on 1 May exist. Some sources also cite impressions in green ink. An estimated 2,000 covers were registered over the five days.

Lesser events treated to special postmarks were, perhaps predictably, less popular than the capital city exhibitions. Half a century on, the 1971 (and 1972) exhibition postmarks are scarcer, though they are regularly offered on online sales sites. It is worth hunting down impressions on registered covers as these can be rare. For example, the 1971 Combined Philatelic Societies Display, Toombul 4012, produced only 12 such covers.

The seventies progressed, and stamp collecting and investing became increasingly popular. As promotional exercises, the National Stamp Weeks, with their associated exhibitions, drew more collectors into the hobby and 'lapsed' collectors returned. The set of seven postmarks for 1974, one for each capital city (except Darwin), featured the states' symbols and made an attractive set. The official statistics tell us that between 3,000 and 6,700 impressions of each were made. Again, registered covers are rare, some existing only in single figures.

The National Stamp Week concept was a big deal in the 1970s, and commemorative postmark collectors have plenty of variations to hunt for. The 1976 set of seven for each capital city (still neglecting Darwin) was expanded with coincident exhibitions. The 1976 Queensland Philatelic Exhibition, Toombul 4012, and SPRINGPEX '76, Sydney 2000, add another element to the series. In particular, the National Stamp Week miniature sheet (SG MS634) was included in a Souvenir Booklet. This was overprinted AUSTRALIAN STAMP PROMOTION COUNCIL, numbered and rouletted down the left side. Notably, the sheet is 5mm wider than the standard version. Of course, it exists with the SPRINGPEX '76 postmark. This wider version is missing from most Australian decimal collections.

The omission of Darwin in the National Stamp Week series was rectified in 1977. The statistics show a significant decrease in interest compared to the previous year. Melbourne and Brisbane were well patronised, but Adelaide saw only 1,254 impressions and Darwin a mere 487, making it one of the scarcer commemorative postmarks of the era.

Collectors with a penchant for coloured postmarks will be delighted with STAMP SHOW '78, held in Adelaide in September 1978. With the regular black ink impressions, examples in red, green and dark blue can be found. Two dateline sizes were made, 2mm and approximately 3.5mm high. If pigeon-post fits in an aerophilately theme, then STAMP SHOW '78 delivers. A souvenir cover postmarked 25 September (in red) included a 'Pigeon Gram Flimsy' adding to the bird theme. The show was commemorated with a 20c stamp (SG 694) and miniature sheet (SG MS695) depicting the 1928 three-pence kookaburra stamp.

The biggest event of 1980 was SYDPEX 80, held in Sydney. Despite the moniker – SYDPEX rather than ANPEX – this was a National Philatelic Exhibition. The event was accompanied by a set of five stamps (SG 752-6) and a miniature sheet (SG MS757) for National Stamp Week, and a dedicated SYDPEX 80 pre-stamped envelope (PSE). The latter depicted three Sydney Views stamps of New South Wales, issued in 1850. Three postmarks were produced, including a massive (9.5cm) rectangular design intended to cancel the se-tenant strip of five stamps with a single application.

In a nod to tradition, postmarks were applied in green ink on the first day, red on the last day, and black on other days. With the variations provided by these colours, the availability of stamps, and a PSE, an extensive collection can be assembled for this event alone. It is no wonder that over 600,000 impressions of the three postmarks were recorded.

At the same time, a special postmark was also provided for the Queensland Philatelic Exhibition in Brisbane and Rundle Mall, Adelaide, had its own National Stamp Week design. Ever progressive, South Australia saw off 1980 with its Christmas Stamp Fair. This provides a bright end-point for a collection that concludes with that year. For most of the 1980s, Australia Post's output of commemorative postmarks was prodigious, some would say excessive. Despite this, specialising in philatelic exhibitions or similar postmarks allows collectors to assemble an inexpensive album of such items.

The emphasis of this book is on postmarks to 1980. Limiting a postmark collection to philatelic exhibitions post-1980 provides an outlet for those wanting to secure 'new issues' without the expense and effort of buying many more items than would otherwise be the case.

1950 – 1954

EVENTS

056	26 Apr 1950	South Burnett Centenary
057	22 Sep 1950	Central Queensland Industries Fair
058	4 Oct 1950	Australian National Philatelic Exhibition (ANPEX)
059	13 Dec 1950	Redlands-Cleveland Centenary
060	2 Jul 1951	Bendigo Philatelic Exhibition
061	3 May 1952	American Memorial Opening
062	8 May 1952	Geelong Philatelic Exhibition (GEEBEX)
063	29 Dec 1952	4th Pan-Pacific Scout Jamboree
064	13 Jan 1953	ICAO Meetings
065	3 Sep 1953	Brighton Philatelic Exhibition (BRIPEX)
066	24 Sep 1953	Returned and Servicemen's League Golf Tournament
067	1 Feb 1954	Royal Visit
068	2 Aug 1954	Western Australian Philatelic Exhibition (WAPEX)

Recurring events.
See the original event number entry for the first occurrence.

022	Aug 1950	*Brisbane Exhibition*
017	Sep 1950	*Royal Melbourne Show*
055	5 Sep 1951	*Royal Adelaide Show*
046	5 Mar 1952	*Royal Adelaide Exhibition*
053	26 Apr 1952	*Queensland Industries Fair*
022	8 Aug 1952	*Brisbane Exhibition*
055	3 Sep 1952	*Royal Adelaide Show*
022	Aug 1953	*Brisbane Exhibition*
017	Sep 1953	*Royal Melbourne Show*
022	Aug 1954	*Brisbane Exhibition*
055	Sep 1954	*Royal Adelaide Show*

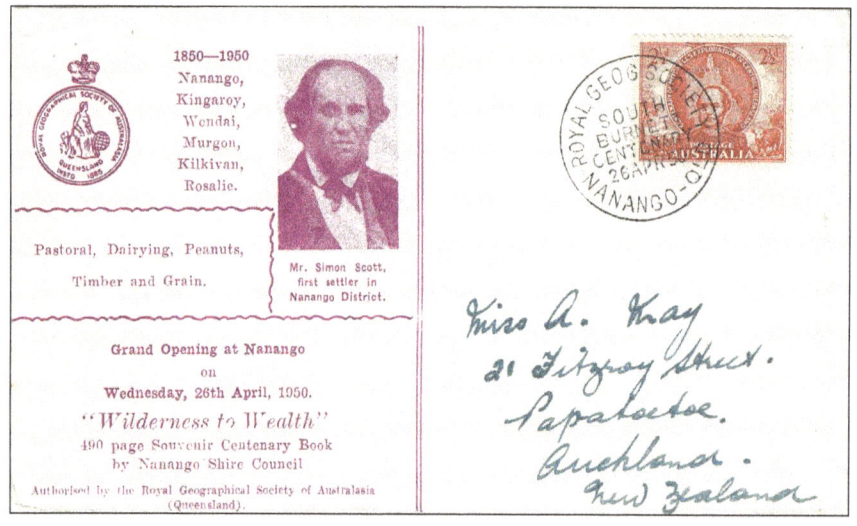

056.1 | 26 April 1950

South Burnett Centenary

1950

056   **1950 SOUTH BURNETT CENTENARY**
    Nanango, Qld
    26 Apr 1950

056.1   Royal Geographic Society cover 15.00

022   ***1950 BRISBANE EXHIBITION***
    Brisbane, Qld
    Aug 1950

022B.1.50   plain cover 30.00
022C.1.50   plain cover 30.00

057   **1950 CENTRAL QUEENSLAND INDUSTRIES FAIR**
    Rockhampton, Qld
    22 – 30 Sep 1950

057.1   souvenir cover 30.00

This post office appears to have operated before the Fair opened.

058A.3 | 4 October 1950

Stamp Centenary and ANPEX

The original printing of this cover shows the full text on the stamps depicted. A reprint has the wording obliterated.

058B.2 | 10 October 1950

ANPEX On To Melbourne Official Cover From "ANPEX".

Two On To Melbourne covers were produced with inscriptions reading:

- OFFICIAL COVER FROM "ANPEX" OCT. 4–14, 1950
- OFFICIAL FIRST DAY COVER FROM "ANPEX".

Both were printed in various colours.

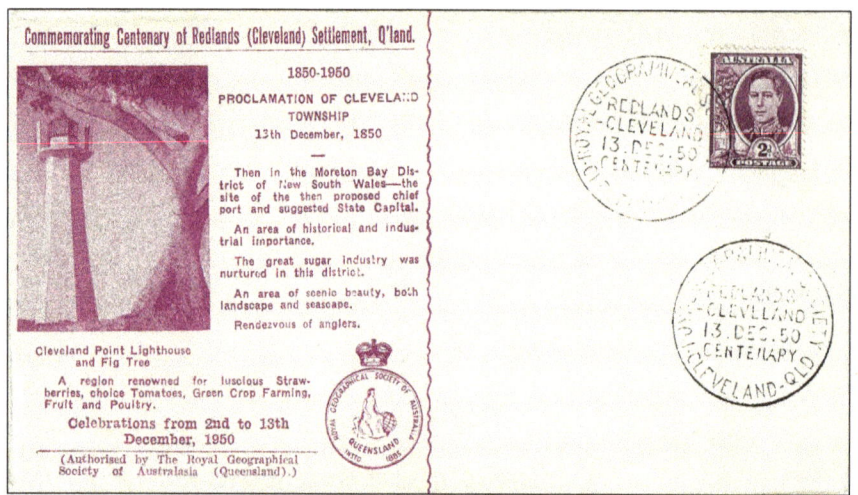

059.1 | 13 December 1950

Redlands-Cleveland Centenary

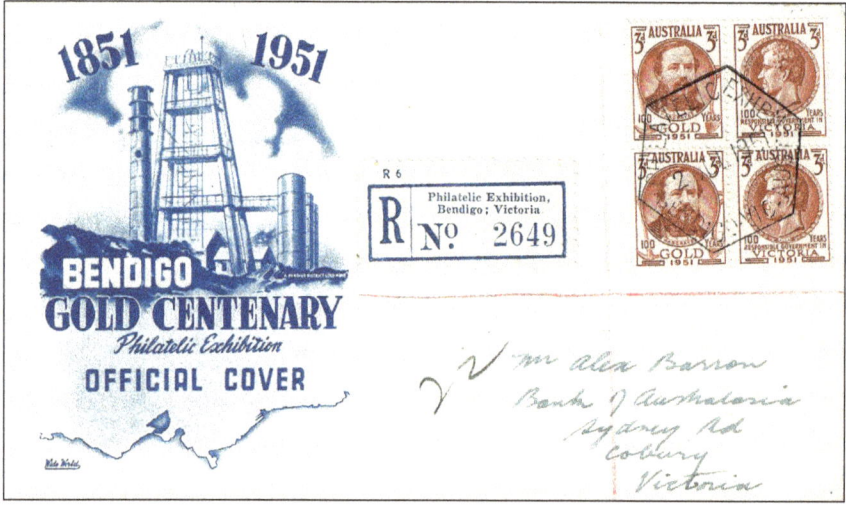

060.1R | 2 July 1951

Bendigo Philatelic Exhibition

The majority of Registered covers are dated 2 July 1951, the exhibition's first day.

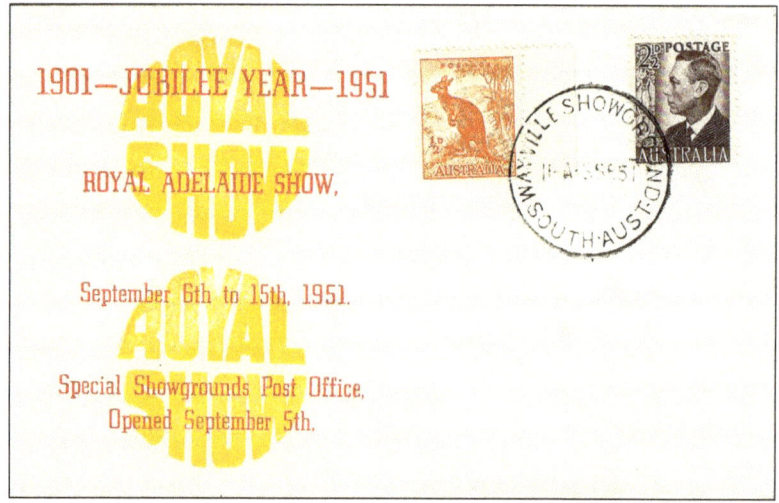

055A.1.51 | 5 September 1951

Royal Adelaide Show

017 1950 ROYAL MELBOURNE SHOW

Show Grounds, Melbourne, Vic
Sep 1950

Type 017B
(see illustration under 1949)

017B.1.50	plain cover	50.00
017B.1.50R	plain cover Registered	75.00

058A | 4 Oct 1950   058B | 5–14 Oct 1950

058 1950 AUSTRALIAN NATIONAL PHILATELIC EXHIBITION (ANPEX)

Melbourne, Vic
4 – 14 Oct 1950

ordinary cover

058A.1	On To Melbourne Official FDC from "ANPEX"	5.00
058A.2	On To Melbourne Official Cover from "ANPEX"	5.00
058A.3	Stamp Centenary and ANPEX Souvenir Cover – original *	5.00
058A.4	Stamp Centenary and ANPEX Souvenir Cover – reprint *	5.00

Registered cover   Qty: est. 10,000**

058A.#R	Any ANPEX cover	10.00

ordinary cover

058B.1	On To Melbourne Official FDC from "ANPEX"	5.00
058B.2	On To Melbourne Official Cover from "ANPEX"	5.00
058B.3	Stamp Centenary and ANPEX Souvenir Cover – original *	5.00
058B.4	Stamp Centenary and ANPEX Souvenir Cover – reprint *	5.00

Registered cover   Qty: est. 10,000**

058B.#R	Any ANPEX cover	10.00

* Published by Wide World, the reprinted souvenir cover showed NSW and Victorian stamps with main lettering obliterated.

** The estimated quantity is a combined figure for both postmarks. The highest numbered R6 label sighted is 9065, on a cover dated 13 October 1950. High numbered labels seen on covers cancelled with the 4 October circular postmark indicates that they were not used in strict numerical sequence. The highest 4 October R6 label sighted by the editor is 8118. The lowest number R6 label seen with the hexagonal postmark is 1691 on a cover dated 6 October.

Related stamp issue:
27 Sep 1950 – 2 x 2½d Centenary of First Adhesive Postage Stamps in Australia (SG239-40)

059

059 1950 REDLANDS-CLEVELAND CENTENARY

Cleveland, Qld
13 Dec 1950

059.1	Royal Geographic Society cover	15.00

1951

060

060 1951 BENDIGO PHILATELIC EXHIBITION

Bendigo, Vic
2 – 4 Jul 1951

Ordinary cover

060.1	Exhibition Official Cover	15.00
060.2	Any other illustrated cover	10.00

Registered cover   Qty: est. 3,000*

060.1R	Exhibition Official Cover	30.00
060.2R	Any other illustrated cover	25.00

* Highest R6 number sighted: 2649 (2 Jul 1951)

055 1951 ROYAL ADELAIDE SHOW

Wayville Showgrounds, SA
5 – 15 Sep 1951

Type 055A (see illustration under 1949)

055A.1.51	Royal Adelaide Show souvenir cover	50.00
055A.2.51	plain cover	30.00

1952

046 ROYAL ADELAIDE EXHIBITION

Adelaide, SA
5 Mar – 3 May 1952

Type 046 (see illustration under 1947)

ordinary cover

046.1.52	Exhibition souvenir cover	40.00
046.2.52	plain cover	25.00

Registered cover

046.1.52R	Exhibition souvenir cover	60.00
046.2.52R	plain cover	40.00

046.1.52 | 5 March 1952

Royal Adelaide Exhibition

061.1 | 3 May 1952

American Memorial Opening

062.1 | 8 May 1952

Geelong Philatelic Exhibition

053 1952 QUEENSLAND INDUSTRIES FAIR
Brisbane, Qld
26 Apr – 17 May 1952

Type 053 (see illustration under 1949)

053.1.52   plain cover 25.00

061 1952 AMERICAN MEMORIAL OPENING
Brisbane, Qld
3 May 1952

061.1   Australian-American Association cover 10.00

062 1952 GEELONG PHILATELIC EXHIBITION (GEEBEX)
Geelong, Vic
8 – 10 May 1952

ordinary cover
062.1   Geelong Philatelic Society GEEBEX cover 15.00
062.2   plain cover 10.00

Registered cover   Qty: est. <600*
062.1R   Geelong Philatelic Society GEEBEX cover 40.00
062.2R   plain cover 30.00

* Highest R6 number sighted: 0560 (10 May 1952)

022 1952 BRISBANE EXHIBITION
Brisbane, Qld
8 – 11 Aug 1952

Type 022C (see illustration under 1950)

022C.1.52   plain cover 30.00
022C.1.52R   plain cover Registered 75.00

055 1952 ROYAL ADELAIDE SHOW
Wayville Showgrounds, SA
3 – 15 Sep 1952

Type 055A (see illustration under 1949)

055A.1.52   plain cover 30.00

063 1952-53 4TH PAN-PACIFIC SCOUT JAMBOREE
Greystanes, NSW
29 Dec 1952 – 9 Jan 1953

ordinary cover
063A.1   Pan-Pacific Scout Jamboree cover 15.00
063A.2   any other illustrated cover 15.00
063A.3   plain cover 10.00

Registered cover   Qty: est. 1,000*
063A.1R   Pan-Pacific Scout Jamboree cover 50.00

ordinary cover
063B.1   Pan-Pacific Scout Jamboree cover 15.00
063B.2   any other illustrated cover 15.00
063B.3   plain cover 10.00

Registered cover   Qty: est. 1,000*
063B.1R   Pan-Pacific Scout Jamboree cover 50.00

* Highest R6 number sighted: 0899 (9 Jan 1953).

Most Registered covers are dated 29 December 1952, with the highest number sighted on that date being 0698. The estimated 1,000 covers is for both postmarks combined.

'Pan-Pacific' appears hyphenated and unhyphenated.

Related stamp issue:
19 Nov 1952 – 3½d, Pan-Pacific Jamboree, Greystanes (SG254)

1953

064 1953 ICAO MEETINGS
Melbourne, Vic
13 Jan – 9 Feb 1953

ordinary cover
064A.1   any illustrated cover $100
064A.2   plain cover 50.00
064B.1   any illustrated cover $100
064B.2   plain cover 50.00

Registered cover
064A.1R   any illustrated cover $150
064A.2R   plain cover $100
064B.1R   any illustrated cover $150
064B.2R   plain cover $100

063B.1R | 9 January 1953

4th Pan-Pacific Scout Jamboree

064B.2R | 13 January 1953

ICAO Meetings

065.2R | 3 September 1953

Brighton Philatelic Exhibition (BRIPEX)

ICAO = International Civil Aviation Organisation

Meetings:
064A – 2nd S.E. Asia Air Navigation Meeting
064B – Limited South Pacific Regional Air Navigation Meeting.

022 1953 BRISBANE EXHIBITION

Brisbane, Qld
Aug 1953

Type 022C (see illustration under 1950)

022C.1.53	plain cover	30.00
022C.1.53R	plain cover Registered	75.00

065 1953 BRIGHTON PHILATELIC EXHIBITION (BRIPEX)

Brighton, Vic
3 – 5 Sep 1953

	ordinary cover	Qty: 17,522
065.1	BRIPEX cover	10.00
065.2	Young Farmers' Clubs FDC	10.00
065.3	any other illustrated cover	10.00
065.4	plain cover	5.00
	Registered cover	Qty: est. 850*
065.1R	BRIPEX cover	20.00
065.2R	Young Farmers' Clubs FDC	20.00
065.3R	any other illustrated cover	20.00
065.4R	plain cover	10.00

* Despite the published quantity of 850 Registered covers, R6 label number 2656 has been sighted.

Coincidental stamp issue:
3 Sep 1953 – 3½d, 25th Anniversary of Young Farmers' Clubs of Australia (SG267)

066 1953 RETURNED AND SERVICEMEN'S LEAGUE GOLF TOURNAMENT

Field P.O. (Eastern Golf Club, Doncaster), Vic
24 Sep 1953

066.1	any illustrated cover	50.00
066.2	plain cover	30.00

017 1953 ROYAL MELBOURNE SHOW

Show Grounds, Melbourne, Vic

Sep 1953

Type 017B (see illustration under 1949)

017B.1.53	plain cover	50.00
017B.1.53R	plain cover Registered	75.00

1954

067 1954 ROYAL VISIT

Camp Royal, Canberra, ACT
1 – 17 Feb 1954

		Qty: 9,904
067.1	plain cover	20.00
067.1R	plain cover Registered	50.00

Related stamp issue:
2 Feb 1954 – 3½d, 7½d and 2s, Royal Visit (SG272-4

Princess Elizabeth was to visit Australia in 1952, when that tour was cut short due to the death of her father, King George VI. Two years later, as Queen Elizabeth II, she became the first reigning monarch to visit Australia, although several royal visits had taken place since 1867.

With the Duke of Edinburgh, in 1954 the queen visited each state and the Australian Capital Territory, where she opened Parliament in Canberra. She also attended an event at the Melbourne Cricket Ground where 70,000 ex-servicemen and women assembled for the visit.

068 1954 WESTERN AUSTRALIAN PHILATELIC EXHIBITION (WAPEX)

Perth, WA
2 – 6 Aug 1954

Type 068A	2 Aug	red ink
Type 068B	3-6 Aug	green ink

	ordinary cover	Qty: 12,142
068A.1	WAPEX cover	10.00
068A.2	WA Stamp Centenary FDC	10.00
068A.3	any other illustrated cover	8.00
068B.1	WAPEX cover	10.00
068B.2	WA Stamp Centenary FDC	10.00
068B.3	any other illustrated cover	8.00

		Registered cover	Qty: 1,332*	
068A.1R		WAPEX cover		25.00
068A.2R		WA Stamp Centenary FDC		25.00
068A.3R		any other illustrated cover		20.00
068B.1R		WAPEX cover		25.00
068B.2R		WA Stamp Centenary FDC		25.00
068B.3R		any other illustrated cover		20.00

* R6 label number 1506 has been sighted.

Related stamp issue:
2 Aug 1954 – 3½d, Western Australian Postage Stamp Centenary (SG277)

022   1954 BRISBANE EXHIBITION

Brisbane, Qld
Aug 1954

Type 022B (see illustration under 1940)

022B.1.54	plain cover	25.00
022B.1.54R	plain cover Registered	75.00

055   1954 ROYAL ADELAIDE SHOW

Wayville Showgrounds, SA
Sep 1954

Type 055A (see illustration under 1949)

055A.1.54	plain cover	30.00

068A.1 | 2 August 1954

Western Australian Philatelic Exhibition (WAPEX)

068B.1R | 2 August 1954

Western Australian Philatelic Exhibition (WAPEX)

1955 – 1959

EVENTS

069	17 Oct 1955	Australasian National Philatelic Exhibition (ANPEX)
070	27 Dec 1955	5th Pan-Pacific Scout Jamboree
071	15 Oct 1956	16th Olympic Games
072	12 Nov 1956	Olympic Philatelic Exhibition (OLYMPEX)
073	27 Dec 1957	Greenbank Corroboree
074	17 Feb 1958	14th British Empire League Service Conference
075	7 Mar 1958	Second Australian Industries Fair
076	Apr 1958	Toowoomba Agricultural Show
077	29 Sep 1958	French Trade Fair
078	2 Feb 1959	Australian National Philatelic Exhibition (ANPEX)
079	26 Feb 1959	International Trade Fair
080	9 Mar 1959	ECAFE Conference
081	5 Jun 1959	Queensland Centenary Stamp Exhibition (QUCEX)
082	29 Jul 1959	Inauguration QANTAS Jet Services

Recurring events.
See the original event number entry for the first occurrence.

053	9 Apr 1955	*Queensland Industries Fair*
022	Aug 1955	*Brisbane Exhibition*
046	Apr 1957	*Royal Adelaide Exhibition*
053	14 May 1957	*Queensland Industries Fair*
053	2 May 1959	*Queensland Industries Fair*
082	27 Oct 1959	*Inauguration QANTAS Jet Services*

1955

053 **1955 QUEENSLAND INDUSTRIES FAIR**
Brisbane, Qld
9 Apr – 2 May 1955

Type 053 (see illustration under 1949)

053.1.55	plain cover	25.00

022 **1955 BRISBANE EXHIBITION**
Brisbane, Qld
Aug 1955

Type 022C (see illustration under 1950)

022C.1.55	plain cover	25.00
022C.1.55R	plain cover Registered	75.00

069 **1955 AUSTRALASIAN NATIONAL PHILATELIC EXHIBITION (ANPEX)**
Adelaide, SA
17 – 22 Oct 1955

069A

069B

Type 069A | 17 Oct | red ink
Type 069B | 18 – 22 Oct | purple ink

	ordinary cover	Qty: 17,468	
069A.1	ANPEX Official cover		15.00
069A.2	SA Stamp Centenary FDC cover		15.00
	Registered cover	Qty: 1,362	
069A.1R	ANPEX Official cover		25.00
069A.2R	SA Stamp Centenary FDC cover		25.00
	ordinary cover	Qty: 3,892	
069B.1	ANPEX Official cover		25.00
069B.2	SA Stamp Centenary FDC cover		25.00
	Registered cover	Qty: 211	
069B.1R	ANPEX Official cover		40.00
069B.2R	SA Stamp Centenary FDC cover		40.00

069B.1R | 21 October 1955

Australasian National Philatelic Exhibition (ANPEX)

Of the 1,573 items sent by Registered mail, most were posted on the opening day. Only 211 were posted between 18 and 22 October.

070A/C.5R | 10 January 1956

Pan-Pacific Scout Jamboree

071J.2R | 22 November 1956

16th Olympic Games

Related stamp issue:
17 Oct 1955 – 3½d, South Australian Postage Stamp Centenary (SG288)

070 1955-56 5TH PAN-PACIFIC SCOUT JAMBOREE
Sydney, NSW
27 Dec 1955 – 10 Jan 1956

070A 070B 070C

	ordinary cover	
070A.1	Pan-Pacific Jamboree cover	10.00
070A.2	Pan-Pacific Jamboree Official Opening Day Cover (30 Dec)	20.00
070A.3	Pan-Pacific Jamboree postcard	10.00
070A.4	any other illustrated cover	8.00
070A.5	plain cover	5.00
070A.#R	Registered cover .... Qty: est. 200*	40.00

	ordinary cover	
070B.1	Pan-Pacific Jamboree cover	10.00
070B.2	Pan-Pacific Jamboree Official Opening Day Cover (30 Dec)	20.00
070B.3	Pan-Pacific Jamboree postcard	10.00
070B.4	any other illustrated cover	8.00
070B.5	plain cover	5.00
070B.#R	Registered cover .... Qty: est. 200*	40.00

	ordinary cover	
070C.1	Pan-Pacific Jamboree cover	10.00
070C.2	Pan-Pacific Jamboree Official Opening Day Cover (30 Dec)	20.00
070C.3	Pan-Pacific Jamboree postcard	10.00
070C.4	any other illustrated cover	8.00
070C.5	plain cover	5.00
070C.#R	Registered cover .... Qty: est. 200*	40.00

* Quantity is for all postmarks combined.
Highest R6 number sighted: 182 (10 Jan 1956)

1956

071 1956 16TH OLYMPIC GAMES
15 Oct – 2 Dec 1956
Ballarat Village

Type 071A	Rowing (coxless pair)
Type 071B	Rowing (single sculls)
Type 071C	Canoeing

	ordinary cover	
071A.1 to C.1	Official Souvenir Cover	20.00
071A.2 to C.2	any other Illustrated cover	15.00
	Registered cover Qty: 216*	
071A.1R to C.1R	Official Souvenir Cover	80.00

* Quantity is a combined total for the three postmarks.

22 Nov – 6 Dec 1956
Exhibition Building

Type 071D	Basketball
Type 071E	Weightlifting
Type 071F	Wrestling

	ordinary cover	
071D.1 to F.1	Official Souvenir Cover	20.00
071D.2 to F.2	any other Illustrated cover	15.00
	Registered cover Qty: 177*	
071D.1R to F.1R	Official Souvenir Cover	80.00

* Quantity is a combined total for the three postmarks.

23 Nov – 1 Dec 1956
Lake Wendouree

Type 071G	Kayaking
Type 071H	Rowing

	ordinary cover	
071G.1 to H.1	Official Souvenir Cover	20.00
071G.2 to H.2	any other Illustrated cover	15.00
	Registered cover Qty: 99*	
071G.1R to H.1R	Official Souvenir Cover	$175

* Quantity is a combined total for both postmarks.

22 Nov – 8 Dec 1956
Main Stadium

Type 071J	Main stadium
Type 071Jv	Main stadium (US style date)
Type 071K	Men's high jump
Type 071L	Men's walking
Type 071M	Men's running
Type 071N	Pole vault
Type 071P	Shotput
Type 071Q	Women's relay running
Type 071R	Women's running

	ordinary cover	
071J.1 to R.1	Official Souvenir Cover	15.00
071Jv.1	Official Souvenir Cover	25.00
071J.2 to R.2	any other Illustrated cover	10.00
071Jv.2	any other Illustrated cover	25.00
	Registered cover Qty: 1,301*	
071J.1R to R.1R	Official Souvenir Cover	50.00

* Quantity is a combined total for all eight postmarks.

22 Nov – 8 Dec 1956
Main Stadium (Press)

Type 071S	Olympic rings, torch and map
Type 071T	Winners' podium

Ballarat Village

Exhibition Building

Lake Wendouree

Main Stadium

Main Stadium (Press)

Melbourne Airport

Mobile Post Office No. 1

Mobile Post Office No. 2

Olympic Park | Olympic Park (Press)

Olympic Village

Richmond Park

St Kilda Pier   St. Kilda Town Hall   Station Pier

	ordinary cover	
071S.1 to T.1	Official Souvenir Cover	20.00
071S.2 to T.2	any other Illustrated cover	15.00
	Registered cover Qty: 1,858*	
071S.1R to T.1R	Official Souvenir Cover	50.00

* Quantity is a combined total for both postmarks.

5 Nov – 15 Dec 1956
Melbourne Airport

Type 071U | Torch

	ordinary cover	
071U.1	Official Souvenir Cover	20.00
071U.2	any other Illustrated cover	15.00
	Registered cover Qty: 95	
071U.1R	Official Souvenir Cover	$100

22 Nov – 8 Dec 1956
Mobile Post Office No. 1

Type 071V | Parallel bars
Type 071W | Pistol shooting
Type 071X | Rifle shooting

	ordinary cover	
071V.1 to X.1	Official Souvenir Cover	20.00
071V.2 to X.2	any other Illustrated cover	15.00
	Registered cover *	
071V.1R to X.1R	Official Souvenir Cover	$100

* No figures recorded for Registered covers.

22 Nov – 8 Dec 1956
Mobile Post Office No. 2

Type 071Y | Clay pigeon shooting
Type 071Z | Equestrian
Type 071AA | Marathon

	ordinary cover	
071Y.1 to AA.1	Official Souvenir Cover	20.00
071Y.2 to AA.2	any other Illustrated cover	15.00
	Registered cover *	
071Y.1R to AA.1R	Official Souvenir Cover	$100

* No figures recorded for Registered covers.

22 Nov – 8 Dec 1956
Olympic Park

Type 071AB | Cycling
Type 071AC | Football (soccer)
Type 071AD | Hockey
Type 071AE | Men's swimming
Type 071AF | Stadiums
Type 071AG | Swimming stadium
Type 071AH | Water polo
Type 071AJ | Women's diving

	ordinary cover	
071AB.1 to AJ.1	Official Souvenir Cover	20.00
071AB.2 to AJ.2	any other Illustrated cover	15.00
	Registered cover Qty: 436*	
071AB.1R to AJ.1R	Official Souvenir Cover	70.00

* Quantity is a combined total for all eight postmarks.

23 Nov – 8 Dec 1956
Olympic Park (Press)

Type 071AK | Diving and swimming
Type 071AL | Vaulting horse

	ordinary cover	
071AK.1 to AL.1	Official Souvenir Cover	20.00
071AK.2 to AL.2	any other Illustrated cover	15.00
	Registered cover Qty: 352*	
071AK.1R to AL.1R	Official Souvenir Cover	80.00

* Quantity is a combined total for both postmarks.

15 Oct – 18 Dec 1956
Olympic Village

Type 071AM | Cycling and running
Type 071AN | Entrance to village
Type 071AP | Javelin throwing
Type 071AQ | Long jump
Type 071AR | Tandem cycling
Type 071AS | Torch bearer
Type 071AT | View of village

	ordinary cover	
071AM.1 to AT.1	Official Souvenir Cover	15.00
071AM.2 to AT.2	any other Illustrated cover	10.00
	Registered cover Qty: 2,995*	
071AM.1R to AT.1R	Official Souvenir Cover	50.00

* Quantity is a combined total for all seven postmarks.

22 Nov – 8 Dec 1956
Richmond Park

Type 071AU | Boxing
Type 071AV | Discus
Type 071AW | Hammer throw
Type 071AX | Hurdles
Type 071AY | Running
Type 071AZ | Triple jump

	ordinary cover	
071AU.1 to AZ.1	Official Souvenir Cover	20.00
071AU.2 to AZ.2	any other Illustrated cover	15.00
	Registered cover Qty: 440*	
071AU.1R to AZ.1R	Official Souvenir Cover	70.00

* Quantity is a combined total for all six postmarks.

26 Nov – 5 Dec 1956
St Kilda Pier

Type 071BA | Sailing 1
Type 071BB | Sailing 2

	ordinary cover	
071BA.1 to BB.1	Official Souvenir Cover	20.00
071BA.2 to BB.2	any other Illustrated cover	15.00
	Registered cover *	
071BA.1R to BB.1R	Official Souvenir Cover	$100

* No figures recorded for Registered covers.

072B.11R | 17 November 1956

Olympic Philatelic Exhibition (OLYMPEX)

23 Nov – 6 Dec 1956
St. Kilda Town Hall

Type 071BC | Fencing

	ordinary cover	
071BC.1	Official Souvenir Cover	20.00
071BC.2	any other Illustrated cover	15.00

	Registered cover	Qty: 80
071BC.1R	Official Souvenir Cover	$100

19 Nov – 8 Dec 1956
Station Pier

Type 071BD | Torch and Olympic rings

	ordinary cover	
071BD.1	Official Souvenir Cover	20.00
071BD.2	any other Illustrated cover	15.00

	Registered cover	*
071BD.1R	Official Souvenir Cover	$100

* No figures recorded for Registered covers.

Related stamp issue:
31 Oct 1956 – 4d, 7½d, 1s and 2s Olympic Games (SG290-293)

To avoid confusion with numerals '1' and '0', letters 'I' and 'O' were not used when allocating the alphabetical suffix to the Olympic Games postmarks.

072A   072B

072   1956 OLYMPIC PHILATELIC EXHIBITION (OLYMPEX)
Melbourne, Vic
12 – 24 Nov 1956

Type 072A	12 Nov 1956	Red ink
Type 072A	13 – 24 Nov 1956	Black ink
Type 072B	12 Nov 1956	Red ink
Type 072B	13 – 24 Nov 1956	Black ink

	ordinary cover	Qty: 55,038*
072A.1	Olympex cover – red ink	15.00
072A.2	Olympex cover – black ink	15.00
072A.3	any other illustrated cover – red ink	10.00
072A.4	any other illustrated cover – black ink	10.00

	Registered cover	Qty: 1,381*
072A.1R	Olympex cover – red ink	80.00
072A.2R	Olympex cover – black ink	80.00
072A.3R	any other illustrated cover – red ink	80.00
072A.4R	any other illustrated cover – black ink	80.00

	Certified cover	Qty: 140*
072A.#C	Any cover	$100

	ordinary cover	Qty: 55,038*
072B.1	Olympex cover – red ink	15.00
072B.2	Olympex cover – black ink	15.00
072B.3	any other illustrated cover – red ink	10.00
072B.4	any other illustrated cover – black ink	10.00

	Registered cover	Qty: 1,381*
072B.1R	Olympex cover – red ink	80.00
072B.2R	Olympex cover – black ink	80.00
072B.3R	any other illustrated cover – red ink	80.00
072B.4R	any other illustrated cover – black ink	80.00

	Certified cover	Qty: 140*
072B.#C	Any cover	$100

* The quantities quoted are for both types of postmarks (in both colours) of ordinary, Registered and Certified covers respectively. Despite the quoted quantity of impressions on Registered covers, R6 label number 5192 has been sighted.

Related stamp issue:
31 Oct 1956 – 4d, 7½d, 1s and 2s Olympic Games (SG290-293)

1957

046 **1957 ROYAL ADELAIDE EXHIBITION**
Adelaide, SA
3 Apr – 4 May 1957

Type 046 (see illustration under 1947)

046.1.57	Exhibition souvenir cover	60.00
046.2.57	plain cover	40.00

053 **1957 QUEENSLAND INDUSTRIES FAIR**
Brisbane, Qld
from 14 May 1957

Type 053 (see illustration under 1949)

053.1.57   plain cover 25.00

073

073 **1957-58 GREENBANK CORROBOREE**
Greenbank, Qld
27 Dec 1957 – 6 Jan 1958

ordinary cover
073.1   Corroboree souvenir cover 30.00
073.2   any other illustrated cover 25.00
073.#R   Registered cover 80.00

1958

074

074 **1958 14TH BRITISH EMPIRE LEAGUE SERVICE CONFERENCE**
Canberra, ACT
17 – 21 Feb 1958

ordinary cover   Qty: 9,405
074.1   Official Conference FDC 15.00
074.2   any other illustrated cover 10.00

Registered cover   Qty: 63
074.1R   Official Conference FDC 50.00
074.2R   any other illustrated cover 40.00

075

075 **1958 SECOND AUSTRALIAN INDUSTRIES FAIR**
Melbourne, Vic
7 – 29 Mar 1958

Type 075A | 1958 Fair

ordinary cover   Qty: 8,621
075A.1   any illustrated cover 40.00
075A.2   plain cover 25.00

Registered cover   Qty: est. 100*
075A.1R any illustrated cover 75.00
075A.2R plain cover 60.00

* Highest R6 number sighted: 83 (25 March 1958)

076

076 **1958 TOOWOOMBA AGRICULTURAL SHOW**
Toowoomba, Qld
Apr 1958

076.1.58   plain cover 10.00

077

077 **1958 FRENCH TRADE FAIR**
Melbourne, Vic
29 Sep – 11 Oct 1958

ordinary cover   Qty: 9,834
077.1   French Fair souvenir cover 17.50
077.2   any other illustrated cover 12.00

Registered cover   Qty: 174
077.1R   French Fair souvenir cover 60.00
077.2R   any other illustrated cover 50.00

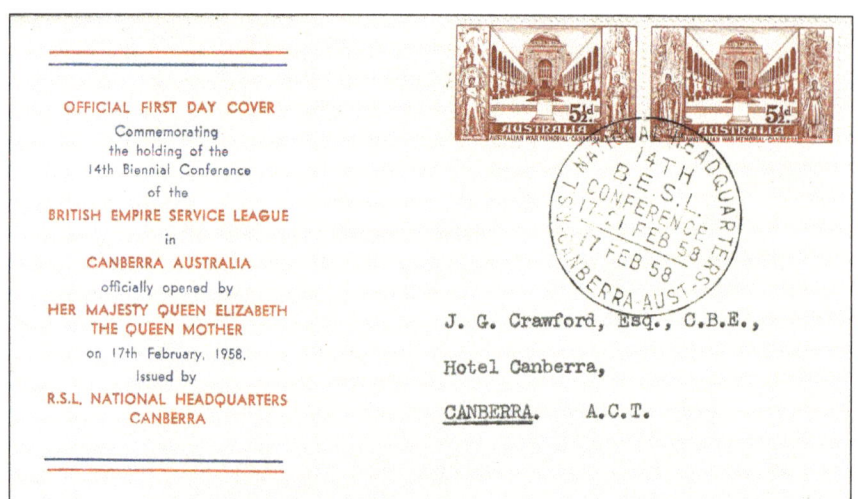

074.1 | 17 February 1958

14th British Empire League Service Conference

Most BESL Conference covers appear to be franked with one or both of the 5½d Australian War Memorial stamps, issued on 10 February 1958.

077.1R | 4 October 1958

French Trade Fair

078AC.1R | 6 February 1959

Australian National Philatelic Exhibition (ANPEX)

1959

078A   078B

078 1959 AUSTRALIAN NATIONAL PHILATELIC EXHIBITION (ANPEX)

Sydney, NSW
2 – 7 Feb 1959

Type 078A		Town Hall	
	078AA	2 Feb | red ink	Qty: 31,347*
	078AB	3 Feb | green ink	Qty: 3,478*
	078AC	4–7 Feb | black ink	Qty: 17,595*

Type 078B		Aeroplane and Aborigine	
	078BA	2 Feb | red ink	*
	078BB	3 Feb | green ink	*
	078BC	4–7 Feb | black ink	*

* Quantities are for red, green and black inks of both postmarks.

	ordinary cover	Qty: 52,420
078AA.1	ANPEX cover	10.00
078AB.1	ANPEX cover	15.00
078AC.1	ANPEX cover	12.00
078BA.1	ANPEX cover	10.00
078BB.1	ANPEX cover	15.00
078BC.1	ANPEX cover	12.00
078AA.2	any other illustrated cover	8.00
078AB.2	any other illustrated cover	12.00
078AC.2	any other illustrated cover	10.00
078BA.2	any other illustrated cover	8.00
078BB.2	any other illustrated cover	12.00
078BC.2	any other illustrated cover	10.00

	Registered cover	**Qty: 801**
	2 Feb	594
	3 Feb	75
	4–7 Feb	132
078AA.1R	ANPEX cover	25.00
078AB.1R	ANPEX cover	35.00
078AC.1R	ANPEX cover	30.00
078BA.1R	ANPEX cover	25.00
078BB.1R	ANPEX cover	35.00
078BC.1R	ANPEX cover	30.00
078AA.2R	any other illustrated cover	25.00
078AB.2R	any other illustrated cover	35.00
078AC.2R	any other illustrated cover	30.00
078BA.2R	any other illustrated cover	25.00
078BB.2R	any other illustrated cover	35.00
078BC.2R	any other illustrated cover	30.00
078#.#C	any Certified cover ...... Qty: 18	$200

Coincidental stamp issue:
2 Feb 1959 – 1d and 4d, Queen Elizabeth II definitives (SG308, 313)

079

079 1959 INTERNATIONAL TRADE FAIR

Melbourne, Vic
26 Feb – 14 Mar 1959

	ordinary cover	
079.1	International Trade Fair souvenir cover	25.00
079.2	any other illustrated cover	15.00
079.3	plain cover	12.00
079.#R	Registered cover	40.00

080A   080B

080C   080D

080 1959 ECAFE CONFERENCE

Broadbeach, Qld
9 – 21 Mar 1959

Type 080A	| 1
Type 080B	| 2
Type 080C	| 3
Type 080D	| 4

	ordinary cover	
080A.1	ECAFE Conference cover	30.00
080B.1	ECAFE Conference cover	30.00
080C.1	ECAFE Conference cover	30.00
080D.1	ECAFE Conference cover	30.00
080A.2	any other illustrated cover	20.00
080B.2	any other illustrated cover	20.00
080C.2	any other illustrated cover	20.00
080D.2	any other illustrated cover	20.00
080A to D.#R	Any Registered cover ...... Qty est: 250*	60.00

* Highest R6 number sighted: 108 (9 March 1959)

080A.1R | 9 March 1959 | ECAFE Conference

053.1.59 | 2 May 1959 | Queensland Industries Fair

081BA.1R | 5 June 1959

Queensland Centenary Stamp Exhibition (QUCEX)

053 (see also illustration under 1949)

053   1959 QUEENSLAND INDUSTRIES FAIR
Brisbane, Qld
2 – 23 May 1959

053.1.59	Queensland Industries Fair souvenir cover	30.00
053.1.59R	Queensland Industries Fair souvenir Registered cover	75.00

081A   081B

081   1959 QUEENSLAND CENTENARY STAMP EXHIBITION (QUCEX)
Brisbane, Qld
5 – 6 Jun 1959

Type 081A | CITY HALL / BRISBANE / (date) / QUCEX
081AA | 5 Jun | violet ink   Qty: 17,506*
081AB | 6 Jun | black ink   Qty: 3,160*

	ordinary cover	
081AA.1	Exhibition Official Cover	10.00
081AB.1	Exhibition Official Cover	10.00
081AA.2	any other illustrated cover	8.00
081AB.2	any other illustrated cover	8.00
081A#.#R	Registered cover.........Qty: 62*	25.00

Type 081B | QUCEX / (date) / CITY HALL / BRISBANE
081BA | 5 Jun | violet ink *
081BB | 6 Jun | black ink *

	ordinary cover	
081BA.1	Exhibition Official Cover	20.00
081BB.1	Exhibition Official Cover	20.00
081BA.2	any other illustrated cover	15.00
081BB.2	any other illustrated cover	15.00
081B#.#R	Registered cover.............*	75.00

* Quantities are for both postmarks combined.

Related stamp issue:
5 Jun 1959 – 4d, Centenary of Self-government in Queensland (SG332)

082A | 29 July 1959

082   1959 INAUGURATION QANTAS JET SERVICE
Sydney, NSW
29 Jul 1959

Type 082A | Sydney to San Francisco

	ordinary cover	Qty: 14,674
082AA.1	QANTAS cover addressed to Nadi, Fiji	12.00
082AA.2	QANTAS cover addressed to Honolulu, Hawaii	12.00
082AA.3	QANTAS cover addressed to San Francisco, USA	8.00
082AA.4	any other illustrated cover	8.00

Figures for covers carried are:
 Fiji 2,060
 Hawaii 1,947
 San Francisco 9,360
 others 102
Another 1,205 covers made the return trip on 31 July.

082A | 27 Oct 1959   29 Oct 1959 backstamp

082   1959 INAUGURATION QANTAS JET SERVICE
Sydney, NSW
27 Oct 1959

Type 082A | Sydney to London via Singapore
(see illustration under 29 Jul 1959)

	ordinary cover	Qty: 3,474
082AB.1	QANTAS cover	8.00
082AB.2	any other illustrated cover	8.00
082AB.1R	QANTAS cover Registered	45.00

Commemorative Postmarks on Registered Covers

Not your regular mail

Gordon

I was fortunate recently to win a Registered cover through eBay. It was a nice, tidy example of the 1968 PAN AM First Direct Service Sydney to Bangkok, and it didn't cost much. I needed it to fill a gap in my 1968 series of commemorative postmarks, and it now sits safely in its clear, acid-free sleeve, keeping company with the ECAFE Conference and State Girl Guide Camp of that year.

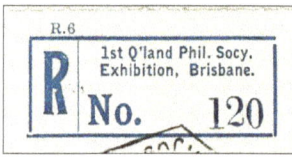

It's my practice to tick off each cover from my 'must acquire' list as it fills its space. Imagine my delight when I saw that only five covers were sent by Registered post on that 1968 PAN AM flight. That figure makes it genuinely rare and virtually impossible to find. There's no telling how many of those five covers have survived the half-century since the event, nor how permanently each sits in their owners' collections. Anyone looking for an example may be searching for a long time before they come across one for sale.

One of the joys of collecting commemorative postmarks on Registered covers is really two joys. First, some are scarce and, therefore, hard to find. Adding one to your collection is very satisfying, especially if it has taken some time. Second, when you do locate them on the market, chances are the price won't reflect their scarcity. You can own a genuinely rare item without paying hundreds of dollars.

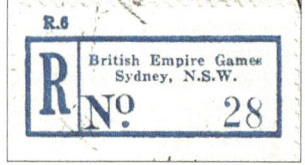

Collecting commemorative postmarks is a niche sector of our hobby and not for everyone, though most cover collectors would have one or two examples. For this reason, while some savvy collectors recognise value when they see it, most would not. Even relatively common postmarks exist only in the low thousands, at least on 'ordinary' covers. Such a postmark with a quantity listed as 5,000 may have been applied to fewer than several dozen Registered covers.

Another aspect of Registered covers that I enjoy is the backstamps, postmarks applied to the back of an envelope at each post office that handled it on its way to the addressee.

Providing you can read the dates, you can gauge the route and timing of delivery of your cover. It is an interesting piece of postal history. My PAN AM flight cover is backstamped Bangkok, proving it was on that first flight from Sydney to Thailand.

Now over 90 years old is the 1928 ANPEX commemorative postmark. While this cancel is still easy to come by, Registered covers are much scarcer. The highest R6 label I've seen is number 627 on a 31 October cover. This suggests that a maximum of 700 items were sent by Registered post, as the exhibition closed the following day. Expect to pay $150

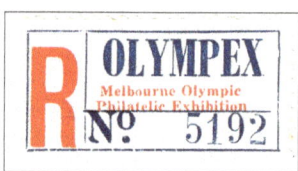

or more for such a cover. The 1932 Opening of the Sydney Harbour Bridge postmarks, one each for the northeast and southeast pylons, are slightly easier to find but still scarce.

The decade of the 1930s was a 'happy time' for commemorative postmarks. Collectors who seek out Registered covers will find that most of the nearly 50 events had registration facilities at the post offices using these cancellers. Philatelic exhibitions feature prominently in the 1930s, and Registered covers can be found cheaply. Other events are not so common. For example, the 1938 Christian Endeavour Convention, despite being held over eight days, accounted for only about 130 Registered covers. I have seen only plain (unillustrated) covers; a registered example would be worth about $150 if you can find one. The R6 label for this event is an early example of a generic label being rubber-stamped for source identification.

Coloured R6 labels add a further element of interest to Registered covers. While the standard printing of labels was in blue, the 1950 Melbourne ANPEX was a multicolour affair in blue, green and red. Five years later, Registered covers of the 1955 ANPEX held in Adelaide have a red and black label, which really stands out. The 1956 OLYMPEX label is in blue and red, while the 1959 Sydney ANPEX label is all red. The violet label produced for the 1959 Queensland Centenary Stamp Exhibition complemented the 5 June (first day) violet postmark.

An unusual variation to generic labels is the one provided for the 1962 Hobart Corroboree. Someone took the trouble to use a typewriter to fill the blank space. Perhaps the rubber stamp didn't arrive in time. Other variations a collector might search for are Registered aerogrammes and postcards with commemorative postmarks. Collectors would have sent these only to secure the R6 label and postmark.

I started this article with an example of a very scarce Registered cover for which only five can exist. Plenty of other commemorative postmarks can be found on fewer than 20 covers. As recently as 1980 – where my collection stops – the Centenary of Local Government, Euroa postmark was applied to only one Registered

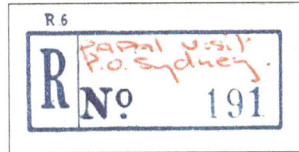

cover. What it might fetch if it came on the market is anyone's guess. At the other end of the spectrum, the SYDPEX 80 postmarks cancelled stamps on at least 4195 covers, the highest number I have seen for this event. More recently, with the cost of the service

increasing, collectors seem not to have bothered much with Registered covers, and they are again becoming scarce.

To conclude, I'll mention that to complete a Registered cover, a collector should ideally also have the R24 Receipt. This would show the same commemorative postmark as the cover. In my experience, very few collectors thought to retain these little souvenirs. Keep an eye out; they are sometimes hidden inside the envelope.

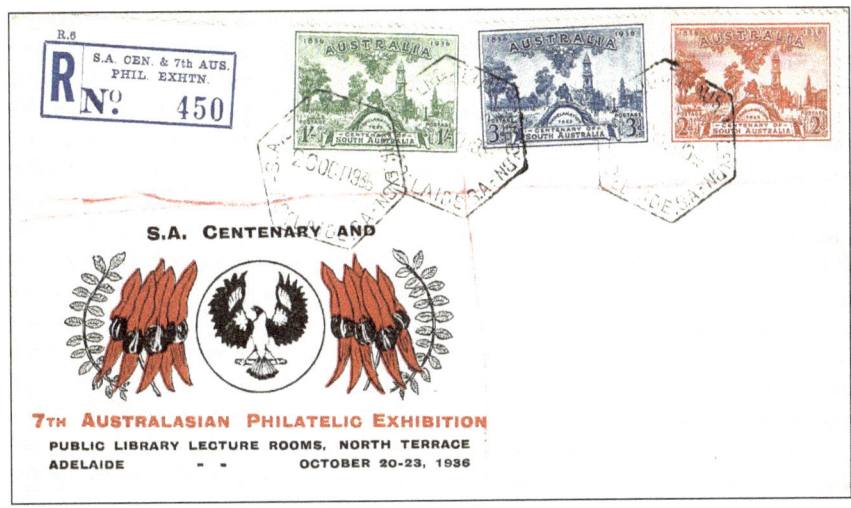

1960

EVENTS

083	22 Feb	12th International Congress of Scientific Management (CIOS)
084	4 Mar	Moomba Festival
085	15 Aug	IUPAC Symposium
086	29 Sep	South Australian Philatelic Exhibition (SAPEX)
087	1 Nov	Queensland Stamp Centenary Exhibition (QUSCEX)
088	29 Dec	6th Australian Scout Jamboree

Recurring event.
See the original event number entry for the first occurrence.

076	Mar	Toowoomba Agricultural Show
055	Sep	Royal Adelaide Show

083E.2 | 3 March 1960

12th International Congress of Scientific Management

The issue of a commemorative aerogramme for this congress creates something of a challenge for the postmark collector wanting a 'complete' collection of the event.

083E.4R | 29 February 1960

12th International Congress of Scientific Management

083

083　12TH INTERNATIONAL CONGRESS OF SCIENTIFIC MANAGEMENT

Sydney, NSW
22 – 29 Feb 1960

Type 083A	No. 1-1 with large lettering
Type 083B	No. 2-2 with large lettering
Type 083C	No. 1-1 with small lettering
Type 083D	No. 2-2 with small lettering

    ordinary cover　　Qty: 1,908
083A.1　CIOS souvenir cover 10.00
083B.1　CIOS souvenir cover 10.00
083C.1　CIOS souvenir cover 10.00
083D.1　CIOS souvenir cover 10.00
083A.2　CIOS aerogramme 10.00
083B.2　CIOS aerogramme 10.00
083C.2　CIOS aerogramme 10.00
083D.2　CIOS aerogramme 10.00
083A.3　any other illustrated cover 5.00
083B.3　any other illustrated cover 5.00
083C.3　any other illustrated cover 5.00
083D.3　any other illustrated cover 5.00
083#.4　plain cover 4.00
083#.#R　Registered cover .... Qty: 33 .... $150

Melbourne, Vic
29 Feb – 4 Mar 1960

Type 083E	No. 1-1 with large lettering
Type 083F	No. 2-2 with large lettering
Type 083G	No. 1-1 with small lettering
Type 083H	No. 2-2 with small lettering

    ordinary cover　　Qty: 2,046
083E.1　CIOS souvenir cover 10.00
083F.1　CIOS souvenir cover 10.00
083G.1　CIOS souvenir cover 10.00
083H.1　CIOS souvenir cover 10.00
083E.2　CIOS aerogramme 10.00
083F.2　CIOS aerogramme 10.00
083G.2　CIOS aerogramme 10.00
083H2　CIOS aerogramme 10.00
083E.3　any other illustrated cover 5.00
083F.3　any other illustrated cover 5.00
083G.3　any other illustrated cover 5.00
083H.3　any other illustrated cover 5.00
083#.4　plain cover 4.00
083#.#R　Registered cover .... Qty: 31 .... $150

084A

084　1960 MOOMBA FESTIVAL

Melbourne, Vic
4 – 12 Mar 1960

    ordinary cover　　Qty: 7,519
084A.1.60　Moomba cover 10.00
084A.2.60　Moomba aerogramme 10.00
084A.3.60　any other illustrated cover 10.00
084A.#.60R　Registered cover .... Qty: 72 .... 50.00

076　1960 TOOWOOMBA AGRICULTURAL SHOW

Toowoomba, Qld
Mar 1960

Type 076 (see illustration under 1958)

076.1.60　plain cover 30.00

085A | Melbourne　　　085B | Sydney

085　1960 IUPAC SYMPOSIUM

Melbourne
15 – 18 Aug 1960

    ordinary cover　　Qty: 4,832
085A.1　any illustrated cover 15.00
085A.2　plain cover 10.00
085A.#R　Registered cover .... Qty: 39 .... $100

    ordinary cover　　Qty: 1,509
085B.1　any illustrated cover 15.00
085B.2　plain cover 10.00
085B.#R　Registered cover .... Qty: 38 .... $100

IUPAC = International Union of Pure and Applied Chemistry

084A.1.60R | 4 March 1960

Moomba Festival

086.1R | 30 September 1960

South Australian Philatelic Exhibition (SAPEX)

087.1R | 2 November 1960

Queensland Stamp Centenary Exhibition (QUSCEX)

055A (see also illustration under 1949)

055 1960 ROYAL ADELAIDE SHOW
Wayville Showgrounds, SA
5 – 15 Sep 1960

055A.1.60	Royal Adelaide Show cover	50.00
055A.2.60	any othr illustrated cover	30.00
055A.3.60	plain cover	15.00

086

086 1960 SOUTH AUSTRALIAN PHILATELIC EXHIBITION (SAPEX)
Adelaide, SA
29 Sep – 1 Oct 1960

	ordinary cover	Qty: 7,400
086.1	SAPEX cover	10.00
086.2	any other illustrated cover	8.00
086.#R	Registered cover .... Qty: 304	25.00

Coincidental stamp issue:
30 Sep 1960 – 6d, Banded Anteater definitive (SG316)

087

087 1960 QUEENSLAND STAMP CENTENARY EXHIBITION (QUSCEX)
Brisbane, Qld
1 – 5 Nov 1960

	ordinary cover	Qty: 18,016
087.1	Exhibition cover	7.50
087.2	Exhibition folded maximum card	7.50
087.3	Queensland Stamp Centenary cover	7.50
087.4	any other illustrated cover	5.00
087.#R	Registered cover .... Qty: 492	20.00

Related stamp issue:
2 Nov 1960 – 5d, Centenary of First Queensland Postage Stamp (SG337)

088

088 1960-61 6TH AUSTRALIAN SCOUT JAMBOREE
Sydney, NSW
29 Dec 1960 – 9 Jan 1961

	ordinary cover	Qty: 61,000
088.1	Scout Jamboree cover	10.00
088.2	any other illustrated cover	6.00
088.#R	Registered cover	40.00

088.1 | 29 December 1960

6th Australian Scout Jamboree

089.2R | 19 February 1961

Last Tram Mail

Some covers were additionally rubber stamped with a 'N.S.W. Tramway Historical Association' cachet in purple.

091.1R | 30 June 1961

Royal Sydney Philatelic Exhibition

093A.1 | 4 August 1961

Sydney Trade Fair

1961

EVENTS

089	19 Feb	Last Tram Mail
090	17 Apr	International Council of Nurses 12th Quadrennial Congress
091	19 Jun	Royal Sydney Philatelic Exhibition
092	10 Jul	Antarctic Treaty First Consultative Meeting
093	1 Aug	Sydney Trade Fair
094	23 Oct	17th International Air Transport Association Annual General Meeting
095	27 Dec	7th World Rover Scout Moot

Recurring events.
See the original event number entry for the first occurrence.

084	3 Mar	*Moomba Festival*
027	Mar	*Royal Easter Show*
055	Sep	*Royal Adelaide Show*
082	14 Nov	*Inauguration QANTAS Jet Service*

089

089 **1961 LAST TRAM MAIL**

Sydney, NSW
19 Feb 1961

	ordinary cover	Qty: 15,820	
089.1	Last Tram Mail 'Last Day Cover'		10.00
089.2	any other illustrated cover		7.50
089.#R	Registered cover	Qty: 33	75.00

084 **1961 MOOMBA FESTIVAL**

Melbourne, Vic
3 – 13 Mar 1961

Type 084A (see illustration under 1960)

	ordinary cover	Qty: 5,070	
084A.1.61	Moomba cover		15.00
084A.2.61	Moomba aerogramme		15.00
084A.3.61	any other illustrated cover		15.00
084A.#.61R	Registered cover	Qty: 69	50.00

027B

027 **1961 ROYAL EASTER SHOW**

Sydney, NSW
Mar 1961

027B.1.61	plain cover	40.00

090

090 **1961 INTERNATIONAL COUNCIL OF NURSES 12TH QUADRENNIAL CONGRESS**

Melbourne, Vic
17 – 22 Apr 1961

	ordinary cover	Qty: 12,685	
090.1	any illustrated cover		10.00
090.2	plain cover		7.50
090.#R	Registered cover	Qty: 38	75.00

094.1R | 24 October 1961

17th International Air Transport Association Annual General Meeting

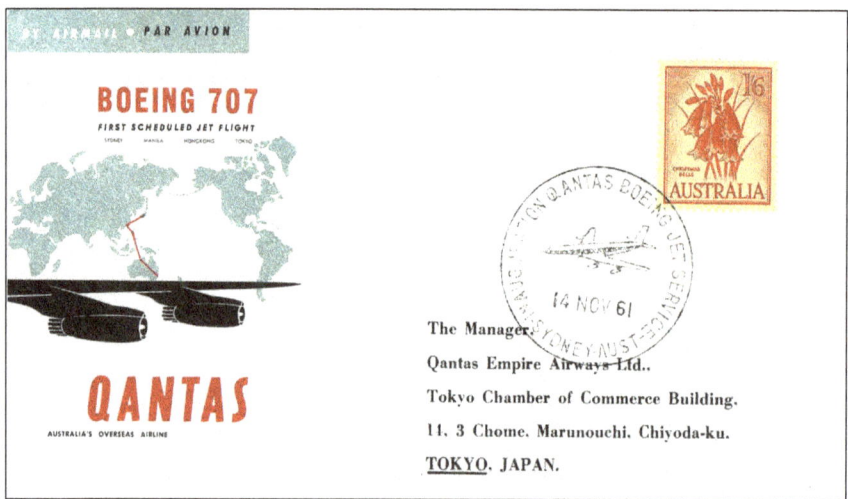

082AC.1 | 14 November 1961

Inauguration QANTAS Jet Service – Sydney to Tokyo

095.1 | 28 December 1961

7th World Rover Scout Moot

091

091 1961 ROYAL SYDNEY PHILATELIC EXHIBITION
Sydney, NSW
19 – 30 Jun 1961

	ordinary cover	Qty: 10,621
091.1	Royal Sydney Philatelic Club souvenir cover	10.00
091.2	Colombo Plan stamp FDC (30 Jun)	8.00
091.3	any other illustrated cover	5.00
091.#R	Registered cover.......... Qty: 174	25.00

Coincidental stamp issue:
30 Jun 1961 – 1/-, Colombo Plan (SG339)

The majority of covers are dated 19 or 30 June.

092

092 1961 ANTARCTIC TREATY FIRST CONSULTATIVE MEETING
Canberra, ACT
10 – 24 Jul 1961

	ordinary cover	Qty: 2,391
092.1	any illustrated cover	20.00
092.2	plain cover	15.00

093A

093 1961 SYDNEY TRADE FAIR
Sydney, NSW
1 – 12 Aug 1961

	ordinary cover	Qty: 11,862
093A.1	Sydney Trade Fair cover – Opening Day (4 Aug)	10.00
093A.2	Sydney Trade Fair cover	10.00
093A.3	any other illustrated cover	5.00
093A.#R	Registered cover.......... Qty: 81	50.00

055 1961 ROYAL ADELAIDE SHOW
Wayville Showgrounds, SA
Sep 1961

Type 055A (see illustrations under 1949 and 1960)

055A.1.61	plain cover	40.00

094

094 1961 17TH INTERNATIONAL AIR TRANSPORT ASSOCIATION ANNUAL GENERAL MEETING
Canberra, ACT
23 – 27 Oct 1961

	ordinary cover	Qty: 1,529
094.1	any illustrated cover	20.00
094.2	plain cover	15.00
094.#R	Registered cover.......... Qty: est. 100	50.00

082 1961 INAUGURATION QANTAS JET SERVICE
Sydney, NSW
14 Nov 1961

Type 082A | Sydney to Tokyo (see illustration under 1959)

	ordinary cover	Qty: 3,231
082AC.1	QANTAS cover	10.00
082AC.2	any other illustrated cover	8.00

095

095 1961-62 7TH WORLD ROVER SCOUT MOOT
Clifford Park, Vic
27 Dec 1961 – 7 Jan 1962

	ordinary cover	Qty: 12,236
095.1	7th World Rover Scout Moot cover	20.00
095.2	any other illustrated cover	15.00
095.#R	Registered cover.......... Qty: 222	75.00

096.1.62 | 28 February 1962

Maitland Agricultural and Horticultural Show

084A.1.62R | 2 March 1962

Moomba Festival

097.2R | 2 June 1962

ECAFE Railway Sub-committee 7th Session

1962

EVENTS

096	28 Feb	Maitland Agricultural and Horticultural Show
097	28 May	ECAFE Railway Sub-committee 7th Session
098	10 Aug	12th World's Poultry Congress
099	20 Sep	Australia's First Automatic Post Office
100	2 Oct	Associated Country Women of the World – World Conference
101	19 Oct	6th World Power Conference
102	30 Oct	14th Colombo Plan Conference
103	1 Nov	7th British Empire and Commonwealth Games
104	26 Nov	ILO 5th Asian Regional Conference
105	27 Dec	Hobart Corroboree

Recurring events.
See the original event number entry for the first occurrence.

084	2 Mar	Moomba Festival
053	28 Apr	Queensland Industries Fair

096

096 1962 MAITLAND AGRICULTURAL AND HORTICULTURAL SHOW

Maitland Showground, NSW
28 Feb – 12 Mar 1962

ordinary cover
096.1.62	any illustrated cover	15.00
096.2.62	plain cover	10.00

084 1962 MOOMBA FESTIVAL

Melbourne, Vic
2 – 12 Mar 1962

Type 084A (see illustration under 1960)

ordinary cover Qty: 4,539
084A.1.62	Moomba cover – boomerang and tiger cat	10.00
084A.2.62	Moomba cover – boomerang and music	10.00
084A.3.62	Moomba aerogramme	15.00
084A.4.62	any other illustrated cover	10.00
084A.#.62R	Registered cover Qty: 86	50.00

053 1962 QUEENSLAND INDUSTRIES FAIR

Brisbane, Qld
from 28 April 1962

Type 053 (see illustration under 1949)

053.1.62	plain cover	25.00
053.2.62R	plain cover Registered *	75.00

* Highest R6 label sighted is 101

097

097 1962 ECAFE RAILWAY SUB-COMMITTEE 7TH SESSION

Melbourne, Vic
28 May – 5 Jun 1962

ordinary cover Qty: 2,155
097.1	any illustrated cover	15.00
097.2	plain cover	10.00
097.#R	Registered cover Qty: 44	50.00

098

098 1962 12TH WORLD'S POULTRY CONGRESS

Sydney, NSW
10 – 18 Aug 1962

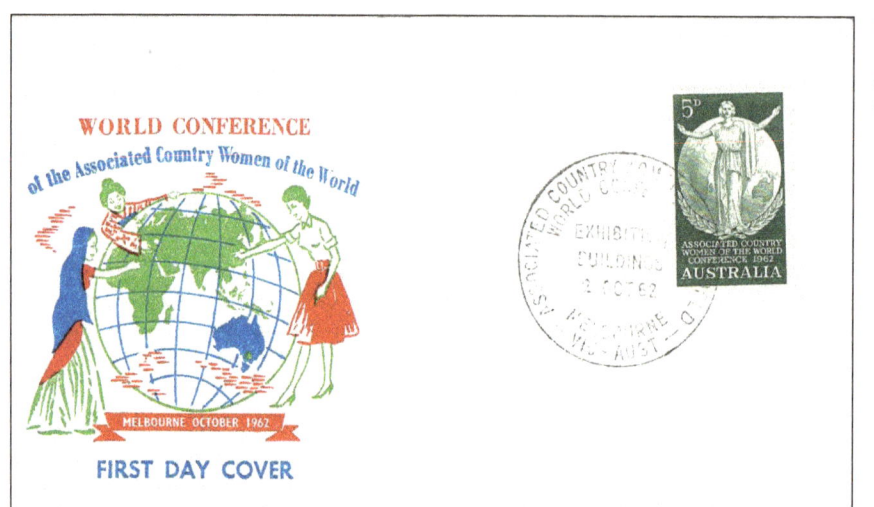

100.1 | 2 October 1962

Associated Country Women of the World – World Conference

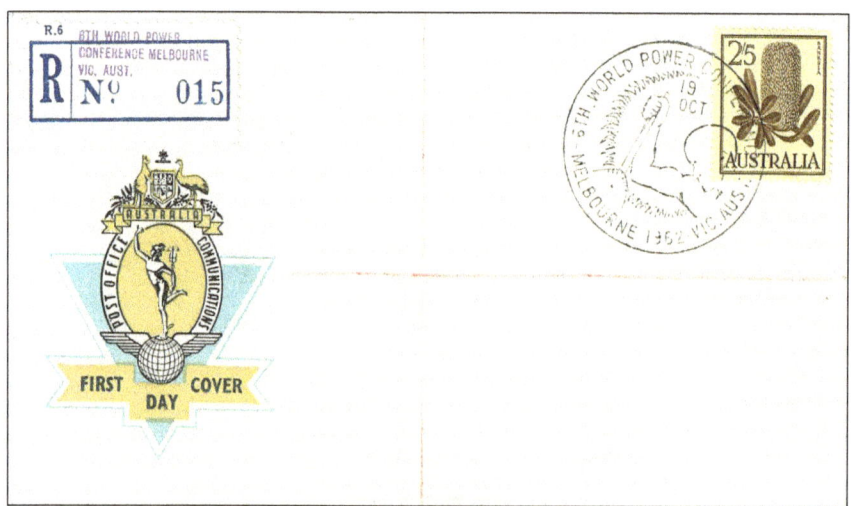

101.2R | 19 October 1962

6th World Power Conference

103N.1R | 1 November 1962

7th British Empire and Commonwealth Games

	ordinary cover	Qty: 5,734
098.1	Poultry Congress cover	20.00
098.2	any illustrated cover	15.00
098.#R	Registered cover........... Qty: 67	40.00

099

099 1962 AUSTRALIA'S FIRST AUTOMATIC POST OFFICE

Melbourne, Vic
20 – 29 Sep 1962

	ordinary cover	
099.1	First Automatic Post Office PSE	$100
099.2	First Automatic Post Office Postal Card	$150
099.3	any other illustrated cover	60.00
099.4	plain cover	30.00

Fewer than 2,000 overprinted stamped envelopes and fewer than 1,150 postal cards were sold at the post office. Not all were postmarked.

100

100 1962 ASSOCIATED COUNTRY WOMEN OF THE WORLD – WORLD CONFERENCE

Melbourne, Vic
2 – 12 Oct 1962

	ordinary cover	Qty: 3,873
100.1	World Conference FDC	15.00
100.2	any other illustrated cover	12.00
100.#R	Registered cover........... Qty: 39	40.00

Related stamp issue:
26 Sep 1962 – 5d, Associated Country Women of the World (SG344)

101

101 1962 6TH WORLD POWER CONFERENCE

Melbourne, Vic
19 – 27 Oct 1962

 ordinary cover Qty: 4,917

101.1	World Power Conference aerogramme	15.00
101.2	any other illustrated cover	10.00
101.#R	Registered cover........... Qty: 69	40.00

Total ordinary items includes 53 parcels and 1,377 packets.

102

102 1962 14TH COLOMBO PLAN CONFERENCE

Melbourne, Vic
29 Oct – 17 Nov 1962

	ordinary cover	Qty: 4,419
102.1	any illustrated cover	15.00
102.#R	Registered cover........... Qty: 45	50.00

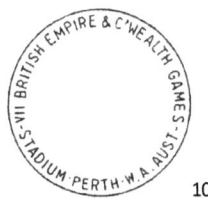
103

103 1962 7TH BRITISH EMPIRE AND COMMONWEALTH GAMES

Stadium, Perth, WA
1 Nov – 1 Dec 1962

Type 103A	Female Runner
Type 103B	Games Emblem
Type 103C	Male runner
Type 103D	Marathon
Type 103E	Relay
Type 103F	Winners' podium

 ordinary cover Qty: est. 32,300

103A.1 to F.1	Commonwealth Games cover	6.00
103A.2 to F.2	Commonwealth Games aerogramme	10.00
103A.3 to F.3	any other illustrated cover	4.00
103A.#R to F.#R	Registered cover........ Qty: 309	30.00

Games Village, Perth
1 Nov – 15 Dec 1962

Type 103G	Boxing
Type 103H	Discus
Type 103J	Hammer throw
Type 103K	High jump
Type 103L	Hurdling
Type 103M	Javelin
Type 103N	Long jump
Type 103P	Pole vault
Type 103Q	Shot put
Type 103R	Village scene
Type 103S	Weight lifting
Type 103T	Wrestling

Stadium Perth:

103A  103B  103C  103D

103E  103F

Games Village Perth:

103G  103H

103J  103K  103L  103M  103N

103P  103Q  103R  103S  103T

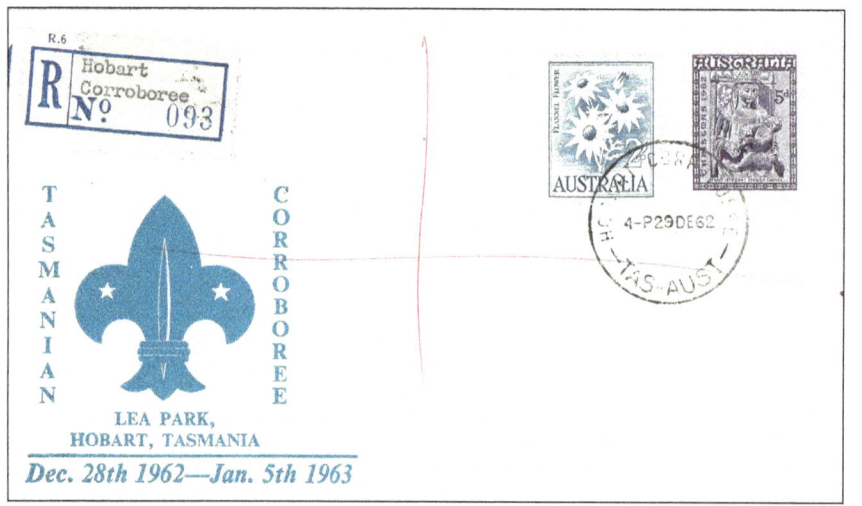

105.1R | 29 December 1962

Hobart Corroboree

	ordinary cover	Qty: est. 64,800
103G.1 to T.1	Commonwealth Games cover	6.00
103G.2 to T.2	Commonwealth Games aerogramme	10.00
103G.3 to T.3	any other illustrated cover	5.00
103G.#R to T.#R	Registered cover............ Qty: 702	30.00

103U

Rink, Dalkeith
19 – 30 Nov 1962

Type 103U | Lawn bowls

	ordinary cover	Qty est.: 2,400
103U.1	Commonwealth Games cover	6.00
103U.2	Commonwealth Games aerogramme	10.00
103U.3	any other illustrated cover	5.00
103U.#R	Registered cover............ Qty: 31	$200

103V

Fremantle Harbour North Wharf
19 Nov – 3 Dec 1962

Type 103V | Sailing

	ordinary cover	Qty est. 14,700
103V.1	Commonwealth Games cover	6.00
103V.2	Commonwealth Games aerogramme	10.00
103V.3	any other illustrated cover	5.00
103V.#R	Registered cover............ Qty: 79	50.00

103W   103X

Aquatic Centre, Perth
23 – 30 Nov 1962

Type 103W | Diving
Type 103X | Swimming

	ordinary cover	Qty est. 6,098
103W.1	Commonwealth Games cover	6.00
103W.2	Commonwealth Games aerogramme	10.00
103W.3	any other illustrated cover	5.00
103X.1	Commonwealth Games cover	6.00
103X.2	Commonwealth Games aerogramme	10.00
103X.3	any other illustrated cover	5.00
	Registered cover	Qty 72
103W.#R	any cover	50.00
103X.#R	any cover	50.00

103Y

Canning River
24 – 27 Nov 1962

Type 103Y | Rowing

	ordinary cover	Qty est. 2,800
103Y.1	Commonwealth Games cover	6.00
103Y.2	Commonwealth Games aerogramme	10.00
103Y.3	any other illustrated cover	5.00
103Y.#R	Registered cover............ Qty: 27	80.00

103Z

Velodrome, Perth
26 – 29 Nov 1962

Type 103Z | Cycling

	ordinary cover	Qty est. 2,500
103Z.1	Commonwealth Games cover	6.00
103Z.2	Commonwealth Games aerogramme	10.00
103Z.3	any other illustrated cover	5.00
103Z.#R	Registered cover............ Qty: 27	80.00

103AA

Drill Hall, Victoria Park
29 – 30 Nov 1962

Type 103AA | Fencing

	ordinary cover	Qty est. 2,800
103AA.1	Commonwealth Games cover	6.00
103AA.2	Commonwealth Games aerogramme	10.00
103AA.3	any other illustrated cover	5.00
103AA.#R	Registered cover............ Qty: 39	75.00

103AB

Kings Park, WA
1 Dec 1962

Type 103AB | Cycling

	ordinary cover	Qty est. 2,098	
103AB.1	Commonwealth Games cover		6.00
103AB.2	Commonwealth Games aerogramme		10.00
103AB.3	any other illustrated cover		5.00
103AB.#R	Registered cover	Qty: 77	50.00

Set of 26 illustrated covers
Set A	Games cover with 5d Games stamp	$100
Set B	Games cover with 5d and 2/3 Games	$200
Set C	Games aerogramme	$200

Related stamp issue:
1 Nov 1962 – 5d and 2/3, 7th British Empire and Commonwealth Games (SG346-7).

The majority of covers were franked with the 5d Commonwealth Games stamp. Registered covers will normally be franked with the 2/3 value.

104   1962 ILO 5TH ASIAN REGIONAL CONFERENCE
Melbourne, Vic
26 Nov – 8 Dec 1962

	ordinary cover	Qty: 4,569	
104.1	any illustrated cover		10.00
104.#R	Registered cover	Qty: 55	40.00

105   1962-63 HOBART CORROBOREE
Hobart, Tas
27 Dec 1962 – 7 Jan 1963

	ordinary cover	Qty: 7,276	
105.1	Tasmanian Corroboree cover		30.00
105.2	any other illustrated cover		20.00
105.3	plain cover		15.00
105.#R	Registered cover		$100

1963

EVENTS

106	27 Feb	2nd Melbourne International Trade Fair
107	7 Oct	Melbourne International Philatelic Exhibition (MIPEX)
108	22 Nov	Canberra Philatelic Exhibition

Recurring events.
See the original event number entry for the first occurrence.

084	1 Mar	*Moomba Festival*
027	Apr	*Royal Easter Show*
093	24 Jul	*Sydney Trade Fair*
022	Aug	*Brisbane Exhibition*
055	4 Sep	*Royal Adelaide Show*

106

106 1963 2ND MELBOURNE INTERNATIONAL TRADE FAIR

Melbourne, Vic
27 Feb – 16 Mar 1963

	ordinary cover	Qty: 3,897	
106.1	any illustrated cover		10.00
106.2	plain cover		5.00
106.#R	Registered cover	Qty: 80	50.00

084 1963 MOOMBA FESTIVAL

Melbourne, Vic
1 – 9 Mar 1963

Type 084A (see illustration under 1960)

	ordinary cover	Qty: 4,014	
084A.1.63	Moomba cover		7.50
084A.2.63	Moomba cover with FDI Canberra stamp o/p		12.00
084A.3.63	Moomba aerogramme		20.00
084A.4.63	any other illustrated cover		6.00
084A.5.63	plain cover		4.00
084A.#.63R	Registered cover	Qty: 55	50.00

Coincidental stamp issue:
8 Mar 1963 – 5d, 50th Anniversary of Canberra (SG35)

027C

027 1963 ROYAL EASTER SHOW

Sydney, NSW
Apr 1963

	ordinary cover	
027C.1.63	any illustrated cover	30.00
027C.2.63	plain cover	25.00
027C.#.63R	Registered cover	$100

093B

093 1963 SYDNEY TRADE FAIR

Sydney, NSW
24 Jul – 13 Aug 1963

	ordinary cover	Qty: 8,681	
093B.1	any illustrated cover		10.00
093B.2	plain cover		6.00
093B.#R	Registered cover	Qty: 130	40.00

022 1963 BRISBANE EXHIBITION

Brisbane, Qld
Aug 1963

Type 022B (see illustration under 1940)

022B.1.63	plain cover	20.00
022B.1.63R	plain cover Registered	50.00

055 1963 ROYAL ADELAIDE SHOW

Wayville Showgrounds, SA
4 – 12 Sep 1963

Type 055A (see illustration under 1949)

055A.1.63	Royal Adelaide Show souvenir cover	40.00
055A.2.63	any other illustrated cover	30.00
055A.2.63	plain cover	20.00

107A   107B

107 1963 MELBOURNE INTERNATIONAL PHILATELIC EXHIBITION (MIPEX)

Melbourne, Vic
7 – 12 Oct 1963

Type 107A | 'IV' postmark

107AA	7 Oct	green ink
107AB	8 Oct	red ink
107AC	9-11 Oct	black ink
107AD	12 Oct	purple ink

Type 107B | 'Barred 1' postmark

107BA	7 Oct	green
107BB	8 Oct	red
107BC	9-11 Oct	black
107BD	12 Oct	purple

	ordinary cover	Qty: 27,798*	
107AA.1 to AD.1	MIPEX cover		8.00
107BA.1 to BD.1	MIPEX cover		8.00
107AA.2 to AD.2	any other illustrated cover		6.00
107BA.2 to BD.2	any other illustrated cover		6.00
	Registered cover	Qty: 1,189*	
107AA.1R to AD.1R	MIPEX cover		15.00
107BA.1R to BD.1R	MIPEX cover		15.00
107AA.2R to AD.2R	any other illustrated cover		12.00
107BA.2R to BD.2R	any other illustrated cover		12.00

084A.2.63 | 8 March 1963

Moomba Festival

055A.1.63 | 4 September 1963

Royal Adelaide Show

107BB.3C | 8 October 1963

Melbourne International Philatelic Exhibition (MIPEX) – First Australian Hovercraft Mail

	Certified cover	Qty: 47*
107AA.#C to BD.#C	Certified cover..50.00

First Australian Hovercraft Mail

	Official Souvenir Cover	Qty: 7,166**
107AB.3	8 Oct IV postmark..10.00
107AB.3R	8 Oct IV postmark Registered *.................35.00
107AB.3C	8 Oct IV postmark Certified *....................60.00
107BB.3	8 Oct Barred 1 postmark...............................10.00
107BB.3R	8 Oct Barred 1 postmark Registered cover *......35.00
107BB.3C	8 Oct Barred 1 postmark Certified cover *......60.00

* The number of ordinary, Registered and Certified Hovercraft Mail covers is presumed to be included in the MIPEX totals.

** Nelson Eustis records 7,166 souvenir covers, 50 aerogrammes and 12 newspaper wrappers.

Red and black impressions of both postmarks are known with 'incorrect' dates.

Coincidental stamp issues:
9 Oct 1963 – 5d, Queen Elizabeth II definitive (SG354).
9 Oct 1963 – 4/-, Abel Tasman definitive (SG355).

108

108	**1963 CANBERRA PHILATELIC EXHIBITION**
	Canberra, ACT
	22 – 25 Nov 1963

	ordinary cover	Qty: 2,661
108.1	Canberra Philatelic Exhibition cover 12.00
108.2	any other illustrated cover 8.00
108.#R	Registered cover............................Qty: 58 ....50.00

107AD.1 | 12 October 1963

Melbourne International Philatelic Exhibition (MIPEX)

108.1R | 22 November 1963 | Canberra Philatelic Exhibition

1964

EVENTS

109	10 Jan	Church of England Boys Society (CEBS) Golden Jubilee
110	20 Jan	ANZAAS Congress
111	23 Mar	Grand Easter Show
112	25 Sep	British Exhibition 1964
113	29 Dec	7th Australian Scout Jamboree

Recurring events.
See the original event number entry for the first occurrence.

084	*3 Mar*	*Moomba Festival*
076	*Apr*	*Toowoomba Agricultural Show*
017	*Sep*	*Royal Melbourne Show*
082	*26 Nov*	*Inauguration QANTAS Jet Service*

112.1R | 6 October 1964

British Exhibition

113.1 | 1 January 1965

7th Australian Scout Jamboree

109A

109 1964 CHURCH OF ENGLAND BOYS SOCIETY (CEBS) CAMP

Loftus, NSW
10 – 20 Jan 1964

	ordinary cover	Qty: 3,767	
109A.1	any illustrated cover		12.00
109A.2	plain cover		10.00
109A.#R	Registered cover	Qty: 44	50.00

110A

110 1964 37TH ANZAAS CONGRESS

Canberra, ACT
20 – 24 Jan 1964

	ordinary cover	Qty: 1,584	
110A.1	any illustrated cover		20.00
110A.2	plain cover		15.00
110A.#R	Registered cover	Qty: 20	75.00

084 **1964 MOOMBA FESTIVAL**

Melbourne, Vic
3 – 12 Mar 1964

Type 084A (see illustration under 1960)

	ordinary cover	Qty: 4,089	
084A.1.64	Moomba cover		8.00
084A.2.64	any other illustrated cover		6.00
084A.#64R	Registered cover	Qty: 74	50.00

111

111 1964 GRAND EASTER SHOW

Melbourne, Vic
23 Mar – 4 Apr 1964

	ordinary cover	Qty: 398	
111.1	any illustrated cover		$100
111.#R	Registered cover	Qty: 20	$150

076 **1964 TOOWOOMBA AGRICULTURAL SHOW**

Toowoomba, Qld
Apr 1964

Type 076 (see illustration under 1958)

076.1.64	plain cover	30.00
076.1.64R	plain cover Registered	50.00

112

112 1964 BRITISH EXHIBITION

Sydney, NSW
25 Sep – 10 Oct 1964

	ordinary cover	Qty: 6,558	
112.1	British Exhibition 1964 cover		10.00
112.2	any other illustrated cover		7.50
112.#R	Registered cover	Qty: 118	35.00

017 **1964 ROYAL MELBOURNE SHOW**

Show Grounds, Melbourne, Vic
Sep 1964

Type 017B (see illustration under 1949)

017B.1.64	plain cover	10.00

082 **1964 INAUGURATION QANTAS JET SERVICE**

Sydney, NSW
26 Nov 1964

082A | Sydney to London via Mexico
(see illustration under 1959)

	ordinary cover	Qty: 3,327	
082AD.1	QANTAS cover – addressed to Mexico		20.00
082AD.2	QANTAS cover – addressed to Bermuda		20.00
082AD.3	QANTAS cover – addressed to London		15.00
082AD.4	any other illustrated cover		10.00

113

113 1964-65 7TH AUSTRALIAN SCOUT JAMBOREE

Dandenong, Vic
29 Dec 1964 – 11 Jan 1965

	ordinary cover	Qty: 124,700	
113.1	Australian Scout Jamboree cover		8.00
113.2	any other illustrated cover		5.00
113.#R	Registered cover	Qty: 406	80.00

1965

EVENTS

114	7 Feb	18th International Banking Summer School
115	19 Mar	Bathurst Sesquicentenary
116	16 Aug	International Crystallographic Meeting
117	19 Aug	15th Convention of the International Federation of University Women
118	23 Aug	3rd Commonwealth and Empire Law Conference
119	20 Nov	Junior Chamber of Commerce International 20th World Congress
120	29 Dec	1st National Senior Scout Venture

Recurring events.
See the original event number entry for the first occurrence.

084	3 Mar	Moomba Festival
075	4 Mar	Australian Industries Fair
082	31 Mar	Inauguration QANTAS Boeing Jet Service
082	5 Apr	Inauguration QANTAS Boeing Jet Service
082	10 Apr	Inauguration QANTAS Boeing Jet Service
082	4 Sep	Inauguration QANTAS Boeing Jet Service
017	Sep	Royal Melbourne Show
093	18 Oct	Sydney Trade Fair

114.1R | 19 February 1965

18th International Banking Summer School

114

114 1965 18TH INTERNATIONAL BANKING SUMMER SCHOOL

Melbourne, Vic
7 – 20 Feb 1965

	ordinary cover	Qty: 3,233
114.1	any illustrated cover	15.00
114.2	plain cover	7.50
114.#R	Registered cover	Qty: 55 .... 75.00

084 1965 MOOMBA FESTIVAL

Melbourne, Vic
3 – 13 Mar 1965

Type 084A (see illustration under 1960)

	ordinary cover	Qty: 4,113
084A.1.65	Moomba cover	8.00
084A.2.65	any other illustrated cover	6.00
084A.#.65R	Registered cover	Qty: 66 .... 50.00

075B

075 1965 AUSTRALIAN INDUSTRIES FAIR

Melbourne, Vic
4 – 20 Mar 1965

	ordinary cover	Qty: 1,152
075B.1	any illustrated cover	40.00
075B.2	plain cover	20.00
075B.#R	Registered cover	Qty: 39 .... $120

An Australian Industrial Fair was held in 1949 and was followed by several similar shows. These included the Made in Australia Exhibition in 1952 and the First Australian Industries Fair in 1955.

115

115 1965 BATHURST SESQUICENTENARY

Bathurst, NSW
19 – 27 Mar 1965

	ordinary cover	Qty: 6,737
115.1	Evans Memorial cover	15.00
115.2	any other illustrated cover	10.00
115.#R	Registered cover	Qty: 106 .... 50.00

082 1965 INAUGURATION QANTAS JET SERVICE

Sydney, NSW
31 Mar 1965

Type 082A | Sydney to Vienna via Singapore
(see illustration under 1959)

	ordinary cover		
082AE.1	QANTAS cover – one way	Qty: 2,009*	25.00
082AE.2	QANTAS cover – return	Qty: 151*	75.00
082AE.3	any other illustrated cover	*	20.00

Sydney, NSW
5 Apr 1965

Type 082A | Sydney to Vienna via Hong Kong
(see illustration under 1959)

	ordinary cover		
082AF.1	QANTAS cover – one way	Qty: 1,452*	30.00
082AF.2	QANTAS cover – return	Qty: 145*	80.00
082AF.3	any other illustrated cover	*	25.00

Sydney, NSW
10 Apr 1965

Type 082A | Sydney to Christchurch
(see illustration under 1959)

	ordinary cover		
082AG.1	QANTAS cover – one way	Qty: 3,084*	10.00
082AG.2	QANTAS cover – return	Qty: 126*	80.00
082AG.3	any other illustrated cover	*	8.00

* Quantities are for all types of cover.

1965 BIRTH CENTENARY OF SIR JOHN MONASH
23 June 1965

On 23 June 1965, a five-pence stamp (SG378) was issued to mark the birth centenary of General Sir John Monash. FDCs can be found postmarked with the regular Monash University cds. This appears to have been used as an appropriate venue to release the stamp rather than for the event described (i.e. the anniversary) and is not listed here. Some 5,200 ordinary and 98 Registered covers were processed. The ordinary event-specific cover is valued at $12.

116

116 1965 INTERNATIONAL CRYSTALLOGRAPHIC MEETING

Melbourne, Vic
16 – 25 Aug 1965

082AE.1 | 31 March 1965

Inauguration QANTAS Jet Service
– Sydney to Vienna via Singapore

082AG.1 | 10 April 1965

Inauguration QANTAS Jet Service
– Sydney to Christchurch

118.1R | 31 August 1965

3rd Commonwealth and Empire
Law Conference

	ordinary cover	Qty: 1,426
116.1	any illustrated cover	20.00
116.1R	Registered cover............Qty: 47	80.00

117

117 1965 15TH CONVENTION OF THE INTERNATIONAL FEDERATION OF UNIVERSITY WOMEN

Brisbane, Qld
19 – 26 Aug 1965

	ordinary cover	Qty: 2,888
117.1	any illustrated cover	15.00
117.2	plain cover	10.00
117.#R	Registered cover............Qty: 3	*

* No established value

118

118 1965 3RD COMMONWEALTH AND EMPIRE LAW CONFERENCE

Sydney, NSW
23 Aug – 2 Sep 1965

	ordinary cover	Qty: 2,992
118.1	Law Conference aerogramme	40.00
118.2	any other illustrated cover	30.00
118.3	plain cover	25.00
	Registered cover	Qty: 92
118.1R	Law Conference aerogramme	60.00
118.2R	any other illustrated cover	50.00

082 1965 INAUGURATION QANTAS JET SERVICE

Sydney, NSW
4 Sep 1965

Type 082A | Sydney to London via Kuala Lumpur
(see illustration under 1959)

	ordinary cover		
082AH.1	QANTAS cover – one way to KL	Qty: 2,026*	10.00
082AH.2	QANTAS cover – one way to London	Qty: 40*	$200
082AH.3	QANTAS cover – return	Qty: 119*	80.00
082AH.4	any other illustrated cover	*	8.00

* Quantities are for all types of cover.

017 1965 ROYAL MELBOURNE SHOW

Show Grounds, Melbourne, Vic
Sep 1965

Type 017B (see illustration under 1949)

017B.1.65 plain cover 25.00

093C

093 1965 SYDNEY TRADE FAIR

Sydney, NSW
18 Oct – 1 Nov 1965

	ordinary cover	Qty: 2,722
093C.1	any illustrated cover	20.00
093C.2	plain cover	15.00
093C.#R	Registered cover............Qty: 60	60.00

119

119 1965 JUNIOR CHAMBER OF COMMERCE INTERNATIONAL 20TH WORLD CONGRESS

Sydney, NSW
20 – 27 Nov 1965

	ordinary cover	Qty: 1,494
119.1	any illustrated cover	40.00
119.2	plain cover	20.00
119.#R	Registered cover............Qty: 45	80.00

120

120 1965-66 1ST NATIONAL SENIOR SCOUT VENTURE

Perth, WA
29 Dec 1965 – 8 Jan 1966

	ordinary cover	Qty: 3,753
120.1	Scouting illustrated cover	20.00
120.2	any other illustrated cover	15.00
120.#R	Registered cover............Qty: 229	35.00

082AJ.1 | 28 March 1966

Inauguration QANTAS Jet Service – Sydney to Mexico City

121.4 | 6 April 1966

Inaugural Flight to Singapore

124A.1 | 24 May 1966

Europa 1 Rocket Launch – Flight 4

The Europa rocket launches proved to be popular with souvenir cover producers and collectors, with several designs available over the course of the program.

Part 2
The Decimal Years
1966
EVENTS

121	3 Mar	Air New Zealand Inaugural Flights to Hong Kong and Singapore
122	11 Apr	Inter-Parliamentary Meetings
123	13 May	31st National Christian Endeavour Convention
124	24 May	Europa 1 Rocket Launch
125	23 Jun	11th SEATO Council Meetings
126	22 Aug	11th International Congresses Haematology and Blood Transfusion
127	19 Sep	7th Regional Conference Water Resources Development ECAFE
128	24 Oct	Western Australian Philatelic Exhibition (WAPEX)
129	2 Nov	Universal Postal Union's Consultative Committee for Postal Studies
130	5 Nov	Back To Braidwood – Local Government Since 1891
131	28 Dec	Australian Scout Corroboree

Recurring events.
See the original event number entry for the first occurrence.

084	*3 Mar*	*Moomba Festival*
082	*28 Mar*	*Inauguration of QANTAS Boeing Jet Service*
021	*Oct*	*Royal Show Hobart*
124	*15 Nov*	*Europa 1 Rocket Launch*

121

121   AIR NEW ZEALAND INAUGURAL FLIGHTS TO HONG KONG AND SINGAPORE

Sydney, NSW
3 Mar 1966 | Hong Kong flight

   ordinary cover
121.1   Air New Zealand cover .... Qty: 1,509 .... 10.00
121.2   return cover .... Qty: 632 .... 20.00
121.3   any other illustrated cover .... * 8.00

   6 Apr 1966 | Singapore flight

   ordinary cover
121.4   Air New Zealand cover .... Qty: 1,624 .... 10.00
121.5   return cover .... Qty: 494 .... 20.00
121.6   any other illustrated cover .... * 8.00

* Quantities included in figures listed.

084   **1966 MOOMBA FESTIVAL**

Melbourne, Vic
3 – 13 Mar 1966

Type 084A (see illustration under 1960)

   ordinary cover   Qty: 4,372
084A.1.66   Moomba cover 8.00
084A.2.66   any other illustrated cover 6.00
084A.#.66R Registered cover .... Qty: 71 .... 50.00

082   **1966 INAUGURATION QANTAS JET SERVICE**

Sydney, NSW
28 Mar 1966

Type 082A | Sydney to Mexico via Auckland
(see illustration under 1959)

   ordinary cover
082AJ.1   QANTAS cover .... Qty: 1,511* 10.00
082AJ.2   QANTAS cover – return .... Qty: 615* 20.00
082AJ.3   any other illustrated cover .... * 8.00
082AJ.#R   Registered cover............................ Qty: 1 .... **

* Quantities are for all types of cover.
** No established value.

124A.1 | 24 May 1966

Europa 1 Rocket Launch – Flight 4

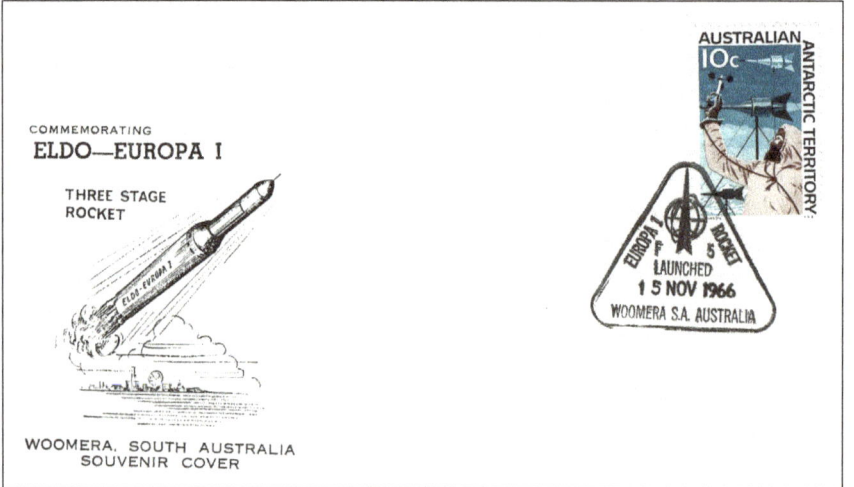

124B.1 | 15 Nov 1966

Europa 1 Rocket Launch – Flight 5

128A.1 | 24 Oct 1966

Western Australian Philatelic Exhibition – WAPEX

122 1966 INTER-PARLIAMENTARY MEETINGS
Canberra, ACT
11 – 17 Apr 1966

	ordinary cover	Qty: est. 2,000	
122.1	any illustrated cover		15.00
122.2	plain cover		8.00
122.#R	Registered cover		35.00

123 1966 31ST NATIONAL CHRISTIAN ENDEAVOUR CONVENTION
Launceston, Tas
13 – 21 May 1966

	ordinary cover	Qty: 5,028	
123.1	any illustrated cover		15.00
123.2	plain cover		10.00
123.#R	Registered cover	Qty: 73	40.00

 124A | Flight 4

124 1966 EUROPA 1 ROCKET LAUNCH
Woomera, SA
24 May 1966

	ordinary cover	Qty: 14,941	
124A.1	Europa 1 illustrated cover		15.00
124A.2	any other illustrated cover		8.00

125 1966 11TH SEATO COUNCIL MEETINGS
Canberra, ACT
23 – 29 Jun 1966

	ordinary cover	Qty: 2,100	
125.1	any illustrated cover		15.00
125.2	plain cover		10.00
125.#R	Registered cover	Qty: 58*	50.00

126 1966 11TH INTERNATIONAL CONGRESSES HAEMATOLOGY AND BLOOD TRANSFUSION
Sydney, NSW
22 – 29 Aug 1966

	ordinary cover	Qty: 4,916	
126.1	any illustrated cover		10.00
126.2	plain cover		8.00
126.#R	Registered cover	Qty: 47	50.00

127 1966 7TH REGIONAL CONFERENCE WATER RESOURCES DEVELOPMENT ECAFE
Canberra, ACT
19 – 26 Sep 1966

	ordinary cover	Qty: 2,074	
127.1	any illustrated cover		15.00
127.2	plain cover		10.00
127.#R	Registered cover	Qty: 43	50.00

 021B

021 1966 ROYAL SHOW HOBART
Hobart, Tas
Oct 1966

021B.1.66	plain cover		10.00

128A   128B

128   1966 WESTERN AUSTRALIAN PHILATELIC EXHIBITION (WAPEX)

Perth, WA
24 – 29 Oct 1966

Type 128A | 24 Oct | red ink

	ordinary cover	Qty: 10,197*	
128A.1	Official WAPEX II cover		5.00
128A.2	Dirk Hartog Anniversary FDC		5.00
128A.3	any other illustrated cover		4.00
128A.#R	Registered cover	Qty: 406*	45.00

* Quantities are combined for red and black inks.

Type 128B | 25 – 29 Oct | black ink

	ordinary cover	*	
128B.1	Official WAPEX II cover		5.00
128B.2	Dirk Hartog Anniversary FDC		5.00
128B.3	any other illustrated cover		4.00
128B.#R	Registered cover	*	60.00

Coincidental stamp issue:
24 Oct 1966 – 4c, 350th Anniversary of Dirk Hartog's Landing in Australia (SG408)

129

129   1966 UPU CONSULTATIVE COMMITTEE FOR POSTAL STUDIES

Sydney, NSW
2 – 18 Nov 1966

	ordinary cover	Qty: 5,696	
129.1	Event-specific illustrated cover		5.00
129.2	any other illustrated cover		4.00
129.#R	Registered cover*	Qty: est 150	35.00

* Highest R6 label sighted: 069 (8 Nov 1966). Generic R6 label used with C.C.P.S. handwritten.

130

130   1966 BACK TO BRAIDWOOD – LOCAL GOVERNMENT SINCE 1891

Braidwood, NSW
5 – 26 Nov 1966

	ordinary cover	Qty: 10,317	
130.1	any illustrated cover		4.00
130.#R	Registered cover		25.00

124B | Flight 5

124   1966 EUROPA 1 ROCKET LAUNCH

Woomera, SA
15 Nov 1966

	ordinary cover	Qty: 10,975	
124B.1	Europa 1 illustrated cover		10.00
124B.2	any other illustrated cover		6.00
124B.#R	Registered cover		35.00

131

131   1966-67 AUSTRALIAN SCOUT CORROBOREE

Woodhouse, SA
28 Dec 1966 – 7 Jan 1967

	ordinary cover	Qty: 24,771	
131.1	Corroboree of Discovery Official Cover		5.00
131.2	any other illustrated cover		4.00
131.#R	Registered cover	Qty: 388	25.00

1967

EVENTS

132	27 Feb	50th Anniversary First Air Mail Mt Gambier to Melbourne
133	8 Mar	5th U.N. Regional Cartographic Conference for Asia and Far East
134	12 Apr	F.A.O. World Symposium – Man Made Forests
135	13 May	All Australia Guide Friendship Camp
136	3 Jul	G.P.O. Centenary, Melbourne
137	4 Aug	2nd World Tournament of Women's Basketball
138	14 Aug	Y.M.C.A. World Council Meeting
139	21 Aug	13th International Conference of Agricultural Economists
140	5 Sep	Aviation Exhibition
141	11 Sep	Commissioning U.S. Naval Communications Station
142	21 Oct	50th Anniversary Trans-Australian Railway
143	1 Nov	G.P.O. Centenary, Adelaide
144	23 Nov	50th Anniversary First Air Mail Within South Australia
145	29 Nov	First Australian Satellite
146	27 Dec	8th Australian Boy Scout Jamboree

Recurring events.
See the original event number entry for the first occurrence.

109	6 Jan	CEBS National Camp
110	16 Jan	ANZAAS Congress
084	3 Mar	Moomba Festival
082	30 Mar	Inauguration QANTAS Boeing Jet Service
082	2 Apr	Inauguration QANTAS Boeing Jet Service
124	4 Aug	Europa Rocket Launch
022	Aug	Brisbane Exhibition
021	Oct	Royal Show Hobart
124	6 Dec	Europa Rocket Launch

109B

109 **1967 CHURCH OF ENGLAND BOYS SOCIETY (CEBS) CAMP**

Langwarrin, Vic
6 – 16 Jan 1967

	ordinary cover	Qty: 3,028	
109B.1	any illustrated cover		15.00
109B.2	plain cover		10.00
109B.#R	Registered cover	Qty: 53	50.00

110B

110 **1967 39TH ANZAAS CONGRESS**

Melbourne, Vic
16 – 20 Jan 1967

	ordinary cover	Qty: 2,488	
110B.1	any illustrated cover		15.00
110B.2	plain cover		10.00
110B.#R	Registered cover	Qty: 60	50.00

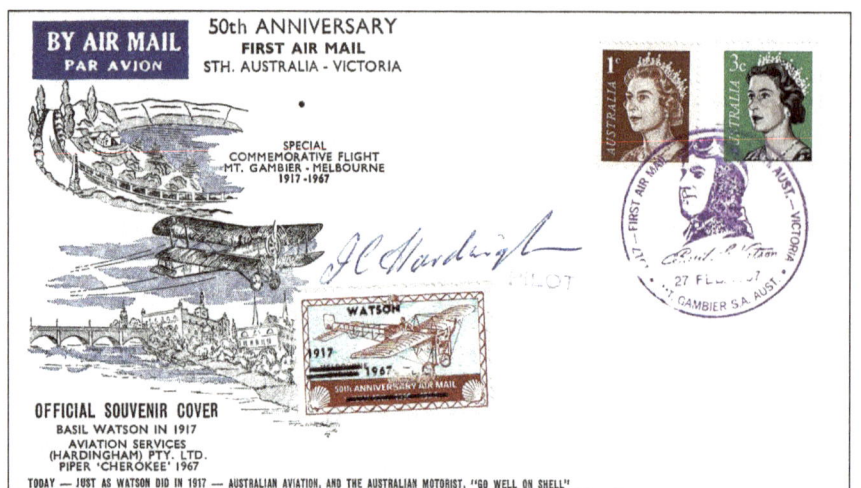

132B.1 | 27 February 1967

50th Anniversary First Air Mail
Mt Gambier to Melbourne

136A.1 | 8 July 1967

G.P.O. Centenary, Melbourne

140.1 | 5 September 1967

Aviation Exhibition

132A 132B

132   1967 50TH ANNIVERSARY FIRST AIR MAIL MT GAMBIER TO MELBOURNE

Mt. Gambier, SA
27 Feb 1967

Type 132A | black ink

	ordinary cover	Qty: 7,888*	
132A.1	Official Souvenir Cover		6.00
132A.2	any other illustrated cover		5.00
132A.#R	Registered cover	Qty: 80*	35.00

Type 132B | violet ink

	ordinary cover		*
132B.1	Official Souvenir Cover		6.00
132B.2	any other illustrated cover		5.00
132B.#R	Registered cover		* ... 35.00

* Quantities are for both colours combined.

084   1967 MOOMBA FESTIVAL

Melbourne, Vic
3 – 13 Mar 1967

Type 084A (see illustration under 1960)

	ordinary cover	Qty: 4,964
084A.1.67	Moomba cover	7.50
084A.2.67	Moomba aerogramme	15.00
084A.3.67	any other illustrated cover	6.00
084A.#.67R	Registered cover	Qty: 118 ... 50.00

133A 133B

133   1967 5TH U.N. REGIONAL CARTOGRAPHIC CONFERENCE FOR ASIA AND FAR EAST

Canberra, ACT
8 – 22 Mar 1967

Type 133A | black ink

	ordinary cover	Qty: 1,621*
133A.1	any illustrated cover	40.00
133A.2	plain cover	20.00
133A.#R	Registered cover	75.00

Type 133B | purple ink

	ordinary cover	*
133B.1	any illustrated cover	40.00
133B.2	plain cover	20.00
133B.#R	Registered cover	75.00

* Total is for both colours combined.

082   1967 INAUGURATION QANTAS JET SERVICE

Sydney, NSW
30 Mar 1967

Type 082A | Sydney to London via Amsterdam
(see illustration under 1959)

	ordinary cover		
082AK.1	QANTAS souvenir cover	Qty: 2,074*	10.00
082AK.2	QANTAS souvenir cover – return	Qty: 347*	40.00
082AK.3	any other illustrated cover	*	8.00
082AK.#R	Registered cover		$100

* Quantities are for all types of cover.

2 Apr 1967

Type 082A | Sydney to Johannesburg
(see illustration under 1959)

	ordinary cover		
082AL.1	QANTAS souvenir cover	Qty: 1,298*	10.00
082AL.2	QANTAS souvenir cover – return	Qty: 152*	80.00
082AL.3	any other illustrated cover	*	8.00
082AL.#R	Registered cover		$100

* Quantities are for all types of cover.

134

134   1967 F.A.O. WORLD SYMPOSIUM – MAN MADE FORESTS

Canberra, ACT
12 – 24 Apr 1967

	ordinary cover	Qty: 2,290
134.1	any illustrated cover	15.00
134.2	plain cover	10.00

135

135   1967 ALL AUSTRALIA GUIDE FRIENDSHIP CAMP

Redland Bay, Qld
13 – 20 May 1967

	ordinary cover	Qty: 7,487
135.1	Friendship Camp illustrated cover	5.00

135.2	any other illustrated cover	4.00
135.#R	Registered cover.......... Qty: 101 .... 30.00	

136A   136B

136 1967 G.P.O. CENTENARY, MELBOURNE
Melbourne, Vic
3 – 15 Jul 1967

Type 136A | black ink

	ordinary cover	Qty: 5,551*
136A.1	Melbourne GPO Centenary cover	5.00
136A.2	any other illustrated cover	4.00

Type 136B | violet ink

	ordinary cover	*
136B.1	Melbourne GPO Centenary cover	5.00
136B.2	any other illustrated cover	4.00

* Quantity is combined for both colours.

137

137 1967 2ND WORLD TOURNAMENT OF WOMEN'S BASKETBALL
Perth, WA
4 – 26 Aug 1967

	ordinary cover	Qty: 3,577
137.1	World Tournament souvenir	35.00
137.2	any other illustrated cover	10.00
137.#R	Registered cover.......... Qty: 57 .... $125	

124C | Flight 6/1

124 1967 EUROPA 1 ROCKET LAUNCH
Woomera, SA
4 Aug 1967

	ordinary cover	Qty: 18,189
124C.1	Europa 1 illustrated cover	6.00
124C.2	any other illustrated cover	5.00
124C.#R	Registered cover.......... Qty: 84 .... 35.00	

138

138 1967 Y.W.C.A. WORLD COUNCIL MEETING
Melbourne, Vic
14 Aug – 1 Sep 1967

	ordinary cover	Qty: 8,630
138.1	World Council Meeting illustrated cover	6.00
138.2	any other illustrated cover	4.00
138.#R	Registered cover.......... Qty: 29 .... 60.00	

A first day of issue (FDI) postmark was provided on 21 August 1967 for the 4c YWCA stamp (SG412). It is identical to the design here except for the addition of text 'FIRST DAY / OF' above, and 'ISSUE' below the date line. That postmark is outside the scope of this guide and is mentioned as a matter of record only. Impressions: 1,530 ordinary articles and 62 Registered.

Related stamp issue:
21 Aug 1967 – 4c, Y.W.C.A. World Council Meeting (SG412)

139

139 1967 13TH INTERNATIONAL CONFERENCE OF AGRICULTURAL ECONOMISTS
Sydney, NSW
21 – 30 Aug 1967

	ordinary cover	Qty: 4,007
139.1	Conference cover	6.00
139.2	any other illustrated cover	4.00
139.#R	Registered cover.......... Qty: 27 .... 75.00	

022 1967 BRISBANE EXHIBITION
Brisbane, Qld
Aug 1967

Type 022B (see illustration under 1940)

022B.1.67	plain cover	20.00
022B.1.67R	plain cover Registered	50.00

140

138.1R | 21 August 1967 | Y.W.C.A. World Council Meeting

140	**1967 AVIATION EXHIBITION**

Melbourne, Vic
5 – 12 Sep 1967

	ordinary cover	Qty: 2,461	
140.1	Aviation Exhibition cover		6.00
140.2	any other illustrated cover		4.00
140.#R	Registered cover	Qty: 43	50.00

141

141	**1967 COMMISSIONING U.S. NAVAL COMMUNICATIONS STATION**

Exmouth, WA
11 – 16 Sep 1967

	ordinary cover	Qty: 3,225	
141.1	Naval Communications Station cover		10.00
141.2	any other illustrated cover		6.00
141.#R	Registered cover	Qty: 56	50.00

142A   142B

142	**1967 50TH ANNIVERSARY TRANS-AUSTRALIAN RAILWAY**

Port Pirie, SA
21 Oct 1967

Type 142A | Port Pirie

	ordinary cover	Qty: 4,332	
142A.1	official souvenir cover		6.00
142A.2	any other illustrated cover		4.00
142A.#R	Registered cover	Qty: 35	55.00

Kalgoorlie, WA
22 Oct 1967

Type 142B | Kalgoorlie

	ordinary cover	Qty: 4,494	
142B.1	official souvenir cover		6.00
142B.2	any other illustrated cover		4.00
142B.#R	Registered cover	Qty: 35	55.00

021	**1967 ROYAL SHOW HOBART**

Hobart, Tas
Oct 1966

Type 021B (see illustration under 1966)

021B.1.67	plain cover	10.00

143

143	**1967 G.P.O. CENTENARY, ADELAIDE**

Adelaide, SA
1 – 14 Nov 1967

142B.1 | 22 October 1967

50th Anniversary of the Trans-Australian Railway, Kalgoorlie

143.1 | 1 November 1967

G.P.O. Centenary, Adelaide

144.1 | 23 November 1967

50th Anniversary First Air Mail Within South Australia

	ordinary cover	Qty: 4,464
143.1	GPO Adelaide cover	6.00
143.2	any other illustrated cover	4.00
143.#R	Registered cover	$100

144

144   1967 50TH ANNIVERSARY FIRST AIR MAIL WITHIN SOUTH AUSTRALIA

Adelaide, SA
23 Nov 1967

	ordinary cover	Qty: 9,518
144.1	official souvenir cover	5.00
144.2	any other illustrated cover	4.00
144.#R	Registered cover	Qty: 46 .... 50.00

145

145   1967 FIRST AUSTRALIAN SATELLITE

Adelaide, SA
29 Nov 1967

	ordinary cover	Qty: 7,179
145.1	WRESAT-1 Launch cover	25.00
145.2	any other illustrated cover	15.00
145.#R	Registered cover	Qty: 34 .... 60.00

124D | Flight 6/2

124   1967 EUROPA 1 ROCKET LAUNCH

Woomera, SA
6 Dec 1967

	ordinary cover	Qty: 10,919
124D.1	Europa 1 illustrated cover	10.00
124D.2	any other illustrated cover	6.00
124D.#R	Registered cover	Qty: 36 .... 50.00

146

146   1967-68 8TH AUSTRALIAN BOY SCOUT JAMBOREE

Jindalee, Qld
27 Dec 1967 – 8 Jan 1968

	ordinary cover	Qty: 51,352
146.1	official souvenir cover	5.00
146.2	any other illustrated cover	4.00
146.#R	Registered cover	Qty: 327 .... 25.00

146.1R | 27 December 1967

8th Australian Boy Scout Jamboree

This is the last commemorative postmark that could legitimately be used to cancel pre-decimal stamps, which were invalidated on Wednesday, 14 February 1968.

147.1 | 17 April 1968

24th Session ECAFE

153.1R | 24 August 1968

State Girl Guide Camp

154A.1 | 25 September 1968

21st Anniversary QANTAS Sydney to Norfolk Island Air Service

1968

EVENTS

147	17 Apr	24th Session ECAFE
148	18 May	Opening of Batman Bridge
149	19 Jul	Trade Fair and Motor Show
150	30 Jul	Asian and Pacific Council 3rd Ministerial Meeting
151	6 Aug	9th International Congress of Soil Science
152	10 Aug	Joint Annual Meeting / 3rd Australian BMA/AMA Medical Congress
153	24 Aug	State Girl Guide Camp
154	25 Sep	21st Anniversary Direct Air Service Sydney to Norfolk Island
155	14 Oct	Indo-Pacific Fisheries Council 13th Session
156	27 Nov	150th Anniversary Macquarie Lighthouse
157	4 Dec	PAN AM First Direct Service Sydney to Bangkok

Recurring events.
See the original event number entry for the first occurrence.

084	1 Mar	Moomba Festival
124	30 Nov	Europa Rocket Launch

---

084 *1968 MOOMBA FESTIVAL*

Melbourne, Vic
1 – 11 Mar 1968

Type 084A (see illustration under 1960)

	ordinary cover	Qty: 4,163	
084A.1.68	Moomba cover		7.50
084A.2.68	Moomba aerogramme		15.00
084A.3.68	any other illustrated cover		6.00
084A.#.68R	Registered cover	Qty: 40*	50.00

* Some sources quote 60 Registered covers.

147

147 **1968 24TH SESSION ECAFE**

Canberra 2600, ACT
17 – 30 Apr 1968

	ordinary cover	Qty: 6,421	
147.1	ECAFE 24th Session aerogramme		8.00
147.2	any other illustrated cover		6.00
147.3	plain cover		4.00
	Registered cover	Qty: 96	
147.1R	ECAFE 24th Session aerogramme		40.00
147.2R	any other illustrated cover		35.00
147.3R	plain cover		30.00

From this event, postmarks usually include the postcode.

148

148 **1968 OPENING OF BATMAN BRIDGE**

Beaconsfield 7251 and Georgetown 7253, Tas
18 May 1968

	ordinary cover	Qty: 8,286	
148.1	Batman Bridge Souvenir Cover		6.00
148.2	any other illustrated cover		4.00
148.#R	Registered cover	Qty: 18	75.00

149

149 **1968 TRADE FAIR AND MOTOR SHOW**

Geelong 3220, Vic
19 – 27 Jul 1968

	ordinary cover	Qty: 1,105	
149.1	any illustrated cover		50.00
149.2	plain cover		30.00
149.#R	Registered cover	Qty: 47	60.00

150

150 1968 ASIAN AND PACIFIC COUNCIL 3RD INISTERIAL MEETING

Canberra 2600, ACT
30 Jul – 1 Aug 1968

	ordinary cover	Qty: 907	
150.1	any illustrated cover		60.00
150.2	plain cover		40.00
150.#R	Registered cover	Qty: 31	80.00

151

151 1968 9TH INTERNATIONAL CONGRESS OF SOIL SCIENCE

Adelaide 5000, SA
6 – 16 Aug 1968

	ordinary cover	Qty: 8,385	
151.1	Soil Science Congress cover		4.00
151.2	any other illustrated cover		3.00
151.#R	Registered cover	Qty: 90	35.00

Related stamp issue:
6 Aug 1968 – 5c, International Soil Science Congress (SG426)

152

152 1968 JOINT ANNUAL MEETING / THIRD AUSTRALIAN BMA/AMA MEDICAL CONGRESS

Sydney 2000, NSW
10 – 16 Aug 1968

	ordinary cover	Qty: 2,905	
152.1	World Medical Association Assembly cover		12.00
152.2	any other illustrated cover		8.00
152.#R	Registered cover	Qty: 52	40.00

Related stamp issue:
6 Aug 1968 – 5c, World Medical Association Assembly (SG427)

153

153 1968 STATE GIRL GUIDE CAMP

Lismore 2480, NSW
24 – 31 Aug 1968

	ordinary cover	Qty: 6,687	
153.1	NSW State Camp cover		10.00
153.2	any other illustrated cover		8.00
153.#R	Registered cover	Qty: 249	40.00

156A.1 | 27 November 1968

150th Anniversary Macquarie Lighthouse, North Ryde

154A 154B

154 1968 21ST ANNIVERSARY QANTAS SYDNEY TO NORFOLK ISLAND AIR SERVICE

Sydney 2000, NSW
25 Sep 1968

Type 154A | black ink

	ordinary cover	
154A.1	QANTAS Air Service cover	12.00
154A.1	QANTAS Air Service aerogramme	12.00
154A.3	any other illustrated cover	8.00

Type 154B | purple ink

	ordinary cover	
154B.1	QANTAS Air Service cover	12.00
154B.2	QANTAS Air Service aerogramme	12.00
154B.3	any other illustrated cover	8.00

155

155 1968 INDO-PACIFIC FISHERIES COUNCIL 13TH SESSION

Brisbane 4000, Qld
14 – 25 Oct 1968

	ordinary cover	Qty: 5,094	
155.1	any illustrated cover		5.00
155.#R	Registered cover	Qty: 39	40.00

156A 156B

156 1968 150TH ANNIVERSARY MACQUARIE LIGHTHOUSE

27 – 30 Nov 1968

Type 156A | North Ryde 2113, NSW

	ordinary cover	Qty: 1,975	
156A.1	Macquarie Lighthouse FDC		20.00
156A.2	any other illustrated cover		15.00

Type 156B | Vaucluse 2030, NSW

	ordinary cover	Qty: 4,635	
156B.1	Macquarie Lighthouse FDC		10.00
156B.2	any other illustrated cover		8.00

Related stamp issue:
27 Nov 1968 – 5c, 150th Anniversary of Macquarie Lighthouse (SG436)

124E | Flight 7

124 1968 EUROPA 1 ROCKET LAUNCH

Woomera, SA
30 Nov 1968

	ordinary cover	Qty: 23,638	
124E.1	Europa 1 illustrated cover		10.00
124E.2	any other illustrated cover		6.00
124E.#R	Registered cover	Qty: 74	75.00

157

157 1968 PAN AM FIRST DIRECT SERVICE SYDNEY TO BANGKOK

Sydney 2000, NSW
4 Dec 1968

	ordinary cover		
157.1	souvenir cover	Qty: 112	$100
157.2	souvenir cover – return trip	484	50.00
157.#R	Registered cover	Qty: 5	$200

1969

EVENTS

158	3 Mar	International Association of Ports and Harbors 6th Biennial Conference
159	9 Apr	Asian Development Bank Board of Governors 2nd Annual Meeting
160	12 May	Railway Centenary Celebrations
161	11 Jun	Fixing of States' Common Corner Queensland, NSW and SA
162	19 Jun	Five Power Meeting
163	7 Aug	Portland Trade Fair
164	10 Aug	50th Anniversary First Airmail Adelaide to Minlaton
165	11 Aug	International Symposium of Electron and Nuclear Magnetic Resonance
166	20 Aug	International Union of Pure and Applied Chemistry 22nd Congress
167	28 Aug	6th Asian Youth Hostels Conference and Rally
168	11 Sep	6th World Orchid Conference
169	21 Oct	Dandenong Trade Fair
170	27 Oct	4th ECAFE Symposium – Petroleum Resources Development
171	12 Dec	50th Anniversary First Flight England to Australia
172	29 Dec	2nd Australian Senior Scout Venture Camp

Recurring events.
See the original event number entry for the first occurrence.

084	28 Feb	*Moomba Festival*
027	Apr	*Royal Easter Show*
124	3 Jul	*Europa 1 Rocket Launch*
082	8 Aug	*Inauguration QANTAS Jet Service*
110	18 Aug	*ANZAAS Congress*

084B

084   1969 MOOMBA FESTIVAL

Melbourne 3002, Vic
28 Feb – 10 Mar 1969

	ordinary cover	Qty: 3,674
084B.1.69	Moomba cover	8.00
084B.2.69	any other illustrated cover	6.00
084B.#.69R	Registered cover . . . . .Qty: 53 . . . . . . 50.00	

158

158   1969 INTERNATIONAL ASSOCIATION OF PORTS AND HARBORS – 6TH BIENNIAL CONFERENCE

Melbourne 3000, Vic
3 – 8 Mar 1969

	ordinary cover	Qty: 784
158.1	6th Biennial Conference illustrated cover	75.00
158.2	any other illustrated cover	60.00
158.3	plain cover	40.00
158.#R	Registered cover .... Qty: 65 .... $125	

Related stamp issue:
26 Feb 1969 – 5c, International Ports and Harbors Conference (SG438)

159

159   1969 ASIAN DEVELOPMENT BANK BOARD OF GOVERNORS 2ND ANNUAL MEETING

Sydney 2000, NSW
9 – 12 Apr 1969

	ordinary cover	Qty: 2,392
159.1	any illustrated cover	20.00
159.#R	Registered cover........................... Qty: 54 .... 50.00	

158.1 | 3 March 1969

International Association of Ports and Harbors – 6th Biennial Conference

027   1969 ROYAL EASTER SHOW
Sydney, NSW
Apr 1969

Type 027C (see illustration under 1963)

027C.1.69   plain cover 25.00

160

160   1969 RAILWAY CENTENARY CELEBRATIONS
Muswellbrook 2333, NSW
12 – 18 May 1969

	ordinary cover	Qty: 5,666	
160.1	Official Souvenir Cover		5.00
160.2	any other illustrated cover		4.00
160.#R	Registered cover	Qty: 91	30.00

161

161   1969 FIXING OF STATES' COMMON CORNER QUEENSLAND, NSW, SA
Cameron Corner *
11 Jun 1969

	ordinary cover	Qty: 1,603	
161.1	any illustrated cover		30.00
161.2	plain cover		20.00
161.#R	Registered cover	Qty: 16	$100

* There is no town or post office at Cameron Corner, and therefore no postcode. It is simply the point at which the states of Queensland, New South Wales and South Australia connect.

162

162   1969 FIVE POWER MEETING
Canberra Parliament House 2600, ACT
19 – 20 June 1969

	ordinary cover	Qty: 1,064	
162.1	Event-specific illustrated cover		40.00
162.2	any other illustrated cover		35.00
162.3	plain cover		25.00
162.#R	Registered cover	Qty: 46	60.00

124F | Flight 8

124   1969 EUROPA 1 ROCKET LAUNCH
Woomera, SA
3 Jul 1969

	ordinary cover	Qty: 17,988	
124F.1	Europa 1 illustrated cover		10.00
124F.2	any other illustrated cover		6.00
124F.#R	Registered cover	Qty: 67	40.00

124F.1 | 3 July 1969

Europa 1 Rocket Launch Flight 8

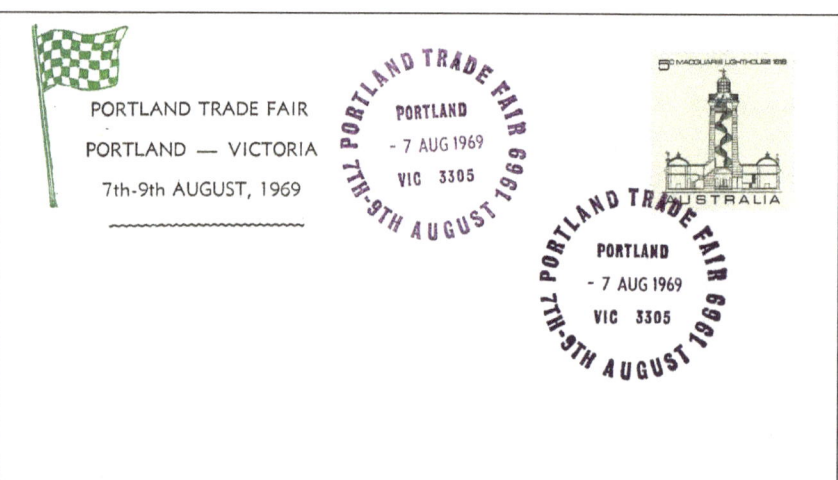

163.1 | 7 August 1969

Portland Trade Fair

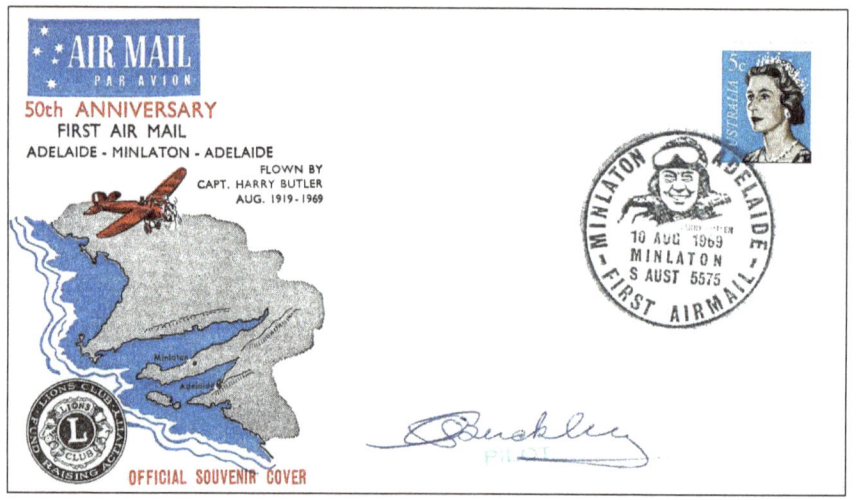

164B.1 | 10 August 1969

50th Anniversary First Airmail Adelaide to Minlaton

163

163 1969 PORTLAND TRADE FAIR
Portland 3305, Vic
7 – 9 Aug 1969

	ordinary cover	Qty: 963	
163.1	Trade Fair cover		50.00
163.2	any illustrated cover		40.00
163.3	plain cover		30.00
163.#R	Registered cover	Qty: 26	80.00

082 1969 INAUGURATION QANTAS JET SERVICE
Sydney, NSW
8 Aug 1969

Type 082A | Sydney to London via Bali
(see illustration under 1959)

	Ordinary cover		
082AM.1	QANTAS cover – addressed to Bali	Qty: 1,500*	15.00
082AM.2	QANTAS cover – return	201*	60.00
082AM.3	any other illustrated cover	*	12.00
082AM.#R	Registered cover	Qty: 8	$200

* Quantities are for all types of cover.

164A   164B

164 1969 50TH ANNIVERSARY FIRST AIRMAIL ADELAIDE TO MINLATON
10 Aug 1969

Type 164A | Adelaide 5000, SA

	ordinary cover	Qty: 4,343	
164A.1	official souvenir cover		6.00
164A.2	souvenir aerial post card		6.00
164A.1R	Registered cover	Qty: 51	40.00

Type 164B | Minlaton 5575, SA

	ordinary cover	Qty: 6,536	
164B.1	official souvenir cover		6.00
164B.2	souvenir aerial post card		6.00
164B.1R	Registered cover	Qty: 64	40.00

165

165 1969 INTERNATIONAL SYMPOSIUM OF ELECTRON AND NUCLEAR MAGNETIC RESONANCE
Monash University 3170, Vic
11 – 14 Aug 1969

	ordinary cover	Qty: 1,455	
165.1	any illustrated cover		25.00
165.2	plain cover		15.00
165.#R	Registered cover	Qty: 28	60.00

110C

110 1969 41ST ANZAAS CONGRESS
Adelaide 5000, SA
18 – 22 Aug 1969

	ordinary cover	Qty: 1,552	
110C.1	any illustrated cover		20.00
110C.2	plain cover		15.00
110C.#R	Registered cover	Qty: 54	50.00

166

166 1969 INTERNATIONAL UNION OF PURE AND APPLIED CHEMISTRY 22ND CONGRESS
Sydney 2000, NSW
20 – 27 Aug 1969

	ordinary cover	Qty: 2,300	
166.1	Congress souvenir cover		25.00
166.2	any other illustrated cover		15.00
166.#R	Registered cover	Qty: 36*	80.00

Despite the quoted number of 36 Registered items, the editor has sighted R6 labels numbered 040 and 047, both dated 20 August 1969.

167

167   1969 6TH ASIAN YOUTH HOSTELS CONFERENCE AND RALLY

Canberra 2600, ACT
28 Aug – 3 Sep 1969

	ordinary cover	Qty: 1,242	
167.1	any illustrated cover		30.00
167.2	plain cover		20.00
167.#R	Registered cover	Qty: 34	60.00

168

168   1969 6TH WORLD ORCHID CONFERENCE

Sydney 2000, NSW
11 – 16 Sep 1969

	ordinary cover	Qty: 3,732	
168.1	Orchid Conference souvenir cover		15.00
168.2	any other illustrated cover		10.00
168.#R	Registered cover	Qty: 52	40.00

169

169   1969 DANDENONG TRADE FAIR

Dandenong 3175, Vic
21 – 24 Oct 1969

	ordinary cover	Qty: 1,050	
169.1	any illustrated cover		25.00
169.2	plain cover		15.00
169.#R	Registered cover	Qty: 36	60.00

170

170   1969 4TH ECAFE SYMPOSIUM – PETROLEUM RESOURCES DEVELOPMENT

Canberra 2600, ACT
27 Oct – 10 Nov 1969

	ordinary cover	Qty: 2,203	
170.1	ECAFE Symposium air letter		30.00
170.2	any other illustrated cover		20.00
170.#R	Registered cover	Qty: 12	$100

171A   171B   171C

171   1969 50TH ANNIVERSARY FIRST FLIGHT ENGLAND TO AUSTRALIA

12 – 14 Dec 1969

Type 171A | Cloncurry 4824, Qld

12 Dec 1969

	ordinary cover	Qty: 2,802	
171A.1	official souvenir cover		8.00
171A.2	any other illustrated cover		8.00
171A.#R	Registered cover	Qty: 30	60.00

Type 171B | Darwin 5790, NT

12 Dec 1969

	ordinary cover	Qty: 6,048	
171B.1	official souvenir cover		8.00
171B.2	any other illustrated cover		8.00
171B.#R	Registered cover	Qty: 37	60.00

Type 171C | Melbourne (3000), Vic

14 Dec 1969

	ordinary cover		
171C.1	official souvenir cover		8.00

171C was a cachet applied to covers on arrival of the re-enactment flight. It is included here for clarification purposes.

Related stamp issue:
12 Nov 1969 – 3 x 5c, 50th Anniversary of First England to Australia Flight (SG450-2)

172

172   2ND AUSTRALIAN SENIOR SCOUT VENTURE CAMP

29 Dec 1969 – 8 Jan 1970

	ordinary cover	Qty: 6,620	
172.1	Venture cover		20.00
172.2	any other illustrated cover		15.00
172.#R	Registered cover	Qty: 192	40.00

1970

EVENTS

173	6 Jan	International Guide Camp
174	12 Jan	Congress of Australian Pharmacy Students
175	23 Feb	Standard Gauge Rail Link Inaugural Train
176	12 Mar	Centenary of Local Government, Wagga Wagga
177	31 Mar	Royal Visit
178	2 Apr	Inaugural Flight Cathay Pacific Perth to Hong Kong and Tokyo
179	4 Apr	10th International Rally for Veteran and Vintage Cars
180	10 Apr	11th International Grassland Congress
181	20 Apr	Captain Cook Bicentenary Celebrations
182	27 Apr	Captain Cook Bicentenary Celebrations and ANPEX 1970
183	16 May	Thunderbolt Centenary Celebrations
184	6 Jun	Pacific Festival
185	1 Jul	Melbourne Airport Opening
186	22 Aug	3rd State Girl Guide Camp
187	14 Sep	Commencement of Overland Telegraph Line 1890
188	19 Sep	3rd Asian and Australasian Congress of Anesthesiology
189	12 Oct	18th International Dairy Congress
190	16 Nov	QANTAS 50th Anniversary
191	30 Nov	Papal Visit 1970
192	29 Dec	9th Australian Scout Jamboree

Recurring events.
See the original event number entry for the first occurrence.

084	27 Feb	*Moomba Festival*
096	4 Mar	*Maitland Agricultural and Horticultural Show*
027	16 Mar	*Royal Easter Show*
124	12 Jun	*Europa 1 Rocket Launch*

175.2 | 23 February 1970

Standard Rail Gauge Link Inaugural Train

084.1.70 | 27 February 1970

Moomba Festival

177B.2 | 2 April 1970

Royal Visit, Hobart

179B.1 | 16 April 1970

10th International Rally for Veteran and Vintage Cars, Canberra

173

173 1970 INTERNATIONAL GUIDE CAMP

Britannia Park 3797, Vic
6 – 15 Jan 1970

	ordinary cover	Qty: 3,287	
173.1	official souvenir cover		20.00
173.2	any other illustrated cover		10.00
173.#R	Registered cover	Qty: 84	60.00

174

174 1970 CONGRESS OF AUSTRALIAN PHARMACY STUDENTS

Coolum Beach 4561, Qld
12 – 17 Jan 1970

	Ordinary cover	Qty: 3,436	
174.1	official souvenir cover		15.00
174.2	any other illustrated cover		10.00
174.#R	Registered cover	Qty: 37	50.00

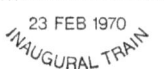

175

175 1970 STANDARD GAUGE RAIL LINK INAUGURAL TRAIN

Sydney 2000, NSW
23 Feb 1970

	ordinary cover	Qty: 23,723	
175.1	Official First Trip cover		10.00
175.2	Rail Link FDC		8.00
175.3	any other illustrated cover		4.00
175.#R	Registered cover	Qty: 47	40.00

Related stamp issue:
11 Feb 1970 – 5c, Sydney to Perth Standard Gauge Rail Link (SG453)

084 1970 MOOMBA FESTIVAL

Melbourne, Vic
27 Feb – 9 Mar 1970

Type 084B (see illustration under 1969)

	ordinary cover	Qty: 2,733	
084B.1.70	Moomba cover		15.00
084B.2.70	any other illustrated cover		10.00
084B.#.70R	Registered cover	Qty: 35	60.00

096 1970 MAITLAND AGRICULTURAL AND HORTICULTURAL SHOW

Maitland Showground, NSW
4 – 7 Mar 1970

Type 096 (see illustration under 1962)

	ordinary cover		
096.1.70	any illustrated cover		15.00

176

176 1970 CENTENARY OF LOCAL GOVERNMENT, WAGGA WAGGA

Wagga Wagga 2650, NSW
12 – 21 Mar 1970

	ordinary cover	Qty: 10,508	
176.1	Centenary of Local Government cover		6.00
176.2	any other illustrated cover		4.00
176.#R	Registered cover	Qty: 39	65.00

First day of use was 12 March 1970 but postmark is inscribed "14-22nd … March 1970".

027 1970 ROYAL EASTER SHOW

Sydney, NSW
16 – 20 Mar 1970

Type 027C (see illustration under 1963)

027C.1.70	plain cover	25.00

177

177 1970 ROYAL VISIT

31 Mar – 2 May 1970

Type			
177A	31 Mar – 2 Apr 29 Apr – 2 May	Sydney 2000, NSW	Qty: 9,335
177B	2 – 3 Apr	Hobart 7000, Tas	4,475
177C	4 Apr	Launceston 7250, Tas	4,747
177D	6 – 8 Apr	Melbourne 3000, Vic	4,461

177E	7 Apr	Portland 3305, Vic	4,935
177F	7 Apr	Swan Hill 3585, Vic	5,607
177G	10 Apr	Newcastle 2300, NSW	5,016
177H	10 Apr	Port Kembla 2505, NSW	4,675
177J	10 Apr	Wollongong 2500, NSW	5,861
177K	11 Apr	Coffs Harbour 2450, NSW	5,451
177L	11 Apr	Grafton 2460, NSW	4,575
177M	13 – 15 Apr	Brisbane 4000, Qld	5,507
177N	15 Apr	Longreach 4730, Qld	5,126
177P	15 – 16 Apr	Mount Isa 4825, Qld	4,361
177Q	16 Apr	Mackay 4740, Qld	4,484
177R	17 – 19 Apr	Proserpine 4800, Qld	4,433
177S	20 Apr	Townsville 4810, Qld	6,795
177T	22 Apt	Cooktown 4895, Qld	4,431
177U	23 Apr	Cairns 4870, Qld	5,105
177V	23 – 28 Apr	Canberra 2600, ACT	5,760
177W	28 Apr	Armidale 2350, NSW	5,363
177X	30 Apr	Orange 2800, NSW	4,585

            ordinary cover (APO souvenir cover)

177A to X.1	with 5c Royal Visit stamp .... each 6.00
177A to X.2	with 5c and 30c Royal Visit stamps ... each 12.00
177A to X.1 set A	with 5c Royal Visit stamp .... set $100
177A to X.2 set B	with 5c and 30c Royal Visit stamps .... set $200

Set A was sold by APO at $3.52
Set B was sold by APO at $10.12

            Registered cover

| 177A to X.#R | APO souvenir cover .... each 75.00 |

Related stamp issue:
31 Mar 1970 – 5c and 30c, Royal Visit (SG456-7)

178   1970 INAUGURAL FLIGHT CATHAY PACIFIC PERTH TO HONG KONG AND TOKYO

Perth 6000, WA
2 Apr 1970

Hong Kong flight

            ordinary cover

178.1	souvenir cover .... Qty: 2,091* 15.00
178.2	souvenir cover return flight.............. 327* 50.00
178.3	aerogramme... 15 .... 60.00
178.4	aerogramme return flight .... 3 .... $200
178.5	any other illustrated cover .... * 12.00
178.6	any other illustrated cover return flight . * 40.00
178.#R	Registered cover... 75.00

Tokyo flight

            ordinary cover

178.7	souvenir cover .... Qty: 2,188* 15.00
178.8	souvenir cover return flight.............. 478* 50.00
178.9	aerogramme... 14 .... 60.00
178.10	aerogramme return flight .... 5 .... $200
178.11	any other illustrated cover .... * 12.00
178.12	any other illustrated cover return flight . * 40.00
178.#R	Registered cover... 75.00

* Quantities for 'other illustrated covers' are included in 'souvenir cover' figures.

                                        179#b   179#p

179   1970 10TH INTERNATIONAL RALLY FOR VETERAN AND VINTAGE CARS
4 – 16 Apr 1970

Type 179A | Sydney 2000, NSW
4 Apr 1970

        ordinary cover   Qty: 5,182

179A.1	VCCA commemorative cover – black ink................5.00
179A.2	any other illustrated cover – black ink 3.00
179A.#R	Registered cover........................... Qty: 20 ....75.00

Type 179B | Canberra 2600, ACT
5 – 7 Apr 1970

        ordinary cover   Qty: 6,207

179B.1	VCCA commemorative cover – black ink................5.00
179B.2	any other illustrated cover – black ink 3.00
179B.#R	Registered cover .... Qty: 10 ....$150

Type 179C | Wagga Wagga 2650, NSW
8 – 10 Apr 1970

        ordinary cover   Qty: 4,508

179C.1b	VCCA commemorative cover – black ink................5.00
179C.1p	VCCA commemorative cover – purple ink..............5.00
179C.2b	any other illustrated cover – black ink 3.00
179C.2p	any other illustrated cover – purple ink 3.00
179C.#R	Registered cover........................... Qty: 6 ....$200

Type 179D | Albury 2640, NSW
11 – 12 Apr 1970

        ordinary cover   Qty: 5,515

179D.1b	VCCA commemorative cover – black ink................5.00
179D.1p	VCCA commemorative cover – purple ink..............5.00
179D.2b	any other illustrated cover – black ink 3.00
179D.2p	any other illustrated cover – purple ink 3.00
179D.#R	Registered cover........................... Qty: 7 ....$200

Type 179E | Shepparton 3630, Vic
13 – 15 Apr 1970

        ordinary cover   Qty: 5,544

179E.1b	VCCA commemorative cover – black ink................5.00
179E.1p	VCCA commemorative cover – purple ink..............5.00
179E.2b	any other illustrated cover – black ink 3.00
179E.2p	any other illustrated cover – purple ink 3.00
179E.#R	Registered cover........................... Qty: 8 ....$200

Type 179F | Melbourne 3000, Vic
16 Apr 1970

	ordinary cover	Qty: 4,148	
179F.1	VCCA commemorative cover – black ink		5.00
179F.2	any other illustrated cover – black ink		3.00
179A to F.1	Set of 6 VCCA commemorative covers		20.00

Postmarks exist in black and purple ink as listed above. Purple postmarks for Sydney, Canberra and Melbourne have not been sighted by the editor but will be listed if their existence can be verified.

VCCA = Veteran Car Club of Australia.

180

180 1970 11TH INTERNATIONAL GRASSLAND CONGRESS

Surfers Paradise 4217, Qld
10 – 24 Apr 1970

	ordinary cover	Qty: 4,273	
180.1	Grassland Congress FDC		15.00
180.2	any other illustrated cover		10.00
180.#R	Registered cover	Qty: 24	40.00

Related stamp issue:
13 Apr 1970 – 5c, 11th International Grassland Congress (SG458)

181A-Mb   181A-Mp

181 1970 CAPTAIN COOK BICENTENARY CELEBRATIONS

20 Apr – 22 Aug 1970

Type				
181A	20 Apr	Point Hicks 3889, Vic	Qty: 8,269
181B	27 Apr – 2 May	Kurnell 2231, NSW	21,009
181C	27 Apr – 1 May	Bulli 2516, NSW	8,690
181D	27 Apr – 2 May	Botany 2019, NSW	8,448
181E	27 Apr – 2 May	Laurieton 2443, NSW	7,915
181F	4 – 16 May	The Entrance 2261, NSW	6,674
181G	13 – 19 May	Coolangatta 4225, Qld	6,870
181H	20 – 26 May	Gladstone 4680, Qld	7,328
181J	25 – 30 May	Rockhampton 4700, Qld	7,085
181K	1 – 6 Jun	Mackay 4740, Qld	7,030
181L	15 – 20 Jun	Cooktown 4895, Qld	6,927
181M	17 – 22 Aug	Thursday Island 4875, Qld	6,468

ordinary cover (APO Cook Bicentenary cover)
Black ink

181A to M.1b	with 5c stamp	each 10.00
181A to M.2b	with 5 x 5c stamps	each 12.00
181A to M.3b	with 30c stamp	each 15.00
181A to M.4b	with 5 x 5c and 30c stamps	each 20.00
181A to M.5b	miniature sheet, not on cover	each 15.00
181A to M.1b set A	12 covers 5c stamp	set 70.00
181A to M.2b set B	12 covers 5 x 5c stamps	set 90.00
181A to M.3b set C	12 covers 30c stamp	set $120
181A to M.4b set D	12 covers 5 x 5c and 30c stamps	set $200
181A to M.5b set E	12 miniature sheets, not on cover	set $120

Set A was sold by APO at $1.92
Set B was sold by APO at $4.32
Set C was sold by APO at $4.92
Set D was sold by APO at $7.92
Set E was sold by APO at $6.96

Purple ink

181A to M.1p	with 5c stamp	each 10.00
181A to M.2p	with 5 x 5c stamps	each 12.00
181A to M.3p	with 30c stamp	each 15.00
181A to M.4p	with 5 x 5c and 30c stamps	each 20.00
181A to M.5p	miniature sheet, not on cover	each 15.00

Postmarks sighted in purple ink: The Entrance, Coolangatta, Gladstone, Rockhampton, Mackay, Cooktown, Thursday Island.

Related stamp issue:
20 Apr 1970 – 5 x 5c and 30c, Captain Cook Bicentenary (SG459-64).

182A

182B

182 1970 CAPTAIN COOK BICENTENARY CELEBRATIONS AND ANPEX 1970

Sydney 2000, NSW
27 Apr – 1 May 1970

Type 182A | 27 Apr | red ink (shades)

	ordinary cover	Qty: 155,593*	
182A.1	ANPEX cover		2.00
182A.2	any other illustrated cover		2.00
182A.#R	Registered cover	Qty: est 2,000*	30.00

Type 182B | 28 Apr – 1 May | black ink

	ordinary cover	*	
182B.1	ANPEX cover		2.00
182B.1	any other illustrated cover		2.00
182B.#R	Registered cover	*	30.00

* Quantities are totals for both colours. The highest numbered R6 label sighted by the editor is 1593.

182A.1R | 1 May 1970

Captain Cook Bicentenary Celebrations and ANPEX 1970

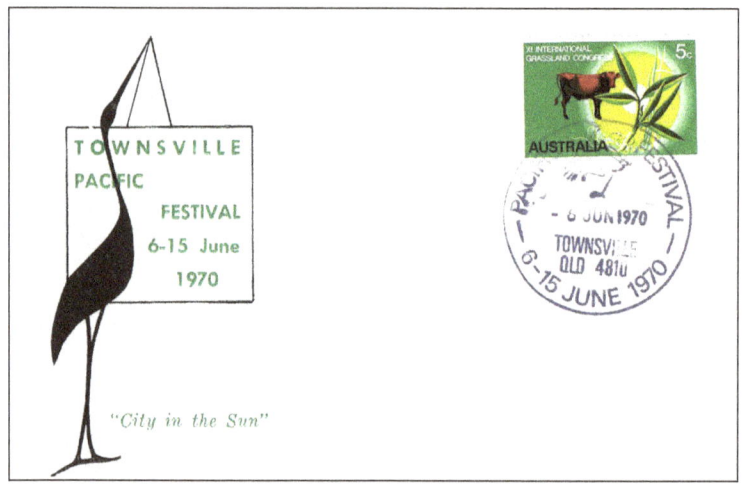

184A.1 | 6 June 1970

Pacific Festival

185.1 | 1 July 1970

Melbourne Airport Opening

Some sources cite 1 May in green ink but the editor has not been able to locate any such examples. 1 May impressions are known in red ink.

Related and coincidental stamp issues:
20 Apr 1970 – 5 x 5c and 30c, Captain Cook Bicentenary (SG459-64)
27 Apr 1970 – 4c and 5c, flower definitive coil stamps (SG466-7)

183 1970 THUNDERBOLT CENTENARY CELEBRATIONS
Uralla 2358, NSW
16 – 25 May 1970

	ordinary cover	Qty: 4,588	
183.1	Thunderbolt Centenary cover		10.00
183.2	any other illustrated cover		6.00
183.#R	Registered cover	Qty: 41	40.00

184 1970 PACIFIC FESTIVAL
Townsville 4810, Qld
6 – 15 Jun 1970

	ordinary cover	Qty: 2,015	
184A.1	Pacific Festival cover		15.00
184A.2	any other illustrated cover		10.00
184A.#R	Registered cover	Qty: 8	$175

124 1970 EUROPA 1 ROCKET LAUNCH
Woomera, SA
12 Jun 1970

Type 124G | Flight 9

	ordinary cover	Qty: 23,566	
124G.1	Europa 1 illustrated cover		10.00
124G.2	any other illustrated cover		6.00
124G.#R	Registered cover	Qty: 69	40.00

185 1970 MELBOURNE AIRPORT OPENING
Melbourne 3000, Vic
1 Jul 1970

	ordinary cover		
185.1	QANTAS cover – one way	Qty: 2,557	12.50
185.2	QANTAS cover – return	Qty: 649	20.00
185.3	aerogramme – one way	Qty: 23	$100
185.4	aerogramme – return	Qty: 63	75.00
185.5	Cook miniature sheet on cover		25.00

This postmark was used on covers carried on the first commercial QANTAS Melbourne to London flight via USA. It is also found on the unofficially overprinted Captain Cook Bicentenary miniature sheet.

186 1970 3RD STATE GIRL GUIDE CAMP
Windsor 2756, NSW
22 – 29 Aug 1970

	ordinary cover	Qty: 11,308	
186.1	Girl Guide Camp cover		8.00
186.2	any other illustrated cover		5.00
186.#R	Registered cover	Qty: 131	35.00

187 1970 COMMENCEMENT OF OVERLAND TELEGRAPH LINE 1890
14 Sep – 10 Oct 1970

Type 187A
14 – 19 Sep 1970 | Darwin 5790, NT

	ordinary cover	Qty: 3,292	
187A.1	Overland Telegraph cover		10.00
187A.2	any other illustrated cover		7.50
187A.#R	Registered cover	Qty: 25	60.00

189.1 | 15 October 1970

18th International Dairy Congress

191A.1 | 2 December 1970

Papal Visit

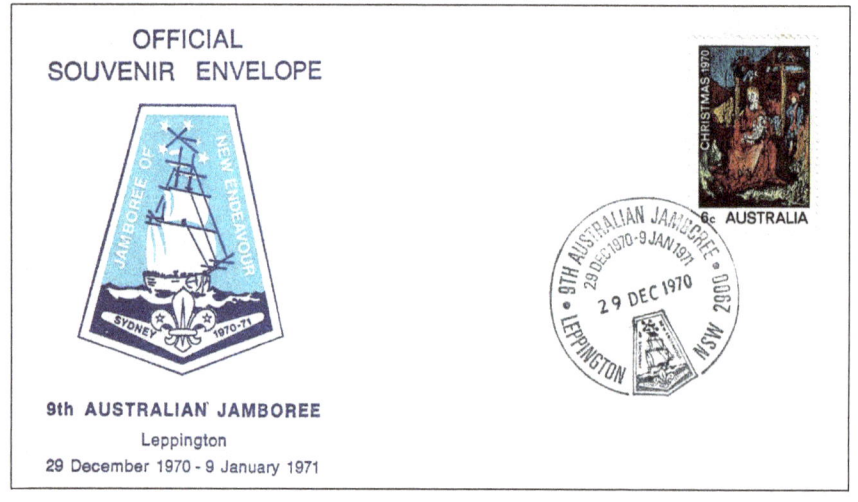

192.1 | 29 December 1970

9th Australian Scout Jamboree

Type 187B

5 – 10 Oct 1970 | Port Augusta 5700, SA

	ordinary cover	Qty: 2,565	
187B.1	Overland Telegraph cover – black ink		10.00
187B.2	Overland Telegraph cover – purple ink		10.00
187B.3	any other illustrated cover – black ink		7.50
187B.4	any other illustrated cover – purple ink		7.50
187B.#R	Registered cover	Qty: 40	50.00

188

188 1970 3RD ASIAN AND AUSTRALASIAN CONGRESS OF ANESTHESIOLOGY

Canberra 2600, ACT
19 – 22 Sep 1970

	ordinary cover	Qty: 3,773	
188.1	any illustrated cover		10.00
188.#R	Registered cover	Qty: 39	50.00

189

189 1970 18TH INTERNATIONAL DAIRY CONGRESS

Sydney Showground 2021, NSW
12 – 16 Oct 1970

	ordinary cover	Qty: 8,754	
189.1	Dairy Congress souvenir cover		15.00
189.2	Dairy Congress FDC		10.00
189.3	any other illustrated cover		8.00
189.#R	Registered cover	Qty: 46	50.00

Related stamp issue:
7 Oct 1970 – 6c, 18th International Dairy Congress (SG474)

190

190 1970 QANTAS 50TH ANNIVERSARY

Sydney 2000, NSW
16 Nov 1970

	ordinary cover		
	QANTAS Commemorative Cover		
190.1	addressed to London	Qty: 8,190	10.00
190.2	addressed to Australia	Qty: 2,641	12.00
190.3	any other address	Qty: 214	30.00
	QANTAS Commemorative aerogramme		
190.4	addressed to London	Qty: 249	30.00
190.5	addressed to Australia	Qty: 591	20.00
190.6	any other address	Qty: 161	40.00

Related stamp issue:
2 Nov 1970 – 6c and 30c, 50th Anniversary of QANTAS Airline (SG477-8)

191A
Small dateline

191B
Large dateline

191 1970 PAPAL VISIT

Sydney 2000, NSW
30 Nov – 3 Dec 1970

Type 191A | Small dateline

	ordinary cover	Qty: 74,514*	
191A.1	Papal Visit cover		10.00
191A.2	any other illustrated cover		6.00
191A.#R	Registered cover **	Qty: 92*	60.00

Type 191B | Large dateline

	ordinary cover	*	
191B.1	Papal Visit cover		10.00
191B.2	any other illustrated cover		6.00

* Quantities are for both types of postmark combined.

** Registered covers exist with either the standard 'Queen Victoria Bldgs (A) / NEW SOUTH WALES' R6 label, a blank label or a handwritten generic label with 'Papal Visit / P.O. Sydney'. Type 191B on a Registered cover has not been verified

Covers franked with Vatican stamps are known.

192

192 1970-71 9TH AUSTRALIAN SCOUT JAMBOREE

Leppington 2900, NSW
29 Dec 1970 - 9 Jan 1971

	ordinary cover	Qty: 56,515	
192.1	Jamboree Official Souvenir Envelope		7.50
192.2	any other illustrated cover		5.00
192.#R	Registered cover	Qty: 164	40.00

1971
EVENTS

193	6 Jan	28th International Congress of Orientalists
194	3 Feb	5th Commonwealth Education Conference
195	10 Feb	Centenary Train Launceston to Deloraine
196	22 Feb	5th Congress – International Plastic and Reconstructive Surgery
197	24 Feb	Newcastle Regional Show
198	8 Mar	Alice Springs Centenary
199	6 Apr	Lufthansa's Inaugural Flight Sydney to Bombay
200	10 Apr	Railway Centenary Celebrations - Scone
201	30 Apr	Goondiwindi Stamp and Coin Club Exhibition
202	5 May	Sydney Stock Exchange Centenary
203	15 May	62nd Rotary International Convention
204	17 May	Rotary Philatelic Exhibition
205	6 Jun	Centenary of Railways in Western Australia
206	9 Jun	50th Anniversary of R.A.A.F.
207	24 Jul	Presentation of Land Title to Aboriginal Trust
208	26 Jul	Australian Federation of Travel Agents Convention
209	27 Jul	Opening Day – Philatelic Sales Centre, Sydney
210	16 Aug	12th International Conference on Cosmic Rays
211	18 Aug	12th Pacific Science Congress
212	23 Aug	9th International Conference – Medical and Biological Engineering
213		[reserved]
214	6 Sep	Melbourne Conference – World Council of Young Men's Service Clubs
215	9 Sep	TAA Silver Jubilee Anniversary Flight
216	10 Sep	Opening of Martin Place
217	1 Oct	9th General Assembly – International Fellowship of Former Scouts and Guides
218	29 Oct	41st ASTA World Travel Congress
219	18 Nov	Combined Philatelic Societies Display
220	19 Nov	Presentation of the Queen's Colour to the R.S.T.T.
221	22 Nov	Radiology – 1st Asian and Oceanian Congress
222	5 Dec	50th Anniversary of First Regular Air Mail Service – Geraldton to Derby

Recurring events.
See the original event number entry for the first occurrence.

084	*26 Feb*	*Moomba Festival*
082	*17 Sep*	*Inauguration QANTAS Jet Service*

Note:
From the 1971 listings, postmarks provided in colours other than black are usually not illustrated in those colours.

193   1971 28TH INTERNATIONAL CONGRESS OF ORIENTALISTS

Canberra 2600, ACT
6 – 12 Jan 1971

	ordinary cover	Qty: 4,120	
193.1	Congress of Orientalists FDC – black ink		10.00
193.2	Congress of Orientalists FDC – violet ink		10.00
193.3	any other illustrated cover – black ink		5.00
193.4	any other illustrated cover – violet ink		5.00
193.5	plain cover – black ink		3.00
193.6	plain cover – violet ink		3.00
193.#R	Registered cover	Qty: 76*	60.00

* R6 label 082 has been sighted.

Related stamp issue:
6 Jan 1971 – 6c, 15c and 20c, 'Australia Asia' 28th International Congress of Orientalists (SG483-5)

194   1971 5TH COMMONWEALTH EDUCATION CONFERENCE

Canberra 2600, ACT
3 – 17 Feb 1971

	ordinary cover	Qty: 2,692	
194.1	official souvenir cover – black ink		20.00
194.2	official souvenir cover – violet ink		20.00
194.3	any other illustrated cover – black ink		8.00
194.4	any other illustrated cover – violet ink		8.00
194.5	plain cover – black ink		4.00
194.6	plain cover – violet ink		4.00
194.#R	Registered cover	Qty: 21	75.00

195   1971 CENTENARY TRAIN LAUNCESTON TO DELORAINE

Launceston 7250, Tas
10 Feb 1971

	ordinary cover	Qty: 4,632	
195.1	souvenir cover		40.00
195.2	any other illustrated cover		12.00
195.3	plain cover		6.00
195.#R	Registered cover	Qty: 6	$200

196   1971 5TH CONGRESS – INTERNATIONAL PLASTIC AND RECONSTRUCTIVE SURGERY

Melbourne 3000, Vic
22 – 26 Feb 1971

	ordinary cover	Qty: 3,998	
196.1	any illustrated cover – black ink		20.00
196.2	any illustrated cover – violet ink		20.00
196.3	plain cover – black ink		10.00
196.4	plain cover – violet ink		10.00
196.#R	Registered cover	Qty: 29	75.00

197   1971 NEWCASTLE REGIONAL SHOW

Newcastle, NSW
22 – 27 Feb 1971

	ordinary cover	
197.1	any illustrated cover	20.00
197.2	plain cover	10.00

084   1971 MOOMBA FESTIVAL

Melbourne, Vic
26 Feb – 8 Mar 1971

Type 084B (see illustration under 1969)

	ordinary cover	Qty: 4,631	
084B.1.71	Moomba cover – black ink		6.00
084B.2.71	Moomba cover – violet ink		6.00
084B.3.71	any other illustrated cover – black ink		4.00
084B.4.71	any other illustrated cover – violet ink		4.00
084B.5.71	plain cover – black ink		3.00
084B.6.71	plain cover – violet ink		3.00
084B.#R.71R	Registered cover	Qty: 35	60.00

084B.2.71 | 26 February 1971

Moomba Festival

198.1 | 11 March 1971

Alice Springs Centenary

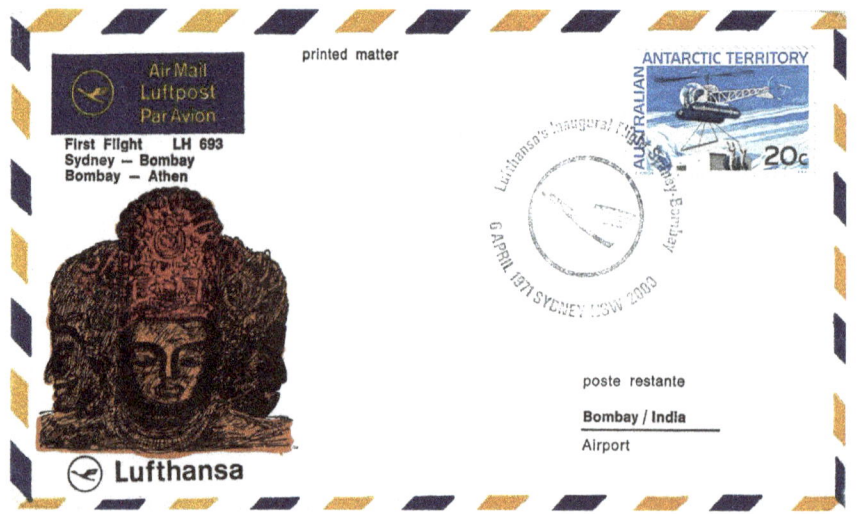

199.1 | 6 April 1971

Lufthansa's Inaugural Flight Sydney to Bombay

198   1971 ALICE SPRINGS CENTENARY

Alice Springs 5750, NT
8 – 21 Mar 1971

	ordinary cover	Qty: 5,695
198.1	Alice Springs Centenary cover	10.00
198.2	Pack Horse Mail cover	10.00
198.3	any other illustrated cover	5.00
198.#R	Registered cover .... Qty: 24	75.00

199   1971 LUFTHANSA'S INAUGURAL FLIGHT SYDNEY TO BOMBAY

Sydney 2000, NSW
6 Apr 1971

	ordinary cover	
199.1	Lufthansa Flight cover – one way	10.00
199.2	Lufthansa Flight cover – return	20.00
199.3	any other illustrated cover – one way	8.00
199.4	any other illustrated cover – return	15.00
199.5	aerogramme – one way	40.00
199.6	aerogramme – return	40.00
199.7	plain cover – one way	5.00
199.8	plain cover – return	5.00
199.#R	Registered cover	50.00

Quantities:
covers one way   4,050
covers return   1,510
aerogrammes one way 105
aerogrammes return 86

Ordinary covers were carried on the flight to India and backstamped at Bombay. The editor has not sighted any registered covers backstamped, suggesting that none were carried.

200   1971 RAILWAY CENTENARY CELEBRATIONS

Scone 2337, NSW
10 – 18 Apr 1971

	ordinary cover	Qty: 6,490
200.1	Scone Railway Centenary cover	7.50
200.2	any other illustrated cover	5.00
200.#R	Registered cover .... Qty: 44	50.00

201   1971 GOONDIWINDI STAMP AND COIN CLUB EXHIBITION

Goondiwindi 4390, Qld
30 Apr – 1 May 1971

	ordinary cover	Qty: 3,921
201.1	Exhibition cover	7.50
201.2	any other illustrated cover	5.00
201.#R	Registered cover .... Qty: 30	70.00

202   1971 SYDNEY STOCK EXCHANGE CENTENARY

Sydney 2000, NSW
5 – 11 May 1971

	ordinary cover	Qty: 136,119
202.1	Official PO FDC (Sydney Stock Exchange building)	2.50
202.2	Official PO FDC (Stock Exchange traders)	2.50
202.3	any other FDC	2.50
202.4	any other illustrated cover	2.00

Similar postmarks were provided for Melbourne, Brisbane, Adelaide and Perth. However, these were FDI postmarks and are outside the scope of this guide.

Related stamp issue:
5 May 1972 – 6c, Centenary of Sydney Stock Exchange (SG487)

203   1971 62ND ROTARY INTERNATIONAL CONVENTION

Sydney Showgrounds 2041, NSW
15 – 20 May 1971

Type 203A | black ink

	ordinary cover	Qty: 29,853*
203A.1	Official PO FDC (Rotary logo)	3.00
203A.2	Official PO FDC ('50th' design)	3.00
203A.3	any other FDC	3.00
203A.4	any other illustrated cover	3.00
203A.#R	Registered cover	25.00

Type 203B | purple ink

	ordinary cover	*
203B.1	Official PO FDC (Rotary logo)	3.00
203B.2	Official PO FDC ('50th' design)	3.00
203B.3	any other FDC	3.00
203B.4	any other illustrated cover	3.00
203B.#R	Registered cover	25.00

* Quantity is for both colours combined.

Related stamp issue:
17 May 1971 – 6c, 50th Anniversary of Rotary International in Australia (SG488)

Type 204B | purple ink

	ordinary cover	*
204B.1	Official PO FDC (Rotary logo)	6.50
204B.2	Official PO FDC ('50th' design)	6.50
204B.3	any other FDC	6.50
204B.4	any other illustrated cover	5.00

Related stamp issue:
17 May 1971 – 6c, 50th Anniversary of Rotary International in Australia (SG488)

* Quantity is for both colours combined.

205

204

204   1971 ROTARY PHILATELIC EXHIBITION

Kilkenny North 5009, SA
17 – 23 May 1971

Type 204A | black ink

	ordinary cover	Qty: 6,741*
204A.1	Official PO FDC (Rotary logo)	6.50
204A.2	Official PO FDC ('50th' design)	6.50
204A.3	any other FDC	6.50
204A.4	any other illustrated cover	5.00

205   1971 CENTENARY OF RAILWAYS IN WESTERN AUSTRALIA

Bunbury 6230, WA
6 Jun 1971

	ordinary cover	Qty: 10,913
205.1	Railway Centenary illustrated cover	6.00
205.2	any other illustrated cover	4.00
205.#R	Registered cover	Qty: 31 ... 70.00

| 206A | 206B | 206C |

201.1 | 1 May 1971 | Goondiwindi Stamp and Coin Club Exhibition

206D 206E

Related stamp issue:
9 Jun 1971 – 6c, 50th Anniversary of R.A.A.F. (SG489).

207

206 1971 50TH ANNIVERSARY OF R.A.A.F.
9 Jun 1971

Type 206A | Amberley 4305, Qld

	ordinary cover	Qty: 11,958	
206A.1	Official PO FDC (airmen design)		4.00
206A.2	Official PO FDC (helmets design)		4.00

Type 206B | Edinburgh 5111, SA

	ordinary cover	Qty: 10,582	
206B.1	Official PO FDC (airmen design)		4.00
206B.2	Official PO FDC (helmets design)		4.00

Type 206C | Pearce 6035, WA

	ordinary cover	Qty: 10,312	
206C.1	Official PO FDC (airmen design) – black ink		4.00
206C.2	Official PO FDC (airmen design) – violet ink		4.00
206C.3	Official PO FDC (helmets design) – black ink		4.00
206C.4	Official PO FDC (helmets design) – violet ink		4.00

Type 206D | Point Cook 3029, Vic

	ordinary cover	Qty: 11,181	
206D.1	Official PO FDC (airmen design)		4.00
206D.2	Official PO FDC (helmets design)		4.00

Type 206E | Richmond 2755, NSW

	ordinary cover	Qty: 12,574	
206E.1	Official PO FDC (airmen design)		4.00
206E.2	Official PO FDC (helmets design)		4.00

207 1971 PRESENTATION OF LAND TITLE TO ABORIGINAL TRUST

Lake Tyers 3887, Vic
24 Jul 1971

	ordinary cover	Qty: 19,532	
207.1	Aboriginal Trust Souvenir Cover		6.00
207.2	any other illustrated cover		4.00

208

208 1971 AUSTRALIAN FEDERATION OF TRAVEL AGENTS CONVENTION

Perth 6000, WA
26 – 28 Jul 1971

	ordinary cover	Qty: 840	
208.1	any illustrated cover		50.00
208.1R	Registered cover	Qty: 21	$100

204B.3 | 17 May 1971

Rotary Philatelic Exhibition

206C.4 | 9 June 1971

50th Anniversary of R.A.A.F.

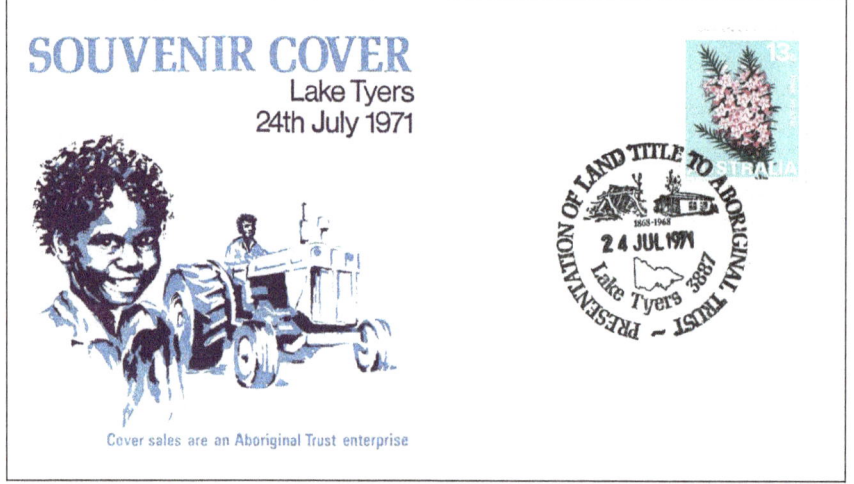

207.1 | 24 July 1971

Presentation of Land Title to Aboriginal Trust

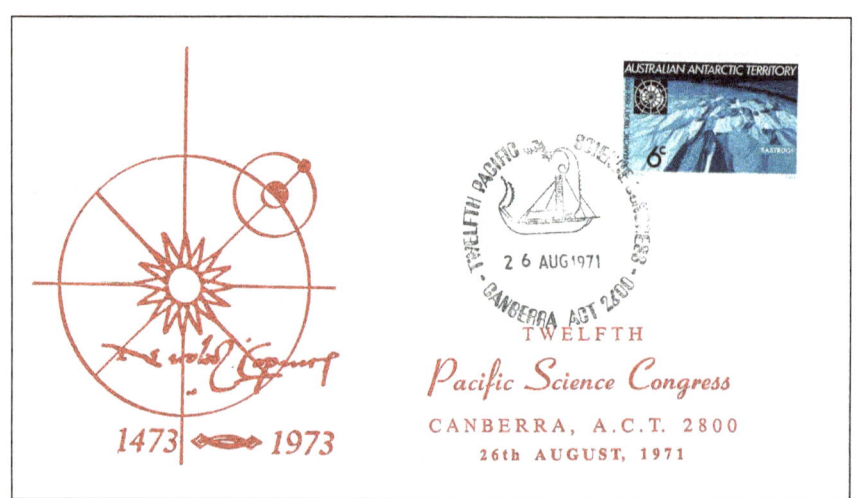

211.1 | 26 August 1971

12th Pacific Science Congress

209

209 1971 OPENING DAY – PHILATELIC SALES CENTRE, SYDNEY

Sydney 2000, NSW
27 Jul 1971

	ordinary cover	
209.1	PO Sydney Philatelic Centre souvenir cover	15.00
209.2	any other illustrated cover	10.00

210

210 1971 12TH INTERNATIONAL CONFERENCE ON COSMIC RAYS

Hobart 7000, Tas
16 – 26 Aug 1971

	ordinary cover	Qty: 3,705
210.1	Conference souvenir cover	15.00
210.2	any other illustrated cover	10.00
210.#R	Registered cover.......... Qty: 39	75.00

211

211 1971 12TH PACIFIC SCIENCE CONGRESS

Canberra 2600, ACT
18 – 27 Aug 1971

	ordinary cover	Qty: 3,667
211.1	Pacific Science Congress cover	15.00
211.2	any other illustrated cover	10.00
211.#R	Registered cover.......... Qty: 46	60.00

212

212 1971 9TH INTERNATIONAL CONFERENCE – MEDICAL AND BIOLOGICAL ENGINEERING

Melbourne 3000, Vic
23 – 27 Aug 1971

	ordinary cover	Qty: 1,597
212.1	any illustrated cover	25.00
212.2	plain cover	15.00
212.#R	Registered cover.......... Qty: 14	$100

16th Biennial Conference – Library Association of Australia
Sydney University, NSW – 24 August 1971
The editor has not been able to verify if this postmark was put into use. No image is available. Number 213 has been reserved.

214

214 1971 MELBOURNE CONFERENCE – WORLD COUNCIL OF YOUNG MEN'S SERVICE CLUBS

St. Kilda Road, Central 3004, Vic
6 – 13 Sep 1971

	ordinary cover	Qty: 6,963
214.1	Conference souvenir cover	15.00
214.2	any other illustrated cover	10.00
214.#R	Registered cover.......... Qty: 24	75.00

215

215 1971 TAA SILVER JUBILEE ANNIVERSARY FLIGHT

Laverton 3028, Vic
9 Sep 1971

	ordinary cover	Qty: 11,302
215.1	TAA souvenir cover	8.00
215.2	any other illustrated cover	5.00

216

216 1971 OPENING OF MARTIN PLACE

Sydney 2000, NSW
10 Sep 1971

	ordinary cover	Qty: 6,021
216.1	Martin Place Opening cover..................................10.00
216.2	any other illustrated cover 5.00
216.#R	Registered cover............................ Qty: 12 ....$125

082B

082   1971 INAUGURATION QANTAS JET SERVICE
Sydney, NSW
17 Sep 1971

Type 082B | Sydney to Singapore

ordinary cover
082B.1	QANTAS cover – one way ..... Qty: 2,446 ....15.00
082B.2	QANTAS cover – return .... Qty: 1,117 ....25.00
082B.3	QANTAS aerogramme – one way Qty: 13 ....60.00
082B.4	QANTAS aerogramme – return ... Qty: 26 ....30.00

Registered cover
| 082B.1R | QANTAS cover – one way .... Qty: 4 ....$200 |
| 082B.2R | QANTAS cover – return .... Qty: 4 ....$200 |

This postmark was applied with black and purple inks. Black has been sighted on aerogrammes and purple on covers, but specific usage is subject to further research.

217

217   1971 9TH GENERAL ASSEMBLY – INTERNATIONAL FELLOWSHIP OF FORMER SCOUTS AND GUIDES
Melbourne 3000, Vic
1 – 4 Oct 1971

	ordinary cover	Qty: 4,464
217.1	Official souvenir cover...5.00
217.2	any other illustrated cover 4.00
217.#R	Registered cover............................ Qty: 9 ....$150

218A

218   1971 41ST ASTA WORLD TRAVEL CONGRESS
Sydney 2000, NSW
29 Oct – 5 Nov 1971

Type 218A | black ink

	ordinary cover	Qty: 4,388*
218A.1	any illustrated cover 5.00

Type 218B | purple ink

	ordinary cover	*
218B.1	any illustrated cover 5.00
218B.#R	Registered cover............................ Qty: 24 ....$100

* Quantity is for both colours combined.

219

219   1971 COMBINED PHILATELIC SOCIETIES DISPLAY
Toombul 4012, Qld
18 – 20 Nov 1971

	ordinary cover	Qty: 6,206
219.1	Combined Philatelic Display cover 12.50
219.2	any other illustrated cover 8.00

220A

220   1971 PRESENTATION OF THE QUEEN'S COLOUR TO THE R.S.T.T.
Wagga Wagga 2651, NSW
19 Nov 1971

Type 220A | black ink

	ordinary cover	Qty: 7,204*
220A.1	Presentation of Colours souvenir cover 10.00
220A.2	any other illustrated cover 6.00

Type 220B | purple ink

	ordinary cover	*
220B.1	Presentation of Colours souvenir cover 10.00
220B.2	any other illustrated cover 6.00

	Registered cover	Qty: 4*
220A/B.#R	black or purple ink $200

* Quantity is for both colours combined. The editor has no information regarding postmark colours on Registered covers.

RSST = R.A.A.F. School of Technical Training

 221  222

221 **1971 RADIOLOGY – 1ST ASIAN AND OCEANIAN CONGRESS**

Melbourne 3000, Vic
22 – 26 Nov 1971

	ordinary cover	Qty: 3,671	
221.1	Event-specific illustrated cover		15.00
221.2	any other illustrated cover		10.00
221.#R	Registered cover	Qty: 14	$150

222 **50TH ANNIVERSARY OF FIRST REGULAR AIR MAIL SERVICE – GERALDTON TO DERBY**

Geraldton 6538, WA
5 Dec 1971

	ordinary cover	Qty: 5,416	
222.1	Event-specific illustrated cover		15.00
222.2	any other illustrated cover		10.00
222.#R	Registered cover	Qty: 33	60.00

217.1 | 24 July 1971

9th General Assembly – International Fellowship of Former Scouts and Guides

1972

EVENTS

223	22 Jan	Opening Salamanca Market
224	21 Feb	1st Australian Child Care Conference
225	21 Feb	1st Conference – Commonwealth Pharmaceutical Association
226	30 Mar	5th National Australian Convention of Amateur Astronomers
227	17 Apr	ICOLD – 40th Executive Meeting
228	7 May	Jarrahdale WA Centenary
229	8 May	4th Confederation Asian Chambers Commerce and Industry
230	8 May	20th Convention Lions International Multiple District 201
231	8 May	Philas 1972 – Philatelic Association of N.S.W. Exhibition
232	14 Aug	6th Biennial Conference – Australian Road Research Board
233	15 Aug	Centenary of Overland Telegraph
234	22 Aug	Centenary of Overland Telegraph – ANPEX 1972
235	22 Aug	14th International Congress of Entomology
236	27 Aug	12th World Rehabilitation Congress
237	28 Sep	Centenary of Brisbane General Post Office
238	2 Oct	5th World Conference on General Practice
239	9 Oct	Western Australia Philatelic Exhibition (WAPEX)
240	12 Oct	Glen Innes Municipal Centenary – GLENPEX 72
241	16 Oct	10th International Congress of Accountants
242	9 Nov	Combined Philatelic Societies Display
243	27 Dec	3rd Australian Senior Scout Venture
244-245		[numbers not allocated]

Recurring events.
See the original event number entry for the first occurrence.

084	3 Mar	Moomba Festival
184	3 Jun	Pacific Festival
110	14 Aug	44th ANZAAS Congress
021	Oct	Royal Show Hobart

223.1 | 22 January 1972

Opening of Salamanca Market, Hobart

223

223　1972 OPENING OF SALAMANCA MARKET

Hobart 7000, Tas
22 Jan 1972

	ordinary cover	Qty: 5,109
223.1	Salamanca Place cover	6.00
223.2	any other illustrated cover	4.00

224

224　1972 1ST AUSTRALIAN CHILD CARE CONFERENCE

Melbourne 3000, Vic
21 – 25 Feb 1972

	ordinary cover	Qty: 2,698
224.1	any illustrated cover	15.00

225

225　192 1ST CONFERENCE – COMMONWEALTH PHARMACEUTICAL ASSOCIATION

Melbourne 3000, Vic
21 – 25 Feb 1972

	ordinary cover	Qty: 2,820
225.1	Pharmaceutical Association cover	15.00
225.2	any other illustrated cover	10.00

084　1972 MOOMBA FESTIVAL

Melbourne, Vic
3 – 13 Mar 1972

Type 084B (see illustration under 1969)

	ordinary cover	Qty: 6,520
084B.1.72	Moomba cover	7.50
084B.2.72	any other illustrated cover	5.00
084B.#.72R	Registered cover	Qty: 22	$100

226

226　1972 5TH NATIONAL AUSTRALIAN CONVENTION OF AMATEUR ASTRONOMERS

Melbourne 3002, Vic
30 Mar – 4 Apr 1972

	ordinary cover	Qty: 11,029
226.1	souvenir cover	5.00
226.2	any other illustrated cover	3.00
226.#R	Registered cover	Qty: 12	$125

227

227　1972 ICOLD – 40TH EXECUTIVE MEETING – CIGB

Melbourne 3000, Vic
17 – 19 Apr 1972

	ordinary cover	Qty: 2,489
227.1	any illustrated cover	15.00

ICOLD = International Commission on Large Dams.
CIGB = Commission Internationale des Grands Barrages.

228

228　1972 JARRAHDALE WA CENTENARY

Jarrahdale 6203, WA
7 May 1972

	ordinary cover	Qty: 3,449
228.1	Jarrahdale Centenary cover	10.00
228.2	any other illustrated cover	7.50

229

230.1 | 12 May 1972

20th Convention Lions International Multiple District 201

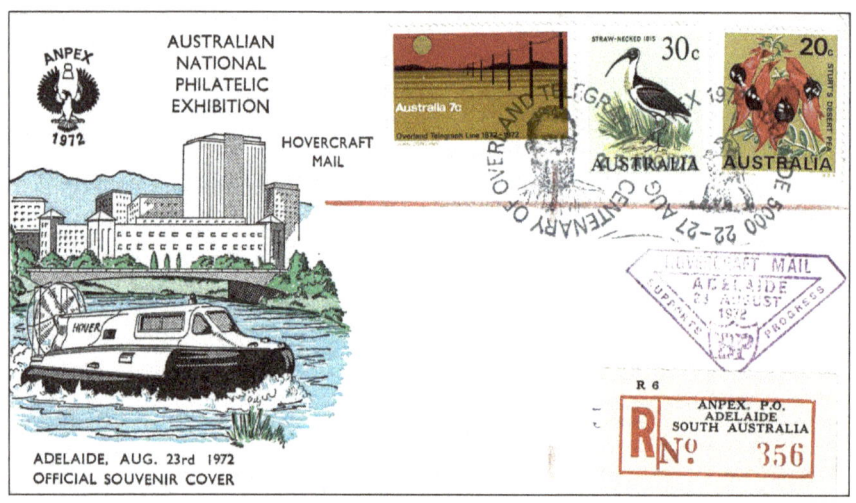

234B.2R | 23 August 1972

Centenary of Overland Telegraph – ANPEX 1972, Hovercraft Mail

239A.1 | 9 Oct 1972

Western Australian Philatelic Exhibition – WAPEX 72

229 **1972 4TH CONFEDERATION ASIAN CHAMBERS COMMERCE AND INDUSTRY**

Perth 6000, WA
8 – 11 May 1972

	ordinary cover	Qty: 1,985	
229.1	Event-specific illustrated cover		20.00
229.2	any other illustrated cover		15.00
229.3	plain cover		10.00
229.#R	Registered cover	Qty: 15	$125

230 **1972 20TH CONVENTION LIONS INTERNATIONAL MULTIPLE DISTRICT 201**

Perth 6000, WA
8 – 12 May 1972

	ordinary cover	Qty: 4,888	
230.1	Lions 25th Australian Anniversary cover		10.00
230.2	any other illustrated cover		7.50
230.#R	Registered cover	Qty: 19	$100

231 **PHILAS 1972 – PHILATELIC ASSOCIATION OF N.S.W. EXHIBITION**

Sydney 2000, NSW
8 – 13 May 1972

	ordinary cover	Qty: 2,121	
231.1	Philas cover		20.00
231.2	any other illustrated cover		10.00
231.#R	Registered cover	Qty: 18	$100

184 **1972 PACIFIC FESTIVAL**

Townsville 4810, Qld
3 – 13 Jun 1972

	ordinary cover	Qty: 1,956	
184B.1	Pacific Festival cover		15.00
184B.2	any other illustrated cover		10.00
184B.3	plain cover		5.00

232 **1972 6TH BIENNIAL CONFERENCE – AUSTRALIAN ROAD RESEARCH BOARD**

Canberra 2600, ACT
14 – 18 Aug 1972

	ordinary cover	Qty: 2,290	
232.1	souvenir cover		20.00
232.2	any other illustrated cover		15.00
232.#R	Registered cover	Qty: 16	$125

110 **1972 44TH ANZAAS CONGRESS**

Sydney 2000, NSW
14 – 18 Aug 1972

	ordinary cover	Qty: 4,151	
110D.1	any illustrated cover		10.00
110D.#R	Registered cover	Qty: 23	75.00

233 **1972 CENTENARY OF OVERLAND TELEGRAPH**
15 – 30 Aug 1972

Type 233A | 22 – 27 Aug | Centenary of Overland Telegraph Exhibition, Adelaide 5000, SA

	ordinary cover	Qty: 10,773
233A.1	PO Overland Telegraph FDC (Morse key and map)	2.50
233A.2	PO Overland Telegraph FDC (Darwin camp)	2.50
233A.3	any other illustrated cover	2.00
233A.#R	Registered cover.......... Qty: 69	40.00

Type 233B | 15 – 30 Aug | Chief Telegraph Office, Adelaide, SA

	ordinary	Qty: 2,567
233B.1	souvenir telegram	10.00

Type 233C | 22 Aug | Alice Springs Old Telegraph Station 5750, NT

	ordinary cover	Qty: 8,862
233C.1	PO Overland Telegraph FDC (Morse key and map)	3.00
233C.2	PO Overland Telegraph FDC (Darwin camp)	3.00
233C.3	any other illustrated cover	2.00
233C.#R	Registered cover.......... Qty: 26	75.00

Type 233D | 22 – 25 Aug | Frews Ironstone Ponds 5760, NT

	ordinary cover	Qty: 9,108
233D.1	PO Overland Telegraph FDC (Morse key and map)	3.00
233D.2	PO Overland Telegraph FDC (Darwin camp)	3.00
233D.3	any other illustrated cover	2.00
233D.#R	Registered cover.......... Qty: 41	75.00

Related stamp issue:
22 Aug 1972 – 7c, Centenary of Overland Telegraph (SG517)

234 1972 CENTENARY OF OVERLAND TELEGRAPH – ANPEX 1972

Adelaide 5000, SA
22 – 27 Aug 1972

Type 234A | 22 Aug | red ink

	ordinary cover	Qty: 20,171*
234A.1	Exhibition official souvenir cover	2.50
234A.2	PO Telegraph FDC (Morse key and map)	2.50
234A.3	PO Telegraph FDC (Darwin camp)	2.50
234A.4	any other illustrated cover	2.50
234A.#R	Registered cover........... Qty: 681***	15.00

Type 234B | 23 – 26 Aug | black ink

	ordinary cover	*
234B.1	Exhibition official souvenir cover	2.50
234B.2	23 Aug	Hovercraft cover (Qty: 3,887**)	10.00
234B.3	23 Aug	Hovercraft aerogramme (Qty: 25)	80.00
234B.4	PO Telegraph FDC (Morse key and map)	2.50
234B.5	PO Telegraph FDC (Darwin camp)	2.50
234B.6	any other illustrated cover	2.50
234B.7	23 Aug	Hovercraft mailbag label (Qty: 25)	80.00

	Registered cover	***
234B.2R	23 Aug Hovercraft Mail official souvenir cover	35.00
234B.#R	23 – 26 Aug	any other cover	15.00

Type 234C | 27 Aug | green ink

	ordinary cover	*
234C.1	Exhibition official souvenir cover	2.50
234C.2	PO Telegraph FDC (Morse key and map)	2.50
234C.3	PO Telegraph FDC (Darwin camp)	2.50
234C.4	any other illustrated cover	2.50
234C.#R	Registered cover.............. ***	15.00

Related stamp issue:
22 Aug 1972 – 7c, Centenary of Overland Telegraph (SG517)

*   Quantity is for all colours combined.

**   Australian Post Office Philatelic Bulletin (Dec 1972) does not state whether the 3,887 Hovercraft Mail items are included in the total impressions of the postmark.

*** Quantity is for all colours combined. The number of Registered Hovercraft Mail covers is probably included in the total of 681.

235 1972 14TH INTERNATIONAL CONGRESS OF ENTOMOLOGY

Canberra 2600, ACT
22 – 30 Aug 1972

	ordinary cover	Qty: 6,912
235.1	any illustrated cover	10.00
235.#R	Registered cover.......... Qty: 42	75.00

236 1972 12TH WORLD REHABILITATION CONGRESS

Sydney 2000, NSW
27 Aug – 1 Sep 1972

	ordinary cover	Qty: 4,286
236.1	Official PO Rehabilitation FDC	10.00
236.2	any other illustrated cover	7.00
236.#R	Registered cover.......... Qty: 40	75.00

Related stamp issue:
2 Aug 1972 – 12c, 18c and 24c, Rehabilitation (SG514-6)

237   cachet

237   **1972 CENTENARY OF BRISBANE GENERAL POST OFFICE**

Brisbane 4000, Qld
28 Sep 1972

	ordinary cover	Qty: 10,252*	
237.1	souvenir cover		15.00
237.2	any other illustrated cover **		10.00
237.#R	Registered cover	Qty: 28	80.00

* Quantity comprises 9,625 items treated with a suitable cachet and carried on a 'Packhorse Mail' and 627 items processed with the commemorative postmark only.

** Many plain covers were submitted to be carried on the Packhorse Mail. If provided in time, they were stamped with the cachet shown here, effectively making such covers 'illustrated'.

238   **1972 5TH WORLD CONFERENCE ON GENERAL PRACTICE**

Melbourne 3000, Vic
2 – 6 Oct 1972

	ordinary cover	Qty: 4,899	
238.1	souvenir cover		10.00
238.2	any other illustrated cover		7.00
238.#R	Registered cover	Qty: 24	$100

239   **1972 WESTERN AUSTRALIAN PHILATELIC EXHIBITION (WAPEX)**

Perth 6000, WA
9 – 15 Oct 1972

Type 239A | 9 Oct | red ink

	ordinary cover	Qty: 5,702*	
239A.1	WAPEX 72 cover		10.00
239A.2	any other illustrated cover		7.00
239A.#R	Registered cover	Qty: 139*	50.00

Type 239B | 10 – 14 Oct | black ink

	ordinary cover	*	
239B.1	WAPEX 72 cover		10.00
239B.2	any other illustrated cover		7.00
239B.#R	Registered cover	*	50.00

Type 239C | 15 Oct | green ink

	ordinary cover	*	
239C.1	WAPEX 72 cover		10.00
239C.2	any other illustrated cover		7.00
239C.#R	Registered cover	*	50.00

* Quantities are for all colours combined.

Green postmark also sighted dated 14 October.

240   **1972 GLEN INNES MUNICIPAL CENTENARY – GLENPEX 72**

Glen Innes 2390, NSW
12 – 14 Oct 1972

	ordinary cover	Qty: 2,523	
240.1	GLENPEX '72 cover		20.00
240.2	any other illustrated cover		15.00
240.#R	Registered cover	Qty: 30	80.00

241   **1972 10TH INTERNATIONAL CONGRESS OF ACCOUNTANTS**

Sydney 2000, NSW
16 – 21 Oct 1972

	ordinary cover	Qty: 7,630	
241.1	Official PO FDC (numbers design)		10.00
241.2	Official PO FDC (abacus design)		10.00
241.3	any other illustrated cover		7.00
241.#R	Registered cover	Qty: 26	$100

Related stamp issue:
16 Oct 1972 – 7c, 10th International Congress of Accountants (SG522)

021   *1972 ROYAL SHOW HOBART*

Hobart, Tas
Oct 1972

Type 021B (see illustration under 1966)

021B.1.72	plain cover		10.00

242   1972 COMBINED PHILATELIC SOCIETIES DISPLAY
Toombul 4012, Qld
9 – 11 Nov 1972

	ordinary cover	Qty: 3,327	
242.1	Combined Philatelic Display cover		15.00
242.2	any other illustrated cover		10.00
242.#R	Registered cover	Qty: 15	$125

243   1972-73 3RD AUSTRALIAN SENIOR SCOUT VENTURE
Samford 4520, Qld
27 Dec 1972 – 6 Jan 1973

	ordinary cover	Qty: 4,135	
243.1	Scouting cover		15.00
243.2	any other illustrated cover		10.00
243.#R	Registered cover	Qty: 144	40.00

240.1 | 14 Oct 1972

Glenn Innes Municipal Centenary – GLENPEX 72

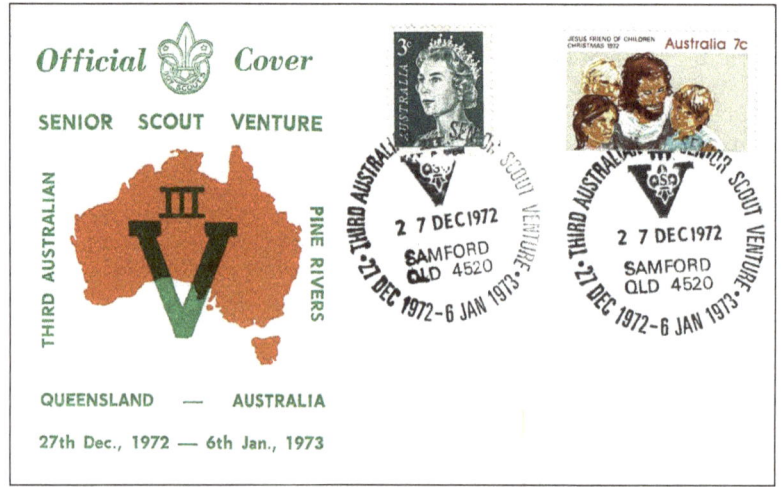

243.1 | 27 December 1972

3rd Australian Senior Scout Venture

1973

EVENTS

246	12 Feb	40th International Eucharistic Congress
247	17 Feb	500th Anniversary of Nicolaus Copernicus – POLPHIL '73
248	18 Apr	Opening of Henry Kendall Memorial Park
249	12 May	50 Years of Ranger Guides in N.S.W.
250	21 May	International Real Estate Federation 24th Annual Congress
251	22 May	3rd World Conference on Animal Production
252	16 Jun	90th Anniversary of Cape York Telegraph Route Expedition
253	16 Jul	International Dental Congress
254	3 Aug	50th Anniversary of Discovery of Mount Isa Orefield
255	20 Aug	15th General Assembly of International Astronomical Union Assembly
256	26 Aug	4th Girl Guide Muster
257	24 Sep	50th Anniversary of Inland Mission Hospital
258	4 Oct	45th Annual Conference of Legacy Clubs
259	8 Oct	25th Anniversary World Mental Health Congress
260	11 Oct	Queensland Philatelic Exhibition
261	17 Oct	Opening of Sydney Opera House
262	12 Nov	80th Anniversary of Rosebery Zinc Discovery
263	10 Dec	Centenary of Death of Sir Paul Strzelecki
264	29 Dec	10th Australian Scout Jamboree

Recurring events.
See the original event number entry for the first occurrence.

109	5 Jan	*CEBS National Camp*
084	2 Mar	*Moomba Festival*

109C

246

109 **1973 CHURCH OF ENGLAND BOYS SOCIETY NATIONAL CAMP**

Swanleigh 6056, WA
5 – 15 Jan 1973

	ordinary cover	Qty: 3,542	
109C.1	CEBS National Camp cover		15.00
109C.2	any other illustrated cover		10.00
109C.#R	Registered cover	Qty: 20	$100

246 **1973 40TH INTERNATIONAL EUCHARISTIC CONGRESS**

Melbourne 3000, Vic
12 – 28 Feb 1973

	ordinary cover	Qty: 15,457	
246.1	any illustrated cover		3.00
246.#R	Registered cover	Qty: 54	60.00

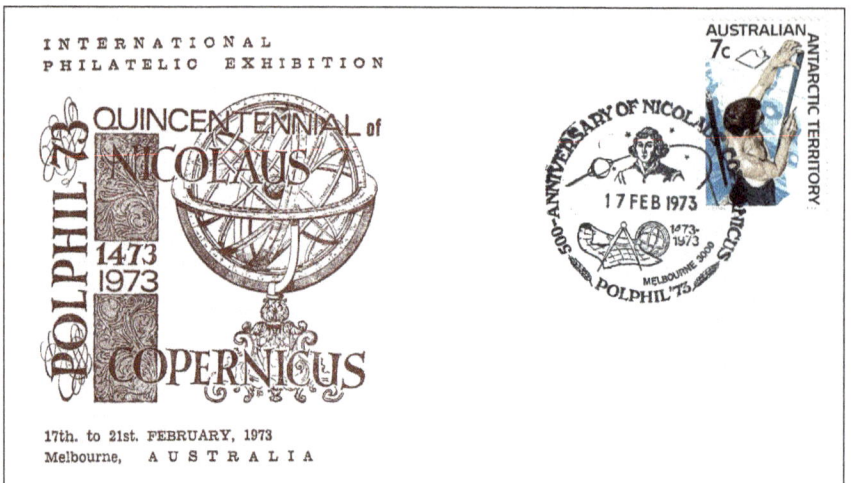

247.1 | 17 February 1973

500th Anniversary of Nicolaus Copernicus – POLPHIL 73

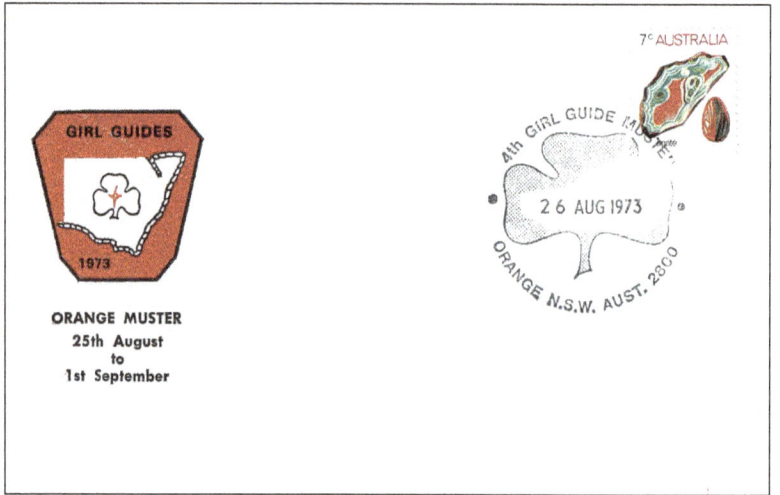

256.1 | 26 August 1973

4th Girl Guide Muster

258.1 | 4 October 1973

45th Annual Conference of Legacy Clubs

247 1973 500TH ANNIVERSARY OF NICOLAUS COPERNICUS – POLPHIL '73

Melbourne 3000, Vic
17 – 21 Feb 1973

	ordinary cover	Qty: 8,043	
247.1	Copernicus / POLPHIL cover		10.00
247.2	any other illustrated cover		5.00
247.#R	Registered cover	Qty: 59	50.00

084 1973 MOOMBA FESTIVAL

Melbourne, Vic
2 – 12 Mar 1973

	ordinary cover	Qty: 8,900	
084C.1.73	Moomba cover		7.50
084C.2.73	any other illustrated cover		5.00
084C.#.73R	Registered cover	Qty: 38	50.00

248 1973 OPENING OF HENRY KENDALL MEMORIAL PARK

Kendal 2439, NSW
18 Apr 1973

	ordinary cover	Qty: 3,416	
248.1	any illustrated cover		10.00
248.#R	Registered cover	Qty: 10	$150

249 1973 50 YEARS OF RANGER GUIDES IN N.S.W.

Turramurra 2074, NSW
12 – 19 May 1973

	ordinary cover	Qty: 5,170	
249.1	any illustrated cover		15.00
249.#R	Registered cover	Qty: 27	80.00

250 1973 INTERNATIONAL REAL ESTATE FEDERATION 24TH ANNUAL CONGRESS

Sydney 2000, NSW
21 – 25 May 1973

	ordinary cover	Qty: 2,735	
250.1	any illustrated cover		15.00
250.#R	Registered cover	Qty: 25	80.00

251 1973 3RD WORLD CONFERENCE ON ANIMAL PRODUCTION

Melbourne 3000, Vic
22 – 30 May 1973

	ordinary cover	Qty: 2,056	
251.1	any illustrated cover		15.00
251.#R	Registered cover	Qty: 18	$100

252 1973 90TH ANNIVERSARY OF CAPE YORK TELEGRAPH ROUTE EXPEDITION

Laura 4871, Qld
16 Jun 1973

	ordinary cover	Qty: 2,607	
252.1	any illustrated cover		15.00
252.2	souvenir lettergram		30.00
252.#R	Registered cover	Qty: 18	$100

262.1 | 21 November 1973

80th Anniversary of Rosebery Zinc Discovery

263.1 | 10 December 1973

Centenary of Death of Paul Strzelecki

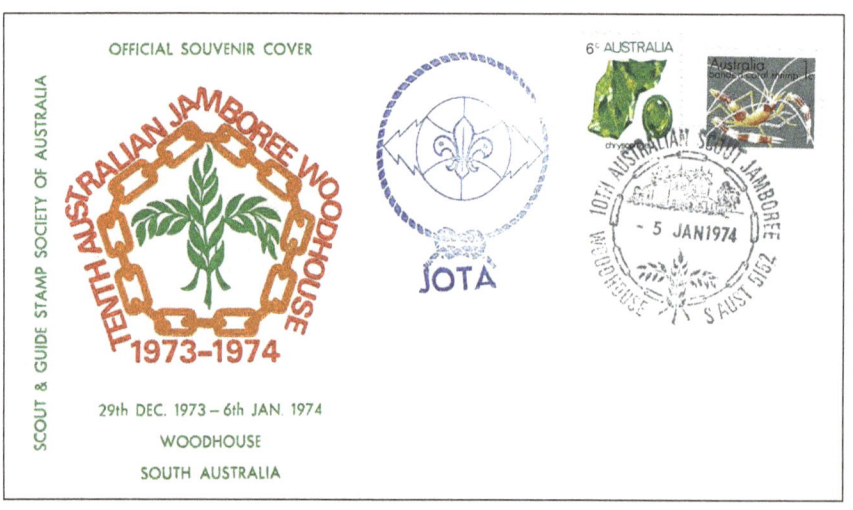

264.1 | 5 January 1974

10th Australian Scout Jamboree

253 1973 INTERNATIONAL DENTAL CONGRESS

Sydney 2000, NSW
16 – 20 Jul 1973

		ordinary cover	Qty: 3,953	
253.1		any illustrated cover		10.00
253.#R		Registered cover	Qty: 34	75.00

254 1973 50TH ANNIVERSARY OF DISCOVERY OF MOUNT ISA OREFIELD

Mt Isa 4825, Qld
3 – 13 Aug 1973

Type 254A | black ink

	ordinary cover	Qty: 4,693*	
254A.1	any illustrated cover		15.00
254A.#R	Registered cover	Qty: 12*	$150

Type 254B | purple ink

	ordinary cover	*	
254B.1	any illustrated cover		15.00
254B.#R	Registered cover	*	$150

* Quantities are for both colours combined.

255 1973 15TH GENERAL ASSEMBLY OF INTERNATIONAL ASTRONOMICAL UNION ASSEMBLY

Sydney 2000, NSW
20 – 30 Aug 1973

	ordinary cover	Qty: 5,862	
255.1	any illustrated cover		7.50
255.#R	Registered cover	Qty: 43	75.00

256 1973 4TH GIRL GUIDE MUSTER

Orange 2800, NSW
26 – 31 Aug 1973

	ordinary cover	Qty: 6,143	
256.1	Girl Guide Muster cover		12.00
256.2	any other illustrated cover		8.00
256.#R	Registered cover	Qty: 110	40.00

257 1973 50TH ANNIVERSARY OF INLAND MISSION HOSPITAL

Birdsville 4482, Qld
24 Sep 1973

	ordinary cover	Qty: 3,679	
257.1	any illustrated cover		16.00
257.#R	Registered cover	Qty: 18	$100

258 1973 45TH ANNUAL CONFERENCE OF LEGACY CLUBS

Melbourne 3000, Vic
4 – 6 Oct 1973

	ordinary cover	Qty: 4,689	
258.1	Legacy souvenir (APO 'wattle') cover		20.00
258.2	APO Legacy FDC (hand holding torch)		15.00
258.3	APO Legacy FDC (Legacy torch)		15.00
258.4	any other illustrated cover		10.00
258.#R	Registered cover	Qty: 16	$110

Related stamp issue:
5 Sep 1973 – 7c, 50th Anniversary of Legacy (SG553).

259 1973 25TH ANNIVERSARY WORLD MENTAL HEALTH CONGRESS

Sydney 2000, NSW
8 – 12 Oct 1973

	ordinary cover	Qty: 1,971	
259.1	APO WHO FDC (WHO logo design)		30.00
259.2	APO WHO FDC (anniversary design)		30.00
259.3	any other illustrated cover		30.00
259.#R	Registered cover	Qty: 14	$120

Related stamp issue:
4 Apr 1973 – 7c, 25th Anniversary of World Health Organisation (SG553)

260 1973 QUEENSLAND PHILATELIC EXHIBITION

Toombul 4012, Qld
11 – 14 Oct 1973

	ordinary cover	Qty: 3,352	
260.1	Exhibition souvenir cover		15.00
260.2	any other illustrated cover		10.00
260.#R	Registered cover	Qty: 19	$100

261A | Ballerina   261B | Orchestra

261 1973 OPENING OF SYDNEY OPERA HOUSE

Sydney 2000, NSW
17 Oct – 13 Nov 1973

	ordinary cover	Qty: 103,282	
261A.1	APO Opera House souvenir cover		3.00
261A.2	APO Architecture FDC (Opera House design)		5.00
261A.3	APO Architecture FDC (architecture design)		5.00
261A.4	any other illustrated cover		3.00
261A.#R	Registered cover	Qty: 250	25.00
	ordinary cover	Qty: 96,450	
261B.1	APO Opera House souvenir cover		3.00
261B.2	APO Architecture FDC (Opera House design)		5.00
261B.3	APO Architecture FDC (architecture design)		5.00
261B.4	any other illustrated cover		3.00
261B.#R	Registered cover	Qty: 323	25.00

Related stamp issue:
17 Oct 1973 – 7c, Sydney Opera House (SG556).

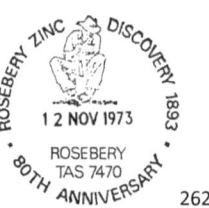

262 1973 80TH ANNIVERSARY OF ROSEBERY ZINC DISCOVERY

Rosebery 7470, Tas
12 – 23 Nov 1973

	ordinary cover	Qty: 8,134	
262.1	Rosebery Zinc Finder cover		10.00
262.2	any other illustrated cover		7.00

263 1973-74 CENTENARY OF DEATH OF SIR PAUL STRZELECKI

Mt Kosciusko, NSW
10 Dec – 1 Apr 1974

	ordinary cover	Qty: 13,484	
263.1	Sir Paul Strzelecki cover		15.00
263.2	any other illustrated cover		10.00
263.#R	Registered cover	Qty: 7	$150

264 1973-74 10TH AUSTRALIAN SCOUT JAMBOREE

Woodhouse 5152, SA
29 Dec 1973 – 6 Jan 1974

	ordinary cover	Qty: 40,299	
264.1	Jamboree souvenir cover		9.00
264.2	any other illustrated cover		5.00
264.#R	Registered cover	Qty: 284	30.00

1974

EVENTS

265	6 Jan	14th World Gliding Championship
266	16 Mar	Matthew Flinders Bicentenary
267	6 Apr	Golden Jubilee Scottish Festival
268	8 Apr	50 Years Re-enactment of Round Australia Flight
269	13 May	Supreme Court of NSW Commemoration
270	15 Jun	Centenary of Sisters of Perpetual Adoration
271	1 Aug	Centenary of Telecommunication Society of Australia
272	5 Aug	11th International Society for Music Education Conference
273	12 Aug	16th International Ornithological Congress
274	19 Aug	7th Biennial Conference of Australian Road Research Board
275	26 Aug	8th International Congress of Electron Microscopy
276	26 Aug	Fusion Festival – Illawarra Philatelic Society Exhibition
277	10 Sep	Last Flying Boat Mail to Lord Howe Island
278	16 Sep	6th Postal Telegraph and Telephone International Asian Regional Conference
279	7 Oct	National Stamp Week
280	8 Oct	Centenary of UPU - PHILAS 74 - National Stamp Week Exhibition
281	8 Oct	14th Triennial Conference of Association of Country Women of the World
282	9 Oct	Queensland Philatelic Exhibition – Centenary of UPU
283	14 Oct	150th Anniversary of Hume and Hovell Expedition

Recurring events.
See the original event number entry for the first occurrence.

084	1 Mar	Moomba Festival
027	Apr	Royal Easter Show

265.1 | 27 January 1974

14th World Gliding Championship

084C.1.74 | 4 March 1974

Moomba Festival

266F.1 | 16 March 1974

Matthew Flinders Bidentenary

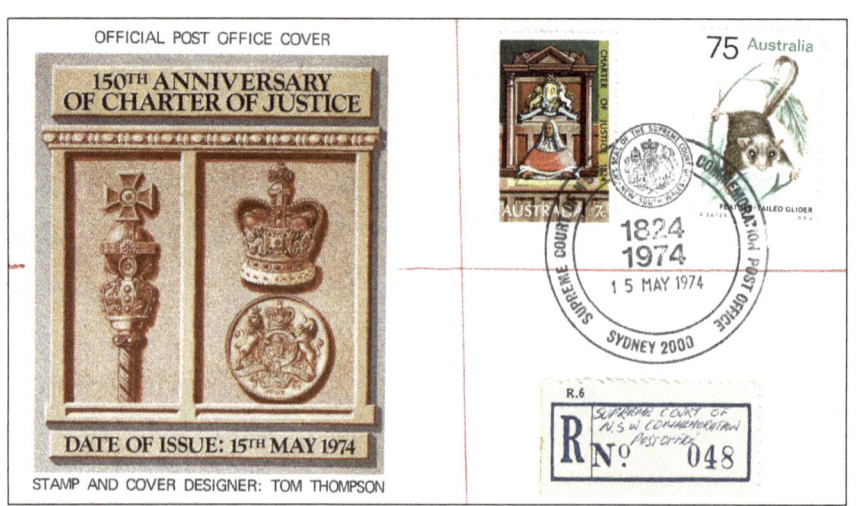

269.2R | 15 May 1974

Supreme Court of NSW Commemoration

265

265 1974 14TH WORLD GLIDING CHAMPIONSHIP
Waikerie 5300, SA
6 – 27 Jan 1974

	ordinary cover	Qty: 27,027	
265.1	Gliding Championship cover		12.00
265.2	any other illustrated cover		7.00
265.#R	Registered cover	Qty: 32	80.00

084 1974 MOOMBA FESTIVAL
Melbourne, Vic
1 – 11 Mar 1974

Type 084C (see illustration under 1973)

	ordinary cover	Qty: 6,471	
084C.1.74	Moomba cover		7.50
084C.2.74	any other illustrated cover		5.00
084C.#.74R	Registered cover	Qty: 25	$100

266E

266 1974 MATTHEW FLINDERS BICENTENARY
16 Mar 1974

Type 266A | Albany 6330, WA

	ordinary cover	Qty: 7,049
	black ink	
266A.1	APO Flinders souvenir cover ($1 Flinders stamp)	7.50
266A.2	APO Flinders souvenir cover (7c stamp)	5.00
266A.3	any other illustrated cover	4.00
	violet ink	
266A.4	APO Flinders souvenir cover ($1 Flinders stamp)	7.50
266A.5	APO Flinders souvenir cover (7c stamp)	5.00
266A.6	any other illustrated cover	4.00

Type 266B | Arthur's Seat 3936, Vic

	ordinary cover	Qty: 8,112
266B.1	APO Flinders souvenir cover ($1 Flinders stamp)	7.50
266B.2	APO Flinders souvenir cover (7c stamp)	5.00
266B.3	any other illustrated cover	4.00

Type 266C | Lake Illawarra 2528, NSW

	ordinary cover	Qty: 7,775
266C.1	APO Flinders souvenir cover ($1 Flinders stamp)	7.50
266C.2	APO Flinders souvenir cover (7c stamp)	5.00
266C.3	any other illustrated cover	4.00

Type 266D | Pialba 4655, Qld

	ordinary cover	Qty: 6,637
	black ink	
266D.1	APO Flinders souvenir cover ($1 Flinders stamp)	7.50
266D.2	APO Flinders souvenir cover (7c stamp)	5.00
266D.3	any other illustrated cover	4.00
	violet ink	
266D.4	APO Flinders souvenir cover ($1 Flinders stamp)	7.50
266D.5	APO Flinders souvenir cover (7c stamp)	5.00
266D.6	any other illustrated cover	4.00

Type 266E | Port Lincoln 5606, SA

	ordinary cover	Qty: 6,650
266E.1	APO Flinders souvenir cover ($1 Flinders stamp)	7.50
266E.2	APO Flinders souvenir cover (7c stamp)	5.00
266E.3	any other illustrated cover	4.00

Type 266F | Whitemark 7255, Tas

	ordinary cover	Qty: 10,986
266F.1	APO Flinders souvenir cover ($1 Flinders stamp)	7.50
266F.2	APO Flinders souvenir cover (7c stamp)	5.00
266F.3	any other illustrated cover	4.00

266A-F.1 set A	6 covers Flinders PO souvenir cover ($1 Flinders stamp)	40.00
266A-F.2 set B	6 covers Flinders PO souvenir cover (7c stamp)	25.00

Related stamp issue:
14 Feb 1966 – $1, Matthew Flinders definitive (SG401)

The use of violet ink at towns other than Albany and Pialba is subject to further research.

267

267 1974 GOLDEN JUBILEE SCOTTISH FESTIVAL
Melbourne 3000, Vic
6 – 16 Apr 1974

	ordinary cover	Qty: 4,242	
267.1	Victorian Highland Pipe Band ('wattle') cover		7.50
267.2	any other illustrated cover		5.00
267.#R	Registered cover	Qty: 10	$125

268

268 1974 50 YEARS RE-ENACTMENT OF ROUND AUSTRALIA FLIGHT

Amberley 4305, Qld
8 Apr 1974

	ordinary cover	Qty: 9,746	
268.1	Round Australia Flight cover		10.00
268.2	any other illustrated cover		7.00
268.#R	Registered cover	Qty: 46	60.00
268.#C	Certified cover	Qty: 5	$200

 Cachet applied to APO 'wattle' cover.

027   1974 ROYAL EASTER SHOW

Sydney, NSW
Apr 1974

Type 027C (see illustration under 1963)

027C.1.74   Royal Easter Show ('wattle') cover 20.00

269   1974 SUPREME COURT OF NSW COMMEMORATION

Sydney 2000, NSW
13 – 17 May 1974

	ordinary cover	Qty: 10,290	
269.1	APO Supreme Court FDC (staff design)		5.00
269.2	APO Supreme Court FDC (seal of court design)		5.00
269.3	any other illustrated cover		4.00
269.#R	Registered cover	Qty: 74	40.00

Related stamp issue:
15 May 1974 – 7c, 150th Anniversary of Charter of Justice (SG568)

270   1974 CENTENARY OF SISTERS OF PERPETUAL ADORATION

Brisbane 4000, Qld
15 Jun 1974

	ordinary cover	Qty: 3,508	
270.1	any illustrated cover		10.00

271   1974 CENTENARY OF TELECOMMUNICATION SOCIETY OF AUSTRALIA

Sydney 2000, NSW
1 Aug 1974

	ordinary cover	Qty: 7,487	
271.1	Telecommunications Society of Australia cover		15.00
271.2	any other illustrated cover		5.00
271.#R	Registered cover	Qty: 4	$225

272   1974 11TH INTERNATIONAL SOCIETY FOR MUSIC EDUCATION CONFERENCE

Perth 6000, WA
5 – 12 Aug 1974

	ordinary cover	Qty: 3,476	
272.1	University of WA cover		20.00
272.2	any other illustrated cover		15.00

273   1974 16TH INTERNATIONAL ORNITHOLOGICAL CONGRESS

Canberra 2600, ACT
12 – 17 Aug 1974

	ordinary cover	Qty: 4,540	
273.1	any illustrated cover		10.00
273.#R	Registered cover	Qty: 10	$125

274 1974 7TH BIENNIAL CONFERENCE OF AUSTRALIAN ROAD RESEARCH BOARD

Flinders University 5042, SA
19 – 23 Aug 1974

	ordinary cover	Qty: 1,796
274.1	any illustrated cover	30.00
274.#R	Registered cover Qty: 12	$125

275 1974 8TH INTERNATIONAL CONGRESS OF ELECTRON MICROSCOPY

Canberra 2600, ACT
26 – 31 Aug 1974

	ordinary cover	Qty: 3,590
275.1	any illustrated cover	20.00
275.#R	Registered cover Qty: 9	$130

The postcode does not appear on this postmark.

276 1974 FUSION FESTIVAL – ILLAWARRA PHILATELIC SOCIETY EXHIBITION

Wollongong 2500, NSW
26 Aug – 6 Sep 1974

	ordinary cover	Qty: 2,668
276.1	Illawarra Philatelic Society souvenir cover	20.00
276.2	any other illustrated cover	15.00
276.#R	Registered cover Qty: 12	$125

277 1974 LAST FLYING BOAT MAIL TO LORD HOWE ISLAND

Rose Bay – Lord Howe Island, NSW
10 Sep 1974

	ordinary cover	Qty: 9,276
277.1	Last Flying Boat Mail cover	50.00
277.2	any other illustrated cover	5.00
277.#R	Registered cover Qty: 18	$100

The postcode does not appear on this postmark.

278 1974 6TH POSTAL TELEGRAPH AND TELEPHONE INTERNATIONAL ASIAN REGIONAL CONFERENCE

271.1 | 1 August 1974

Centenary of Telecommunications Society of Australia

Melbourne 3000, Vic
16 – 20 Sep 1974

	ordinary cover	Qty: 2,964	
278.1	any illustrated cover		15.00
278.#R	Registered cover	Qty: 21	75.00

279 1974 NATIONAL STAMP WEEK
7 – 14 Oct 1974

Type 279A | Adelaide 5000, SA

	ordinary cover	Qty: 4,627	
279A.1	UPU Centenary Pigeon Post cover		10.00
279A.2	any other illustrated cover		4.50
279A.#R	Registered cover	Qty: 11	$125

Type 279B | Brisbane 4000, Qld

	ordinary cover	Qty: 3,199	
279B.1	any illustrated cover		4.50

Type 279C | Canberra 2600, ACT

	ordinary cover	Qty: 6,721	
279C.1	National Stamp Week (PS of Canberra) cover		10.00
279C.2	any other illustrated cover		4.50
279C.#R	Registered cover	Qty: 12	$125

Type 279D | Hobart 7000, Tas

	ordinary cover	Qty: 5,346	
279D.1	any illustrated cover		4.50
279D.#R	Registered cover	Qty: 2	*

* No established value.

Type 279E | Melbourne 3000, Vic

	ordinary cover	Qty: 6,640	
279E.1	any illustrated cover		4.50
279E.#R	Registered cover	Qty: 29	$85

Type 279F | Sydney 2000, NSW

	ordinary cover	Qty: 3,085	
279F.1	any illustrated cover		4.50
279F.#R	Registered cover	Qty: 3	*

* No established value.

Type 279G | Perth 6000, WA

	ordinary cover	Qty: 3,016	
279G.1	any illustrated cover		4.50

Coincidental stamp issues:
9 Oct 1974 – 7c and 30c, Universal Postal Union Centenary (SG576-7)
9 Oct 1974 – 7c, 150th Anniversary of Australia's First Independent Newspaper (SG578)

280 1974 CENTENARY OF UPU – PHILAS 74 – NATIONAL STAMP WEEK EXHIBITION

Sydney 2000, NSW
8 – 11 Oct 1974

	ordinary cover	Qty: 2,725	
280.1	UPU Centenary FDC		10.00
280.2	any other illustrated cover		8.00
280.#R	Registered cover	Qty: 70	35.00

Related stamp issue:
9 Oct 1974 – 7c and 30c, Universal Postal Union Centenary (SG576-7)

Coincidental stamp issue:
9 Oct 1974 – 7c, 150th Anniversary of Australia's First Independent Newspaper (SG578)

281 1974 14TH TRIENNIAL CONFERENCE OF ASSOCIATION OF COUNTRY WOMEN OF THE WORLD

Perth 6000, WA
8 – 18 Oct 1974

	ordinary cover	Qty: 11,074	
281.1	any illustrated cover		10.00
281.#R	Registered cover	Qty: 19	$100

Related stamp issue:
18 Apr 1972 – 7c, 50th Anniversary of CWA (SG509)

282 | **1974 QUEENSLAND PHILATELIC EXHIBITION – CENTENARY OF UPU**

Toombul 4012, Qld
9 – 11 Oct 1974

	ordinary cover	Qty: 5,030
282.1	Queensland Philatelic Exhibition cover	10.00
282.2	APO UPU Centenary FDC	10.00
282.3	any other illustrated cover	7.00

Related stamp issue:
9 Oct 1974 – 7c and 30c, Universal Postal Union Centenary (SG576-7)

283 | **1974 150TH ANNIVERSARY OF HUME AND HOVELL EXPEDITION**

Gunning 2581, NSW
14 –21 Oct 1974

	ordinary cover	Qty: 10,613
283.1	Hume & Hovell Expedition 150th Year cover	6.00
283.2	any other illustrated cover	4.00
283.#R	Registered cover	Qty: 17	$100

277.1 | 10 September 1974

Last Flying Boat Mail to Lord Howe Island

280.1R | 9 October 1974

Centenary of UPU – PHILAS 74 – National Stamp Week Exhibition

1975

EVENTS

284	15 Feb	Leisuretime Show '75
285	9 Apr	2nd Australian Rose Convention
286	14 Apr	14th Annual Conference of IFATCA
287	5 May	2nd Australasian-Asian Regional Conference of ISRRT
288	12 May	1st Pacific Conference of Psychiatry
289	16 Jul	50th Anniversary of De Pinedo's Flight Italy to Australia
290	21 Aug	Royal Australian College of General Practitioners Convention
291	24 Aug	5th Girl Guide Muster
292	25 Aug	5th International Convention on Atomic Spectroscopy
293	1 Sep	6th Triennial Convention of Australian Institute of Medical Technologists
294	7 Oct	Commonwealth Educational Broadcasting Conference
295	11 Oct	Opening of Launceston Mall
296	15 Oct	Centenary of State Education in South Australia
297	19 Oct	3rd Congress of Asian Oceanic Postal Union
298	1 Dec	Centenary of GPO Clock Adelaide
299	4 Dec	Centenary of Death of Governor La Trobe

Recurring events.
See the original event number entry for the first occurrence.

084	*28 Feb*	*Moomba Festival*
027	*Mar*	*Royal Easter Show*
082	*5 Jun*	*1st Regular QANTAS Sydney to Paris*
022	*13 Aug*	*Brisbane Exhibition*
017	*Sep*	*Royal Melbourne Show*

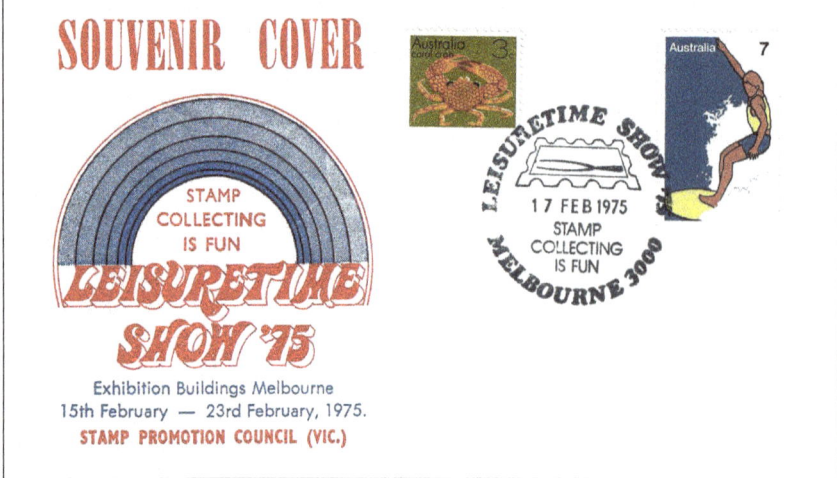

284.1 | 17 February 1975

Leisuretime Show '75

284

284   LEISURETIME SHOW '75
Melbourne 3000, Vic
15 – 23 Feb 1975

	ordinary cover	Qty: 4,339	
284.1	Leisuretime Show '75 cover		12.00
284.2	any other illustrated cover		8.00
284.#R	Registered cover	Qty: 14	$120

084   1975 MOOMBA FESTIVAL
Melbourne, Vic
28 Feb – 10 Mar 1975

Type 084C (see illustration under 1973)

	ordinary cover	Qty: 8,413	
084C.1.75	Moomba cover		5.00
084C.2.75	any other illustrated cover		4.00
084C.#.75R	Registered cover	Qty: 24	$100

027   1975 ROYAL EASTER SHOW
Sydney, NSW
Mar 1975

Type 027C (see illustration under 1963)

027C.1.75	any illustrated cover	15.00

285

285   1975 2ND AUSTRALIAN ROSE CONVENTION
Melbourne 3000, Vic
9 – 13 Apr 1975

	ordinary cover	Qty: 2,761	
285.1	any illustrated cover		20.00
285.#R	Registered cover	Qty: 9	$175

286

286   1975 14TH ANNUAL CONFERENCE OF IFATCA
Melbourne 3000, Vic
14 – 18 Apr 1975

	ordinary cover	Qty: 4,014	
286.1	any illustrated cover		15.00
286.#R	Registered cover	Qty: 2	*

IFATCA = International Federation of Air Traffic Controllers' Associations
* No established value.

287

287   1975 2ND AUSTRALASIAN-ASIAN REGIONAL CONFERENCE OF ISRRT
Sydney 2000, NSW
5 – 9 May 1975

	ordinary cover	Qty: 3,342	
287.1	Institute of Radiography cover		20.00
287.2	any other illustrated cover		15.00
287.#R	Registered cover	Qty: 12	$125

ISRRT = International Society of Radiographers and Radiological Technologists

288

288   1975 1ST PACIFIC CONFERENCE OF PSYCHIATRY
Melbourne 3000, Vic
12 – 16 May 1975

	ordinary cover	Qty: 3,242	
288.1	any illustrated cover		15.00
288.#R	Registered cover	Qty: 16	$150

082C

082   1975 INAUGURATION QANTAS JET SERVICE
Sydney, NSW
5 Jun 1975

082C.1 | 5 June 1975

Inauguration QANTAS Jet Service – Sydney to Paris

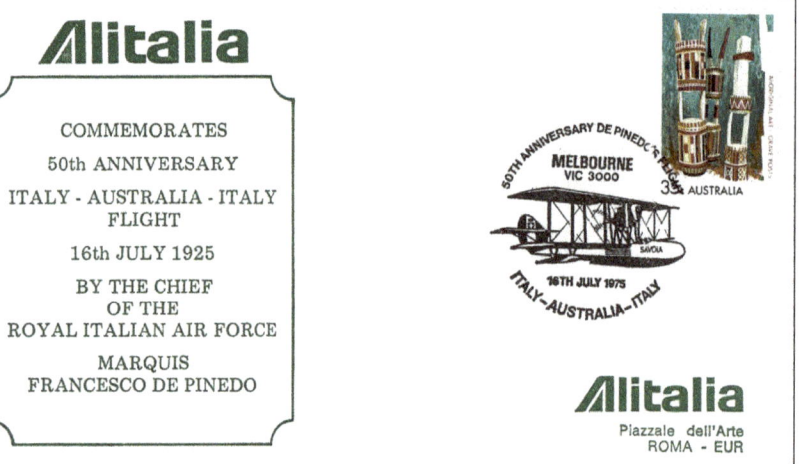

289.1 | 16 July 1975

50th Anniversary De Pinedo Flight – Italy to Australia

298.1 | 2 December 1975

Centenary of GPO Clock, Adelaide

Type 082C | Sydney to Paris

	ordinary cover	Qty: 3,752	
082C.1	QANTAS cover		8.00
082C.2	any other illustrated cover		8.00
082C.#R	Registered cover	Qty: 13	$100

289   1975 50TH ANNIVERSARY OF DE PINEDO'S FLIGHT – ITALY TO AUSTRALIA

Melbourne 3000, Vic
16 Jul 1975

	ordinary cover		
	One way	Qty: 3,223	
289.1	souvenir flight cover		8.00
289.2	any other illustrated cover		8.00
	Return flight	Qty: 3,239	
289.3	souvenir flight cover		8.00
289.4	any other illustrated cover		8.00
289.#R	Registered cover	Qty: 15	$110

022   1975 BRISBANE EXHIBITION

Brisbane, Qld
13 Aug 1975

	ordinary cover	Qty: *20,930	
022D.1.75	Exhibition (short 'wattle') cover – pmk and cachet		5.00
022D.2.75	Exhibition (long 'wattle') cover – pmk and cachet		5.00
022D.3.75	any other illustrated cover – pmk and cachet		5.00
022D.4.75	any other illustrated cover – pmk only		20.00
022D.#.75R	Registered cover	Qty: 65	50.00

* Quantity comprises 20,765 covers on which a Cobb & Co pictorial cachet was applied, and carried on a re-enactment coach mail run. 165 covers were processed with the postmark only.

290   1975 ROYAL AUSTRALIAN COLLEGE OF GENERAL PRACTITIONERS CONVENTION

Lindfield 2070, NSW
21 – 29 Aug 1975

	ordinary cover	Qty: 10,250	
290.1	any illustrated cover		6.00
290.#R	Registered cover	Qty: 26	80.00

291   1975 5TH GIRL GUIDE MUSTER

Fairfield 2165, NSW
24 – 29 Aug 1975

	ordinary cover	Qty: 5,635	
291.1	Guiding souvenir cover		10.00
291.2	any other illustrated cover		8.00
291.#R	Registered cover	Qty: 85	40.00

292   1975 5TH INTERNATIONAL CONVENTION ON ATOMIC SPECTROSCOPY

Melbourne 3000, Vic
25 – 29 Aug 1975

	ordinary cover	Qty: 3,841	
292.1	any illustrated cover		10.00
292.#R	Registered cover	Qty: 5	$200

Related Stamp Issue:
14 May 1975 – 11c, Atomic Absorption Spectrophotometry (SG596)

293   1975 6TH TRIENNIAL CONVENTION OF AUSTRALIAN INSTITUTE OF MEDICAL TECHNOLOGISTS

Melbourne 3000, Vic
1 – 8 Sep 1975

	ordinary cover	Qty: 2,204
293.1	any illustrated cover	20.00
293.#R	Registered cover......... Qty: 4	$200

017 1975 ROYAL MELBOURNE SHOW
Show Grounds, Melbourne, Vic
Sep 1975

Type 017B (see illustration under 1949)

017B.1.75	souvenir ('wattle') cover	10.00

294 1975 COMMONWEALTH EDUCATIONAL BROADCASTING CONFERENCE
Sydney 2000, NSW
7 – 16 Oct 1975

	ordinary cover	Qty: 3,521
294.1	any illustrated cover	10.00
294.#R	Registered cover......... Qty: 5	$200

295 1975 OPENING OF LAUNCESTON MALL
Launceston 7250, Tas
11 – 30 Oct 1975

	ordinary cover	Qty: 6,690
295.1	any illustrated cover	8.00
295.#R	Registered cover......... Qty: 5	$200

296 1975 CENTENARY OF STATE EDUCATION IN SOUTH AUSTRALIA
Adelaide 5000, SA
15 Oct – 4 Nov 1975

	ordinary cover	Qty: 1,664
296.1	any illustrated cover	20.00
296.2	plain cover	10.00
296.#R	Registered cover......... Qty: 19	$100

297 1975 3RD CONGRESS OF ASIAN OCEANIC POSTAL UNION
Melbourne 3000, Vic
19 – 27 Nov 1975

	ordinary cover	Qty: 2,166
297.1	any illustrated cover	20.00
297.#R	Registered cover......... Qty: 19	$100

298 1975 CENTENARY OF GPO CLOCK ADELAIDE
Adelaide 5000, SA
1 – 12 Dec 1975

	ordinary cover	Qty: 1,831
298.1	1870s King William Street postcard	30.00
298.2	any illustrated cover	20.00
298.3	plain cover	10.00
298.#R	Registered cover......... Qty: 2	*

* No established value.

299 1975 CENTENARY OF DEATH OF GOVERNOR LA TROBE
Melbourne 3000, Vic
4 Dec 1975

	ordinary cover	Qty: 5,336
299.1	souvenir cover	10.00
299.2	any other illustrated cover	8.00
299.#R	Registered cover......... Qty: 6	$200

1976

EVENTS

300	29 Jan	Youth Expo '76
301	9 Feb	29th International Banking Summer School
302	16 Feb	Centenary of Local Government, Mount Gambier
303	5 Mar	Centenary of Local Government, Wodonga
304	13 May	Toastmasters Downunder Conference
305	24 May	7th International Coal Preparation Congress
306	29 May	Leisuretime Show '76
307	16 Aug	25th International Geological Congress
308	3 Sep	Centenary of Birth of C.J. Dennis
309	27 Sep	50th Anniversary of Australia/Pacific/Australia Flight
310	27 Sep	National Stamp Week
311	27 Sep	Queensland Philatelic Exhibition
312	27 Sep	Springpex '76 – National Stamp Week Exhibition
313	1 Oct	Centenary of Local Government, Tatiara
314	6 Oct	Pharmaceutical Society of NSW Centenary Seminar
315	8 Oct	Centenary of Thornborough to Cairns Packhorse Mail
316	20 Oct	Australian Air Race
317	23 Oct	Solar Eclipse
318	16 Nov	8th International Teletraffic Congress
319	30 Dec	11th Australian Scout Jamboree

Recurring events.
See the original event number entry for the first occurrence.

084	26 Feb	*Moomba Festival*
110	10 May	*ANZAAS Conference*
017	Sep	*Royal Melbourne Show*

300   YOUTH EXPO '76

Melbourne 3000, Vic
29 Jan – 2 Feb 1976

	ordinary cover	Qty: 1,912	
300.1	any illustrated cover		20.00
300.2	plain cover		10.00
300.#R	Registered cover	Qty: 5	$200

301   1976 29TH INTERNATIONAL BANKING SUMMER SCHOOL

Melbourne 3000, Vic
9 – 20 Feb 1976

	ordinary cover	Qty: 965	
301.1	any illustrated cover		30.00
301.2	plain cover		20.00
301.#R	Registered cover	Qty: 4	$200

301.1 | 9 February 1976

29th International Banking Summer School

110E.2 | 10 May 1976

47th ANZAAS Congress

An unusual (possibly unique) cover combining the 47th Congress postmark with the 42nd, held in Port Moresby, Papua & New Guinea, in 1970.

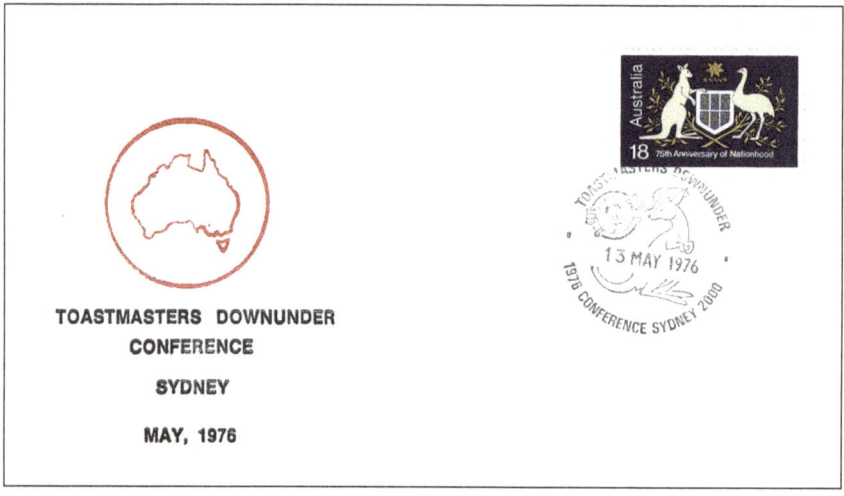

304.1 | 13 May 1976

Toastmasters Downunder Conference

302 1976 CENTENARY OF LOCAL GOVERNMENT, MOUNT GAMBIER

Mount Gambier 5290, SA
16 – 27 Feb 1976

	ordinary cover	Qty: 2,160	
302.1	any illustrated cover		15.00
302.#R	Registered cover	Qty: 1	*

* No established value.

084 1976 MOOMBA FESTIVAL

Melbourne, Vic
26 Feb – 8 Mar 1976

Type 084C (see illustration under 1973)

	ordinary cover	Qty: 5,678	
084C.1.76	Moomba cover		5.00
084C.2.76	any other illustrated cover		4.00
084C.#.76R	Registered cover	Qty: 4	$200

303 1976 CENTENARY OF LOCAL GOVERNMENT, WODONGA

Wodonga 3690, Vic
5 – 12 Mar 1976

	ordinary cover	Qty: 3,516	
303.1	official souvenir cover		20.00
303.2	any other illustrated cover		15.00
303.#R	Registered cover	Qty: 6	$200

110 1976 47TH ANZAAS CONGRESS

Hobart 7000, Tas
10 – 14 May 1976

| | ordinary cover | Qty: 4,763 |

110E.1	official souvenir cover	20.00
110E.2	any other illustrated cover	15.00
110E.#R	Registered cover .... Qty: 22	75.00

304 1976 TOASTMASTERS DOWNUNDER CONFERENCE

Sydney 2000, NSW
13 – 18 May 1976

	ordinary cover	Qty: 914	
304.1	Toastmasters Downunder Conference cover		40.00
304.2	any other illustrated cover		30.00
304.3	plain cover		20.00
304.#R	Registered cover	Qty: 7	$175

305 1976 7TH INTERNATIONAL COAL PREPARATION CONGRESS

Sydney 2000, NSW
24 – 28 May 1976

	ordinary cover	Qty: 1,473	
305.1	Congress souvenir cover		30.00
305.2	any other illustrated cover		20.00
305.3	plain cover		10.00
305.#R	Registered cover	Qty: 6	$200

306 LEISURETIME SHOW '76

Melbourne 3000, Vic
29 May – 6 Jun 1976

	ordinary cover	Qty: 1,281	
306.1	Leisuretime Show cover		30.00
306.2	any other illustrated cover		20.00
306.3	plain cover		10.00
306.#R	Registered cover	Qty: 6	$200

307

307 1976 25TH INTERNATIONAL GEOLOGICAL CONGRESS

Sydney 2000, NSW
16 – 25 Aug 1976

	ordinary cover	Qty: 10,425
307.1	Event-specific illustrated cover	10.00
307.2	any other illustrated cover	6.00
307.#R	Registered cover......... Qty: 20 ....$100

308

308 1976 CENTENARY OF BIRTH OF C.J. DENNIS

Healesville 3777, Vic
3 – 7 Sep 1976

	ordinary cover	Qty: 2,826
308.1	C.J. Dennis Centenary cover	20.00
308.2	any other illustrated cover	15.00
308.#R	Registered cover............ Qty: 4 ....$200

309

309 1976 50TH ANNIVERSARY OF AUSTRALIA/ PACIFIC/AUSTRALIA FLIGHT

Melbourne 3000, Vic
27 Sep 1976

	ordinary cover	Qty: 7,508*
309.1	Anniversary Flight cover	15.00
309.2	Anniversary Flight aerogramme	30.00
309.3	any other illustrated cover	10.00

* Statistics by destination:	Letters	Aerogrammes
Daru	22	201
Port Moresby	134	20
Kieta	1	-
Honiara	605	7
Port Vila	537	6
Noumea	26	6
Norfolk Island	41	2
Lord Howe Island	2	4
Melbourne (return flight)	5,545	349
TOTAL	**6,913**	**595**

310

309.2 | 27 September 1976 | 50th Anniversary of Australia/Pacific/Australia Flight

310   1976 NATIONAL STAMP WEEK
27 Sep – 1 Oct 1976

Type 310A | Adelaide 5000, SA (from 26 Sep 1976)

ordinary cover   Qty: 9,968

310A.1	AP NSW FDC (text design)	4.00
310A.2	AP NSW FDC (Blamire Young design)	4.00
310A.3	AP NSW FDC (miniature sheet)	5.00
310A.4	any other illustrated cover	3.00
310A.5	miniature sheet only	5.00
310A.6	NSW Festival Centre PIGEON POST cover	10.00
310A.#R	Registered cover............ Qty: 4	$200

Type 310B | Brisbane 4000, Qld

ordinary cover   Qty: 7,833

310B.1	AP NSW FDC (text design)	4.00
310B.2	AP NSW FDC (Blamire Young design)	4.00
310B.3	AP NSW FDC (miniature sheet)	5.00
310B.4	any other illustrated cover	3.00
310B.5	miniature sheet only	5.00

Type 310C | Canberra 2600, ACT

ordinary cover   Qty: 2,993

310C.1	AP NSW FDC (text design)	4.00
310C.2	AP NSW FDC (Blamire Young design)	4.00
310C.3	AP NSW FDC (miniature sheet)	5.00
310C.4	any other illustrated cover	3.00
310C.5	miniature sheet only	5.00
310C.#R	Registered cover............ Qty: 7	$175

Type 310D | Hobart 7000, Tas

ordinary cover   Qty: 7,553

310D.1	AP NSW FDC (text design)	4.00
310D.2	AP NSW FDC (Blamire Young design)	4.00
310D.3	AP NSW FDC (miniature sheet)	5.00
310D.4	any other illustrated cover	3.00
310D.5	miniature sheet only	5.00
310D.#R	Registered cover............ Qty: 6	$200

Type 310E | Melbourne 3000, Vic

ordinary cover   Qty: 9,775

310E.1	AP NSW FDC (text design)	4.00
310E.2	AP NSW FDC (Blamire Young design)	4.00
310E.3	AP NSW FDC (miniature sheet)	5.00
310E.4	any other illustrated cover	3.00
310E.5	miniature sheet only	5.00
310E.#R	Registered cover............ Qty: 6	$200

Type 310F | Perth 6000, WA

ordinary cover   Qty: 7,138

310F.1	AP NSW FDC (text design)	4.00
310F.2	AP NSW FDC (Blamire Young design)	4.00
310F.3	AP NSW FDC (miniature sheet)	5.00
310F.4	any other illustrated cover	3.00
310F.5	miniature sheet only	5.00

Type 310G | Sydney 2000, NSW

ordinary cover   Qty: 43,467

310G.1	AP NSW FDC (text design)	4.00
310G.2	AP NSW FDC (Blamire Young design)	4.00
310G.3	AP NSW FDC (miniature sheet)	5.00
310G.4	any other illustrated cover	3.00
310G.5	miniature sheet only	5.00

The quantity of items processed using the Canberra postmark is quoted as '3,000 articles, including seven registered', an unlikely round number. As the other cities' usage was noticeably greater, the Canberra figure is in doubt.

The use of coloured inks for these postmarks is subject to further research.

Related stamp issue:
27 Sep 1976 – 18c, National Stamp Week (SG633)
27 Sep 1976 – 4 x 18c, National Stamp Week miniature sheet (SGMS634)

310A.4 | 26 September 1976

National Stamp Week

311 1976 QUEENSLAND PHILATELIC EXHIBITION

Toombul 4012, Qld
27 Sep – 2 Oct 1976

	ordinary cover	Qty: 4,995	
311.1	Exhibition souvenir cover		10.00
311.2	AP NSW FDC (text design)		6.00
311.3	AP NSW FDC (Blamire Young design)		6.00
311.4	AP NSW FDC (miniature sheet)		8.00
311.5	any other illustrated cover		5.00

312 1976 SPRINGPEX '76 – NATIONAL STAMP WEEK EXHIBITION

Sydney 2000, NSW
27 Sep – 4 Oct 1976

	ordinary cover	Qty: 18,670	
312.1	Springpex souvenir cover		15.00
312.2	AP NSW FDC (text design)		5.00
312.3	AP NSW FDC (Blamire Young design)		5.00
312.4	AP NSW FDC (miniature sheet)		6.00
312.5	any other illustrated cover		5.00
312.6	miniature sheet		4.00
312.7	miniature sheet in NSW 1976 Souvenir Booklet		25.00
312.#R	Registered cover	Qty: 96	40.00

The National Stamp Week 1976 Souvenir Booklets were produced by the Australian Stamp Promotion Council. The miniature sheets were overprinted (in red) AUSTRALIAN STAMP PROMOTION COUNCIL with a serial number and additionally rouletted vertically on the left side. They are 5mm wider than the regular miniature sheet.

017 1976 ROYAL MELBOURNE SHOW

Show Grounds, Melbourne, Vic
Sep 1976

017C.1.76   souvenir ('wattle') cover 10.00

313 1976 CENTENARY OF LOCAL GOVERNMENT, TATIARA

1 – 8 Oct 1976

Type 313A | Bordertown 5268, SA

	ordinary cover	Qty: 2,452	
313A.1	Centenary of Local Government souvenir cover		25.00
313A.2	any other illustrated cover		15.00

Type 313B | Keith 5267, SA

	ordinary cover	Qty: 1,219	
313B.1	Centenary of Local Government souvenir cover		25.00
313B.2	any other illustrated cover		15.00
313B.3	plain cover		10.00

314 1976 PHARMACEUTICAL SOCIETY OF NSW CENTENARY SEMINAR

Sydney 2000, NSW
6 – 9 Oct 1976

	ordinary cover	Qty: 1,132	
314.1	any illustrated cover		25.00
314.2	plain cover		15.00
314.#R	Registered cover	Qty: 5	$200

315 1976 CENTENARY OF THORNBOROUGH TO CAIRNS PACKHORSE MAIL

Cairns 4870, Qld
8 Oct 1976

	ordinary cover	Qty: 20,299	
315.1	Centenary of Packhorse Mail cover		8.00
315.2	any other illustrated cover		5.00
315.#R	Registered cover	Qty: 4	$200

316   1976 AUSTRALIAN AIR RACE
Perth 6000, WA
20 – 24 Oct 1976

	ordinary cover	Qty: 11,170
316.1	Air Race Official Flight Cover	10.00
316.2	any other illustrated cover	7.50

317   1976 SOLAR ECLIPSE
Melbourne 3000, Vic
23 Oct 1976

	ordinary cover	Qty: 3,108
317.1	any illustrated cover	10.00
317.#R	Registered cover	Qty: 5 $200

318   1976 8TH INTERNATIONAL TELETRAFFIC CONGRESS
Melbourne 3000, Vic
16 – 17 Nov 1976

	ordinary cover	Qty: 2,392
318.1	any illustrated cover	15.00
318.#R	Registered cover	Qty: 5 $200

319   1976-77 11TH AUSTRALIAN SCOUT JAMBOREE
Dandenong 3195, Vic
30 Dec 1976 – 7 Jan 1977

	ordinary cover	Qty: 14,070
319.1	Jamboree souvenir cover	10.00
319.2	Nomad Test Flight cover	15.00
319.3	any other illustrated cover	6.00
319.#R	Registered cover	Qty: 150* 35.00

* Despite the quoted volume of 150 Registered covers, R6 label 0366 has been sighted.

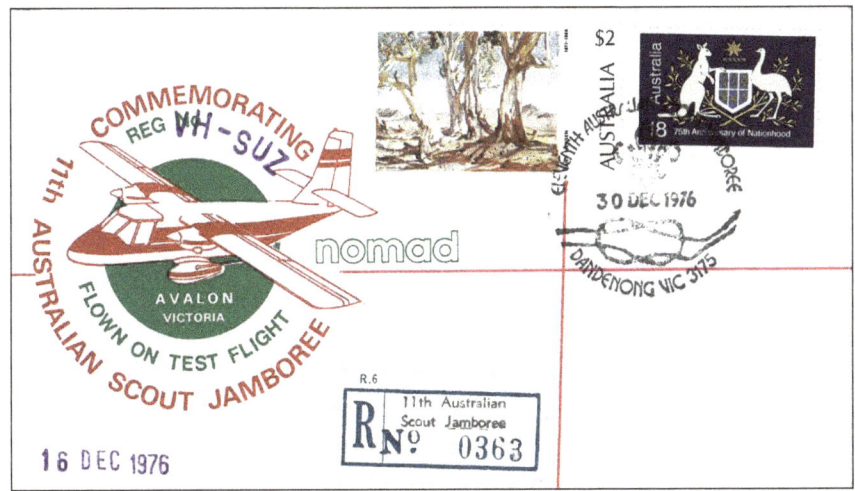

319.2R | 30 December 1976

11th Australian Scout Jamboree – Nomad Test Flight

1977

EVENTS

320	1 Jan	St. John Ambulance Australian Cadet Camp
321	19 Jan	Chinese Exhibition
322	28 Feb	Junior Philatelic Exhibition
323	7 Mar	Royal Visit
324	9 Mar	Test Cricket Centenary
325	21 Mar	21 Years Duke of Edinburgh's Award Scheme
326	28 Mar	150 Years of Albany, W.A
327	11 Apr	1977 Inter-Parliamentary Meetings
328	28 Apr	27th Convention of World's Women's Christian Temperance Union
329	9 May	50th Anniversary of Opening of Parliament House
330	9 May	6th Girl Guide Muster
331	16 May	Royal Australasian College of Surgeons Golden Jubilee
332	1 Jul	75th Anniversary of Australian Army Nursing
333	29 Aug	25th Anniversary of First Jindivik Flight
334	2 Sep	Can-Tiki Expedition
335	10 Sep	5th World Underwater Congress
336	26 Sep	50th Anniversary of 1927 Stamp Booklet
337	26 Sep	National Stamp Week
338	8 Oct	Birth Centenary of Hans Heysen
339	10 Oct	Centenary of Balaklava, S.A.
340	13 Oct	26th International Congress of Apimondia
341	21 Oct	McLaren Vale Wine Bushing Festival
342	22 Oct	Opening of Historic Norfolk Gallery
343	28 Oct	Opening of New Burnie Post Office
344	29 Oct	Centenary of Melbourne to Hamilton Rail Link
345	23 Nov	60th Anniversary of First South Australian Air Mail
346	30 Nov	3rd Pacific Conference Games
347	30 Nov	Australian Music Exposition
348	8 Dec	Centenary of Intercolonial Telegraph Line

Recurring events.
See the original event number entry for the first occurrence.

084	*4 Mar*	*Moomba Festival*
017	*Sep*	*Royal Melbourne Show*

320 **1977 ST. JOHN AMBULANCE AUSTRALIAN CADET CAMP**

Swanleigh 6056, WA
1 – 14 Jan 1977

	ordinary cover	Qty: 2,441	
320.1	St. John Ambulance souvenir cover		20.00
320.2	any other illustrated cover		15.00
320.#R	Registered cover	Qty: 16	$110

321 **1977 CHINESE EXHIBITION**
19 Jan – 29 Jun 1977

Type 321A | 19 Jan – 6 Mar | Melbourne 3000, Vic

	ordinary cover	Qty: 5,855	
321A.1	Chinese Exhibition (long 'wattle') souvenir cover		7.50
321A.2	any other illustrated cover		5.00
321A.#R	Registered cover	Qty: 28	75.00

Type 321B | 9 – 29 Jun* | Adelaide 5000, SA

	ordinary cover	Qty: 16,857	
321B.1	Chinese Exhibition (long 'wattle') souvenir cover		7.50
321B.2	any other illustrated cover		5.00
321B.#R	Registered cover	Qty: 10	$125

* The date range for Adelaide is quoted from the December 1977 Philatelic Bulletin, but examples dated 4 and 7 July have been sighted.

322 **1977 JUNIOR PHILATELIC EXHIBITION**

Kilkenny North 5009, SA
28 Feb – 12 Mar 1977

	ordinary cover	Qty: 1,954	
322.1	Junior Philatelic Exhibition souvenir cover		15.00
322.2	any other illustrated cover		10.00
322.3	plain cover		8.00

084 **1977 MOOMBA FESTIVAL**

Melbourne, Vic
4 – 14 Mar 1977

Type 084C (see illustration under 1973)

	ordinary cover	Qty: 5,985	
084C.1.77	Moomba cover		5.00
084C.2.77	any other illustrated cover		4.00
084C.#.77R	Registered cover	Qty: 4	$200

323 **1977 ROYAL VISIT**
7 – 30 Mar 1977

Type 323A | 7 – 9 Mar | Canberra 2600, ACT

	ordinary cover	Qty: 7,080	
323A.1	AP Royal Visit cover (18c + 45c Jubilee stamps)		7.50
323A.2	AP Royal Visit cover (18c Silver Jubilee stamp)		5.00
323A.3	any other illustrated cover		4.00

Type 323B | 9 Mar | Queanbeyan 2620, ACT

	ordinary cover	Qty: 370	
323B.1	AP Royal Visit cover (18c + 45c Jubilee stamps)		50.00
323B.2	AP Royal Visit cover (18c Silver Jubilee stamp)		35.00
323B.3	any other illustrated cover		30.00
323B.4	plain cover		25.00

Type 323C | 9 – 11 Mar | Brisbane 4000, Qld

	ordinary cover	Qty: 8,996	
323C.1	AP Royal Visit cover (18c + 45c Jubilee stamps)		7.50
323C.2	AP Royal Visit cover (18c Jubilee stamp)		5.00
323C.3	any other illustrated cover		4.00

Type 323D | 11 Mar | Tamworth 2340, NSW

	ordinary cover	Qty: 2,116	
323D.1	AP Royal Visit cover (18c + 45c Jubilee stamps)		10.00
323D.2	AP Royal Visit cover (18c Jubilee stamp)		7.50
323D.3	any other illustrated cover		5.00

Type 323E | 11 Mar | Newcastle 2300, NSW

	ordinary cover	Qty: 5,607	
323E.1	AP Royal Visit cover (18c + 45c Jubilee stamps)		7.50
323E.2	AP Royal Visit cover (18c Jubilee stamp)		5.00
323E.3	any other illustrated cover		4.00

Type 323F | 11 Mar | Launceston 7250, Tas

	ordinary cover	Qty: 1,377	
323F.1	AP Royal Visit cover (18c + 45c Jubilee stamps)		15.00
323F.2	AP Royal Visit cover (18c Jubilee stamp)		12.00
323F.3	any other illustrated cover		10.00
323F.4	plain cover		8.00

322.1 | 2 March 1977

Junior Philatelic Exhibition

323B.2 | 9 March 1977

Royal Visit, Queanbeyan

Despite the popularity of the Royal Visit series, only 370 impressions of the Queanbeyan cancel were recorded, making it a very scarce modern postmark.

332.1 | 1 July 1977

75th Anniversary of Australian Army Nursing

Type 323G | 14 Mar | Sydney 2000, NSW

ordinary cover   Qty: 13,434

323G.1	AP Royal Visit cover (18c + 45c Jubilee stamps)	7.50
323G.2	AP Royal Visit cover (18c Jubilee stamp)	5.00
323G.3	any other illustrated cover	4.00

Type 323H | 14 – 16 Mar | Hobart 7000, Tas

ordinary cover   Qty: 1,268

323H.1	AP Royal Visit cover (18c + 45c Jubilee stamps)	15.00
323H.2	AP Royal Visit cover (18c Jubilee stamp)	12.00
323H.3	Royal Jubilee Military Tattoo cover	12.00
323H.4	any other illustrated cover	10.00
323H.5	plain cover	8.00

Type 323J | 16 – 17 Mar | Melbourne 3000, Vic

ordinary cover   Qty: 27,501

323J.1	AP Royal Visit cover (18c + 45c Jubilee stamps)	7.50
323J.2	AP Royal Visit cover (18c Jubilee stamp)	5.00
323J.3	any other illustrated cover	4.00

Type 323K | 21 – 23 Mar | Adelaide 5000, SA

ordinary cover   Qty: 5,538

323K.1	AP Royal Visit cover (18c + 45c Jubilee stamps)	7.50
323K.2	AP Royal Visit 197 cover (18c Jubilee stamp)	5.00
323K.3	any other illustrated cover	4.00

Type 323L | 21 Mar | Elizabeth 5112, SA

ordinary cover   Qty: 3,226

323L.1	AP Royal Visit cover (18c + 45c Jubilee stamps)	10.00
323L.2	AP Royal Visit cover (18c Jubilee stamp)	7.50
323L.3	any other illustrated cover	5.00

Type 323M | 21 Mar | Nuriootpa 5355, SA

ordinary cover   Qty: 2,609

323M.1	AP Royal Visit cover (18c + 45c Jubilee stamps)	10.00
323M.2	AP Royal Visit cover (18c Jubilee stamp)	7.50
323M.3	any other illustrated cover	5.00

Type 323N | 25 Mar | Darwin 5790, NT

ordinary cover   Qty: 1,713

323N.1	AP Royal Visit cover (18c + 45c Jubilee stamps)	15.00
323N.2	AP Royal Visit cover (18c Jubilee stamp)	12.00
323N.3	any other illustrated cover	10.00
323N.4	plain cover	8.00

Type 323P | 25 Mar | Geraldton 6530, WA

ordinary cover   Qty: 2,740

323P.1	AP Royal Visit cover (18c + 45c Jubilee stamps)	10.00
323P.2	AP Royal Visit cover (18c Jubilee stamp)	7.50
323P.3	any other illustrated cover	5.00

Type 323Q | 28 Mar | Fremantle 6160, WA

ordinary cover   Qty: 2,287

323Q.1	AP Royal Visit cover (18c + 45c Jubilee stamps)	10.00
323Q.2	AP Royal Visit cover (18c Jubilee stamp)	7.50
323Q.3	any other illustrated cover	5.00

Type 323R | 28 – 30 Mar | Perth 6000, WA

ordinary cover   Qty: 6,350

323R.1	AP Royal Visit cover (18c + 45c Jubilee stamps)	7.50
323R.2	AP Royal Visit cover (18c Jubilee stamp)	5.00
323R.3	Royal Flight Australia to England QANTAS cover	20.00
323R.4	any other illustrated cover	4.00

Type 323S | 29 Mar | Albany 6330, WA

ordinary cover   Qty: 2,795

323S.1	AP Royal Visit cover (18c + 45c Jubilee stamps)	10.00
323S.2	AP Royal Visit cover (18c Jubilee stamp)	7.50
323S.3	any other illustrated cover	5.00

323A-S.11 set A	AP Royal Visit cover (18c + 45c stamps)	set $200
323A-S.12 set B	AP Royal Visit cover (18c stamp)	set $150

Related stamp issue:
2 Feb 1977 – 18c and 45c, Silver Jubilee (SG645-6)

324

324   1977 TEST CRICKET CENTENARY

Jolimont 3002, Vic
9 – 17 Mar 1977

ordinary cover   Qty: 101,332

324.1	APO Test Cricket FDC	5.00
324.2	any other illustrated cover	5.00
324.#R	Registered cover .... Qty: 56	$2,500

Related stamp issue:
9 Mar 1977 – 5x18c and 45c, Australia-England Test Cricket Centenary (SG647-52).

325

325   1977 21 YEARS DUKE OF EDINBURGH'S AWARD SCHEME

Wembley 6014, WA
21 Mar – 3 Dec 1977

ordinary cover   Qty: 2,477

325.1	Duke of Edinburgh's Awards souvenir cover	10.00
325.2	any other illustrated cover	8.00
325.#R	Registered cover .... Qty: 10	$150

326

326   **1977 150 YEARS OF ALBANY, WA**

Albany 6330, WA
28 Mar – 30 Dec 1977

	ordinary cover	Qty: 6,300
326.1	Albany 150 Years souvenir cover	10.00
326.2	any other illustrated cover	7.50

327   **1977 INTER-PARLIAMENTARY MEETINGS**

Canberra 2600, ACT
11 – 16 Apr 1977

	ordinary cover	Qty: 14,297
327.1	Inter-Parliamentary Meetings souvenir cover	5.00
327.2	any other illustrated cover	4.00

328   **1977 27TH CONVENTION OF WORLD'S WOMEN'S CHRISTIAN TEMPERANCE UNION**

Sydney 2000, NSW
28 Apr – 4 May 1977

	ordinary cover	Qty: 2,871
328.1	any illustrated cover	20.00
328.#R	Registered cover	Qty: 5 ... $200

329   **1977 50TH ANNIVERSARY OF OPENING OF PARLIAMENT HOUSE**

Canberra 2600, ACT
9 May 1977

	ordinary cover	Qty: 13,940
329.1	Australia Post souvenir cover	5.00
329.2	any other illustrated cover	4.00

Related stamp issue:
13 Apr 1977 – 18c, 50th Anniversary of Opening of Parliament House (SG653)

330   **1977 6TH GIRL GUIDE MUSTER**

The Rock 2655, NSW
9 – 15 May 1977

	ordinary cover	Qty: 3,016
330.1	official Guides souvenir cover	15.00
330.2	any other illustrated cover	12.50
330.#R	Registered cover	Qty: 159 ... 40.00

337D.1 | 26 September 1977

National Stamp Week, Darwin

The surprisingly low number of impressions of the National Stamp Week series is highlighted by a mere 487 for Darwin, making another scarce modern postmark.

331 **1977 ROYAL AUSTRALASIAN COLLEGE OF SURGEONS GOLDEN JUBILEE**

Melbourne 3000, Vic
16 – 20 May 1977

	ordinary cover	Qty: 3,770	
331.1	Event-specific illustrated cover		17.50
331.2	any other illustrated cover		12.50
331.#R	Registered cover	Qty: 10	$150

332 **1977 75TH ANNIVERSARY OF AUSTRALIAN ARMY NURSING**

Sydney 2000, NSW
1 Jul 1977

	ordinary cover	Qty: 10,853
332.1	Australian Army Nursing cover	7.50
332.2	any other illustrated cover	5.00

333 **1977 25TH ANNIVERSARY OF FIRST JINDIVIK FLIGHT**

Jervis Bay 2540, ACT
29 Aug 1977

	ordinary cover	Qty: 4,972	
333.1	Jindivik souvenir cover		10.00
333.2	any other illustrated cover		7.00
333.#R	Registered cover	Qty: 7	$175

334 **1977 CAN-TIKI EXPEDITION**

Darwin 5794, NT
2 Sep 1977

	ordinary cover	Qty: 7,210
334.1	Can-Tiki souvenir cover	10.00
334.2	any other illustrated cover	7.00

335 **1977 5TH WORLD UNDERWATER CONGRESS**

Brisbane 4000, Qld
10 – 14 Sep 1977

	ordinary cover	Qty: 793
335.1	any illustrated cover	60.00
335.2	plain cover	50.00

017 *1977 ROYAL MELBOURNE SHOW*

Show Grounds, Melbourne, Vic
Sep 1977

Type 017B (see illustration under 1949)

017B.1.77	any illustrated cover	10.00

336 **1977 50TH ANNIVERSARY OF 1927 STAMP BOOKLET**

Canberra 2600, ACT
26 Sep 1977

	ordinary cover	Qty: 2,736
336.1	any illustrated cover	20.00
336.2	Reprint of 1927 Canberra booklet *	4.00

* Produced by the Australian Stamp Promotion Council, this souvenir booklet is found with the 18c Parliament House stamp affixed to the inside cover and cancelled with postmark type 336.

Related stamp issue:
13 Apr 1977 – 18c, 50th Anniversary of Opening of Parliament House (SG653)

337F

337   1977 NATIONAL STAMP WEEK
26 Sep – 2 Oct 1977

Type 337A | Adelaide 5000, SA

	ordinary cover	Qty: 1,254	
337A.1	any illustrated cover		20.00
337A.2	plain cover		10.00

Type 337B | Brisbane 4000, Qld

	ordinary cover	Qty: 3,732	
337B.1	Queensland Philatelic Exhibition souvenir cover		10.00
337B.2	any other illustrated cover		10.00

Type 337C | Canberra 2600, ACT

	ordinary cover	Qty: 2,575	
337C.1	any illustrated cover		15.00

Type 337D | Darwin 5794, NT

	ordinary cover	Qty: 487	
337D.1	any illustrated cover		60.00
337D.2	plain cover		40.00

Type 337E | Hobart 7000, Tas

	ordinary cover	Qty: 2,250	
337E.1	any illustrated cover		15.00

Type 337F | Melbourne 3000, Vic

	ordinary cover	Qty: 4,180	
337F.1	any illustrated cover		3.00
337F.#R	Registered cover	Qty: 4	$200

Type 337G | Perth 6000, WA

	ordinary cover	Qty: 2,672	
337G.1	any illustrated cover		15.00

Type 337H | Sydney 2000, NSW

	ordinary cover	Qty: 2,770	
337H.1	any illustrated cover		15.00
337A-H.1 set	any illustrated cover		set $140

338

338   1977 BIRTH CENTENARY OF HANS HEYSEN
Adelaide 5000, SA
8 Oct 1977

	ordinary cover	Qty: 4,144	
338.1	any illustrated cover		7.50
338.#R	Registered cover	Qty: 47	60.00

339

339   1977 CENTENARY OF BALAKLAVA, SA
Balaklava 5461, SA
10 – 16 Oct 1977

339.1 | 15 October 1977

Centenary of Balaklava, South Australia

	ordinary cover	Qty: 4,094
339.1	Centenary Committee souvenir cover	10.00
339.2	any other illustrated cover	7.50
339.#R	Registered cover............ Qty: 7	$175

340

340 1977 26TH INTERNATIONAL CONGRESS OF APIMONDIA
Adelaide 5000, SA
13 – 19 Oct 1977

	ordinary cover	Qty: 5,224
340.1	souvenir cover	10.00
340.2	any other illustrated cover	7.50
340.#R	Registered cover............ Qty: 8	$175

341A

341 1977 MCLAREN VALE WINE BUSHING FESTIVAL
McLaren Vale 5171, SA
21 – 30 Oct 1977

Type 341A | 1977 Festival

	ordinary cover	Qty: 3,678
341A.1	Festival Committee souvenir cover	25.00
341A.2	any other illustrated cover	15.00
341A.#R	Registered cover............ Qty: 6	$200

342

342 1977 OPENING OF HISTORIC NORFOLK GALLERY
Port Arthur 7182, Tas
22 Oct 1977

	ordinary cover	Qty: 4,168
342.1	souvenir cover	10.00
342.2	any other illustrated cover	7.50

343

343 1977 OPENING OF NEW BURNIE POST OFFICE
Burnie 7320, Tas
28 Oct 1977

	ordinary cover	Qty: 3,799
343.1	APO Official Opening cover	20.00
343.#R	Registered cover............ Qty: 1	*

* No established value.

344

344 1977 CENTENARY OF MELBOURNE TO HAMILTON RAIL LINK
Hamilton 3300, Vic
29 Oct 1977

	ordinary cover	Qty: 3,271
344.1	souvenir cover	15.00
344.2	any other illustrated cover	10.00
344.#R	Registered cover............ Qty: 2	*

* No established value.

345A   345B

345 1977 60TH ANNIVERSARY OF FIRST SOUTH AUSTRALIAN AIR MAIL
23 Nov 1977

Type 345A | Adelaide 5000, SA

	ordinary cover	Qty: 4,310
345A.1	Flight Committee souvenir cover	20.00
345A.2	any other illustrated cover	10.00
345A.#R	Registered cover............ Qty: 6	$200

Type 345B | Gawler 5118, SA

	ordinary cover	Qty: 4,215
345B.1	Flight Committee souvenir cover	20.00
345B.2	any other illustrated cover	10.00
345B.#R	Registered cover............ Qty: 6	$200

346   1977 3RD PACIFIC CONFERENCE GAMES

Canberra 2600, ACT
30 Nov – 4 Dec 1977

	ordinary cover	Qty: 3,806
346.1	souvenir cover	15.00
346.2	any other illustrated cover	10.00
346.#R	Registered cover............ Qty: 6 .... $200	

348   1977 CENTENARY OF INTERCOLONIAL TELEGRAPH LINE

Perth 6000, WA
8 Dec 1977

	ordinary cover	Qty: 3,477
348.1	PO Historical Society of WA cover	20.00
348.2	any other illustrated cover	15.00
348.#R	Registered cover............ Qty: 5 .... $200	

347   1977 AUSTRALIAN MUSIC EXPOSITION

Sydney 2000, NSW
30 Nov – 11 Dec 1977

	ordinary cover	Qty: 2,343
347.1	Music Exposition souvenir cover	25.00
347.2	any other illustrated cover	20.00
347.#R	Registered cover............ Qty: 2 ....*	

* No established value.

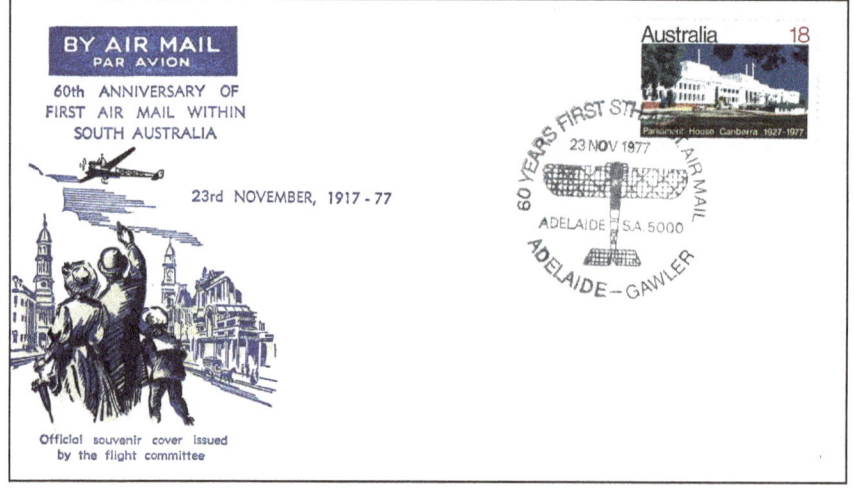

345A.1 | 23 November 1977

60th Anniversary of First South Australian Airmail

1978

EVENTS

349	2 Jan	6th World Jamboree of Lithuanian Scouting
350	24 Feb	1st Visit to Australia of RMS *Queen Elizabeth 2*
351	25 Feb	El Dorado Colombian Gold Exhibition, Adelaide
352	13 Mar	Clare Valley Easter Wine Festival
353	23 Mar	50th Anniversary of Church of England Boys Society in NSW
354	8 Apr	Australian International Veteran and Vintage Motor Rally
355	14 Apr	Centenary of Carrieton, S.A.
356	6 May	Centenary of Xavier College
357	6 May	Opening of Brighton Philatelic Society's Bri-Phil House
358	12 May	Royal Adelaide International Exposition '78
359	15 May	Opening of New Frankston Post office
360	1 Jun	*Loch Ard* Shipwreck Centenary
361	9 Jun	50th Anniversary of First Trans-Pacific Flight
362	10 Jun	Centenary of Street Public Transport, Adelaide
363	19 Jul	Opening of Philas House
364	19 Jul	Centenary of RSPCA
365	23 Jul	Centenary of Royal Zoological Society of South Australia
366	24 Jul	Golden Jubilee of Apprenticeship Industrial Training Commission
367	28 Jul	53rd International Y's Men's Club Convention
368	12 Aug	3rd World Congress of International Society for Education Through Art
369	14 Aug	Opening of Hartley Historic Site
370	15 Aug	20th International Horticultural Congress
371	7 Sep	Geelong Trade Exhibition
372	11 Sep	50th Anniversary of First Flight Australia to New Zealand
373	20 Sep	Centenary of Narracan Shire
374	23 Sep	Stamp Show '78
375	25 Sep	National Stamp Week
376	25 Sep	Queensland Philatelic Exhibition
377	30 Sep	75th Anniversary of Royal Automobile Association of South Australia
378	6 Oct	Opening of City Mall, Hobart
379	13 Oct	Centenary of Snowtown
380	25 Oct	Royal Agricultural Show, Glenorchy
381	15 Nov	Opening of West Gate Bridge
382	28 Nov	Golden Jubilee of Rural Youth Club, Glen Innes

Recurring events.
See the original event number entry for the first occurrence.

084	*3 Mar*	*Moomba Festival*
351	*10 Apr*	*El Dorado Colombian Gold Exhibition, Perth*
351	*26 May*	*El Dorado Colombian Gold Exhibition, Melbourne*
351	*13 Jul*	*El Dorado Colombian Gold Exhibition, Brisbane*
351	*21 Aug*	*El Dorado Colombian Gold Exhibition, Sydney*
017	*20 Sep*	*Royal Melbourne Show*
341	*20 Oct*	*McLaren Vale Wine Bushing Festival*

349

349 1978 6TH WORLD JAMBOREE OF LITHUANIAN SCOUTING

Gembrook 3783, Vic
2 – 15 Jan 1978

	ordinary cover	Qty: 2,987
349.1	official souvenir cover	20.00
349.2	any other illustrated cover	15.00
349.#R	Registered cover............ Qty: 10 ....$150	

350

350 1978 1ST VISIT TO AUSTRALIA OF RMS *QUEEN ELIZABETH 2*

Sydney 2000, NSW
24 – 25 Feb 1978

	ordinary cover	Qty: 4,337
350.1	souvenir cover	15.00
350.2	any other illustrated cover	9.00

351A   Cachet

351 1978 EL DORADO COLOMBIAN GOLD EXHIBITION

Adelaide 5000, SA
25 Feb – 26 Mar 1978

Type 351A | Adelaide

	ordinary cover	Qty: 2,582
351A.1	El Dorado Exhibition cover	20.00
351A.2	any other illustrated cover	15.00

The cachet illustrated was applied to souvenir covers in green ink.

For exhibition postmarks used in other capital cities, see under their respective dates.

084 1978 MOOMBA FESTIVAL

Melbourne, Vic
3 – 13 Mar 1978

Type 084C (see illustration under 1973)

	ordinary cover	Qty: 4,410
084C.1.78	Moomba cover	5.00
084C.2.78	any other illustrated cover	4.00
084C.#.78R	Registered cover .... Qty: 16 ....$125	

352

352 1978 CLARE VALLEY EASTER WINE FESTIVAL

Clare 5453, SA
13 – 23 Mar 1978

	ordinary cover	Qty: 1,983
352.1	Festival Committee souvenir cover	30.00
352.2	any other illustrated cover	20.00
352.3	plain cover	10.00
352.#R	Registered cover............... Qty: 5 ....$200	

353

353 1978 50TH ANNIVERSARY OF CHURCH OF ENGLAND BOYS SOCIETY IN NSW

Barraba 2347, NSW
23 Mar – 14 Apr 1978

	ordinary cover	Qty: 2,963
353.1	souvenir cover	20.00
353.2	any other illustrated cover	15.00
353.#R	Registered cover.............. Qty: 4 ....$200	

354

354 1978 AUSTRALIAN INTERNATIONAL VETERAN AND VINTAGE MOTOR RALLY

Sydney 2000, NSW
8 Apr 1978

	ordinary cover	Qty: 3,685
354.1	Rally Committee souvenir cover	20.00
354.2	any other illustrated cover	15.00

351 1978 EL DORADO COLOMBIAN GOLD EXHIBITION

Perth 6000, WA
10 Apr – 5 May 1978

Type 351B | Perth

	ordinary cover	Qty: 2,451	
351B.1	El Dorado Exhibition cover		25.00
351B.2	any other illustrated cover		20.00
351B.#R	Registered cover	Qty: 5	$200

355 1978 CENTENARY OF CARRIETON, SA

Carrieton 5432, SA
14 – 15 Apr 1978

	ordinary cover	Qty: 1,962	
355.1	souvenir cover		30.00
355.2	any other illustrated cover		20.00
355.3	plain cover		15.00

356 1978 CENTENARY OF XAVIER COLLEGE

Kew 3101, Vic
6 May 1978

	ordinary cover	Qty: 1,919	
356.1	Xavier College souvenir cover		30.00
356.2	any other illustrated cover		20.00
356.3	plain cover		10.00
356.#R	Registered cover	Qty: 6	$200

357 1978 OPENING OF BRIGHTON PHILATELIC SOCIETY'S BRI-PHIL HOUSE

Elsternwick 3185, Vic
6 – 7 May 1978

	ordinary cover	Qty: 3,416	
357.1	Official Opening of Bri-Phil House cover		12.50
357.2	any other illustrated cover		10.00
357.#R	Registered cover	Qty: 25	80.00

358 ROYAL ADELAIDE INTERNATIONAL EXPOSITION '78

Adelaide 5000, SA
12 – 28 May 1978

	ordinary cover	Qty: 3,673	
358.1	International Exposition ('wattle') cover		20.00
358.2	any other illustrated cover		10.00
358.#R	Registered cover	Qty: 9	$175

359 1978 OPENING OF NEW FRANKSTON POST OFFICE

Frankston 3199, Vic
15 May 1978

	ordinary cover	Qty: 2,358	
359.1	souvenir cover		25.00
359.2	any other illustrated cover		15.00
359.#R	Registered cover	Qty: 3	*

* No established value.

351 1978 EL DORADO COLOMBIAN GOLD EXHIBITION

Melbourne 3000, Vic
26 May – 2 Jul 1978

Type 351C | Melbourne

	ordinary cover	Qty: 3,691	
351C.1	El Dorado Exhibition cover		20.00
351C.2	any other illustrated cover		15.00
351C.#R	Registered cover	Qty: 78	30.00

360 1978 *LOCH ARD* SHIPWRECK CENTENARY

Port Campbell 3269, Vic
1 Jun 1978

	ordinary cover	Qty: 8,253
360.1	Shipwreck Centenary souvenir cover	8.00
360.2	any other illustrated cover	5.00

361

361   1978 50TH ANNIVERSARY OF FIRST TRANS-PACIFIC FLIGHT

Brisbane 4000, Qld
9 Jun 1978

	ordinary cover	Qty: 19,357
361.1	Trans-Pacific Flight cover	12.50
361.2	any other illustrated cover	6.00

Related stamp issue:
19 Apr 1978 – 4 x 18c and 4 x 18c miniature sheet, Early Australian Aviators (SG658-61, MS602).

362

362   1978 CENTENARY OF STREET PUBLIC TRANSPORT, ADELAIDE

Adelaide 5000, SA
10 Jun 1978

	ordinary cover	Qty: 5,702
362.1	Adelaide Tramways cover	8.00
362.2	any other illustrated cover	5.00
362.#R	Registered cover	Qty: 6 ...... $200

351   *1978 EL DORADO COLOMBIAN GOLD EXHIBITION*

Brisbane 4000, Qld
13 Jul – 13 Aug 1978

Type 351D | Brisbane

	ordinary cover	Qty: 4,840
351D.1	El Dorado Exhibition cover	15.00
351D.2	any other illustrated cover	10.00

363B

363   1978 OPENING OF PHILAS HOUSE

Sydney 2000, NSW
19 – 24 Jul 1978

Type 363A | 19 Jul | red ink

	ordinary cover	Qty: 8,894*
363A.1	Philas House Opening Official Souvenir Cover	12.00
363A.2	any other illustrated cover	8.00
363A.#R	Registered cover	Qty: 155* 60.00

Type: 363B | 20 – 24 Jul | black ink

	ordinary cover	*
363B.1	Philas House Opening Official Souvenir Cover	10.00
363B.2	any other illustrated cover	6.00
363B.#R	Registered cover	* 60.00

* Quantities are for both colours combined.

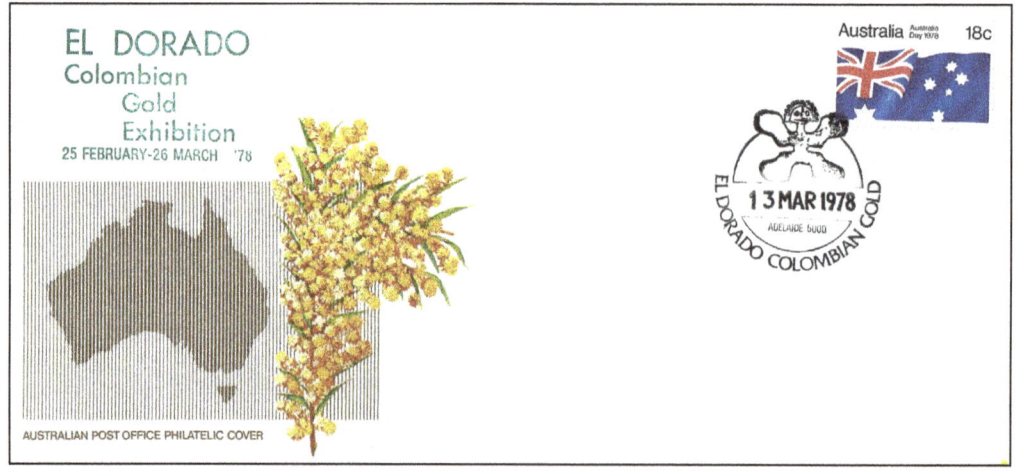

351A.1 | 13 March 1978 | El Dorado Colombian Gold Exhibition, Adelaide

364 **1978 CENTENARY OF RSPCA**

Hobart 7000, Tas
19 Jul – 19 Aug 1978

	ordinary cover	Qty: 3,500
364.1	any illustrated cover.. 15.00	

365 **1978 CENTENARY OF ROYAL ZOOLOGICAL SOCIETY OF SOUTH AUSTRALIA**

Adelaide 5000, SA
23 Jul 1978

	ordinary cover	Qty: 3,271
365.1	Centenary souvenir cover 20.00	
365.2	any other illustrated cover 10.00	
365.#R	Registered cover............................ Qty: 12 .... $125	

366 **1978 GOLDEN JUBILEE OF APPRENTICESHIP INDUSTRIAL TRAINING COMMISSION**

Melbourne 3000, Vic
24 – 30 Jul 1978

	ordinary cover	Qty: 1,174
366.1	any illustrated cover.. 30.00	
366.2	plain cover... 20.00	

367 **1978 53RD INTERNATIONAL Y'S MEN'S CLUB CONVENTION**

Melbourne 3000, Vic
28 Jul – 1 Aug 1978

	ordinary cover	Qty: 1,510
367.1	Y's Men's Club cover.. 30.00	
367.2	any other illustrated cover 25.00	
367.3	plain cover.. 15.00	

368 **1978 3RD WORLD CONGRESS OF INTERNATIONAL SOCIETY FOR EDUCATION THROUGH ART**

Adelaide 5000, SA
12 – 19 Aug 1978

	ordinary cover	Qty: 1,311
368.1	any illustrated cover.. 30.00	
368.2	plain cover... 15.00	
368.#R	Registered cover............................ Qty: 4 .... $200	

369 **1978 OPENING OF HARTLEY HISTORIC SITE**

Hartley 2790, NSW
14 – 28 Aug 1978

	ordinary cover	Qty: 2,118
369.1	Historic Site souvenir cover.................................. 25.00	
369.2	any other illustrated cover 20.00	
369.#R	Registered cover............................ Qty: 18 .... $100	

370 **1978 20TH INTERNATIONAL HORTICULTURAL CONGRESS**

Sydney 2000, NSW
15 – 23 Aug 1978

	ordinary cover	Qty: 5,136
370.1	Congress souvenir cover 8.00	
370.2	any other illustrated cover 5.00	
370.#R	Registered cover............................ Qty: 7 .... $175	

358.1 | 12 May 1978 | Royal Adelaide International Exposition

362.1 | 10 June 1978

Centenary of Street Public Transport, Adelaide

365.1 | 23 July 1978 | Centenary of Royal Zoological Society of South Australia

351   **1978 EL DORADO COLOMBIAN GOLD EXHIBITION**

Sydney 2000, NSW
21 Aug – 1 Oct 1978

Type 351E | Sydney

	ordinary cover	Qty: 1,880	
351E.1	El Dorado Exhibition cover		20.00
351E.2	any other illustrated cover		15.00
351E.3	plain cover		10.00
351E.#R	Registered cover .... Qty: 3		*

* No established value.

371

371   **1978 GEELONG TRADE EXHIBITION**

Geelong 3220, Vic
7 – 9 Sep 1978

	ordinary cover	Qty: 794	
371.1	any illustrated cover		40.00
371.2	plain cover		25.00
371.#R	Registered cover .... Qty: 6		$250

372

372   **1978 50TH ANNIVERSARY OF FIRST FLIGHT AUSTRALIA TO NEW ZEALAND**

Sydney 2000, NSW
11 Sep 1978

	ordinary cover	Qty: 3,198*	
372.1	Event-specific illustrated cover – one way		20.00
372.2	Event-specific illustrated cover – return		30.00
372.3	any other illustrated cover – one way		15.00
372.4	any other illustrated cover – return		20.00

* Quantity includes 1,286 return covers.

373

373   **1978 CENTENARY OF NARRACAN SHIRE**

Trafalgar 3824, Vic
20 Sep 1978

	ordinary cover	Qty: 2,249	
373.1	Shire of Narracan souvenir cover		25.00
373.2	any other illustrated cover		10.00
373.#R	Registered cover .... Qty: 7		$175

017D

017   **1978 ROYAL MELBOURNE SHOW**

Show Grounds 3032, Melbourne, Vic
20 Sep – 1 Oct 1978

	ordinary cover	Qty: 5,632	
017D.1.78	any illustrated cover		5.00
017D.#.78R	Registered cover .... Qty: 12		$150

374A   374B
large dateline   small dateline

374   **STAMP SHOW '78**

Adelaide 5000, SA
23 – 29 Sep 1978

	ordinary cover	Qty: 29,881	
374A.1	Education with Stamps / Stamp Show '78 cover		4.00
374A.2	any other illustrated cover		3.00
374B.1	Education with Stamps / Stamp Show '78 cover		4.00
374B.2	Pigeon Post cover		10.00
374B.3	any other illustrated cover		3.00
	Registered covers	Qty: 12	
374A.#R	any cover		$125
374B.#R	any cover		$125

With the two dateline typefaces, these postmarks were applied in various colours. The 'Education with Stamps' covers were printed in three sizes, the smaller of which exists overprinted with '5th ANNUAL S.A.P.A. CONGRESS 1978' and consecutive numbering. The two larger covers were also numbered.

The editor has sighted the following postmark variations:

large dateline	small dateline
23 Sep – black and green	23 Sep – black
26 Sep – black	24 Sep – green
27 Sep – black	25 Sep – red
28 Sep – black	26 Sep – black
29 Sep – blue	28 Sep – black

The entry for this event will be expanded when fully researched.

367.1 | 29 July 1978

53rd International Y's Men's Club Convention

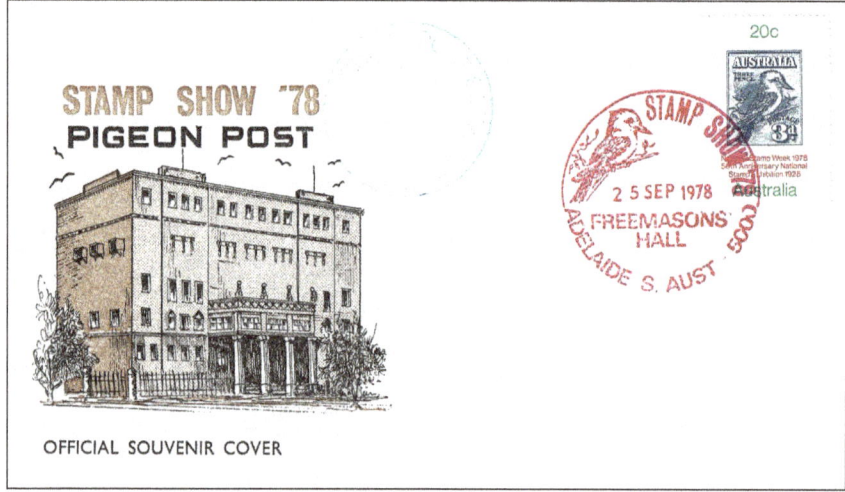

374B.2 | 25 September 1978

Stamp Show '78 Pigeon Post

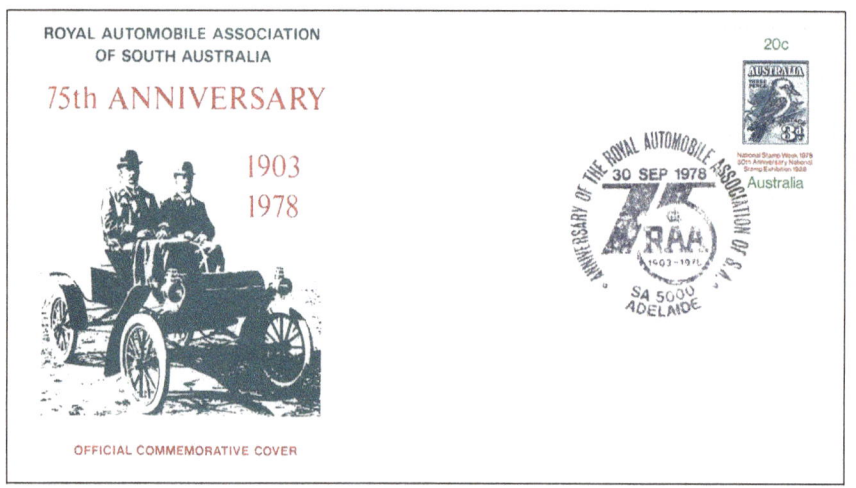

377.1 | 30 September 1978

75th Anniversary of Royal Automobile Association of South Australia

375B

375 1978 NATIONAL STAMP WEEK
25 Sep – 1 Oct 1978

Type 375A | Adelaide 5000. SA
ordinary cover
375A.1	AP NSW FDC (single stamp)	4.00
375A.2	AP NSW FDC (miniature sheet)	6.00

Type 375B | Brisbane 4000, Qld
ordinary cover
375B.1	AP NSW FDC (single stamp)	4.00
375B.2	AP NSW FDC (miniature sheet)	6.00

Type 375C | Canberra 2600, ACT
ordinary cover
375C.1	AP NSW FDC (single stamp)	4.00
375C.2	AP NSW FDC (miniature sheet)	6.00

Type 375D | Darwin 5794, NT
ordinary cover
375D.1	AP NSW FDC (single stamp)	4.00
375D.2	AP NSW FDC (miniature sheet)	6.00

Type 375E | Hobart 7000, Tas
ordinary cover
375E.1	AP NSW FDC (single stamp)	4.00
375E.2	AP NSW FDC (miniature sheet)	6.00

Type 375F | Melbourne 3000, Vic
ordinary cover
375F.1	AP NSW FDC (single stamp)	4.00
375F.2	AP NSW FDC (miniature sheet)	6.00
375F.3	Royal Melbourne Show / NSW FDC with cachet	7.50

Type 375G | Perth 6000, WA
ordinary cover
375G.1	AP NSW FDC (single stamp)	4.00
375G.2	AP NSW FDC (miniature sheet)	6.00

Type 375H | Sydney 2000, NSW
ordinary cover
375H.1	AP NSW FDC (single stamp)	4.00
375H.2	AP NSW FDC (miniature sheet)	6.00

Related stamp issue:
25 Sep 1978 – 20c and 4x20c miniature sheet, National Stamp Week (SG694 and MS695).

376

376 1978 QUEENSLAND PHILATELIC EXHIBITION
Brisbane 4000, Qld
25 Sep – 1 Oct 1978

ordinary cover   Qty: 5,281
376.1	AP National Stamp Week FDC (single stamp)	5.00
376.1	AP National Stamp Week FDC (miniature sheet)	10.00
376.#R	Registered cover .... Qty: 2	*

* No established value.

Related stamp issue:
25 Sep 1978 – 20c and 4x20c, miniature sheet, National Stamp Week (SG694 and MS695)

377

377 1978 75TH ANNIVERSARY OF ROYAL AUTOMOBILE ASSOCIATION OF S.A.
Adelaide 5000, SA
30 Sep 1978

ordinary cover   Qty: 3,021
377.1	75th Anniversary souvenir cover	20.00
377.2	any other illustrated cover	15.00
377.#R	Registered cover .... Qty: 4	$200

378B

378 1978 OPENING OF CITY MALL, HOBART
Hobart 7000, Tas
6 Oct 1978 – 31 Jul 1979

Type 378A | hand cancel
ordinary cover   Qty: 18,231*
378A.1	Hobart City Council souvenir cover	10.00
378A.2	any other illustrated cover	5.00

Type 378B | machine cancel
ordinary cover   *
378B.2	175th Foundation of Hobart PSE (30 May 1979)	10.00

* Quantity is for both postmarks combined.

Related PSE issue:
30 May 1979 – 20c, 175th Anniversary of the Foundation of Hobart.

379   1978 CENTENARY OF SNOWTOWN
Snowtown 5520, SA
13 – 15 Oct 1978

	ordinary cover	Qty: 4,006	
379.1	Snowtown Centenary cover		12.00
379.2	any other illustrated cover		10.00
379.#R	Registered cover	Qty: 4	$200

341   1978 MCLAREN VALE WINE BUSHING FESTIVAL
McLaren Vale 5171, SA
20 – 28 Oct 1978

Type 341B | 1978 Festival

	ordinary cover	Qty: 2,349	
341B.1	Festival Committee souvenir cover		30.00
341B.2	any other illustrated cover		20.00
341B.#R	Registered cover	Qty: 5	$200

380   1978 ROYAL AGRICULTURAL SHOW
Glenorchy 7010, Tas
25 – 28 Oct 1978

	ordinary cover	Qty: 5,582	
380.1.78	any illustrated cover		10.00
380.#.78R	Registered cover	Qty: 6	$200

For earlier Royal Hobart Show entries, see event 021.

381   1978 OPENING OF WEST GATE BRIDGE
Melbourne 3000, Vic
15 Nov 1978

	ordinary cover	Qty: 4,109	
381.1	APO Official Opening souvenir cover		4.00
381.#R	Registered cover	Qty: 4	$200

382   1978 GOLDEN JUBILEE OF RURAL YOUTH CLUB, GLEN INNES
Glen Innes 2370, NSW
28 Nov – 11 Dec 1978

	ordinary cover	Qty: 2,120	
382.1	Jubilee Committee souvenir cover		25.00
382.2	any other illustrated cover		15.00
382.#R	Registered cover	Qty: 14	$110

1980 AND ALL THAT

Leon Trapman

Most collectors who were active in the late 1970s would be aware of the remarkable surge in values of many Australian philatelic items that occurred at that time. Investment booms have taken place throughout the short history of stamp collecting. They are not peculiar to Australia, and collectors in Great Britain, for example, saw the 1929 £1 UPU Congress stamp, catalogued (mint) at £145 in 1975, surge to £1100 in 1980. Five years later, it was a 'mere' £800.

Closer to home in Australia, the 1932 five-shilling Sydney Harbour Bridge was listed in Stanley Gibbons 1975 British Commonwealth catalogue at £60. Five years later, it was valued at £650, nearly 11 times as much, and a nice ten-bagger for a canny investor who bought and sold at the right time. By 1985, it was down to £450. Even the humble 1966 five-cent Elizabeth II definitive raced to £2.25 in 1980 from a modest (and nominal) five pence in 1975. Today, you occasionally see it used on mail by collectors happy – in a manner of speaking – to cut their losses and get some return on their 'investment'.

The late seventies investment boom wasn't limited to stamps. Australia's share market surged when it recovered from the 1970 to 1974 bear market. It peaked in 1980 and spent the next two years in decline. Gold topped out in 1980 at (a now bargain price) of $US850 an ounce but dropped to $US303 in 2002. Even wine found investment followers, and no doubt, some still have their now undrinkable 'collectable' ports sitting at the back of a cupboard.

In some areas, by 1980, the stamp market had reached its inevitable climax, and prices began an inexorable decline. All booms of this nature are followed by a bust. Some values took years to recover. Others never did. The higher face value late pre-decimal commemoratives found eager buyers at $25 in MNH condition. Today, you can find, for example, the 1963 Royal Visit pair for under $4.

The boom of this period coincided with Australia Post's reinvention of its pre-stamped envelopes, which had hitherto not been on most philatelists' radar. From 1978, starting with a new birds definitive set, PSEs captured Australian collectors' imaginations, and values soared. Notably, and of interest to anyone reading this, PSEs with related special postmarks were in great demand. Some of these were natural pairings, but many more were contrived to convince collectors that what they really wanted to be was investors.

Relevant to readers of this guide are the commemorative postmarks found applied to PSEs, some relevant, others not. One I happily paid $25 for 'in 1980' was the 1979 Norman Lindsay with its related Creswick postmark. That postmark was also applied in purple ink, which hit $150 for a short time. It can be found now, although not very often, offered for considerably less over 40 years later.

Another example is the 1979 Blood Donor Service PSE with the 'Billy Blood Drop' cancel. Having reached nose-bleed (sorry!) heights, the price is now back down to earth and can be found for $10 or less. This postmark was machine applied – in other words, printed – in red ink. The scarcer hand-applied versions in red and black are worth seeking out. One 1980 catalogue put the former at $80.

In Australia, a philatelic highlight of 1980 was the Sydpex 80 exhibition. Perversely, it may also have been an indicator of the end of the boom market. Collectors had the concurrent National Stamp Week stamps and miniature sheet to buy, as well as an admittedly attractive PSE. Three commemorative Sydpex postmarks were available, each in black, red and green, so the number of 'products' available was large.

It's worth comparing a few PSE/postmark prices of 1980/81 with the values indicated in this guide:

- 1979 Norman Lindsay (black) $55 $10
- 1979 Norman Lindsay (purple) $125 $50
- 1979 Railway Anniversary $24 $7.50
- 1979 Blood Donors (red – hand) $80 $30
- 1979 Blood Donors (black) $60 $30
- 1979 Scout Jamboree $20 $3

It was in the 1980s that many countries, Australia included, started issuing what most collectors imprecisely call 'too many stamps.' Each successive year seemed to come with a more extensive new issue calendar, and many standing order customers of Australia Post either curtailed

448.1 | 26 – 27 April 1980

Re-enactment of Mail Coach Run Gawler to Mount Pleasant

Some 1980 commemorative postmark products at least related to postal anniversaries. This is one of the 3000 numbered replica Letter Cards suitably overprinted. The Re-enactment and Mt Pleasant postmarks are genuine.

their purchases or stopped altogether. The provision of commemorative postmarks also burgeoned, as can be seen in this Guide. 1979 and 1980 account for over 20% of the country's output for 102 years.

Again, postmark collectors thought twice about their hobby; many would call it a day sometime in the eighties. It is no coincidence that this Guide goes only to 1980.

With the increased popularity of stamps, PSEs and commemorative postmarks to 1980, the quantities of some of those postmarks do present a few surprises. At the high end of the scale are the Sydpex 80 cancels, which account for over 650,000 impressions between them. Little wonder, then, that they are easily found all these years later. High-profile non-philatelic events also produced postmarks in huge numbers. The 1980 Melbourne International Centenary Exhibition postmark was applied 52,300 times, and in Sydney, the 1979 Opening of the Eastern Suburbs Railway postmark cancelled over 45,000 items.

Conversely, some meagre numbers can be found. Witness Melbourne's 1979 International Telecommunications Working Party (349 examples) and Hobart's 1980 World Forestry Day (450), which both command respectable prices today.

Australia's commemorative postmarks of 1979 and 1980 provide a fascinating insight into the peculiar nature of boom markets. They were not only literally a collective product of the period but also a reflection of the trend of temporary popularity. I commend them to you.

390B.1 | 22 February 1979

Centenary of the Birth of Norman Lindsay

Once commanding $150 the 1979 Norman Lindsay PSE with a purple impression of the postmark can now be found at a third of that price.

471B | 29 Sep – 6 Oct 1980

Sydpex 80

An example of the enthusiasm in late 1980, collectors contrived souvenirs with multiple impressions of the postmarks available. This PSE shows the 'square' cancel in green (29 Sep), black (5 Oct) and red (6 Oct).

1979

EVENTS

383	2 Jan	150th Anniversary of Western Australia
384	8 Jan	National Christian Youth Convention
385	19 Jan	Opening of New Kwinana Post Office
386	26 Jan	Australia Day Exhibition 1979
387	1 Feb	175th Anniversary of Tasmania Police
388	5 Feb	Centenary of Horsham Railway
389	19 Feb	Myer British Exhibition
390	22 Feb	Centenary of Birth of Norman Lindsay
391	2 Mar	International Masonic Festival Week
392	9 Mar	150th Anniversary of Founding of Swan River Colony
393	2 Apr	Centenary of Morwell
394	2 Apr	Institution of Engineers Diamond Jubilee Conference
395	13 Apr	Gemboree
396	14 Apr	Centenary of Port Augusta to Quorn Railway
397	23 Apr	Centenary of Royal National Park
398	5 May	27th Convention of Lions International
399	6 May	Rowland Hill Exhibition
400	21 May	Credit Union World Conference
401	26 May	Centenary of Local Government, Lismore
402	4 Jun	Western Australian Philatelic Exhibition (WAPEX)
403	23 Jun	Opening of Eastern Suburbs Railway
404	2 Jul	Centenary of Botanical Gardens, Darwin
405	22 Jul	4th Interflora World Conference
406	6 Aug	50th Anniversary of Ghan Passenger Train
407	12 Aug	60th Anniversary of Adelaide to Minlaton Airmail
408	13 Aug	International Year of the Child
409	18 Aug	35th World Fencing Championships
410	24 Aug	Opening of New Williamstown Post Office
411	28 Aug	Dowerin Machinery Field Days
412	3 Sep	Centenary of Dandenong Post Office
413	16 Sep	125th Anniversary of First Rail Journey: Flinders St to Port Melbourne
414	24 Sep	Perth Royal Show
415	24 Sep	National Stamp Week & Sir Rowland Hill Centenary
416	24 Sep	QUESPEX '79 Philatelic Exhibition
417	24 Sep	ITU Working Party X1/3 – SPC Languages
418	1 Oct	18th General Assembly of International Music Council
419	7 Oct	Dom Polski Society Philatelic Exhibition
420	14 Oct	Opening of Wireless Hill Telecommunications Museum
421	15 Oct	32nd National Convention of Australian Jaycees
422	16 Oct	USSR Old Master Paintings Exhibition
423	3 Nov	Charles Sturt 150th Year Celebrations
424	12 Nov	International Hand Surgery Congress
425	13 Nov	50th Anniversary of Voluntary Blood Donors Service
426	17 Nov	Opening of Electric Railway, Brisbane
427	19 Nov	Opening of New Preston Mail Centre

428	19 Nov	POLPHIL '79 International Philatelic Exhibition
429	22 Nov	Opening of 'Old Town Centre' Community Plaza, Bankstown
430	23 Nov	Opening of New Footscray West Mail Centre
431	28 Aug	150th Anniversary of Western Australia – Parmelia Yacht Race
432	6 Dec	Asian Oceanic Postal Union Meeting
433	16 Dec	50th Anniversary of Glenelg Tram
434	20 Dec	40th Anniversary of Radio Australia
435	29 Dec	4th Asia-Pacific / 12th Australian Jamboree

Recurring events.
See the original event number entry for the first occurrence.

084	2 Mar	Moomba Festival
027	6 Apr	Royal Easter Show
055	31 Aug	Royal Adelaide Show
017	19 Sep	Royal Melbourne Show
380	24 Oct	Royal Agricultural Show, Glenorchy

388.1 | 5 February 1979

Centenary Horsham Railway

391.1 | 10 March 1979

International Masonic Festival Week

383

383 1979 150TH ANNIVERSARY OF WESTERN AUSTRALIA

Perth 6000, WA
2 Jan – 31 Dec 1979

	ordinary cover	Qty: 13,372	
383.1	150th Anniversary souvenir cover		8.00
383.2	any other illustrated cover		5.00

Related stamp issue:
6 Jun 1979 – 20c, 150th Anniversary of Western Australia (SG719)

384

384 1979 NATIONAL CHRISTIAN YOUTH CONVENTION

Perth 6000, WA
8 – 14 Jan 1979

	ordinary cover	Qty: 776	
384.1	any illustrated cover		50.00
384.2	plain cover		35.00
384.#R	Registered cover	Qty: 4	$200

385

385 1979 OPENING OF NEW KWINANA POST OFFICE

Kwinana 6167, WA
19 Jan 1979

	ordinary cover	Qty: 4,515	
385.1	Australia Post souvenir cover		30.00
385.2	any other illustrated cover		7.00
385.#R	Registered cover	Qty: 2	*

* No established value.

386

386 1979 AUSTRALIA DAY EXHIBITION

Melbourne 3000, Vic
26 Jan 1979

	ordinary cover	Qty: 1,037	
386.1	APO Australia Day FDC (pioneer family)		40.00
386.2	APO Australia Day FDC (soldier of NSW Corps)		40.00
386.3	any other illustrated cover		30.00
386.4	plain cover		20.00
386.#R	Registered cover	Qty: 8	$175

Related stamp issue:
26 Jan 1979 – 20c, Australia Day (SG703)

An identical postmark exists, but with text FIRST DAY OF ISSUE above the date. That postmark is outside the scope of this guide.

387

387 1979 175TH ANNIVERSARY OF TASMANIA POLICE

Hobart 7000, Tas
1 Feb 1979

	ordinary cover	Qty: 4,523	
387.1	Tasmania Police souvenir cover		15.00
387.2	any other illustrated cover		10.00

388

388 1979 CENTENARY OF HORSHAM RAILWAY

Horsham 3400, Vic
5 Feb 1979

	ordinary cover	Qty: 2,093	
388.1	Horsham Historical Society souvenir cover		20.00
388.2	any other illustrated cover		15.00
388.#R	Registered cover	Qty: 5	$200

389 1979 MYER BRITISH EXHIBITION

Melbourne 3000, Vic
19 Feb – 2 Mar 1979

	ordinary cover	Qty: 1,363	
389.1	any illustrated cover		30.00
389.2	plain cover		20.00
389.#R	Registered cover	Qty: 9	$175

390 1979 CENTENARY OF BIRTH OF NORMAN LINDSAY

Creswick 3363, Vic
22 Feb 1979

Type 390A | black ink

	ordinary cover	Qty: 8,980	
390A.1	Birth of Norman Lindsay PSE		10.00
390A.2	any other illustrated cover		10.00
390A.#R	Registered cover	Qty: 5	$200

Type 390B | purple ink

	ordinary cover	Qty: est. 500*	
390B.1	Birth of Norman Lindsay PSE		50.00

* Approximately 1,000 impressions of the Norman Lindsay postmark were made in purple ink but this was in error. About half were recalled and destroyed. The editor has not sighted a registered cover with the postmark in purple, nor any examples of a purple impression on any cover other than the Norman Lindsay PSE.

This postmark is occasionally listed on the market in grey ink, but this variation is generally regarded as bogus.

Related PSE issue:
22 Feb 1979 – 20c, Centenary of the Birth of Norman Lindsay.

391 1979 INTERNATIONAL MASONIC FESTIVAL WEEK

Sydney 2000, NSW
2 – 11 Mar 1979

	ordinary cover	Qty: 11,285	
391.1	Opening of the Masonic Centre cover (10 Mar)		5.00
391.2	any other illustrated cover		4.00
391.#R	Registered cover	Qty: 27	90.00

084 1979 MOOMBA FESTIVAL

Melbourne, Vic
2 – 12 Mar 1979

	ordinary cover	Qty: 3,448	
084D.1	Moomba cover		10.00
084D.2	any other illustrated cover		8.00
084D.#R	Registered cover	Qty: 28	75.00

392 1979 150TH ANNIVERSARY OF FOUNDING OF SWAN RIVER COLONY

Perth 6000, WA
9 Mar 1979

	ordinary cover	Qty: 4,374	
392.1	WA Philatelic Association souvenir cover		12.00
392.2	any other illustrated cover		7.00
392.#R	Registered cover	Qty: 1	*

* No established value.

393 1979 CENTENARY OF MORWELL

Morwell 3840, Vic
2 Apr 1979

	ordinary cover	Qty: 2,316	
393.1	souvenir cover		20.00
393.2	any other illustrated cover		15.00
393.#R	Registered cover	Qty: 8	$175

396.1 | 14 April 1979

Centenary of Port Augusta to Quorn Railway

397.1 | 26 April 1979 | Centenary of Royal National Park

398.1 | 10 May 1979

27th Convention of Lions International

394

394   **1979 INSTITUTION OF ENGINEERS DIAMOND JUBILEE CONFERENCE**

Perth 6000, WA
2 – 6 Apr 1979

	ordinary cover	Qty: 1,372	
394.1	any illustrated cover		30.00
394.2	plain cover		20.00
394.#R	Registered cover	Qty: 5	$200

027D

027   *1979 ROYAL EASTER SHOW*

Sydney, NSW
6 – 17 Apr 1979

	ordinary cover	Qty: 9,211	
027D.1.79	any illustrated cover		6.00

395A

395   **1979 GEMBOREE**

Tanunda 5352, SA
13 – 16 Apr 1979

	ordinary cover	Qty: 3,462	
395A.1	Gemboree Committee souvenir cover		15.00
395A.2	any other illustrated cover		12.00
395A.#R	Registered cover	Qty: 7	$175

396

396   **1979 CENTENARY OF PORT AUGUSTA TO QUORN RAILWAY**

Quorn 5433, SA
14 Apr 1979

	ordinary cover	Qty: 3,068	
396.1	Port Augusta – Quorn Railway souvenir cover		20.00
396.2	any other illustrated cover		16.00
396.#R	Registered cover	Qty: 7	$175

397

397   **1979 CENTENARY OF ROYAL NATIONAL PARK**

Sydney 2000, NSW
23 – 29 Apr 1979

	ordinary cover	Qty: 1,886	
397.1	any illustrated cover		30.00
397.2	plain cover		20.00

Related stamp issue:
9 Apr 1979 – 7 x 20c, National Parks (SG708-14)

398

398   **1979 27TH CONVENTION OF LIONS INTERNATIONAL**

Perth 6000, WA
5 – 10 May 1979

	ordinary cover	Qty: 2,033	
398.1	Lions Clubs International Convention cover		30.00
398.2	any other illustrated cover		25.00
398.#R	Registered cover	Qty: 1	*

* No established value.

399

399   **1979 ROWLAND HILL EXHIBITION**

Elsternwick 3185, Vic
6 May 1979

	ordinary cover	Qty: 2,308	
399.1	Rowland Hill Exhibition cover		20.00
399.2	any other illustrated cover		15.00
399.#R	Registered cover	Qty: 26	90.00

400

400   1979 CREDIT UNION WORLD CONFERENCE

Sydney 2000, NSW
21 – 25 May 1979

	ordinary cover	Qty: 2,300	
400.1	any illustrated cover		20.00
400.#R	Registered cover	Qty: 11	$150

401

401   1979 CENTENARY OF LOCAL GOVERNMENT, LISMORE

Lismore 2480, NSW
26 May – 3 Jun 1979

	ordinary cover	Qty: 9,740	
401.1	Lismore 100 overprinted PSE (birds definitive)		4.00
401.2	any other illustrated cover		3.00
401.#R	Registered cover	Qty: 20	$100

402

402   1979 WESTERN AUSTRALIAN PHILATELIC EXHIBITION (WAPEX)

Perth 6000, WA
4 – 9 Jun 1979

	ordinary cover	Qty: 12,344	
402.1	WAPEX cover – black ink		4.00
402.2	WAPEX cover – green ink		4.00
402.3	WAPEX cover – purple ink		4.00
402.4	WAPEX cover – red ink		4.00
402.5	any other illustrated cover		4.00
402.#R	Registered cover	Qty: 75	40.00

The colours known for this postmark were apparently not assigned to particular days. Various applications are recorded but is subject to further research.

403A   403B
Machine cancel   Hand cancel
Small dateline   Large dateline

403   1979 OPENING OF EASTERN SUBURBS RAILWAY

Sydney 2000, NSW
23 Jun 1979

	ordinary cover	Qty: 45,608*	
403A.1	Eastern Suburbs Railway First Train cover		3.00

	ordinary cover	*	
403B.1	Eastern Suburbs Railway First Train cover		10.00

* Quantity is for both styles of postmark combined.

404

404   1979 CENTENARY OF BOTANICAL GARDENS, DARWIN

Darwin 5790, NT
2 Jul 1979

	ordinary cover	Qty: 3,206	
404.1	Darwin Philatelic Society souvenir cover		20.00
404.2	any other illustrated cover		15.00
404.#R	Registered cover	Qty: 4	$200

405

405   1979 4TH INTERFLORA WORLD CONFERENCE

Melbourne 3000, Vic
22 – 28 Jul 1979

	ordinary cover	Qty: 2,851	
405.1	Event-specific illustrated cover		20.00
405.2	any other illustrated cover		15.00

406 1979 50TH ANNIVERSARY OF GHAN PASSENGER TRAIN

Alice Springs 5750, NT
6 Aug 1979

	ordinary cover	Qty: 5,807	
406.1	50th Anniversary of the Ghan souvenir cover		15.00
406.2	any other illustrated cover		10.00
406.#R	Registered cover	Qty: 5	$200

407A | Adelaide 5000, SA

407B | Minlaton 5575, SA

407 1979 60TH ANNIVERSARY OF ADELAIDE TO MINLATON AIRMAIL

12 Aug 1979

	ordinary cover	Qty: 6,764*	
407A.1	souvenir postcard		8.00
407B.1	souvenir postcard		8.00
407#.#R	Registered cover	Qty: 9	$175

* Quantity is for both postmarks combined.

408 1979 INTERNATIONAL YEAR OF THE CHILD

Melbourne 3000, Vic
13 Aug 1979

	ordinary cover	Qty: 70,840	
408.1	APO International Year of the Child FDC		8.00
408.2	any other illustrated cover		5.00

Related stamp issue:
13 Aug 1979 – 20c, International Year of the Child (SG720)

409 1979 35TH WORLD FENCING CHAMPIONSHIPS

Melbourne 3000, Vic
18 – 28 Aug 1979

	ordinary cover	Qty: 2,633	
409.1	Fencing Championships souvenir cover		20.00
409.2	any other illustrated cover		15.00
409.#R	Registered cover	Qty: 7	$175

410 1979 OPENING OF NEW WILLIAMSTOWN POST OFFICE

Williamstown 3016, Vic
24 Aug 1979

	ordinary cover	Qty: 2,119	
410.1	Event-specific illustrated cover		20.00
410.2	any other illustrated cover		15.00
410.#R	Registered cover	Qty: 2	*

* No established value.

411 1979 DOWERIN MACHINERY FIELD DAYS

Dowerin 6461, WA
28 – 30 Aug 1979

	ordinary cover	Qty: 2,060	
411.1	any illustrated cover		25.00

403B.1 | 23 June 1979

Opening of Eastern Suburbs Railway

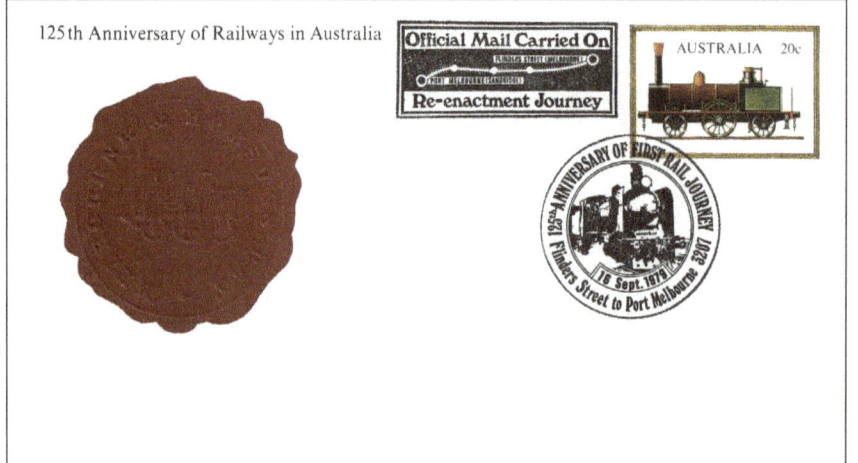

413.1 | 16 September 1979

125th Anniversary of First Rail Journey: Flinders Street to Port Melbourne

431.1 | 25 November 1979

150th Anniversary of Western Australia – Parmelia Yacht Race

055 **1979 ROYAL ADELAIDE SHOW**
Wayville 5034, SA
31 Aug – 8 Sep 1979

    ordinary cover
055B.1.79   any illustrated cover 25.00

412 **1979 CENTENARY OF DANDENONG POST OFFICE**
Dandenong 3175, Vic
3 – 7 Sep 1979

    ordinary cover   Qty: 4,428
412.1   APO Dandenong PO Centenary cover 25.00
412.2   any other illustrated cover 10.00
412.#R   Registered cover .... Qty: 10 .... $150

413 **1979 125TH ANNIVERSARY OF FIRST RAIL JOURNEY: FLINDERS ST TO PORT MELBOURNE**
Port Melbourne 3207, Vic
16 Sep 1979

    ordinary cover   Qty: 4,020
413.1   125th Anniversary of Railways in Australia PSE 7.50
413.2   any other illustrated cover 5.00

Related PSE issue:
12 Sep 1979 – 20c, 125th Anniversary of Railways in Australia

017 **1979 ROYAL MELBOURNE SHOW**
Show Grounds 3032, Melbourne, Vic
19 – 29 Sep 1979

    Type 017D (see illustration under 1978)

    ordinary cover   Qty: 9,189
017D.1.79   any illustrated cover 4.00

414 **1979 PERTH ROYAL SHOW**
Claremont 6010, WA
24 Sep 1979

Type 414A

    ordinary cover   Qty: 1,705
414A.1   any illustrated cover 30.00
414A.2   plain cover 15.00

415 **1979 NATIONAL STAMP WEEK & SIR ROWLAND HILL CENTENARY**
24 – 28 Sep 1979

    Type 415A | Adelaide 5000, SA

    ordinary cover
415A.1   any illustrated cover 5.00

    Type 415B | Brisbane 4000, Qld

    ordinary cover
415B.1   Queensland Philatelic Exhibition cachet cover 8.00
415B.2   any other illustrated cover 5.00

    Type 415C | Canberra 2600, ACT

    ordinary cover
415C.1   any illustrated cover 5.00

    Type 415D | Darwin 5794, NT

    ordinary cover
415D.1   any illustrated cover 5.00

    Type 415E | Hobart 7000, Tas

    ordinary cover
415E.1   any illustrated cover 5.00

    Type 415F | Melbourne 3000, Vic

    ordinary cover
415F.1   any illustrated cover 5.00

    Type 415G | Perth 6000, WA

    ordinary cover
415G.1   any illustrated cover 5.00

    Type 415H | Sydney 2000, NSW

    ordinary cover
415H.1   any illustrated cover 5.00

416

416 QUESPEX '79 PHILATELIC EXHIBITION
Brisbane 4000, Qld
24 – 29 Sep 1979

      ordinary cover   Qty: 1,100
416.1   QUESPEX souvenir cover 40.00
416.2   any other illustrated cover 30.00
416.3   plain cover 15.00

417

417 1979 ITU WORKING PARTY X1/3 – SPC LANGUAGES
Melbourne 3000, Vic
24 Sep – 11 Oct 1979

      ordinary cover   Qty: 349
417.1   any illustrated cover $100
417.2   plain cover 40.00
417.#R Registered cover .... Qty: 1 .... *

* No established value.

418

418 1979 18TH GENERAL ASSEMBLY OF INTERNATIONAL MUSIC COUNCIL
Melbourne 3000, Vic
1 – 5 Oct 1979

      ordinary cover   Qty: 178
418.1   any illustrated cover $150
418.2   plain cover $125

419

419 1979 DOM POLSKI SOCIETY PHILATELIC EXHIBITION
Adelaide 5000, SA
7 – 8 Oct 1979

      ordinary cover   Qty: 2,709
419.1   any illustrated cover 25.00

420

420 1979 OPENING OF WIRELESS HILL TELECOMMUNICATIONS MUSEUM
Melville 6156, WA
14 Oct 1979

      ordinary cover   Qty: 1,461
420.1   Museum Committee souvenir cover 35.00
420.2   any other illustrated cover 25.00
420.3   plain cover 15.00

421

421 1979 32ND NATIONAL CONVENTION OF AUSTRALIAN JAYCEES
Perth 6000, WA
15 – 19 Oct 1979

      ordinary cover   Qty: 3,557
421.1   any illustrated cover 15.00

422

422 1979 USSR OLD MASTER PAINTINGS EXHIBITION
Melbourne 3000, Vic
17 Oct* – 2 Dec 1979

      ordinary cover   Qty: 12,000
422.1   any illustrated cover 5.00

* Australian Stamp Bulletin (October 1979) promoted this postmark as being available on 16 October 1979 and reported its use only on that date in the March 1980 issue of Stamp Bulletin.

380   1979 ROYAL AGRICULTURAL SHOW, GLENORCHY

Glenorchy 7010, Tas
24 – 27 Oct 1979

Type 380 (see illustration under 1978)

ordinary cover
380.1.79   any illustrated cover 10.00

For earlier Royal Hobart Show entries, see event 021.

423   1979 CHARLES STURT 150TH YEAR CELEBRATIONS

Gundagai 2722, NSW
3 – 4 Nov 1979

ordinary cover   Qty: 4,972
423.1   Sturt Sesqui-centenary Celebrations cover 15.00
423.2   any other illustrated cover 10.00
423.#R   Registered cover............................. Qty: 4 .... $200

Some souvenir covers were backstamped Goolwa 5214 on 9 December 1979.

424   1979 INTERNATIONAL HAND SURGERY CONGRESS

Melbourne 3000, Vic
12 – 15 Nov 1979

ordinary cover   Qty: 1,670
424.1   any illustrated cover............................. 35.00
424.2   plain cover... 20.00
424.#R   Registered cover............................ Qty: 5 .... $200

425   1979 50TH ANNIVERSARY OF VOLUNTARY BLOOD DONORS SERVICE

Hobart 7000, Tas
13 Nov 1979

Type 425A | machine cancel

ordinary cover   Qty: 39,640*
425A.1   Voluntary Blood Donor Service PSE – red ink....... 10.00

Type 425B | hand cancel

ordinary cover   *
425B.1   Voluntary Blood Donor Service PSE – red ink....... 30.00
425B.2   Voluntary Blood Donor Service PSE – black ink.... 30.00
425B.3   any other illustrated cover 10.00

* Quantity is for both colours and types of postmark combined.

Related PSE issue:
13 Nov 1979 – 20c, 50th Anniversary of Voluntary Blood Donor Service in Australia

426   1979 OPENING OF ELECTRIC RAILWAY, BRISBANE

Brisbane 4000, Qld
17 Nov 1979

ordinary cover   Qty: 19,500
426.1   Railways PSE....................................... 12.50
426.2   Railways PSE + set of 4 Steam Railway stamps..... 20.00
426.3   any other illustrated cover 5.00

Related PSE issue:
12 Sep 1979 – 20c, 125th Anniversary of Railways in Australia

Related stamp issue:
16 May 1979 – 20c, 35c, 50c, 55c, Steam Railways (SG715-18)

427   1979 OPENING OF NEW PRESTON MAIL CENTRE

Preston 3072, Vic
19 Nov 1979

ordinary cover
427.1   event-specific souvenir cover............................. 10.00
427.2   any other illustrated cover 7.00

428 POLPHIL '79 INTERNATIONAL PHILATELIC EXHIBITION

Melbourne 3000, Vic
19 – 30 Nov 1979

Type 428A | red ink

	ordinary cover	Qty: 3,786*	
428A.1	POLPHIL 79 cover		15.00
428A.2	any other illustrated cover		10.00
428A.#R	Registered cover	Qty: 9*	$200

Type 428B | black ink

	ordinary cover	*	
428B.1	POLPHIL 79 cover		15.00
428B.2	any other illustrated cover		10.00
428B.#R	Registered cover	*	$200

* Quantities are for both colours combined.

429 1979 OPENING OF 'OLD TOWN CENTRE' COMMUNITY PLAZA, BANKSTOWN

Bankstown 2200, NSW
22 – 24 Nov 1979

	ordinary cover	Qty: 4,450
429.1	Bankstown Municipal Council souvenir cover	12.50
429.2	any other illustrated cover	10.00

430 1979 OPENING OF NEW FOOTSCRAY WEST MAIL CENTRE

Footscray West 3012, Vic
23 Nov 1979

	ordinary cover	
430.1	souvenir cover	10.00
430.2	any other illustrated cover	7.00

431 1979 150TH ANNIVERSARY OF WESTERN AUSTRALIA – PARMELIA YACHT RACE

Fremantle 6160, WA
25 Nov 1979

	ordinary cover	Qty: 25,810
431.1	150th Anniversary of Western Australia cover	5.00

Related stamp issue:
6 Jun 1979 – 20c, 150th Anniversary of Western Australia (SG719)

432 1979 ASIAN OCEANIC POSTAL UNION MEETING

Melbourne 3000, Vic
6 – 12 Dec 1979

	ordinary cover	
432.1	any illustrated cover	6.00

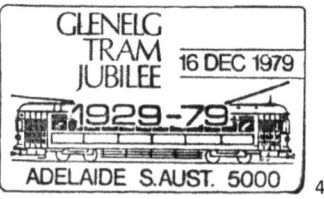

433 1979 50TH ANNIVERSARY OF GLENELG TRAM

Adelaide 5000, SA
16 Dec 1979

	ordinary cover	Qty: 10,230
433.1	50th Anniversary Glenelg Tram souvenir cover	15.00
433.2	any other illustrated cover	10.00

434 1979 40TH ANNIVERSARY OF RADIO AUSTRALIA

Melbourne 3000, Vic
20 Dec 1979

	ordinary cover	Qty: 877
434.1	any illustrated cover	60.00
434.2	plain cover	30.00

435A
Small logo and date

435B
Large logo and date

435 1979-80 4TH ASIA-PACIFIC / 12TH AUSTRALIAN JAMBOREE

Perth 6000, WA
29 Dec 1979 – 8 Jan 1980

Type 435A | small logo and dateline typeface

	ordinary cover	Qty: 24,409*
435A.1	4th Asia-Pacific (12th Australian) Jamboree PSE	3.00
435A.2	any other illustrated cover	2.00
435A.1R	Registered Jamboree PSE .... Qty: 173*	50.00

Type 435B | large logo and dateline typeface

	ordinary cover	*
435B.1	Jamboree PSE	3.00
435B.2	any other illustrated cover	2.00
435B.1R	Registered Jamboree PSE .... *	50.00

* Quantities are for both postmarks combined.

Related PSE issue:
19 Dec 1979 – 20c, 4th Asia-Pacific (12th Australian) Jamboree, Perth 1979-80

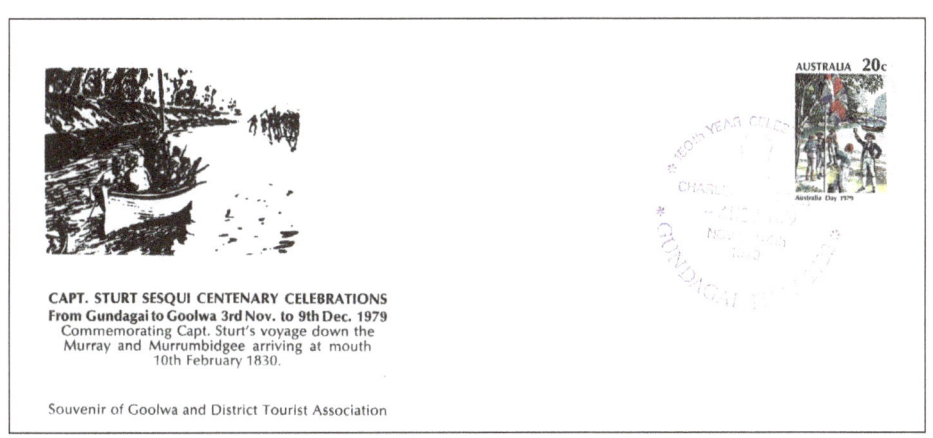

423.1 | 4 November 1979 | Charles Sturt 150th Year Celebrations

433.1 | 16 December 1979 | 150th Anniversary of Glenelg Tram

1980
EVENTS

436	11 Jan	9th Annual National Bottle Show
437	16 Jan	4th World Bowls Championships
438	4 Feb	8th International Thyroid Congress
439	11 Feb	Opening of New Hobart Mail Centre
440	11 Feb	6th International Congress of Endocrinology
441	21 Mar	World Forestry Day
442	22 Mar	Red Earth Festival
443	23 Mar	60th Anniversary of First Flight England to Australia
444	28 Mar	Wangaratta Colonial Festival
445	31 Mar	50th Anniversary of First Brisbane to Townsville Airmail
446	5 Apr	Centenary of Local Government, Euroa
447	10 Apr	Melrose to Adelaide ATHRC Ride-a-thon
448	26 Apr	Re-enactment of Mail Coach Run Gawler to Mount Pleasant
449	4 May	Bri-Phil House Exhibition
450	8 May	Opening of New Willetton Post Office
451	10 May	Guides International Camp
452	14 May	International Museum Day (see notes)
453	28 May	Opening of Melbourne City Square
454	1 Jun	75th Anniversary of Prahran Philatelic Society
455	14 Jun	Air Niugini Coral Sea Air Classic
456	25 Jun	Centenary of Ned Kelly's Last Stand
457	26 Jun	Pompeii AD79 Exhibition
458	1 Jul	Sesquicentenary of Loyal Orange Institution in Australia
459	28 Jul	Opening of New Torquay Post Office
460	5 Aug	400th Anniversary of Lutheran Church
461	13 Aug	Opening of New Mortlake Post Office
462	19 Aug	Ag-Quip Agricultural Exhibition
463	25 Aug	Parkes Centenary Show
464	11 Sep	Centenary of Railway, Roma
465	17 Sep	Salvation Army Centenary Congress
466	23 Sep	Melbourne International Centenary Exhibition
467	29 Sep	Vancouver Day
468	29 Sep	National Stamp Week Adelaide Exhibition
469	29 Sep	Queensland Philatelic Exhibition
470	29 Sep	National Stamp Week
471	29 Sep	Sydpex 80
472	11 Oct	Australian Railway Historical Society Gladstone Centenary
473	25 Oct	1st National Philatelic Convention
474	27 Oct	World Amateur Snooker Championship
475	8 Nov	Christmas Stamp Fair
476	14 Nov	Hand Over Ceremony - Underground Rail Loop, Melbourne
477	16 Nov	12th Asia-Pacific Scout Conference
478	20 Nov	Cambrai Day
479	22 Nov	Southern Cross Air Race
480	24 Nov	Last Old Ghan Trip

481	13 Dec	Centenary of Peterborough Post Office
482	18 Dec	50th Anniversary of Interstate Telephone Service

Recurring events.
See the original event number entry for the first occurrence.

084	29 Feb	Moomba Festival
027	24 Mar	Royal Easter Show
395	4 Apr	Gemboree
022	11 Aug	Brisbane Exhibition
055	3 Sep	Royal Adelaide Show
017	17 Sep	Royal Melbourne Show
414	20 Sep	Perth Royal Show
380	22 Oct	Royal Agricultural Show, Glenorchy

436

436   1980 9TH ANNUAL NATIONAL BOTTLE SHOW

Colac 3250, Vic
11 Jan 1980

	ordinary cover	Qty: 960*	
436.1	Exhibition official cover	Qty: 500*	50.00
436.2	any other illustrated cover		40.00
436.3	plain cover		25.00
436.#R	Registered cover	Qty: 435**	50.00

* The 500 official commemorative covers quantity is included in the total of 960.

** The quantity of Registered covers appears to be unlikely and is subject to further research.

437A   437B

437   1980 4TH WORLD BOWLS CHAMPIONSHIPS

Frankston 3199, Vic
16 Jan – 2 Feb 1980

Type 437A | Small dateline postmark

	ordinary cover	Qty: 22,572*	
437A.1	Bowls Championship PSE (dark print)		3.00
437A.2	Bowls Championship PSE (light print)		3.00
437A.#R	Registered cover	Qty: 934*	20.00

Type 437B | Large dateline postmark

	ordinary cover	*	
437B.1	Bowls Championship PSE (dark print)		6.00
437B.2	Bowls Championship PSE (light print)		6.00
437B.#R	Registered cover	*	20.00

* Quantities are combined for both postmarks.

Related PSE issue:
16 Jan 1980 – 20c, 4th World Bowls Championship (two printings were made, commonly referred to as 'dark' and 'light'.

438

438   1980 8TH INTERNATIONAL THYROID CONGRESS

Sydney 2000, NSW
4 – 8 Feb 1980

	ordinary cover	Qty: 2,773*	
438.1	any illustrated cover		20.00

* Quantity to be confirmed.

439

439   1980 OPENING OF NEW HOBART MAIL CENTRE

Hobart 7000, Tas
11 Feb 1980

Type 439A | machine cancel | blue ink

	ordinary cover	Qty: 35,758	
439A.1	Official Opening PSE – Crimson Rosella		3.50
439A.2	Official Opening PSE – Superb Blue Wren		3.50

Type 439B | hand cancel | black ink

439B.1	any illustrated cover 15.00

437A.1 | 16 January 1980

4th World Bowls Championships

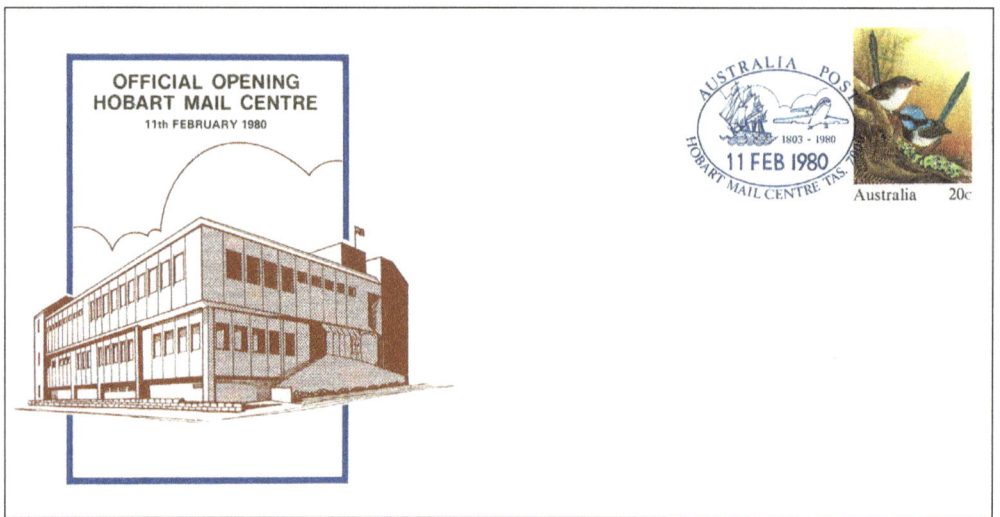

439A.2 | 11 February 1980 | Opening of New Hobart Mail Centre

440.1 | 11 February 1980

6th International Congress of Endocrinology

440

440   1980 6TH INTERNATIONAL CONGRESS OF ENDOCRINOLOGY

Melbourne 3000, Vic
11 – 15 Feb 1980

	ordinary cover	Qty: 3,142	
440.1	Congress cover		20.00
440.2	any other illustrated cover		12.00
440.#R	Registered cover	Qty: 2	*

* No established value.

048E

084   1980 MOOMBA FESTIVAL

Melbourne, Vic
29 Feb – 10 Mar 1980

	ordinary cover	Qty: 3,275	
084E.1	Moomba cover		10.00
084E.2	any other illustrated cover		8.00
084E.#R	Registered cover	Qty: 19	$125

441

441   1980 WORLD FORESTRY DAY

Hobart 7000, Tas
21 Mar – 30 Apr 1980

	ordinary cover	Qty: 450	
441.1	any illustrated cover		60.00
441.2	plain cover		40.00

442

442   RED EARTH FESTIVAL

Mooroolbark 3138, Vic
23 Mar 1980

	ordinary cover	Qty: 2,258	
442.1	Red Earth Festival cover		25.00
442.2	any other illustrated cover		20.00

443

443   1980 60TH ANNIVERSARY OF FIRST FLIGHT ENGLAND TO AUSTRALIA

Northfield 5085, SA
23 Mar 1980

	ordinary cover	Qty: 2,638	
443.1	60th Anniversary First Flight cover		20.00
443.2	any other illustrated cover		15.00

027   1980 ROYAL EASTER SHOW

Sydney, NSW
24 Mar – 8 Apr 1980

Type 027D (see illustration under 1979)

	ordinary cover	Qty: 9,927	
027D.1.80	Royal Easter Show cover		5.00
027D.2.80	any other illustrated cover		3.00

444

444   1980 WANGARATTA COLONIAL FESTIVAL

Wangaratta 3677, Vic
28 Mar 1980

	ordinary cover	Qty: 1,620	
444.1	organising committee souvenir cover		40.00
444.2	any other illustrated cover		35.00
444.3	plain cover		20.00

445

441.1 | 21 March 1980

World Forestry Day

With only 450 impressions recorded, this postmark is scarce on any cover.

443.1 | 23 March 1980

60th Anniversary of First Flight England to Australia

446.1 | 11 April 1980 | Centenary of Local Government, Euroa

445 **1980 50TH ANNIVERSARY OF FIRST BRISBANE TO TOWNSVILLE AIRMAIL**

Brisbane 4000, Qld
31 Mar 1980

	ordinary cover	Qty: 4,088
445.1	50th Anniversary souvenir card 15.00
445.2	any other illustrated cover 10.00

The postcode does not appear on this postmark.

395 **1980 GEMBOREE**

Wanneroo 6065, WA
4 – 7 Apr 1980

	ordinary cover	Qty: 3,119
395B.1	Gemboree Committee souvenir cover 15.00
395B.2	any other illustrated cover 12.00

446 **1980 CENTENARY OF LOCAL GOVERNMENT, EUROA**

Euroa 3666, Vic
5 – 13 Apr 1980

	ordinary cover	Qty: 2,735
446.1	Centenary of Local Government cover 20.00
446.2	any other illustrated cover 15.00
446.#R	Registered cover .... Qty: 1 .... *

* No established value.

447 **1980 MELROSE TO ADELAIDE ATHRC RIDE-A-THON**

Melrose 5483, SA
10 Apr 1980

	ordinary cover	Qty: 3,252
447.1	Adelaide Trail Horse Riders' Club souvenir cover . 15.00
447.2	any other illustrated cover 10.00

448 **1980 RE-ENACTMENT OF MAIL COACH RUN GAWLER TO MOUNT PLEASANT**

Gawler 5118, SA
26 – 27 Apr 1980

	ordinary cover	Qty: 4,000
448.1	Facsimile Letter Card* .... (3,000) 20.00
448.2	any other illustrated cover 15.00

* These letter cards were produced by the Postal Stationery and Postal History Society of Australia. Not all were postmarked.

The postcode does not appear on this postmark.

449 **1980 BRI-PHIL HOUSE EXHIBITION**

Elsternwick 3185, Vic
4 May 1980

	ordinary cover	Qty: 2,348
449.1	'Philatelic Firsts' Exhibition cover 15.00
449.2	any other illustrated cover 10.00
449.#R	Registered cover .... Qty: 9 .... $175

450 **1980 OPENING OF NEW WILLETTON POST OFFICE**

Willetton 6155, WA
8 May 1980

	ordinary cover	Qty: 7,871
450.1	APO Willetton Post office cover 25.00
450.2	any other illustrated cover 5.00
450.#R	Registered cover .... Qty: 3 .... *

* No established value.

450.1 | 8 May 1980 | Opening of New Willetton Post Office

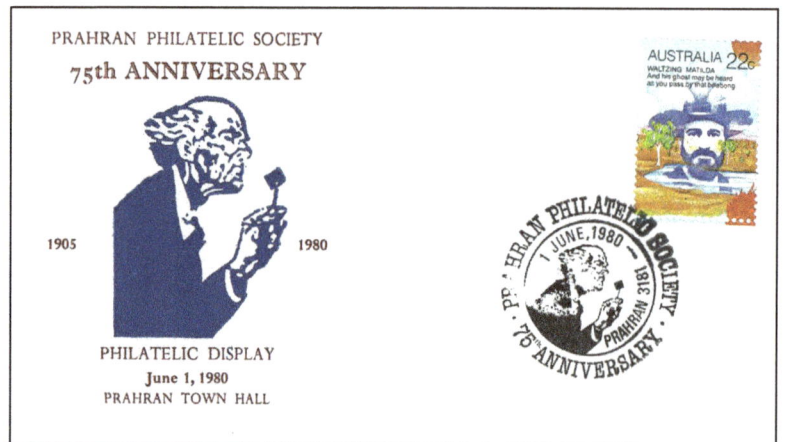

454.1 | 1 June 1980

75th Anniversary of Prahran Philatelic Society

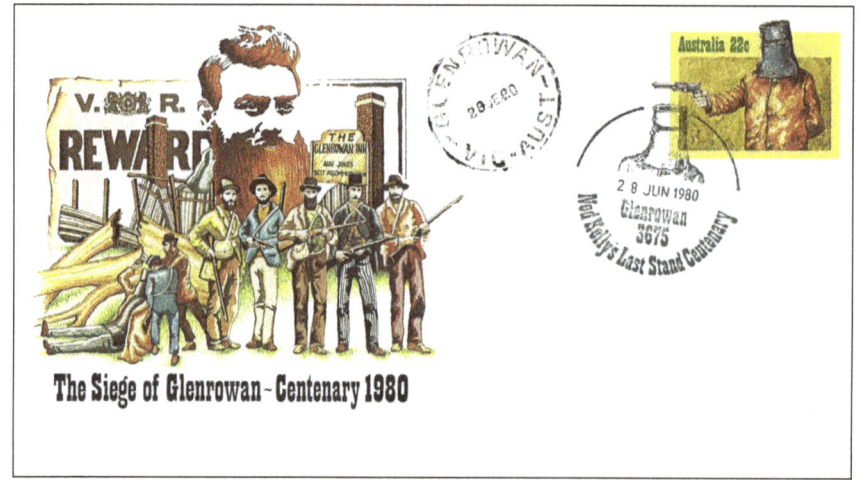

456B.1 | 28 June 1980

Centenary of Ned Kelly's Last Stand

With additional standard Glenrowan circular date stamp.

451

451   1980 GUIDES INTERNATIONAL CAMP
Silverdale 2750, NSW
10 – 17 May 1980

	ordinary cover	Qty: 5,155	
451.1	Camp Kui-Cooinda cover		10.00
451.2	any other illustrated cover		7.00
451.#R	Registered cover		50.00

452   1980 INTERNATIONAL MUSEUM DAY
14 May 1980
Sydney 2000, NSW

The Nov-Dec 1980 issue of Australian Stamp Bulletin records 11,830 impressions of an International Museum Day postmark. There is some doubt as to whether this was the pictorial First Day of Issue cancel, or the same postmark with that wording omitted. Until the existence of the latter can be verified, it is not listed, though number 452 has been reserved.

453

453   1980 OPENING OF MELBOURNE CITY SQUARE
Melbourne 3000, Vic
28 May 1980

	ordinary cover	Qty: 1,540	
453.1	any illustrated cover		30.00
453.2	plain cover		15.00

454

454   1980 75TH ANNIVERSARY OF PRAHRAN PHILATELIC SOCIETY
Prahran 3181, Vic
1 Jun 1980

	ordinary cover	Qty: 2,701	
454.1	Prahran Philatelic Society cover		10.00
454.2	any other illustrated cover		7.00
454.#R	Registered cover	Qty: 12	$150

455

455   1980 AIR NIUGINI CORAL SEA AIR CLASSIC
Wollongong 2527, Vic
14 Jun 1980

	ordinary cover	Qty: 3,013	
455.1	organising committee souvenir cover		15.00
455.2	any other illustrated cover		7.50

456

456   1980 CENTENARY OF NED KELLY'S LAST STAND
Glenrowan 3675, Vic
25 – 28 Jun 1980

Type 456A | machine cancel

	ordinary cover	Qty: 103,157*	
456A.1	Siege of Glenrowan PSE		1.00

Type 456B | hand cancel

	ordinary cover	*	
456B.1	Siege of Glenrowan PSE		2.00
456B.2	any other illustrated cover		5.00

* Quantities are for both versions of the postmark combined.

Related PSE issue:
25 Jun 1980 – 22c, Siege of Glenrowan Centenary

457

457   1980 POMPEII AD79 EXHIBITION
Melbourne 3000, Vic
26 Jun – 4 Aug 1980

	ordinary cover	Qty: 44,398	
457.1	Pompeii AD79 souvenir cover		3.50
457.2	any other illustrated cover		2.50
457.#R	Registered cover	Qty: 6	$200

458

458   1980 SESQUICENTENARY OF LOYAL ORANGE INSTITUTION IN AUSTRALIA

Melbourne 3000, Vic
1 Jul 1980

	ordinary cover	Qty: 3,114
458.1	Loyal Orange Institution souvenir cover	25.00
458.2	any other illustrated cover	15.00

459

459   1980 OPENING OF NEW TORQUAY POST OFFICE

Torquay 3228, Vic
28 Jul 1980

	ordinary cover	Qty: 450
459.1	souvenir cover	60.00
459.2	any other illustrated cover	30.00
459.3	plain cover	20.00
459.#R	Registered cover........... Qty: 641	75.00

The high number of Registered covers seems unlikely but is the figure quoted by Australia Post in the Nov-Dec 1980 issue of Australian Stamp Bulletin.

460

460   1980 400TH ANNIVERSARY OF LUTHERAN CHURCH

North Adelaide 5006, SA
5 – 8 Aug 1980

	ordinary cover	Qty: 6,631
460.1	souvenir cover	10.00
460.2	any other illustrated cover	7.00

022E | postcode 4000   022F | postcode 4029

022   *1980 BRISBANE EXHIBITION*

Brisbane, Qld
11 – 16 Aug 1980

	Type 022E ordinary cover	Qty: 1,220*
022E.1.80	souvenir cover	10.00
022E.2.80	any other illustrated cover	6.00
022E.3.80	plain cover	4.00

	Type 022F ordinary cover	*
022F.1.80	souvenir cover	10.00
022F.2.80	any other illustrated cover	6.00
022F.3.80	plain cover	4.00

* Quantity is for both postmarks combined.

469B.1 | 30 September 1980 | Queensland Philatelic Exhibition

461

461 1980 OPENING OF NEW MORTLAKE POST OFFICE
Mortlake 3272, Vic
13 Aug 1980

	ordinary cover	Qty: 2,728	
461.1	souvenir cover		25.00
461.2	any other illustrated cover		20.00
461.#R	Registered cover	Qty: 8	$175

462

462 1980 AG-QUIP AGRICULTURAL EXHIBITION
Gunnedah 2380, NSW
19 – 26 Aug 1980

	ordinary cover	Qty: 6,000
462.1	APO Ag-Quip souvenir cover	10.00
462.2	any other illustrated cover	7.00

ZEAPEX 80 EXHIBITION
23 Aug 1980

Auckland, New Zealand

The Zeapex 80 International Philatelic Exhibition was held in Auckland, New Zealand from 23 to 31 August. Australia Post applied a cachet to covers for collectors wanting a souvenir of the event.

463

463 1980 PARKES CENTENARY SHOW
Parkes 2870, NSW
25 Aug – 5 Sep 1980

	ordinary cover	Qty: 2,982
463.1	souvenir cover	15.00
463.2	any other illustrated cover	10.00

The August 1980 issue of Australian Stamp Bulletin advised that this postmark was available from a temporary post office at the Parkes Showgrounds on 25, 26 and 27 August, and from the Parkes post office from 25 August till 5 September 1980.

055 1980 ROYAL ADELAIDE SHOW
Wayville 5034, SA
3 – 12 Sep 1980*

Type 055B
(see illustration under 1979)

055B.1.80	Adelaide Show overprinted PSE**	25.00
055B.2.80	any other illustrated cover	20.00

* Impressions dated 1 and 2 September 1980 are known.

** The set of 7 Animals PSEs was rubber-stamped ROYAL ADELAIDE SHOW 1980 on four lines.

464

464 1980 CENTENARY OF RAILWAY, ROMA
Roma 4455, Qld
11 – 18 Sep 1980

	ordinary cover	Qty: 12,800
464.1	100 Years of Railway cover	5.00
464.2	any other illustrated cover	4.00

465

465 1980 SALVATION ARMY CENTENARY CONGRESS
Adelaide 5000, SA
17 – 24 Sep 1980

	ordinary cover	Qty: 16,132
465.1	Centenary Congress cover	8.00
465.2	any other illustrated cover	5.00

Related stamp issue:
11 Aug 1980 – 22c, Salvation Army (part of a Community Welfare set of four stamps (SG748)

017 1980 ROYAL MELBOURNE SHOW
Show Grounds 3032, Melbourne, Vic
17 – 27 Sep 1980

Type 017D
(see illustration under 1978)

	ordinary cover	Qty: 9,979
017D.1.80	any illustrated cover	4.00

414B

414 1980 PERTH ROYAL SHOW
Claremont 6010, WA
20 – 28 Sep 1980

    ordinary cover   Qty: 5,523
414B.1   any illustrated cover 12.00

466

466 1980 MELBOURNE INTERNATIONAL CENTENARY EXHIBITION
Melbourne 3000, Vic
23 Sep – 5 Oct 1980

    ordinary cover   Qty: 52,300
466.1   'One Hundred Years' Centenary Exhibition cover .. 1.50
466.2   Exhibition souvenir miniature sheet (Cinderella) ... 5.00

467

467 1980 VANCOUVER DAY
Albany 6330, WA
29 Sep 1980

    ordinary cover   Qty: 4,043
467.1   Capt. George Vancouver cover 12.00
467.2   any other illustrated cover 8.00
467.#R   Registered cover .... Qty: 3 .... *

* No established value.

468

468 1980 NATIONAL STAMP WEEK ADELAIDE EXHIBITION
Adelaide 5000, SA
29 Sep – 4 Oct 1980

    ordinary cover
468.1   APO National Stamp Week FDC 5.00
468.2   Sydpex 80 PSE 5.00
468.3   any other illustrated cover 4.00

Related stamp issue:
29 Sep 1980 – 5 x 22c, and 3 x 22c miniature sheet, National Stamp Week (SG752-6, MS757)

Related PSE issue:
29 Sep 1980 – 22c, Sydpex 80

469

469 1980 QUEENSLAND PHILATELIC EXHIBITION
Brisbane 4000, Qld
29 Sep – 4 Oct 1980

Type 469A | black ink

    ordinary cover
469A.1   Queensland Philatelic Exhibition cover 4.00
469A.2   APO National Stamp Week FDC 4.00
469A.3   Sydpex 80 PSE 4.00
469A.4   any other illustrated cover 3.00

Type 469B | green ink

    ordinary cover
469B.1   Queensland Philatelic Exhibition cover 4.00
469B.2   APO National Stamp Week FDC 4.00
469B.3   Sydpex 80 PSE 4.00
469B.4   any other illustrated cover 3.00

Type 469C | red ink

    ordinary cover
469C.1   Queensland Philatelic Exhibition cover 4.00
469C.2   APO National Stamp Week FDC 4.00
469C.3   Sydpex 80 PSE 4.00
469C.4   any other illustrated cover 3.00

Related stamp issue:
29 Sep 1980 – 5 x 22c, and 3 x 22c miniature sheet, National Stamp Week (SG752-6, MS757)

Related PSE issue:
29 Sep 1980 – 22c, Sydpex 80

470E

470 1980 NATIONAL STAMP WEEK
29 Sep – 6 Oct 1980

Type 470A | Adelaide 5000, SA
29 Sep – 4 Oct

	ordinary cover	Qty: 10,673*
470A.1	APO National Stamp Week FDC	1.00
470A.2	APO National Stamp Week miniature sheet FDC	2.00
470A.3	Sydpex 80 PSE	1.00
470A.4	any other illustrated cover	1.00

Type 470B | Brisbane 4000, Qld
29 Sep – 4 Oct

	ordinary cover	Qty: 17,888*
470B.1	APO National Stamp Week FDC	1.00
470B.2	APO National Stamp Week miniature sheet FDC	2.00
470B.3	Sydpex 80 PSE	1.00
470B.4	any other illustrated cover	1.00

Type 470C | Canberra 2600, ACT
29 Sep – 6 Oct

ordinary cover
- 470C.1 APO National Stamp Week FDC 1.00
- 470C.2 APO National Stamp Week miniature sheet FDC ... 2.00
- 470C.3 Sydpex 80 PSE 1.00
- 470C.4 any other illustrated cover 1.00

Type 470D | Darwin 5790, NT
29 Sep – 6 Oct

ordinary cover
- 470D.1 APO National Stamp Week FDC 1.00
- 470D.2 APO National Stamp Week miniature sheet FDC ... 2.00
- 470D.3 Sydpex 80 PSE 1.00
- 470D.4 any other illustrated cover 1.00

Type 470E | Hobart 7000, Tas
29 Sep – 6 Oct

ordinary cover
- 470E.1 APO National Stamp Week FDC 1.00
- 470E.2 APO National Stamp Week miniature sheet FDC ... 2.00
- 470E.3 Sydpex 80 PSE 1.00
- 470E.4 any other illustrated cover 1.00

Type 470F | Melbourne 3000, Vic
29 Sep – 3 Oct

	ordinary cover	Qty: 4,885
470F.1	APO National Stamp Week FDC	1.00
470F.2	APO National Stamp Week miniature sheet FDC	2.00
470F.3	Sydpex 80 PSE	1.00
470F.4	any other illustrated cover	1.00

Type 470G | Sydney 2000, NSW
29 Sep – 6 Oct

ordinary cover
- 470G.1 APO National Stamp Week FDC 1.00
- 470G.2 APO National Stamp Week miniature sheet FDC ... 2.00
- 470G.3 Sydpex 80 PSE 1.00
- 470G.4 any other illustrated cover 1.00

Type 470H | Perth 6000, WA
29 Sep – 6 Oct

	ordinary cover	Qty: 5,253
470H.1	APO National Stamp Week FDC	1.00
470H.2	APO National Stamp Week miniature sheet FDC	2.00
470H.3	Sydpex 80 PSE	1.00
470H.4	any other illustrated cover	1.00

* Given the larger quantities for Adelaide and Brisbane, it is possible the numbers include impressions of postmarks for events 468 and 469.

Related stamp issue:
29 Sep 1980 – 5 x 22c, and 3 x 22c miniature sheet, National Stamp Week (SG752-6, MS757)

Related PSE issue:
29 Sep 1980 – 22c, Sydpex 80

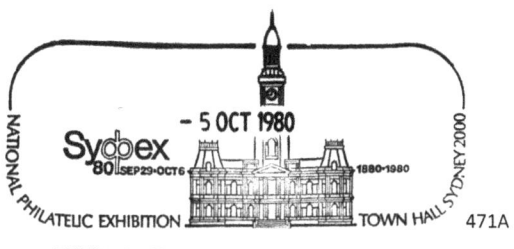
471A

471B

417C

471   SYDPEX 80
Sydney 2000, NSW
29 Sep – 6 Oct 1980

Type 471A | Town Hall

	ordinary cover	Qty: 400,800
471A.1	Sydpex 80 PSE – green ink 29 Sep	1.00
471A.2	Sydpex 80 PSE – black ink 30 Sep – 5 Oct	1.00
471A.3	Sydpex 80 PSE – red ink 6 Oct	1.00
471A.#R	Registered cover *	15.00

Type 471B | square

	ordinary cover	Qty: 201,069
471B.1	Sydpex 80 PSE – green ink 29 Sep	1.00
471B.2	Sydpex 80 PSE – black ink 30 Sep – 5 Oct	1.00
471B.3	Sydpex 80 PSE – red ink 6 Oct	1.00
471B.#R	Registered cover *	15.00

* The Highest R6 label number sighted by the editor is 4195 on a cover dated 6 October 1980. Registered covers exist with both postmarks 471A and 471B applied.

Type 471C | Model K

	ordinary cover	Qty: 54,000
471C.1	Sydpex 80 PSE – green ink 29 Sep	1.00
471C.2	Sydpex 80 PSE – black ink 30 Sep – 5 Oct	1.00
471C.3	Sydpex 80 PSE – red ink 6 Oct	1.00

Related PSE issue:
29 Sep 1980 – 22c, Sydpex 80

The Model K postmark was produced by a hand-cancelling machine. Contradictory in description, it is included in this guide in the interests of completion.

472 1980 AUSTRALIAN RAILWAY HISTORICAL SOCIETY GLADSTONE CENTENARY

Gladstone 4680, Qld
11 Oct 1980

	ordinary cover	Qty: 30,306
472.1	any illustrated cover	5.00

This postmark is generally found in purple. It exists in black, red and green but such covers were produced at the request of a single collector who 'extracted' 100 examples of each. The editor regards these as unofficial and are not listed.

380 1980 ROYAL AGRICULTURAL SHOW, GLENORCHY

Glenorchy 7010, Tas
22 – 25 Oct 1980

Type 380 (see illustration under 1978)

	ordinary cover	
380.1.80	any illustrated cover	10.00

For earlier Royal Hobart Show entries, see event 021.

473 1980 1ST NATIONAL PHILATELIC CONVENTION

Canberra 2600, ACT
25 – 26 Oct 1980

	ordinary cover	Qty: 22,800
473.1	First National Philatelic Convention cover	6.00
473.2	any other illustrated cover	4.00

22c Animals PSEs were overprinted by the Philatelic Society of Canberra.

474 1980 WORLD AMATEUR SNOOKER CHAMPIONSHIP

Launceston 7250, Tas
27 Oct – 9 Nov 1980

	ordinary cover	Qty: 4,224
474.1	any illustrated cover	15.00

475 1980 CHRISTMAS STAMP FAIR

Adelaide 5000, SA
8 – 9 Nov 1980

	ordinary cover	Qty: 9,953
475.1	Christmas Stamp Fair '80 cover	5.00
475.2	any other illustrated cover	4.00

476 1980 HAND OVER CEREMONY – UNDERGROUND RAIL LOOP

Melbourne 3000, Vic
14 Nov 1980

	ordinary cover	Qty: 107,766
476.1	Melbourne Underground Rail Loop cover	2.00
476.2	any other illustrated cover	2.00

477 1980 12TH ASIA-PACIFIC SCOUT CONFERENCE

Melbourne 3000, Vic
16 – 21 Nov 1980

	ordinary cover	Qty: 14,201
477.1	Asia-Pacific Jamboree PSE – one date	4.00
477.2	Asia-Pacific Jamboree PSE – all six dates*	20.00
477.3	any other illustrated cover	3.00

* J.E. Koch *Illustrated Catalogue of Pre-stamped Envelopes* states that 2,000 sets were produced.

Related PSE issue:
19 Dec 1979 – 20c, 4th Asia-Pacific (12th Australian) Jamboree, Perth 1979-1980

 478

478   1980 CAMBRAI DAY
Milpo Puckapunyal 3662, Vic
20 Nov 1980

	ordinary cover	Qty: 10,084
478.1	RAAC Tank Museum souvenir cover	5.00
478.2	any other illustrated cover	4.00
478.#R	Registered cover .... Qty: 361	25.00

 479

479   1980 SOUTHERN CROSS AIR RACE
Sydney 2000, NSW
22 – 23 Nov 1980

	ordinary cover	Qty: 9,914
479.1	Southern Cross Air Race cover	4.00
479.2	any other illustrated cover	3.00

480A   480B   480C

480   1980 LAST OLD GHAN TRIP
24 – 25 Nov 1980

Type 480A | Marree 5733, NT | 24 Nov

	ordinary cover	Qty: 61,448
480A.1	Last Old Ghan cover	2.00
480A.2	any other illustrated cover	1.50

The Australian Philatelic Bulletin of May-June 1981 reported this postmark's statistics with the location listed simply as South Australia. Having been announced in the January-February Bulletin in equally vague terms, it isn't clear whether the Oodnadatta postmarks were official PO productions.

Type 480B is known in magenta as a cachet on a cover cancelled with the Marree postmark. Until the status of the Oodnadatta postmarks is ascertained, they are not listed here, but illustrated for information.

 481

481   1980 CENTENARY OF PETERBOROUGH POST OFFICE
Peterborough 5422, SA
12 Dec 1980

	ordinary cover	Qty: 12,130
481.1	100 Years Peterborough PO cover	5.00
481.2	any other illustrated cover	4.00

 482

482   1980 50TH ANNIVERSARY OF INTERSTATE TELEPHONE SERVICE
Perth 6000, WA
18 Dec 1980

	ordinary cover	Qty: 8,737
482.1	First Commercial Telephone Call cover	7.50
482.2	any other illustrated cover	5.00

1981 – 2023

The following is a summary of postmarks produced to celebrate events and anniversaries after 1980. The distinction of strictly commemorative postmarks is sometimes hazy as other primarily pictorial cancellations were used in a commemorative context. Some have also been used as an FDI postmark, with or without 'First Day of Issue' text. Those without such a notation have been included, even though FDI postmarks are outside the scope of this guide. Excluded are postmarks used exclusively on postal numismatic covers, postal medallion covers, and similar products where there is no evidence that those postmarks were otherwise available. No attempt has been made to identify the use of multiple postmarks for the same event.

Over 1,800 events are listed, and some years present a large number of entries, a carry-over of the production excesses seen in 1979 and 1980. It would be a determined collector who attempted to complete a collection from 1981. More likely, and arguably more interesting, collectors would specialise, targeting a theme such as centenaries, philatelic exhibitions, scouting or their own state or town.

It has not been feasible to illustrate all postmarks in this section, but a small selection for each year is provided. A bullet mark (•) appears against entries with included illustrations.

This list is subject to ongoing work and may be expanded for a future edition of Australian Commemorative Postmarks. The editor invites readers to advise of errors and omissions.

1981

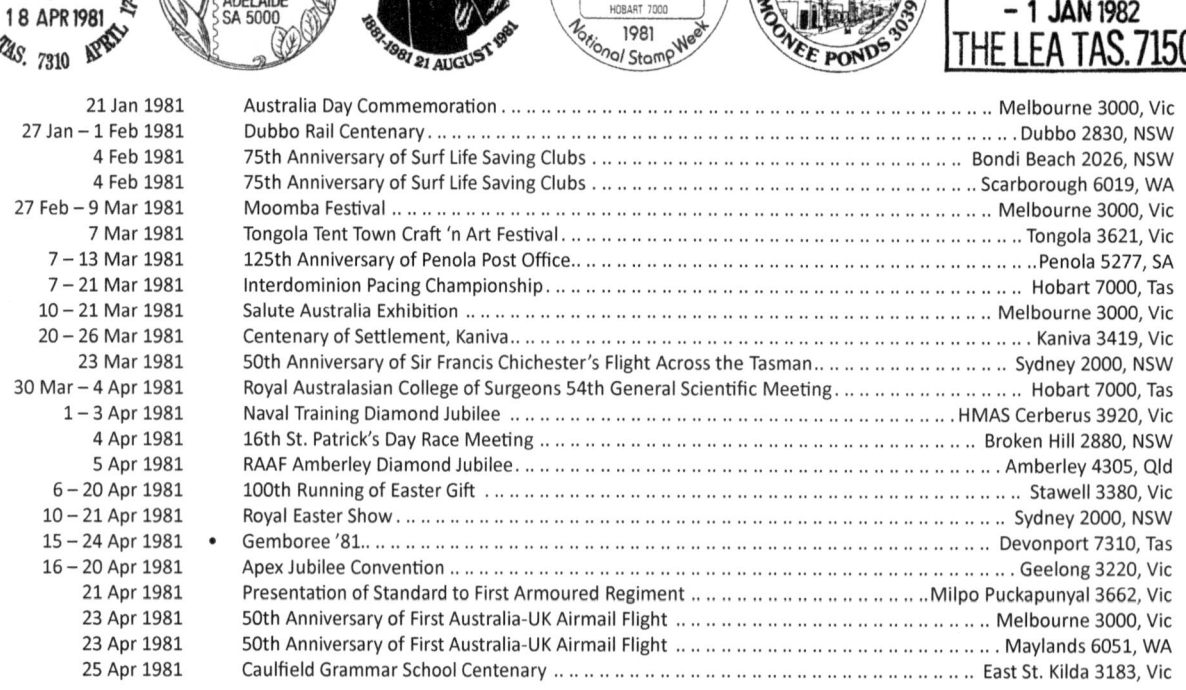

Date	Event	Location
21 Jan 1981	Australia Day Commemoration	Melbourne 3000, Vic
27 Jan – 1 Feb 1981	Dubbo Rail Centenary	Dubbo 2830, NSW
4 Feb 1981	75th Anniversary of Surf Life Saving Clubs	Bondi Beach 2026, NSW
4 Feb 1981	75th Anniversary of Surf Life Saving Clubs	Scarborough 6019, WA
27 Feb – 9 Mar 1981	Moomba Festival	Melbourne 3000, Vic
7 Mar 1981	Tongola Tent Town Craft 'n Art Festival	Tongola 3621, Vic
7 – 13 Mar 1981	125th Anniversary of Penola Post Office	Penola 5277, SA
7 – 21 Mar 1981	Interdominion Pacing Championship	Hobart 7000, Tas
10 – 21 Mar 1981	Salute Australia Exhibition	Melbourne 3000, Vic
20 – 26 Mar 1981	Centenary of Settlement, Kaniva	Kaniva 3419, Vic
23 Mar 1981	50th Anniversary of Sir Francis Chichester's Flight Across the Tasman	Sydney 2000, NSW
30 Mar – 4 Apr 1981	Royal Australasian College of Surgeons 54th General Scientific Meeting	Hobart 7000, Tas
1 – 3 Apr 1981	Naval Training Diamond Jubilee	HMAS Cerberus 3920, Vic
4 Apr 1981	16th St. Patrick's Day Race Meeting	Broken Hill 2880, NSW
5 Apr 1981	RAAF Amberley Diamond Jubilee	Amberley 4305, Qld
6 – 20 Apr 1981	100th Running of Easter Gift	Stawell 3380, Vic
10 – 21 Apr 1981	Royal Easter Show	Sydney 2000, NSW
15 – 24 Apr 1981	• Gemboree '81	Devonport 7310, Tas
16 – 20 Apr 1981	Apex Jubilee Convention	Geelong 3220, Vic
21 Apr 1981	Presentation of Standard to First Armoured Regiment	Milpo Puckapunyal 3662, Vic
23 Apr 1981	50th Anniversary of First Australia-UK Airmail Flight	Melbourne 3000, Vic
23 Apr 1981	50th Anniversary of First Australia-UK Airmail Flight	Maylands 6051, WA
25 Apr 1981	Caulfield Grammar School Centenary	East St. Kilda 3183, Vic

26 – 30 Apr 1981	Lions Clubs International Multiple District 201 29th Convention	Canberra 2600, ACT
6 May 1981	Centenary of Victorian College of Pharmacy	Parkville 3052, Vic
20 May 1981	Tribute to Artist S.T. Gill	Ballarat 3350, Vic
20 May 1981	Camel Mail Re-enactment Trip	Coolgardie 6429, WA
20 May 1981	Camel Mail Re-enactment Trip	Kalgoorlie 6430, WA
1 Jun 1981	Centenary of Lord Howe Island PO	Lord Howe Island 2898, NSW
5 – 7 Jun 1981	St. John's College Golden Jubilee	Lismore 2480, NSW
7 Jun 1981	Golden Anniversary of DH.82 Tiger Moth	Albury 2640, NSW
15 Jun 1981	New Moe PO	Moe 3825, Vic
15 Jun – 10 Jul 1981	21st Australian Legal Convention	Hobart 7000, Tas
27 – 28 Jun 1981 •	Stamp Fair 1981	Adelaide 5000, SA
13 Jul 1981	Airbus Delivery Flight Toulouse-Melbourne	Perth 6000, WA
22 Jul 1981	Inaugural Airbus Flight Melbourne-Sydney	Melbourne Airport 3045, Vic
27 Jul 1981	Centenary Sheep Show	Ballarat 3350, Vic
5 – 15 Aug 1981	Brisbane Exhibition	Brisbane 4029, Qld
11 – 13 Aug 1981	Yorke Peninsula Field Day	Kadina 5554, SA
14 – 19 Aug 1981	11th International Scientific Congress on the Cultivation of Edible Fungus	Sydney 2000, NSW
16 Aug 1981	South Australian Philatelic Association 8th Annual Congress	Snowtown 5520, SA
21 Aug 1981 •	Centenary of Port Fairy PO	Port Fairy 3284, Vic
24 Aug 1981	Botanical Gardens Display	Booragoon 6154, WA
24 – 29 Aug 1981	13th International Botanical Congress	Sydney University 2006, NSW
30 Aug 1981	Festival of Wollongong	Wollongong 2500, NSW
4 – 6 Sep 1981	Tibooburrra Centenary	Tibooburra 2880, NSW
4 – 12 Sep 1981	Royal Adelaide Show	Wayville 5034, SA
5 Sep 1981	Scout Skillorama Day	Redcliffe 4020, Qld
7 Sep 1981	First Scheduled Airbus Service Sydney-Brisbane-Sydney	Sydney 2000, NSW
13 Sep – 4 Oct 1981	Warana Festival	Brisbane 4000, Qld
15 – 18 Sep 1981	150th Anniversary of York	York 6302, WA
16 Sep 1981	25th Anniversary of Outward Bound Australia	Canberra City 2601, ACT
16 Sep 1981	International Year of Disabled Persons	Woden 2606, ACT
16 Sep 1981	International Year for Disabled Persons[1]	Prospect 5082, SA
16 – 26 Sep 1981	Royal Melbourne Show	Ascot Vale 3032, Vic
19 – 20 Sep 1981	First Australian Facetors Forum	Warwick 4370, Qld
22 – 24 Sep 1981	Henty Field Days	Henty 2658, NSW
26 Sep – 4 Oct 1981	Centenary of Local Settlement, Millmerran	Millmerran 4357, Qld
28 Sep – 3 Oct 1981	National Stamp Week Exhibition	Carlingford Shopping Square 2118, NSW
28 Sep – 3 Oct 1981	Queensland Philatelic Exhibition	Brisbane 4000, Qld
28 Sep – 4 Oct 1981 •	National Stamp Week	[7 capital cities]
30 Sep – 7 Oct 1981	Commonwealth Heads of Government Meeting	Melbourne 3000, Vic
1 Oct 1981	Centenary of Thoona PO	Thoona 3726, Vic
1 – 30 Oct 1981	Passionist Fathers and Brothers (25th Anniversary of Order)	Hobart 7000, Tas
2 – 19 Oct 1981	Perth Royal Show	Claremont 6010, WA
6 – 8 Oct 1981	Elmore and District Machinery Fields Days	Elmore 3558, Vic
10 – 23 Oct 1981	Djerriwarrh Festival	Melton 3337, Vic
14 Oct 1981	First 50 Years of Commercial Broadcasting in WA	Perth 6000, WA
14 Oct 1981	Port Augusta Yacht Club Centenary	Port Augusta 5700, SA
14 Oct 1981	America's Cup Challenge 1983	Williamstown 3016, Vic
19 – 24 Oct 1981	International Understanding Week	Rylstone 2849, NSW
22 Oct 1981	Royal Agricultural Show, Glenorchy	Glenorchy 7010, Tas
23 Oct 1981	Opening of New Lakes Entrance PO	Lakes Entrance 3909, Vic
23 Oct 1981	Rostrum State Convention	Orange 2800, NSW
26 Oct 1981	50th Anniversary of DH.82 Tiger Moth	Parafield Airport 5105, SA
26 Oct 1981	STAMPEX '86	Smoky Bay 5680, SA
26 – 31 Oct 1981 •	Centenary Celebrations, Moonee Ponds	Moonee Ponds 3039, Vic
29 Oct 1981	Northern Australia Development Seminar	Katherine 5780, NT
31 Oct 1981	Beersheba Day – Royal Australian Armoured Corps	Milpo Puckapunyal 3662, Vic
2 – 7 Nov 1981	Chinese Exhibition	Sydney 2000, NSW
3 Nov 1981	Melbourne Cup	Flemington 3031, Vic
7 Nov 1981	Arts and Crafts Festival	Stirling 5152, SA
9 – 20 Nov 1981	Centenary of North Eastern Agricultural and Pastoral Society	Scottsdale 7254, Tas
10 Nov 1981	40th Anniversary – Air Training Corps in Australia	Adelaide 5000, SA

---

1   The 16 September 1981 Prospect postmark incorrectly describes the event as International Year "for" Disabled Persons.

14 Nov 1981	28th Victorian Philatelic Association Congress	Blackburn South 3130, Vic
14 – 15 Nov 1981	Christmas Stamp Fair	Adelaide 5000, SA
17 – 19 Nov 1981	Australian National Field Days	Orange 2800, NSW
20 Nov 1981	50th Anniversary of C.A. Butler's England-Australia Flight	Bathurst 2795, NSW
20 Nov 1981	Birthday Commemoration of 2nd Cavalry Regiment RAAC	Milpo Puckapunyal 3662, Vic
23 Nov 1981	Centenary of Peterborough-Orroroo Railway	Peterborough 5422, SA
26 – 28 Nov 1981	Rotary International 1981 Pacific Regional Conference	Melbourne 3000, Vic
28 Dec 1981	Glenelg Commemoration Day Sports Association	Glenelg 5045, SA
29 Dec 1981 – 4 Jan 1982	Tasmanian Fiesta	Hobart 7000, Tas
29 Dec 1981 – 5 Jan 1982	• 5th Tasmanian Corroboree	The Lea 7150, Tas

1982

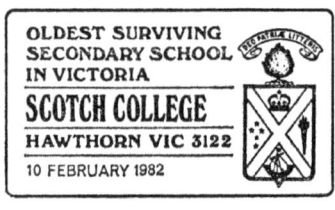    

16 – 18 Jan 1982	Queensland Stamp and Coin Dealers Association Fair	Surfers Paradise 4217, Qld
17 Jan 1982	Birthday Commemoration of 3rd Cavalry Regiment RAAC	Milpo Puckapunyal 3662, Vic
23 – 24 Jan 1982	Annual Stamp Fair	Warrnambool 3280, Vic
26 Jan 1982	Australia Day Family Festival	Nunawading 3131, Vic
27 Jan 1982	Birth Centenary of Peter Dawson	Adelaide 5000, SA
1 Feb 1982	Australia Day Festival	Frankston 3199, Vic
6 Feb 1982	Karingal Stamp and Coin Fayre	Geelong West 3218, Vic
7 – 19 Feb 1982	150th Anniversary of WA Legislative Council	Perth 6000, WA
8 – 12 Feb 1982	International Seminar on Viral Diseases in SE Asia and Western Pacific	Canberra 2600, ACT
8 – 12 Feb 1982	Glenelg Rotarama Festival	Glenelg 5045, SA
10 Feb 1982	• Scotch College Commemoration	Hawthorn 3122, Vic
13 Feb 1982	150th Anniversary of Opening of The Kings School	Parramatta 2150, NSW
15 Feb 1982	Local Government Centenary	Warragul 3820, Vic
17 Feb 1982	Greenpeace – Australian Whales	Adelaide 5000, SA
17 Feb 1982	Queensland Sires Stakes Triad Series	Toowoomba 4350, Qld
24 Feb 1982	Birthday Commemoration of Armoured Centre RAAC	Milpo Puckapunyal 3662, Vic
24 – 26 Feb 1982	Centenary of the Ashes	Macquarie Centre 2113, NSW
26 Feb – 8 Mar 1982	Moomba Festival	Melbourne 3000, Vic
1 Mar 1982	Corny Point Lighthouse Centenary	Warooka 5577, SA
3 Mar 1982	Birthday Commemoration of 1st / 15th Royal NSW Lancers	Milpo Puckapunyal 3662, Vic
6 – 7 Mar 1982	Second National Philatelic Convention	Canberra 2600, ACT
13 Mar 1982	Red Earth Festival	Mooroolbark 3138, Vic
19 – 26 Mar 1982	50th Anniversary of Opening of Sydney Harbour Bridge	Sydney 2000, NSW
27 Mar 1982	17th St. Patrick's Day Race Meeting	Broken Hill 2880, NSW
2 – 13 Apr 1982	Centenary of Royal Agricultural Showgrounds	Sydney Showground 2021, NSW
2 – 13 Apr 1982	Royal Easter Show	Sydney Showground 2021, NSW
8 Apr 1982	Centenary of Public School, Lennox Head	Lennox Head 2478, NSW
21 Apr 1982	Birthday of Queen Elizabeth II	Elizabeth 5112, SA
28 Apr – 11 May 1982	Centenary of Gold Mining at Mt. Morgan	Mt. Morgan 4714, Qld
1 May 1982	Centenary of Pittsworth State Primary School	Pittsworth 4356, Qld
1 – 2 May 1982	The May Festival	Camberwell 3124, Vic
5 May 1982	Birth Centenary of Sir Douglas Mawson	Adelaide 5000, SA
14 May 1982	Centenary of Casterton Cup	Casterton 3311, Vic
19 May 1982	Belmont Rose Display	Cloverdale 6105, WA
31 May – 11 Jun 1982	75th Anniversary of Telephone Service	Sarina 4737, Qld

Date		Event	Location
1 – 2 Jun 1982	•	150th Anniversary of Government Postal Services in Tasmania.	[15 cities / towns]
6 Jun 1982		Centenary of Queensland Rugby Union	Brisbane 4000, Qld
7 Jun 1982	•	50th Anniversary of First Airmail to Flinders Island	Whitemark 7255, Tas
14 – 15 Jun 1982		29th World Ploughing Contest	Longford 7301, Tas
16 Jun 1982		50th Anniversary of Australian Broadcasting Commission	Sydney 2000, NSW
16 Jun 1982		Honouring Radio Australia	Melbourne 3000, Vic
19 – 20 Jun 1982		Communications Stamp Fair 82.	Adelaide 5000, SA
3 Jul 1982		Dimboola Railway Centenary	Dimboola 3414, Vic
5 – 9 Jul 1982		Grainger Museum – Grainger Commemoration Week	University of Melbourne 3052, Vic
7 Jul 1982		Birthday Commemoration of 1st Armoured Regiment	Milpo Puckapunyal 3662, Vic
7 & 31 Jul 1982		Hundred Years of Railway – Local Government	Uralla 2358, NSW
8 Jul 1982		Birthplace of Percy Grainger	North Brighton 3186, Vic
10 Jul 1982		50th Anniversary of Sinking of *SS Casino*.	Apollo Bay 3233, Vic
22 Jul 1982		75th Anniversary of Fremantle Post Office.	Market Street 6160, WA
1 – 20 Aug 1982		XI International Conference on Health Education	University of Tasmania 7005, Tas
4 Aug 1982		Centenary of Hawker Post Office	Hawker 5434, SA
4 – 9 Aug 1982	•	Transpex '82.	Granville 2142, NSW
4 – 13 Aug 1982		Brisbane Exhibition	Brisbane 4000, Qld
4 – 17 Aug 1982		Sesquicentenary of Post Services, Wollongong	Wollongong 2500, NSW
8 Aug 1982		South Australian Philatelic Association 9th Annual Congress.	Aldgate 5154, SA
14 Aug 1982		21st Anniversary of Chartering of Rotary Club of Tara.	Tara 4421, Qld
16 Aug 1982		International Conference of Health Education	Prospect 5082, SA
16 – 20 Aug 1982		12th International Congress of Biochemistry	University Crawley 6009, WA
18 Aug 1982		Centenary of Toora Post Office.	Toora 3962, Vic
23 – 27 Aug 1982		Australian Road Research Board 11th Conference.	Melbourne University 3052, Vic
24 – 27 Aug 1982		10th Australian Ceramic Conference – Austceram 82.	Carlton South 3053, Vic
25 – 26 Aug 1982		St Vincent's Hospital 125th Anniversary.	Darlinghurst 2010, NSW
26 Aug 1982		Ayr Town Centenary.	Ayr 4807, Qld
28 Aug 1982		Rotary's 21st Henley-on-Todd.	Alice Springs 5750, NT
28 Aug – 5 Sep 1982		7th Girl Guide Muster.	Dubbo 2830, NSW
30 Aug 1982		Ashes Obituary Centenary	Melbourne 3000, Vic
2 – 11 Sep 1982		Royal Adelaide Show	Wayville 5034, SA
6 Sep 1982		Australian Administrative Staff College Silver Jubilee	Mt. Eliza 3930, Vic
11 – 12 Sep 1982		Essendon Broadmeadows 1st Exhibition and Stamp Fair	Essendon 3040, Vic
13 – 15 Sep 1982		7th Congress Western Pacific Orthopaedic Association.	Perth 6000, WA
16 – 25 Sep 1982		Royal Melbourne Show.	Ascot Vale 3032, Vic
18 Sep 1982		Western Australian Football League Grand Final	Subiaco Coghlan Road 6008, WA
18 Sep 1982		Orange Blossom Festival	Castle Hill 2154, NSW
21 – 23 Sep 1982		Henty Field Days.	Henty 2658, NSW
22 Sep 1982		Centenary of Hobart and District YMCA Youth Clubs	Hobart 7000, Tas
22 – 26 Sep 1982		Annual Antique and Collectable Exposition	Brisbane 4000, Qld
24 – 28 Sep 1982		7th Australian Orchid Conference	Brisbane 4000, Qld
25 Sep 1982		Victorian Football League Grand Final.	East Melbourne 3002, Vic
26 Sep 1982		Granting of the Freedom of the Shire of Seymour to 1st Armoured Regiment.	Seymour 3660, Vic
27 Sep – 1 Oct 1982		National Stamp Week	[8 capital cities]
27 Sep – 2 Oct 1982		National Stamp Week Exhibition.	Carlingford Shopping Centre 2118, NSW
30 Sep – 9 Oct 1982		12th Commonwealth Games.	Brisbane 4000, Qld + 2
5 – 7 Oct 1982		Elmore and District Machinery Field Days.	Elmore 3558, Vic
8 Oct 1982		Back to Smoky Bay	Smoky Bay 5680, SA
10 Oct 1982		2nd Bunbury and District Philatelic Forum.	Bunbury 6230, WA
11 Oct 1982		Australian Jaycees 35th National Convention	Belmont 3216, Vic
11 Oct 1982		Birthday Commemoration of 4th Cavalry Regiment RAAC	Milpo Puckapunyal 3662, Vic
11 – 17 Oct 1982	•	ANPEX '82.	Brisbane 4000, Qld
12 Oct 1982		Opening of Australian National Gallery	Canberra 2600, ACT
12 – 15 Oct 1982		Chamber of Commerce Centenary.	Townsville 4810, Qld
14 Oct 1982		Bald Hills 125th Anniversary	Bald Hills 4036, Qld
15 Oct 1982		Sandy Hollow – Ulan Railway Opening.	Muswellbrook 2333, NSW
15 Oct 1982		Opening of Rosny Park Post Office	Rosny Park 7018, Tas
16 Oct 1982		Opening of Adelaide International Airport.	Adelaide 5000, SA
20 Oct 1982		Royal Agricultural Show.	Glenorchy 7010, Tas
21 Oct 1982		Arnott-Spiller's National (Greyhound) Championship.	Woolloongabba 4102, Qld
25 Oct 1982		Port Augusta Catholic Parish Centenary	Port August 5700, SA
29 Oct 1982		STAMPEX '86.	Mt. Gambier 5290, SA
29 Oct – 15 Nov 1982		13th Annual Rose Festival.	Benalla 3672, Vic

Date	Event	Location
31 Oct 1982	Birthday Commemoration of 2nd / 14th Queensland Mounted Infantry RAAC	Milpo Puckapunyal 3662, Vic
2 Nov 1982	Melbourne Cup	Flemington 3031, Vic
4 Nov 1982	First International Flight from Adelaide International Airport	Adelaide 5000, Qld
6 – 7 Nov 1982	6th Northern Stamp and Coin Convention	Grafton 2460, NSW
9 Nov 1982	YWCA Centenary	Melbourne 3000, Vic
13 Nov 1982	30th Rhododendron Festival	Blackheath 2785, NSW
13 – 14 Nov 1982	Christmas Stamp Fair	Adelaide 5000, SA
13 – 22 Nov 1982	Centenary Celebrations	Manly 4179, Qld
15 – 18 Nov 1982	Australian National Field Days	Orange 2800, NSW
17 Nov 1982	Centenary of Horsham Municipality	Horsham 3400, Vic
19 – 21 Nov 1982	Fort Queenscliff Centenary	Queenscliff 3225, Vic
26 Nov 1982	50th Anniversary of Opening of Great Ocean Road	Apollo Bay 3233, Vic
27 Nov 1982	125th Anniversary of Local Government, Broadmeadows	Broadmeadows 3047, Vic
1 Dec 1982	Birthday of Royal Corps of Australian Electrical and Mechanical Engineers	Milpo Puckapunyal 3662, Vic
5 Dec 1982	'Circa 1900' (celebrating cycling)	Port Adelaide 5015, SA
8 Dec 1982	Opening of Adelaide-Crystal Brook Standard Gauge Railway	Adelaide 5000, SA
23 Dec 1982	P&O's 50 Years of Cruising	Sydney 2000, NSW
24 Dec 1982	National Skate and Kitty Cat Titles	Ceduna 5690, SA
28 Dec 1982	Glenelg Commemoration Day Sports Association	Glenelg 5045, SA
29 Dec 1982	75th Anniversary of World Scouting	Leichhardt 2040, NSW
29 Dec 1982 – 4 Jan 1983	Tasmanian Fiesta	Hobart 7000, Tas
29 Dec 1982 – 7 Jan 1983	75th Anniversary of Scouting	Redbank Scout Jamboree 4301, Qld

1983

   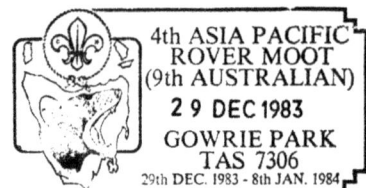

Date	Event	Location
22 – 23 Jan 1983	Annual Stamp Fair	Warrnambool 3280, Vic
26 Jan 1983	Australia Day Family Festival	Nunawading 3131, Vic
26 Jan 1983	Birthplace of Champion Blade Shearer Jackie Howe	Warwick 4370, Qld
26 Jan 1983	Dorothea Mackellar Memorial	Gunnedah 2380, NSW
29 – 31 Jan 1983	Australia Day Stamp Fair	Sydney 2000, NSW
29 – 31 Jan 1983	Australia Day Pageant	Melbourne 3000, Vic
7 – 20 Feb 1983	10th Saltwater River Festival	Footscray 3011, Vic
9 Feb 1983	Try Youth and Community Services Centenary	South Yarra 3141, Vic
14 – 25 Feb 1983	6th Conference of Commonwealth Postal Administrations	Melbourne 3000, Vic
22 Feb 1983	75th Anniversary of Scouting – Lord Baden-Powell Stamp Exhibition	Elsternwick 3185, Vic
28 Feb 1983	Centenary of Local Government, Parkes	Parkes 2870, NSW
28 Feb – 14 Mar 1983	Moomba Festival	Melbourne 3000, Vic
1 – 4 Mar 1983	Victorian Urban Fire Brigade Demonstration	Ballarat 3350, Vic
1 – 31 Mar 1983	Salvation Army Tasmanian Centenary	Launceston 7250, Tas
4 – 11 Mar 1983	1983 International 505 World Championships	Brighton 5048, SA
9 Mar 1983	Commonwealth Day	Corowa 2646, NSW
12 Mar 1983	40th Anniversary of Formation of Australian Army Catering Corps	Milpo Puckapunyal 3662, Vic
14 Mar 1983	Centenary of Adelaide Hills Railway	Aldgate 5154, SA
19 Mar 1983 •	18th St. Patrick's Day Race Meeting	Broken Hill 2880, NSW
19 – 20 Mar 1983	Red Earth Festival	Mooroolbark 3138, Vic
24 Mar 1983	Royal Visit	Canberra 2601, ACT
25 Mar – 5 Apr 1983	Royal Easter Show	Sydney 2000, NSW
26 Mar 1983	Chinchilla School Centenary	Chinchilla 4413, Qld
31 Mar 1983	Commemoration of 4th / 19th Prince of Wales Light Horse Regiment	Milpo Puckapunyal 3662, Vic
1 Apr 1983	Katherine Post Office Centenary	Katherine 5780, NT
1 – 4 Apr 1983	Gemboree '83	Broken Hill 2250, NSW

Date	Event	Location
7 Apr 1983	Rats of Tobruk World Reunion	Gosford 2250, NSW
11 – 16 Apr 1983	50th Anniversary Exhibition – Grace Bros Parramatta Westfield	Westfield 2150, NSW
12 Apr 1983	Opening of Canberra GPO – Australia Post Philatelic Exhibition	Canberra 2600, ACT
16 Apr 1983	Scout Family Fair	Melbourne 3000, Vic
17 – 23 Apr 1983	Lions International Multiple District 201 31st Convention	Mt. Gambier 5290, SA
20 Apr 1983	Birthday of Queen Elizabeth II	Elizabeth 5112, SA
30 Apr – 1 May 1983	The May Festival.	Camberwell 3124, Vic
30 Apr – 1 May 1983	South Australian Philatelic Association 10th Annual Congress	Port Pirie 5540, SA
14 May 1983	Kernewek Lowender (Cornish Festival)	Kadina 5554, SA
18 May 1983	World Communications Year 1983	Sydney 2000, NSW
25 May 1983	Centenary of Agricultural Colleges	Roseworthy 5371, SA
25 May 1983	Centenary of Agricultural Colleges	Richmond 2753, NSW
31 May 1983	World Communications Year "Tin Can Mail".	Rottnest 6161, WA
4 Jun 1983	Presentation of Banner to Royal Australian Corps of Transport	Milpo Puckapunyal 3662, Vic
8 Jun 1983	50th Anniversary of Australian Jaycees	Canberra 2600, ACT
8 Jun 1983 •	50th Anniversary of Australian Jaycees	Perth 6000, WA
8 – 11 Jun 1983	St. John Ambulance Centenary	Miranda Shopping Fair 2228, NSW
11 Jun 1983	Centenary of Completion of Wodonga-Albury Rail Link	Albury 2640, NSW
14 Jun 1983	Centenary of Completion of Melbourne-Sydney Rail Link	Melbourne 3000, Vic
10 Jul 1983	125th Anniversary of Australian Rules Football	Melbourne 3000, Vic
1 Aug 1983	Birthday Commemoration of 12th / 16th Hunter River Lancers RAAC	Milpo Puckapunyal 3662, Vic
3 – 6 Aug 1983	Folklore – "The Sentimental Bloke"	Miranda Shopping Fair 2228, NSW
3 – 12 Aug 1983	Brisbane Exhibition	Brisbane 4000, Qld
7 Aug 1983	City to Surf Fitness Run	Sydney 2000, NSW
8 – 12 Aug 1983	Municipality of Concord Centenary	Concord 2137, NSW
9 – 11 Aug 1983	Yorke Peninsula Field Days	Kadina 5554, SA
12 Aug 1983	STAMPEX '86.	Victor Harbour 5211, SA
15 – 19 Aug 1983	Solar World Congress	University Crawley 6009, WA
17 – 24 Aug 1983	4th International Congress of Plant Pathology	Melbourne University 3052, Vic
22 Aug 1983	World Veterinary Day	Perth 6000, WA
22 – 26 Aug 1983	22nd World Veterinary Congress	Perth 6000, WA
23 – 25 Aug 1983	Ag-quip Agriculture Exhibition	Gunnedah 2380, NSW
26 Aug 1983	Centenary of Dominican Sisters	North Adelaide 5006, SA
31 Aug 1983	Alice Springs Golden Jubilee	Alice Springs 5750, NT
2 – 19 Sep 1983	Royal Adelaide Show	Wayville 5034, SA
5 Sep 1983	Broken Hill Centenary	Broken Hill 2880, NSW
7 Sep 1983	C.J. Dennis Birth Centenary	Auburn 5461, SA
15 Sep 1983	English Speaking Union World Members' Conference	Melbourne 3000, Vic
15 – 24 Sep 1983	Royal Melbourne Show	Ascot Vale 3032, Vic
16 Sep – 2 Oct 1983	Warana Festival	Brisbane 4000, Qld
20 – 22 Sep 1983	Henty Field Days	Henty 2658, Vic
23 Sep – 4 Oct 1983	Lilac Festival and Free Flight Championships	Goulburn 2580, NSW
25 Sep – 1 Oct 1983	Queensland Philatelic Exhibition	Brisbane 4000, Qld
26 Sep 1983	Diamond Jubilee of GPO Perth	Perth 6000, WA
26 Sep 1983	Explorers of Australia – Sir Paul Strzelecki	Cooma 2630, NSW
26 – 30 Sep 1983	World Communications Year	Melbourne 3000, Vic
26 Sep – 1 Oct 1983 •	Explorers of Australia National Stamp Week Exhibition	Carlingford Shopping Centre 2118, NSW
26 Sep – 1 Oct 1983	Australian Photographic Society Apscon 83 Convention	Hobart 7000, Tas
26 Sep – 2 Oct 1983	National Stamp Week 1983	[8 capital cities]
27 Sep 1983	America's Cup Victory	Perth 6000, WA
29 Sep 1983	Nyngan Centenary.	Nyngan 2825, NSW
30 Sep – 8 Oct 1983	Perth Royal Show	Claremont 6010, WA
1 – 2 Oct 1983	Stamp Fair	Adelaide 5000, SA
1 – 3 Oct 1983	ASDA GPO Stamp Fair	Sydney 2000, NSW
3 Oct 1983	Commemoration of 10th Light Horse Regiment RAAC	Milpo Puckapunyal 3662, Vic
4 Oct 1983	200 Years Man in Flight	Bathurst 2795, NSW
4 Oct 1983	Hot Air Ballooning 200th Anniversary	Sydney 2000, NSW
4 – 6 Oct 1983	Elmore and District Machinery Field Days	Elmore 3558, Vic
4 – 7 Oct 1983	Boys Brigade World Centenary	Parramatta Westfield 2150, NSW
4 – 14 Oct 1983	17th World Road Congress	Sydney 2000, NSW
19 Oct 1983	150th Anniversary of Birth of Adam Lindsay Gordon	Mt. Gambier 5290, SA
19 – 22 Oct 1983	Royal Agricultural Show	Glenorchy 7010, Tas
24 – 30 Oct 1983	Legacy in Australia Diamond Jubilee	Hobart 7000, Tas
28 Oct – 5 Nov 1983	Stirling District Council Centenary	Stirling 5152, SA

Date	Event	Location
29 Oct 1983	150th Anniversary of Oatley	Oatley 2223, NSW
29 Oct – 5 Nov 1983	Hobart Fire Brigade Centenary	Hobart 7000, Tas
1 Nov 1983	Melbourne Cup	Flemington 3031, Vic
9 Nov 1983	Commemoration of 8th / 13th Victorian Mounted Rifles RAAC	Milpo Puckapunyal 3662, Vic
14 – 17 Nov 1983	Australian National Field Days	Orange 2800, NSW
18 Nov 1983	75th Anniversary of Birth of Sir Donald Bradman	Cootamundra 2590, NSW
18 Nov 1983	Southern Cross Air Race[2]	Bathurst 2795, NSW
23 Nov 1983	Commemoration of 3rd / 9th South Australian Mounted Rifles RAAC	Milpo Puckapunyal 3662, Vic
24 Nov 1983	Official Opening of Post Office Square Brisbane	Brisbane 4000, Qld
5 Dec 1983	Birth Centenary of Katherine Susannah Prichard	Claremont 6010, WA
27 Dec 1983	Glenelg Commemoration Day Sports Association	Glenelg 5045, SA
29 Dec 1983 – 8 Jan 1984 •	4th Asia Pacific Rover Moot (9th Australian)	Gowrie Park 7306, Tas
30 Dec 1983 – 10 Jan 1984	The Boys' Brigade Centenary Camp	Canberra 2600, ACT

1984

Date	Event	Location
26 Jan 1984	Pioneer Life – Australia Day	Armadale 6112, WA
28 – 30 Jan 1984	Australia Day	Melbourne 3000, Vic
31 Jan 1984	United Trades and Labour Council of South Australia Centenary	Adelaide 5000, SA
13 Feb 1984	Centenary of the Invention of the Stripper Harvester	Raywood 3570, Vic
23 Feb 1984 •	Opening of Bowen Bridge	Hobart 7000, Tas
24 Feb 1984	STAMPEX '86	Port Lincoln 5606, SA
2 – 12 Mar 1984	Moomba Festival	Melbourne 3000, Vic
10 – 11 Mar 1984	3rd National Philatelic Convention	Canberra 2601, ACT
18 – 25 Mar 1984	Golden Jubilee of Sporting Car Club of South Australia	Adelaide 5000, SA
7 Apr 1984	19th St. Patrick's Day Race Meeting	Broken Hill 2880, NSW
13 – 21 Apr 1984	Royal Easter Show	Sydney Showground 2021, NSW
18 Apr 1984	Birthday of Queen Elizabeth II	Elizabeth 5112, SA
21 Apr 1984	20th Gemboree	Mt. Isa 4825, Qld
19 – 26 May 1984	WAPEX '84	Perth 6000, WA
23 May 1984	Maiden Voyage of *Thermopylae* 1868	Williamstown 3016, Vic
2 Jun 1984	Inaugural Airmail Flight Port Headland-Bali	Port Headland 6721, WA
6 Jun 1984	Centenary of Regional Art Galleries	Ballarat 3350, Vic
6 – 8 Jun 1984	Young Artist Exhibition – W.A. Week	Cannington 6107, WA
15 Jun 1984	Opening of Australian National Rail Passenger Terminal	Adelaide 5000, SA
23 – 28 Jun 1984	47th International Convention of Zonta International	Sydney 2000, NSW
30 Jun 1984	150th Anniversary of Founding of South Australian Company	Adelaide 5000, SA
16 Jul 1984	16th Congress of International Association of Medical Laboratory Technologists	Perth 6000, WA
25 Jul 1984	Golden "I" Tourist Award	Kununurra 6743, WA
29 Jul 1984 •	South Australian Philatelic Association 11th Annual Congress	Eastwood 5063, SA
4 – 13 Aug 1984	12th International Cartographic Conference	Perth 6000, WA
6 Aug 1984	Centenary of Coastal Pilot Services	Perth 6000, WA
8 – 18 Aug 1984	Brisbane Exhibition	Brisbane 4000, Qld
13 Aug 1984	Official Opening of Sorell Post Office	Sorell 7172, Tas

---

2   The 18 November 1983 Southern Cross Air Race postmark is the same as 4 October Hot Air Ballooning cancel.

Date	Event	Location
26 – 31 Aug 1984 •	Australian Road Research Board 12th Conference	Sandy Bay 7005, Tas
27 Aug – 2 Sep 1984	Girl Guides Colonial Muster	Silverdale 2750, NSW
31 Aug – 8 Sep 1984	Royal Adelaide Show	Wayville 5034, SA
18 Sep 1984	175th Anniversary of Postal Services Mail Re-enactment	Fremantle 6160, WA
18 Sep 1984	175th Anniversary of Postal Services Mail Re-enactment	Perth 6000, WA
20 – 29 Sep 1984	Royal Melbourne Show	Ascot Vale 3032, Vic
21 – 30 Sep 1984 •	AUSIPEX '84	Melbourne 3000, Vic
22 Sep 1984	Centenary of Alpha	Alpha 4724, Qld
27 Sep – 14 Oct 1984	Warana Festival	Brisbane 4000, Qld
29 Sep – 6 Oct 1984	Perth Royal Show	Claremont 6010, WA
3 Oct 1984 •	50th Anniversary of Perth-Daly Waters Airmail Service	Perth 6000, WA
21 – 27 Oct 1984	22nd International Congress of Actuaries	Sydney 2000, NSW
22 Oct 1984	Completion of Victorian Arts Centre	Melbourne 3000, Vic
31 Oct 1984	St Bartholomew's Church Commemoration	Norwood 5067, SA
3 Nov 1984	150th Anniversary of Wollongong	Wollongong 2500, NSW
3 – 4 Nov 1984	Christmas Stamp Fair	Adelaide 5000, Qld
6 Nov 1984	Melbourne Cup	Flemington 3031, Vic
19 Nov 1984	150th Anniversary of Victoria	[5 cities / towns]
28 Nov – 7 Dec 1984	Indian Ocean Festival	Perth 6000, WA
7 – 12 Dec 1984	Centenary of Test Cricket at Adelaide Oval	Adelaide 5000, SA
27 Dec 1984 – 5 Jan 1985	40th Anniversary of Sydney to Hobart Yacht Race	Hobart 7000, Tas
28 Dec 1984	Glenelg Commemoration Day Sports Association	Glenelg 5045, SA
29 Dec 1984 – 7 Jan 1984	Asia - Pacific Jamborella	Dandenong 3175, Vic

1985

Date	Event	Location
25 Jan 1985	Australia Day	Melbourne 3000, Vic
25 Jan 1985	Inaugural Australia Games	Melbourne 3000, Vic
25 Jan 1985	Birth Centenary of John Curtin	Creswick 3363, Vic
25 Jan 1985	Birth Centenary of John Curtin	Perth 6000, WA
26 – 28 Jan 1985 •	Australia Day Stamp Fair	Sydney 2000, NSW
13 Feb – 2 Mar 1985	5th Women's World Bowls Championship	Reservoir 3073, Vic
25 Feb 1985	QANTAS 50 Years of International Flying	Brisbane 4000, Qld
1 – 11 Mar 1985	Moomba Festival	Melbourne 3000, Vic
13 Mar 1985	Australian Council of Community Nursing Congress	Melbourne 3000, Vic
17 Mar 1985	75th Anniversary of First Powered Flight in Australia	Parafield Airport 5106, SA
20 Mar 1985	Bathurst Centennial City Celebrations	Bathurst 2795, NSW
23 Mar 1985 •	20th St. Patrick's Day Race Meeting	Broken Hill 2880, NSW
25 – 27 Mar 1985	International Electronic Mail Conference	Melbourne 3000, Vic
29 Mar – 9 Apr 1985	Royal Easter Show	Sydney Showground 2021, NSW
17 Apr 1985	Opening of Postal Museum	Adelaide 5000, SA
17 Apr 1985	50th Anniversary of Rotary Club of Unley	Unley 5061, SA
17 Apr 1985	75th Anniversary of Guiding in Australia	Melbourne 3000, Vic
22 Apr 1985	Birthday of Queen Elizabeth II	Elizabeth 5112, SA
28 Apr 1985	STAMPEX '86	Goolwa 5214, SA
8 Jun 1985	Mitchell Railway Centenary	Mitchell 4465, Qld
7 – 16 Aug 1985	Brisbane Exhibition	Brisbane 4000, Qld
12 Aug 1985	28th World Modern Pentathlon Championships	Melbourne 3000, Vic
18 Aug 1985	South Australian Philatelic Association 12th Annual Congress	Kadina 5554, Qld

19 Aug 1985	50th Anniversary of First Adelaide-Darwin Airmail	Adelaide 5000, SA
22 Aug 1985 •	50th Anniversary of First Darwin-Adelaide Airmail	Darwin 5790, NT
30 Aug – 7 Sep 1985	Royal Adelaide Show	Wayville 5034, SA
6 – 10 Sep 1985	Education Department Centenary Celebrations	Hobart 7000, Tas
16- 27 Sep 1985	Salvation Army Queensland Centenary	Brisbane 4000, Qld
18 Sep 1985	75 Years of Farming	Dalwallinu 6609, WA
19 – 28 Sep 1985	Royal Melbourne Show	Ascot Vale 3032, Vic
21 Sep 1985	Western Australian Football League Centenary	Subiaco East 6008, WA
27 Sep – 11 Oct 1985	Warana Festival	Brisbane 4000, Qld
30 Sep – 6 Oct 1985 •	SUNPEX '85	Fortitude Valley 4006, Qld
4 – 7 Oct 1985	Stamp Fair	Sydney 2000, NSW
18 – 20 Oct 1985	Stamp and Coin Show	Melbourne 3000, Vic
22 Oct 1985	Services to Deaf and Blind Children	North Hobart 7000, Tas
31 Oct – 3 Nov 1985	Australian Formula 1 Grand Prix	Adelaide 5000, SA
5 Nov 1985	Melbourne Cup	Flemington 3031, Vic
7 Nov 1985 •	Centenary of *Polly Woodside*	World Trade Centre 3005, Vic
11 Nov 1985	Centenary of Cable Trams	Melbourne 3000, Vic
12 Dec 1985	Centenary of Birth of Rev 'Tubby' Clayton	Maryborough 4650, Qld

1986

2 Jan 1986	South Australia Sesquicentenary	Adelaide 5000, SA
6 – 10 Jan 1986	Girl Guide International Camp	Brisbane 4000, Qld
24 Jan 1986	Introduction of ABC / AUSSAT Satellite Link	Frenchs Forest 2086, NSW
24 Jan – 19 Feb 1986	International 12 Metre World Fleet Racing Championships	Fremantle 6160, WA
24 – 27 Jan 1986	Australia Day Stamp Fair	Sydney 2000, NSW
24 Jan 1986 – 7 Jan 1987	150th Anniversary of Bunbury	Bunbury 6230, WA
19 Feb 1986	South Australian Coastal Mails Commemoration	Port Augusta 5700, SA
23 Feb 1986	South Australian Coastal Mails Commemoration	Wallaroo 5556, SA
28 Feb 1986	South Australian Coastal Mails Commemoration	Port Lincoln 5606, SA
28 Feb 1986	Moomba Festival	Melbourne 3000, Vic
2 Mar 1986	Official Opening Adelaide-O-Bahn Bus	Adelaide 5000, SA
4 Mar 1986	South Australian Coastal Mails Commemoration	Edithburgh 5583, SA
9 – 13 Mar 1986	Royal Visit to South Australia	Adelaide 5000, SA
10 Mar – 5 Jun 1986	150th Anniversary of South Australia – Jubilee Trade Train	TPO, SA
15 Mar 1986	Bullock Train Re-enactment	Naracoorte 5271, SA
15 – 16 Mar 1986	Red Earth Festival	Mooroolbark 3138, Vic
15 – 17 Mar 1986 •	4th National Philatelic Convention	Canberra 2600, ACT
19 Mar 1986	South Australian Coastal Mails Commemoration	Robe 5276, SA
21 – 23 Mar 1986	Stamp and Coin Show	Melbourne 3000, Vic
23 Mar 1986	Anniversary of Ross and Keith Smith Flight	Northfield 5085, SA
21 Mar – 1 Apr 1986	Royal Easter Show	Sydney Showground 2021, NSW
28 – 31 Mar 1986	Gemboree '86	Loxton 5333, SA
2 Apr 1986	Golden Jubilee of City of Warwick	Warwick 4370, Qld
3 & 9 Apr 1986	Halley's Comet	Comet 4702, Qld
9 Apr 1986	Halley's Comet	Alice Springs 5750, NT
18 Apr 1986	Re-enactment of Colonial Pony Mail Perth-Northam	Perth 6000, WA
21 Apr 1986	Birthday of Queen Elizabeth II	Elizabeth 5112, SA
27 Apr 1986	STAMPEX '86	Adelaide 5000, SA
3 May 1986 •	Re-enactment of Stage Coach Mail Mt Pleasant-Adelaide	Mt. Pleasant 5235, SA

Date	Event	Location
14 May 1986	Official Opening Gateway Bridge	Brisbane 4000, Qld
19 May 1986	Opening of Darwin's Performing Arts Centre	Darwin 5790, NT
20 May 1986	• Presentation of the Prince Philip Banner	Milpo Bandiana 3694, Vic
22 – 25 May 1986	6th World Three Day Event Championships	Gawler 5118, SA
24 – 25 May 1986	Murray River Ramble	Morgan 5320, SA
14 Jun 1986	Reintroduction of Horse Trams	Victor Harbour 5211, SA
10 Jul 1986	75th Anniversary of Royal Australian Navy	Hobart 7000, Tas
10 Jul 1986	75th Anniversary of Royal Australian Navy	[8 capital cities + Williamstown 3016, Vic]
14 Jul 1986	70th Anniversary of King Edward Memorial Hospital for Women	Subiaco 6008, WA
21 – 23 Jul 1986	Sheep and Woolcraft Show	Ascot Vale 3032, Vic
27 Jul 1986	150th Anniversary of Arrival of Duke of York	Kingscote 5223, SA
4 – 10 Aug 1986	• STAMPEX '86	Adelaide 5000, SA
10 Aug 1986	South Australian Philatelic Association 13th Annual Congress	Adelaide 5000, SA
25 – 29 Aug 1986	13th ARRB and 5th REAAA Combined Conference	Adelaide University 5000, SA
5 – 13 Sep 1986	Royal Adelaide Show	Wayville 5034, SA
18 Sep 1986	10th Australian Orchid Conference	Adelaide 5000, SA
18 – 27 Sep 1986	Royal Melbourne Show	Ascot Vale 3032, Vic
19 Sep 1986	Re-enactment of Gold Escort Service	Castlemaine 3450, Vic
19 Sep – 3 Oct 1986	Warana Festival	Brisbane 4000, Qld
26 Sep 1986	America's Cup Defence 1986/87	Perth 6000, WA
26 Sep 1986	America's Cup Defence 1986/87	Fremantle 6160, WA
27 Sep – 4 Oct 1986	Perth Royal Show	Claremont 6010, WA
28 Sep 1986	World Planning and Housing Congress	Adelaide 5000, SA
29 Sep – 13 Oct 1986	75th Anniversary of Royal Australian Navy	Woolloomooloo 2011, NSW
1 Oct 1986	Opening of Riverside Complex	Brisbane 4000, Qld
7 Oct 1986	21st International Executive Council Meeting, International Police Association	Adelaide 5000, SA
18 Oct 1986	Re-enactment of Meeting of Baudin and Flinders	Victor Harbour 5211, SA
20 – 24 Oct 1986	WA Children's Week	Perth 6000, WA
23 – 26 Oct 1986	Australian Formula 1 Grand Prix	Adelaide 5000, SA
31 Oct – 2 Nov 1986	Stamp and Coin Show	Sydney Town Hall 2000, NSW
4 Nov 1986	Melbourne Cup 1986	Flemington 3031, Vic
17 Nov 1986	Pac Rim 86 Symposium	Perth 6000, WA
24 – 30 Nov 1986	• Papal Visit	[8 capital cities + Alice Springs 5750, NT]
28 Dec 1986	150th Anniversary of Proclamation Day	Glenelg 5045, SA

1987

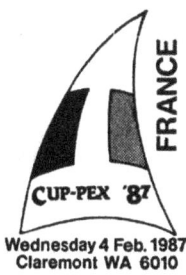   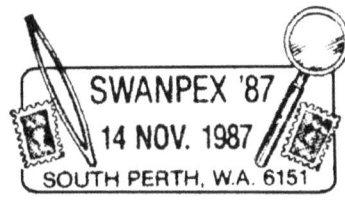 

Date	Event	Location
18 Jan 1987	The Adelaide-Melbourne Overland Centenary	Adelaide 5000, SA
28 Jan 1987	America's Cup Defence	Fremantle 6160, WA
28 Jan 1987	America's Cup Defence	Perth 6000, WA
31 Jan – 8 Feb 1987	• CUP-PEX '87	Claremont 6010, WA
4 Feb 1987	America's Cup Winner	Fremantle 6160, WA
11 Feb 1987	Centenary of Irrigation	Renmark 5341, SA
3 Mar 1987	100 Years of Friends' Society	North Hobart 7002, Tas
13 Mar 1987	Red Earth Festival	Mooroolbark 3138, Vic
19 Mar 1987	WA Garden Week '87	Wembley 6014, WA
20 – 22 Mar 1987	• Stamp and Coin Show	Melbourne 3000, Vic
21 – 28 Mar 1987	World Archery Championships	Adelaide 5000, SA
10 – 21 Apr 1987	Royal Easter Show	Sydney Showground 2021, NSW
21 Apr 1987	Birthday of Queen Elizabeth II	Elizabeth 5112, SA

1 May 1987	Montville Centenary	Montville 4560, Qld
8 May 1987	50th Anniversary of RAAF 23rd Squadron	Amberley 4305, Qld
13 May 1987	First Fleet Departure	Botany 2019, NSW
13 May 1987	First Fleet Departure	Sydney 2000, NSW
16 – 18 May 1987	Kernewek Lowender (Cornish Festival)	Kadina 5554, SA
23 – 24 May 1987	50th Anniversary of Woodville Philatelic Society	Woodville 5011, SA
29 May 1987	Centenary of Irrigation	Mildura 3500, Vic
31 – 31 May 1987	GEORGEPEX '87	Hurstville 2220, NSW
3 Jun 1987	First Fleet at Tenerife, Canary Islands	Sydney 2000, NSW
7 Jun 1987	South Australian Philatelic Association 14th Annual Congress	Renmark 5341, SA
28 Jun 1987	50th Anniversary of Amelia Earhart's Last Flight	Darwin 5790, NT
27 Jul 1987	Tweed Heads Centenary	Tweed Heads 2485, NSW
27 Jul 1987	Twinning of the Cities of Gold Coast and Netanya, Israel	Surfers Paradise 4217, Qld
6 Aug 1987	First Fleet at Rio de Janeiro, Brazil	Sydney 2000, NSW
19 Aug 1987	Achievements in Technology	Melbourne 3000, Vic
24 – 28 Aug 1987 •	57TH ANZAAS Conference	Townsville 4810, Qld
27 Aug 1987	Centenary of Queenscliff Post Office[3]	Queenscliff 3225, Vic
2 Sep 1987	25th Anniversary of the Australian Ballet	Flemington 3031, Vic
4 – 12 Sep 1987	Royal Adelaide Show	Wayville 5034, SA
17 – 26 Sep 1987	Royal Melbourne Show	Ascot Vale 3032, Vic
18 Sep 1987	80th Anniversary of Appointment of First District Nurse	Perth 6000, WA
18 Sep – 4 Oct 1987	Warana Festival	Brisbane 4000, Qld
19 – 27 Sep 1987	Centenary of Longreach	Longreach 4730, Qld
26 Sep 1987	Perth Royal Show	Claremont 6010, WA
29 Sep – 1 Oct 1987	Yorke Peninsula Field Days	Kadina 5554, SA
30 Sep 1987	Post Office Centenary, Bendigo	Bendigo 3550, Vic
3 – 4 Oct 1987	NORPEX '87	Newcastle 2300, NSW
13 Oct 1987	People of the First Fleet	Melbourne 3000, Vic
19 Oct 1987	Centenary of Cooktown Post Office	Cooktown 4871, Qld
23 Oct 1987	Centenary of Healesville Shire	Healesville 3777, Vic
26 Oct 1987	WA Children's Week	Perth 6000, WA
28 Oct 1987	Centenary of Nhill Post Office[4]	Nhill 3418, Vic
30 Oct – 1 Nov 1987	ASDA Stamp and Coin Fair	Brisbane 4000, Qld
6 – 8 Nov 1987	Sydney Stamp and Coin Show	Sydney 2000, NSW
12 – 15 Nov 1987	Australian Formula 1 Grand Prix	Adelaide 5000, SA
14 – 15 Nov 1987 •	SWANPEX '87	South Perth 6151, WA
23 Nov 1987	Centenary of Traralgon Post Office[5]	Traralgon 3844, Vic
28 Nov 1987	7th World Veterans' Games	Melbourne 3000, Vic
8 – 12 Dec 1987	Tall Ships Australia 1988	Fremantle 6160, WA
17 – 24 Dec 1987	Welcome to the First Fleet	Fremantle 6160, WA
22 – 26 Dec 1987	Tall Ships Australia 1988	Port Adelaide 5015, SA
24 Dec 1987	50th Performance of Carols by Candlelight	Melbourne 3000, Vic
29 Dec 1987 – 14 Jan 1988 •	Tall Ships Race	Hobart 7000, Tas
30 Dec 1987 – 2 Jan 1988	Tall Ships Australia 1988	Brisbane 4000, Qld
30 Dec 1987 – 9 Jan 1988	16th World Scouting Jamboree	Campbelltown 2560, NSW
31 Dec 1987 – 5 Jan 1988	Tall Ships Australia 1988	Melbourne 3000, Vic

1988

4 Jan – 30 Nov 1988	Expo '88	South Brisbane 4101, Qld
5 Jan 1988	300th Anniversary of William Dampier's Arrival to Australia	Derby 6728, WA
7 Jan 1988	50 Years of Broadcasting – Six Twelve 4QR	Brisbane 4000, Qld[6]
10 Jan 1988	Tall Ships Australia 1988	Hobart 7000, Tas
11 – 15 Jan 1988	International and Australian White Water Championships	Harvey 6220, WA
11 – 24 Jan 1988	Australian Open (Tennis)	Melbourne 3000, Vic
19 – 25 Jan 1988	Tall Ships Australia 1988	Sydney 2000, NSW
26 Jan 1988	Arrival of First Fleet	Sydney 2000, NSW

---

3 Promoted by Australia Post as a cachet (Stamp Bulletin 191, July 1987).
4 Promoted by Australia Post as a cachet (Stamp Bulletin 192, October 1987)
5 Promoted by Australia Post as a cachet (Stamp Bulletin 193, January 1988)
6 Venue not indicated on postmark.

Date	Event	Location
26 Jan 1988	Australia Day	Adelaide 5000, SA
28 Jan – 26 Feb 1988	*HMAV Bounty*	Sydney 2000, NSW
1 Feb 1988	Australian Bicentennial Exhibition	Mt Gambier 5290, SA
1 – 5 Feb 1988	Hobart Technical College Centenary	Hobart 7000, Tas
8 Feb 1988	14th Commonwealth Universities Congress	PO University Crawley 6009, WA
17 Feb 1988	75th Anniversary of University of Western Australia	Nedlands 6009, WA
20 Feb 1988	Australian Bicentennial Exhibition	Port Pirie 5540, SA
29 Feb 1988	Australian Bicentennial Exhibition	Adelaide 5000, SA
6 Mar 1988	Melbourne Welcomes the First Fleet	Melbourne 3000, Vic
12 Mar 1988	Australian Bicentennial Exhibition	Whyalla 5600, SA
14 – 18 Mar 1988	ICFTU 14th World Congress[7]	Melbourne 3000, Vic
17 Mar 1988	WA Garden Week	Wembley 6017, WA
17 Mar 1988	15th Anniversary of SLSA[8] Helicopter Rescue Service	No venue[9]
19 – 21 Mar 1988	5th National Philatelic Convention	Canberra 2601, ACT
24 Mar 1988	Portland Welcomes the First Fleet	Portland 3305, Vic
25 Mar 1988	Australian Bicentennial Exhibition	Kalgoorlie 6430, WA
25 Mar – 5 Apr 1988	Royal Easter Show	Sydney Showground 2021, NSW
26 Mar – 23 Jun 1988	Giant Pandas Visit	Parkville 3052, Vic
31 Mar 1988	Coach Mail Re-enactment, Bunbury-Greenbushes	Bunbury 6230, WA
1 – 4 Apr 1988	North Queensland Bicentennial Games	Cairns 4870, Qld
1 – 11 Apr 1988	First Fleet Re-enactment Voyage	Port Adelaide 2015, SA
5 Apr 1988	Australian Bicentennial Exhibition	Albany 6330, WA
8 – 10 Apr 1988 •	AEROPEX 88 – National Air Mail Exhibition	Adelaide 5000, SA
14 Apr 1988	Australian Bicentennial Exhibition	Bunbury 6230, WA
17 Apr 1988	Steamfest '88	TPO[10]
21 Apr 1988	Birthday of Queen Elizabeth II	Elizabeth 5112, SA
23 Apr 1988	Australian Bicentennial Exhibition	Perth 6000, WA
23 Apr 1988 •	Re-opening of Forrest Place	Perth 6000, WA
23 Apr – 1 May 1988	CSR Hinkler Bicentennial Air Race	Bundaberg 4670, Qld
26 Apr 1988	Granting of City Status, Burnie	Burnie 7320, Tas
28 Apr 1988	150th Anniversary of SA Police	Adelaide 5000, SA
29 Apr – 1 May 1988	Stamp and Coin Show	Melbourne 3000, Vic
30 Apr – 24 Oct 1988	Expo 88[11]	Brisbane 4000, Qld
4 May 1988	Bicentennial Stage Coach Run	Brisbane 4000, Qld
6 May 1988	Australian Bicentennial Exhibition	Geraldton 6530, WA
13 – 15 May 1988	GPO Stamp Fair	Sydney 2000, NSW
17 May 1988	Australian Bicentennial Exhibition	Port Hedland 6721, WA
29 May 1988	South Australian Philatelic Association 15th Annual Congress	Woodville 5011, SA
1 Jun 1988	Australian Bicentennial Exhibition	Darwin 0800, NT
14 Jun 1988	Australian Bicentennial Exhibition	Alice Springs 0870, NT
4 – 22 Jul 1988	Giant Pandas Visit to Taronga Zoo	Mosman 2088, NSW
21 Jul 1988	Opening of Sydney Monorail	Sydney 2000, NSW
29 Jul 1988	Bicentennial Stage Coach Run	Cairns 4870, Qld
30 Jul – 7 Aug 1988	SYDPEX 88	Sydney 2000, NSW
26 Aug 1988	Amamoor Country Music Muster	Gympie 4570, Qld
2 – 10 Sep 1988 •	Royal Adelaide Show	Wayville 5034, SA
3 Sep 1988	Opera in the Outback	Beltana via Leigh Creek 5730, NT
4 Sep 1988	Albert Shire Bicentennial Packhorse Mail Re-enactment	Nerang 4211, Qld
6 Sep 1988	Royal Adelaide Show	Wayville 5034, SA

---

7 ICFTU = International Confederation of Free Trade Unions
8 SLSA = Surf Life Saving Australia
9 No venue appears on this postmark but is likely to be Sydney 2000
10 Two postmarks were used, TPO Boyanup-Yarloop, and TPO Perth-Yarloop.
11 Appropriately, 88 postmarks were provided to mark this event.

9 – 18 Sep 1988	Warana Festival…………………………………………………	Brisbane 4000, Qld
12 – 16 Sep 1988	Girls Friendly Society Centenary …………………………………	Perth 6000, WA
24 Sep 1988	Royal Perth Show………………………………………………	Claremont Showgrounds 6010, WA
24 Sep – 6 Oct 1988	Bicentennial Re-enactment Goldfields Mail Trek ………………………	8 towns, WA
25 Sep 1988	Southpex 88……………………………………………………	Gosnells 6110, WA
1 Oct 1988	Bicentennial Naval Salute………………………………………	Sydney 2000, NSW
24 Oct 1988	WA Children's Week……………………………………………	Perth 6000, WA
28 – 30 Oct 1988	STAMPEX 88……………………………………………………	Adelaide 5000, SA
10 – 13 Nov 1988	• Australian Formula 1 Grand Prix…………………………………	Adelaide 5000, SA
11 – 13 Nov 1988	Sydney Stamp and Coin Show …………………………………	Sydney 2000, NSW
12 Nov 1988	Declaration of Rockingham as a City………………………………	Rockingham 6168, WA
18 Nov 1988	150th Anniversary of German Immigration ………………………	Klemzig 5087, SA
20 Nov 1988	Centenary of Edinvale…………………………………………	Pinjarra 6208, WA
25 – 27 Nov 1988	• ASDA Stamp and Coin Fair ……………………………………	Brisbane 4000, Qld
30 Dec 1988 – 10 Jan 1989	15th Australian Scout Jamboree …………………………………	Woodhouse 5152, SA

1989

 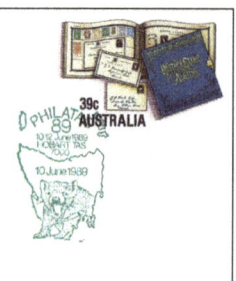  

25 Jan 1989	Australia Day …………………………………………………	Tenterfield 2372, NSW
13 Feb 1989	Announcing STAMPSHOW '89 …………………………………	Melbourne 3000, Vic
12 – 21 Mar 1989	Centenary of the United Grand Lodge of Victoria…………………	East Melbourne 3002, Vic
17 – 28 Mar 1989	Royal Easter Show……………………………………………	Sydney Showground 2021, NSW
23 Mar 1989	25th Anniversary Gemboree 89 …………………………………	Devonport 7301, Tas
28 Apr – 1 May 1989	Queensland Philatelic Council 89 Stamp Show ……………………	Wynnum Central 4178, Qld
13 – 15 May 1989	Kernewek Lowender (Cornish Festival)……………………………	Kadina 5554, SA
2 Jun 1989	60th Anniversary of First Air Mail Adelaide-Perth…………………	Adelaide 5000, SA
6 Jun 1989	60th Anniversary of First Air Mail Perth-Adelaide…………………	Perth 6000, WA
10 – 12 Jun 1989	• PHILATAS 89 Philatelic Convention……………………………	Hobart 7000, Tas
2 Jul 1989	South Australian Philatelic Association 16th Annual Congress ………	Mannum 5238, SA
3 Jul – 29 Sep 1989	50th Anniversary Nos. 10 and 11 Squadrons………………………	RAAF Base Edinburgh 5111, SA
18 Jul 1989	75th Anniversary of First Airmail Service Melbourne-Sydney ………	Melbourne Airport 3045, Vic
6 Aug 1989	70th Anniversary of First Air Mail Adelaide-Minlaton………………	Adelaide 5000, SA
6 Aug 1989	70th Anniversary of First Air Mail Minlaton-Adelaide………………	Minlaton 5575, SA
12 Aug 1989	150th Anniversary of Huonville[12] ………………………………	Huonville 7109, Tas
23 Aug 1989	Centenary of Townsville………………………………………	Townsville 4810, Qld
25 Aug 1989	Amamoor Country Music Muster………………………………	Gympie 4570, Qld
30 Aug 1989	Ashes Victory …………………………………………………	Mosman 2088, NSW
1 – 9 Sep 1989	150th Anniversary of Royal Adelaide Show ………………………	Wayville 5034, SA
8 Sep 1989	Centenary of Postal Services……………………………………	Katanning 6317, WA
8 – 24 Sep 1989	Warana Festival………………………………………………	Brisbane 4000, Qld
15 Sep 1989	St. John First Aid Centenary……………………………………	Brisbane 4000, Qld
19 Sep 1989	Turning on of the Natural Gas Pipeline……………………………	Karratha 6714, WA
26 – 28 Sep 1989	Yorke Peninsula Field Days ……………………………………	Kadina 5554, SA
2 Oct 1989	Australia Post Shop Official Opening……………………………	Brisbane 4000, Qld

---

12 To be confirmed.

11 Oct 1989	Last Tram Mail Re-enactment Trip	Sydney 2000, NSW
14 Oct 1989	Centenary of First Electric Tram Line Box Hill-Doncaster	Box Hill 3128, Vic
18 – 22 Oct 1989	Stampshow '89	Melbourne 3000, Vic
23 Oct 1989	WA Children's Week	Perth 6000, WA
2 – 5 Nov 1989	Australian Formula 1 Grand Prix	Adelaide 5000, SA
3 – 5 Nov 1989	Sydney Stamp and Coin Show	Sydney 2000, NSW
11 – 12 Nov 1989	SWANPEX '89	South Perth 6151, WA
18 Nov 1989	Opening of Bicentennial Conservatory at Botanic Gardens of Adelaide	Adelaide 5000, SA
24 Nov 1989	Arrival in Australia of Yachts Participating in Whitbread Round the World Race	Fremantle 6160, WA
20 Dec 1989	50th Anniversary of Radio Australia	Burwood 3125, Vic

1990

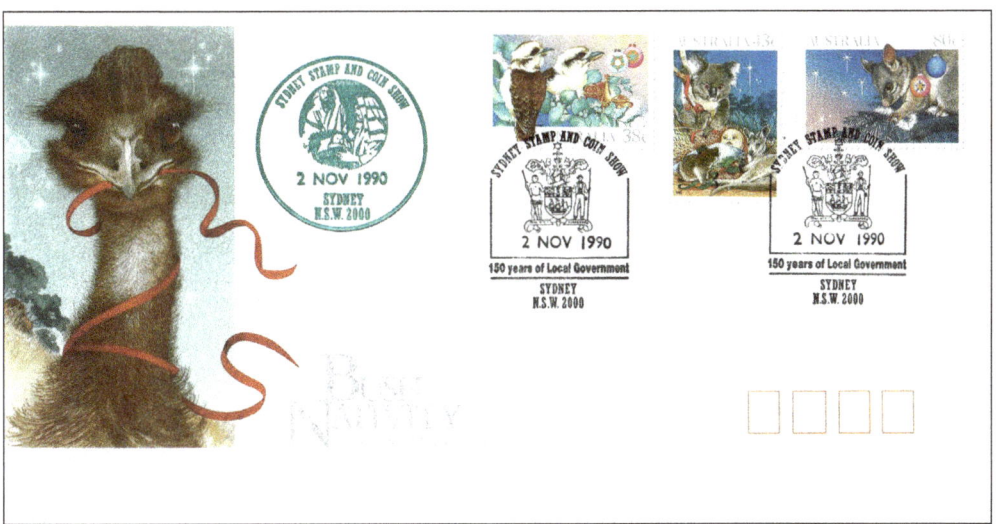

25 Jan 1990	125th Anniversary of *CSS Shenandoah*	Williamstown 3016, Vic
11 Feb 1990	Centenary of Devonport	Devonport 7310, Tas
9 – 10 Mar 1990	Woolorama	Wagin 6315, WA
16 – 19 Mar 1990	AUSTAMP 90 National Philatelic Exhibition	Canberra 2601, ACT
19 Mar 1990	10th Anniversary of State Rescue Helicopter Service	Adelaide 5000, SA
6 – 17 Apr 1990	Royal Easter Show	Sydney Showgrounds 2021, NSW
13 Apr 1990	International Facetors' Challenge	Bundaberg 4670, Qld
13 – 16 Apr 1990	4th North Queensland Games	Mackay 4740, Qld
20 Apr 1990	ANZAC Tradition	Canberra 2601, ACT
25 Apr 1990	Golden Anniversary of Empire Air Training Scheme	Perth 6000, WA
4 May 1990	Maiden Voyage of *Aurora Australis* to the Southern Ocean	Hobart 7000, 7000
7 – 11 May 1990	5th International Chrysanthemum Conference	Booragoon 6154, WA
16 May 1990	First Peel and Stick Stamp	Gumly Gumly 2652, NSW
17 May 1990	Centenary of Baillie Henderson Hospital	Toowoomba 4350, Qld
23 May 1990	Centenary of Flemington Post Office	Flemington 3031, Vic
9 – 11 Jun 1990	Brisbane Stamp Show 90	Brisbane 4000, Qld
26 Jun 1990	Masonic Centenary	Hobart 7000, Tas
6 Jul 1990	50th Anniversary of Story Bridge	Brisbane 4000, Qld
4 Aug 1990	Avon Descent 1990	Northam 6401, WA
15 Aug 1990	Centenary of Responsible Government in WA	Perth 6000, WA
24 Aug 1990	Amamoor Country Music Muster	Gympie 4570, Qld
29 – 30 Aug 1990	Dowerin Machinery Days	Dowerin 6461, WA
14 – 30 Sep 1990	Warana Festival	Brisbane 4000, Qld
18 Sep 1990	Melbourne Bid for 1996 Olympic Games	Melbourne 3000, Vic
29 Sep 1990	Perth Royal Show	Claremont Showgrounds 6010, WA
30 Sep 1990	South Australian Philatelic Association 17th Annual Congress	Goodwood 5034, SA
4 Oct 1990	Stagecoach Mail Re-enactment Gawler-Adelaide	Gawler 5118, SA

6 Oct 1990	Colonial George Street Festival	Brisbane 4000, Qld
8 Oct 1990	National Arts Week	Perth 6000, WA
20 Oct 1990	WA Children's Week	Perth 6000, WA
26 Oct 1990	Centenary of the Salvation Army Devonport Corps	Devonport 7310, Tas
1 – 4 Nov 1990	Australian Formula 1 Grand Prix	Adelaide 5000, SA
2 – 4 Nov 1990 •	Sydney Stamp and Coin Show	Sydney 2000, NSW
8 – 18 Nov 1990	Fremantle Italian Festival	Fremantle 6160, WA
10 – 11 Nov 1990	SWANPEX '90	South Perth 6151, WA
26 Nov – 5 Dec 1990	General Assembly of IUCNNR[13]	Burswood 6000, WA
7 Dec 1990	150th Anniversary of the MUIOOF[14]	Melbourne 3000, Vic
24 Dec 1990	58th Senior Sports Carnival of the Queensland Maccabi[15]	Southport 4215, Qld

1991

2 – 12 Jan 1991	8th Australian Scout Venture	Launceston 7250, Tas
3 – 13 Jan 1991	6th World Swimming Championships	Perth 6000, WA
12 Jan 1991	Centenary of Launceston Post Office	Launceston 7250, Tas
26 Jan 1991	Australia Day	5 capital cities
25 Feb 1991	Edward John Eyre Journey Re-enactment	Fowler's Bay 5690, SA
2 Mar 1991	Opening of the Golden Dragon Museum	Bendigo 3550, Vic
8 – 9 Mar 1991	Woolorama	Wagin 6315, WA
9 – 10 Mar 1991	Rainbow Coast Air Show	Albany 6330, WA
15 – 17 Mar 1991	Indy Car Grand Prix	Surfers Paradise 4217, Qld
17 Mar 1991	Edward John Eyre Journey Re-enactment	Norseman 6443, WA
18 Mar 1991	Board of Works Melbourne Centenary	Melbourne 3000, Vic
19 Mar 1991	Centenary of Nudgee College	Nundah 4012, Qld
22 Mar – 2 Apr 1991	Royal Easter Show	Sydney Showground 2021, NSW
28 Mar 1991	Apex Diamond Jubilee	Perth 6000, WA
20 – 27 Apr 1991	4th Girls World Softball Championship	West Beach 5024, SA
26 Apr 1991	Edward John Eyre Journey Re-enactment	Norseman 6443, WA
4 May 1991	Centenary of Great Shearers' Strike	Barcaldine 4725, Qld
18 – 20 May 1991	Kernewek Lowender (Cornish Festival)	Kadina 5554, SA
18 – 25 May 1991	Arafura Sports Festival	Darwin 0800, NT
21 May 1991	Centenary of National Women's Christian Temperance Union	Adelaide 5000, SA
27 – 31 May 1991	International Golden Oldies Rugby Union Festival	Perth 6000, WA
6 Jun 1991	75th Anniversary of Returned Services League	Melbourne 3000, Vic
8 – 10 Jun 1991	Queensland Stamp Show 1991	Brisbane 4000, Qld
8 – 10 Jun 1991 •	Launceston Stamp Show 1991	Launceston 7250, Tas
17 – 21 Jun 1991	74th Lions International Convention	Brisbane 4000, Qld
19 Jun 1991	Edward John Eyre Journey Re-enactment	Esperance 6450, WA
29 – 30 Jun 1991	Petersham Giant Stamp and Coin Fair	Petersham 2049, NSW
5 Jul 1991	75th Anniversary of King Edward Memorial Hospital for Women	Subiaco 6008, WA
19 – 21 Jul 1991	Stampshow Melbourne '91	Melbourne 3000, Vic
25 Jul 1991	Centenary of Dunolly Post Office	Dunolly 3472, Vic
13 – 19 Sep 1991	Warana Festival	Brisbane 4000, Qld
24 – 26 Sep 1991	Yorke Peninsula Field Days	Kadina 5554, SA
27 – 29 Sep 1991	Queensland Stamp Show '91½	Brisbane 4000, Qld
28 Sep 1991	Perth Royal Show	Claremont 6010, WA

---

13 IUCNNR = International Union for the Conservation of Nature and Natural Resources
14 MUIOOF = Manchester Unity Independent Order of Odd Fellows.
15 To be confirmed.

4 Oct 1991		World Animal Day	7 towns/cities
5 Oct 1991		Colonial George Street Festival	Brisbane 4000, Qld
5 – 6 Oct 1991		NORPEX '91	Newcastle 2300, NSW
10 Oct 1991	•	70th Anniversary of First Airmail Alice Springs-Adelaide	Alice Springs 0870, NT
11 – 13 Oct 1991		STAMPEX '91	Adelaide 5000, SA
19 – 27 Oct 1991		WA Children's Week	Perth 6000, WA
31 Oct – 3 Nov 1991	•	Australian Formula 1 Grand Prix	Adelaide 5000, SA
2 – 3 Nov 1991		SWANPEX '91	Fremantle 6160, WA
25 – 29 Nov 1991		4th Asia-Pacific Vibration Conference	Monash University 3168, Vic
30 Nov 1991		Summer on the Harbour	Darling Harbour 2000, NSW
5 Dec 1991		70th Anniversary of First Regular Airmail Perth-Geraldton	Perth 6000, WA

1992

3 Jan 1992		50th Anniversary of Uncle Bob's Club	Parkville 3052, Vic
3 – 13 Jan 1992		Veterans' World Cup Orienteering	St Helens 7216, Tas
3 – 12 Jan 1992	•	16th Australian Scout Jamboree	Ballarat 3350, Vic
17 – 23 Jan 1992		Great Guide Walkabout	Yarra Junction 3797, Vic
26 Jan 1992		Australia Day	Darling Harbour 2000, NSW
26 Jan 1992		Lions International Convention	Carnarvon 6701, WA
13 Feb 1992		Opening of National Philatelic Centre	Melbourne 3000, Vic
17 Feb 1992		75th Anniversary of First Airmail Mt Gambier-Melbourne	Mt Gambier 5290, SA
22 Feb 1992		10th Anniversary Penny Farthing Championships	Evandale 7212, Tas
3 Mar 1992		50th Anniversary of First Air Raids on Broome	Broome 6725, WA
6 – 7 Mar 1992		Woolorama	Wagin 6315, WA
8 Mar 1992		40th Anniversary of Ringwood Philatelic Society	Ringwood 3134, Vic
8 Mar 1992		25th Anniversary of Hungarian Philatelic Society	Ringwood 3134, Vic
11 Mar 1992	•	Centenary of Collingwood Football Club	Collingwood 3066, Vic
14 – 16 Mar 1992		7th National Philatelic Convention	Canberra 2601, ACT
19 – 22 Mar 1992		Daikyo Indy Car Grand Prix	Surfers Paradise 4217, Qld
25 Mar 1992		Cricket World Cup Final	East Melbourne 3002, Vic
30 Mar 1992		Commissioning of *HMAS Arunta*	HMAS Cerberus 3920, Vic
31 Mar 1992		Centenary of Mudgeeraba State School	Mudgeeraba 4213, Qld
2 – 3 Apr 1992		Rotary District 9500 Conference	Port Lincoln 5606, SA
7 May 1992		50th Anniversary of Battle of the Coral Sea	Bowen 4805, Qld
9 May 1992		Centenary of Cue	Cue 6640, WA
4 – 8 Jun 1992		National Stamp Show	Brisbane 4000, Qld
7 Jun 1992		70th Anniversary of First Scheduled Air Service Geraldton-Derby	Derby 6728, WA
27 Jun 1992		55th Anniversary of Woodville Philatelic Society	Woodville 5011, SA
27 Jun 1992		Victorian Philatelic Association Congress	Frankston 3199, Vic
27 Jun 1992		End of an Era Reunion	Longreach 4730, Qld
1 Jul 1992		Sesquicentenary of Gold Coast	Surfers Paradise 4217, Qld
25 Jul 1992	•	Centenary of Devonport Post Office	Devonport 7310, Tas
10 Aug 1992		Centenary of Royal Philatelic Society of Victoria	South Yarra 3141, Vic
12 Aug 1992		150th Anniversary of City of Melbourne	Melbourne 3000, Vic
24 Aug 1992		Centenary of Pharmaceutical Society of Western Australia	Subiaco 6008, WA
5 – 6 Sep 1992		World Motocross Championships	Manjimup 6258, WA
18 Sep 1992		150th Anniversary of St Marks Old Picton Church	Bunbury 6230, WA
19 – 20 Sep 1992	•	PEELPEX '92	Tamworth 2340, NSW

21 & 27 Sep 1992	Brisbane Broncos – Rugby League Winfield Cup	Brisbane 4000, Qld
25 Sep – 4 Oct 1992	Warana Festival	Brisbane 4000, Qld
3 Oct 1992	Colonial George Street Festival	Brisbane 4000, Qld
10 – 11 Oct 1992	South Australian Philatelic Association 18th Annual Congress	Unley 5061, SA
15 Oct 1992	Centenary of Sheffield Shield Cricket	6 capital cities
21 – 25 Oct 1992	Australian International Air Show and Aerospace Exp.	Lara 3212, Vic
23 – 25 Oct 1992	Brisbane Stamp and Coin Show '92	Brisbane 4000, Qld
30 Oct 1992	Sea World 21st Anniversary	Surfers Paradise 4217, Qld
31 Oct – 1 Nov 1992	SWANPEX 92	Fremantle 6160, WA
2 – 3 Nov 1992	70th Anniversary of Qantas First Airmail and Scheduled Passenger Service	5 towns, Qld
4 – 8 Nov 1992	Australian Formula 1 Grand Prix	Adelaide 5000, SA
6 – 8 Nov 1992	Sydney Stamp and Coin Show	Sydney 2000, NSW
8 Nov 1992	10th Anniversary of Victorian Arts Festival	Melbourne 3000, Vic
18 Nov 1992	Genevieve 500 Veteran and Vintage Car Race	Albany 6330, WA
23 Nov 1992	75th Anniversary of First Adelaide-Gawler Airmail	Adelaide 5000, SA
23 Nov 1992	75th Anniversary of First Gawler-Adelaide Airmail	Gawler 5118, SA
1 Dec 1992	150th Anniversary of Postal Services in Busselton	Busselton 6280, WA
3 Dec 1992 •	350th Anniversary of Abel Tasman's Landing in Tasmania	Dunalley 7177, Tas
4 Dec 1992	5th Anniversary of Cobb & Co. Museum	Toowoomba 4350, Qld
8 Dec 1992	Centenary of Birth of Bert Hinkler	Bundaberg 4670, Qld
18 Dec 1992	Centenary of Sheffield Shield Cricket Match Between SA and NSW	Adelaide 5000, SA

1993

20 Feb 1993	150th Anniversary of St John's School, Richmond	Richmond 7025, Tas
5 – 6 Mar 1993	21st Anniversary of Woolorama	Wagin 6315, WA
18 – 21 Mar 1993	Australian FAI Indy Car Grand Prix	Surfers Paradise 4217, Qld
7 Apr – 31 Aug 1993	Centaur Memorial Unveiling	Tweed Heads 2485, NSW
15 Apr 1993	Inter Dominion Pacing Championship	Albion 4010, Qld
5 – 17 May 1993	Kernewek Lowender (Cornish Festival)	Kadina 5554, SA
22 – 26 May 1993	Rotary International Convention	Melbourne 3000, Vic
6 Jun 1993	Queensland Day	Brisbane 4000, Qld
10 Jun 1993	Centenary of Kalgoorlie-Boulder	Kalgoorlie 6430, WA
12 – 14 Jun 1993	Queensland Stamp Show '93	Brisbane 4000, Qld
19 Jul 1993	Restoration of GPO Perth	Perth 6000, WA
21 – 22 Aug 1993	South Australian Philatelic Council[16] 19th Annual Congress	Noarlunga Centre 5168, SA
28 Aug 1993	Launch of Collins Class Submarine	Port Adelaide 5015, SA
19 Sep 1993	21st Anniversary of City-Bay Fun Run	Glenelg 5045, SA
22 – 26 Sep 1993	WAPEX '93 Gold Centenary Stamp Exhibition	Fremantle 6160, WA
28 – 30 Sep 1993	Yorke Peninsula Field Days	Kadina 5554, SA
1 – 31 Oct 1993	Stamp Collecting Month	Melbourne 3000, Vic
1 – 31 Oct 1993	Stamp Collecting Month	Sydney 2000, NSW
1 – 31 Oct 1993 •	Stamp Collecting Month	Brisbane 4000, Qld

---

16 For earlier Congresses, Philatelic Council was referred to as Philatelic Association.

Date	Event	Location
2 Oct 1993	Colonial George Street Festival	Brisbane 4000, Qld
10 Oct 1993	40th Victorian Philatelic Council Congress	Ballarat 3350, Vic
15 – 17 Oct 1993	Sydney Stamp and Coin Fair	Sydney South 2000, NSW
21 – 21 Oct 1993	Riverland Gadget and Field Days	Barmera 5345, SA
20 – 23 Oct 1993	Royal Hobart Show	Glenorchy 7010, Tas
22 – 24 Oct 1993	Brisbane Stamp Show '93	Brisbane 4000, Qld
28 Oct 1993	150th Anniversary of Postal Services to Port Fairy	Port Fairy 3284, Vic
2 Nov 1993	150th Anniversary of City of Seymour	Seymour 3660, Vic
4 – 7 Nov 1993	Australian Formula 1 Grand Prix	Adelaide 5000, SA
6 Nov 1993	Centenary of St Vincent's Hospital	Fitzroy 3065, Vic
11 Nov 1993	75th Anniversary of Armistice Day	Canberra 2601, ACT
9 Dec 1993	Whitbread Round-the-World Yacht Race	Fremantle 6160, WA
9 Dec 1993	Launch of Replica *HM Bark Endeavour*	Fremantle 6160, WA
30 Dec 1993 – 8 Jan 1994	Arura Rally	North Tamborine 4272, Qld

1994

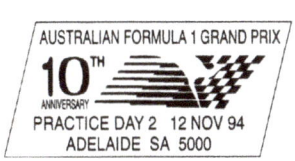    

Date	Event	Location
3 – 12 Jan 1994	1st Asia-Pacific / 9th Australian Venture	Capalaba 4157, Qld
20 Jan 1994	Asian-Pacific Life Saving Championships	Dandenong 3175, Vic
30 Jan – 3 Feb 1994	The Retailers Digest 1st Annual Convention and Exhibition	Broadbeach 4218, Qld
3 Feb 1994	7th World Veterans Table Tennis Championships[17]	Melbourne 3000, Vic
11 – 13 Feb 1994	Stamp and Coin Fair	Melbourne 3000, Vic
25 Feb 1994	50th Anniversary of First Platypus Breeding in Captivity	Healesville 3777, Vic
16 Mar 1994	Centenary of Naming of Lakes Entrance	Lakes Entrance 3909, Vic
19 – 21 Mar 1994	Canberra Stamp Show 94	Canberra 2600, ACT
2 – 3 Apr 1994	Newcastle '94	Newcastle 2300, NSW
19 – 24 Apr 1994	World Gymnastics Championships	Nundah 4012, Qld
22 – 27 Apr 1994	7th World Veterans Table Tennis Championships[18]	Melbourne 3000, Vic
9 May 1994	50th Anniversary of Australian Legion of Ex-servicemen and Women	Melbourne 3000, Vic
11 – 13 Jun 1994	Queensland Stamp and Coin Show	Brisbane 4000, Qld
11 – 13 Jun 1994	PHILATAS 94	Hobart 7000, Tas
16 – 17 Jul 1994	South Australian Philatelic Council 20th Annual Congress	Salisbury 5108, SA
26 – 29 Jul 1994	50th Anniversary of Ladies Silver Country Gold Meeting	Bordertown 5268, SA
28 Jul – 4 Aug 1994	25th South Pacific Forum	Brisbane 4000, Qld
5 – 7 Aug 1994	Stamp and Coin Show	Melbourne 3000, Vic
6 Aug 1994	75th Anniversary of First Airmail Adelaide-Minlaton	Adelaide 5000, SA
6 Aug 1994	75th Anniversary of First Airmail Minlaton-Adelaide	Minlaton 5575, SA
11 Aug 1994	Warana Festival	Brisbane 4000, Qld
18 Aug 1994	Official Opening of Parliament House, Darwin	Darwin 0800, NT
23 Aug 1994	Royal Flying Doctor Service – 60 Years in the Kimberley	Derby 6728, WA
30 Sep – 2 Oct 1994	Sydney Stamp and Coin Show	Sydney 2000, NSW
1 Oct 1994	Colonial George Street Festival	Brisbane 4000, Qld
1 – 15 Oct 1994	Stamp Collecting Month	Adelaide 5000, SA
2 Oct 1994	Victorian Philatelic Congress	Gardenvale 3185, Vic
15 Oct 1994	Menzies Centennial Celebrations	Menzies 6436, WA
19 – 26 Oct 1994	Royal Hobart Show	Glenorchy 7010, Tas
20 – 23 Oct 1994	Talk to the Animals Expo	Caulfield South 3162, Vic
21 – 23 Oct 1994	Brisbane Stamp and Coin Show	Brisbane 4000, Qld
22 Oct 1994	Zootober Stamp Fair	Salisbury 5108, SA

---

17 See also usage from 22 April 1994.
18 See also usage on 3 February 1994.

24 Oct 1994	Catalina Club International Reunion	Nedlands 6009, WA
27 – 30 Oct 1994	Stampshow '94	Melbourne 3000, Vic
29 Oct 1994	Zootober Stamp Fair	Morphett Vale 5162, SA
5 – 6 Nov 1994	Stamp Show '94	Fremantle 6160, WA
10 – 13 Nov 1994 •	10th Australian Formula 1 Grand Prix	Adelaide 5000, SA
18 – 20 Nov 1994 •	AEROPEX 94	Adelaide 5000, SA
8 Dec 1994 – 31 Dec 1995	Cyclone Tracy 20 Years	Darwin 0800, NT
11 Dec 1994 – 26 Dec 1994	Mary Rose Exhibition	Warrnambool 3280, Vic
20 Dec 1994	Opening of Healesville Sanctuary	Healesville 3777, Vic
26 Dec 1994	50th Anniversary of Sydney-Hobart Yacht Race	Sydney 2000, NSW
28 Dec 1994	50th Anniversary of Sydney-Hobart Yacht Race	Hobart 7000, Tas
28 Dec 1994 – 8 Jan 1995	15th Asia-Pacific / 17th Australian Scout Jamboree	Floreat 6014, WA

1995

12 Jan – 31 Dec 1995	Jubilee 150	Burra 5417, SA
14 – 15 Jan 1995	Schützenfest 1995 – German Festival	Adelaide 5000, SA
19 Jan 1995	Beatification of Mary Mackillop	Sydney 2000, NSW
10 – 12 Feb 1995	Stamp and Coin Fair	Melbourne 3000, Vic
12 Feb 1995	Centenary of Shire of Harvey Bay	Harvey Bay 6220, WA
6 Apr 1995	Centenary of Waltzing Matilda	Winton 4735, Qld
13 – 15 May 1995	Kernewek Lowender (Cornish Festival)	Kadina 5554, SA
10 – 12 Jun 1995	Queensland Stamp and Coin Show	Brisbane 4000, Qld
1 Jul 1995	25 Years of Service – Melbourne Airport	Melbourne Airport 3045, Vic
10 – 20 Aug 1995	VP50 Townsville Festival	Townsville 4810, Qld
12 – 13 Aug 1995	South Australian Philatelic Council 21st Annual Congress	Unley 5061, SA
24 – 29 Sep 1995	Australian Universities Games '95	Darwin 0800, NT
26 – 28 Sep 1995	Yorke Peninsula Field Days	Kadina 5554, SA
30 Sep 1995	Warana Festival	Brisbane 4000, Qld
5 – 14 Oct 1995	VicHealth 5th Australian Masters Games	Melbourne 3000, Vic
7 Oct 1995	Victorian Philatelic Congress	Glen Waverley 3160, Vic
8 Oct 1995	Salisbury Stamp Fair	Salisbury 5108, SA
14 – 15 Oct 1995	Adelaide Stamp and Collectibles Fair	Norwood 5067, SA
19 – 22 Oct 1995	Sydney Centrepoint 95 Stampshow	Sydney 2000, NSW
20 – 22 Oct 1995	Brisbane Stamp Show	Brisbane 4000, Qld
21 Oct 1995	Noarlunga Stamp Fair	Noarlunga Centre 5168, SA
21 Oct 1995	Renmark Rose Festival	Renmark 5341, SA
27 – 29 Oct 1995	Stamp and Coin Fair	Melbourne 3000, Vic
28 – 29 Oct 1995	Stamp Show 95 – SWANPEX	Claremont 6010, WA
1 Nov 1995	Royal Adelaide Show	Wayville 5034, SA
9 – 12 Nov 1995 •	Australian Formula 1 Grand Prix	Adelaide 5000, SA
23 Nov 1995	Centenary of Arrival of Sisters of St John of God in Australia	Albany 6330, WA
1 Dec 1995	10th Anniversary of STV *One and All*	Port Adelaide 5015, SA

1996

Date	Event	Location
9 Jan 1996	Lunar New Year – Year of the Rat	Haymarket 2000, NSW
9 Jan 1996	Lunar New Year – Year of the Rat	Cabramatta 2166, NSW
10 Jan 1996	Beam Me Up Spotty Space Exhibition	Melbourne 3000, Vic
17 Jan 1996	Elmore and District Machinery Field Days	Elmore 3558, Vic
26 Jan 1996	Australia Day Tall Ships Race	Sydney 2000, NSW
3 Feb 1996	Arrival of Trans-Pacific Flight by Qantas Super Constellation	Mascot 2020, NSW
23 – 25 Feb 1996 •	Stamp and Coin Fair	Melbourne 3000, Vic
1 Mar 1996	Centenary of Founding of Port Hedland	Port Hedland 6721, WA
16 – 18 Mar 1996	Canberra Stamp Show '96	Canberra 2600, ACT
23 Apr 1996	QBE Sydney Swans	Sydney 2000, NSW
23 Apr 1996	Home of the West Coast Eagles	Subiaco 6008, WA
23 Apr 1996	Brisbane Bears	Brisbane 4000, Qld
2 – 4 May 1996	AGFEST Agricultural Festival	Carrick 7291, Tas
14 May 1996	200 Years of Vaccine Development	Adelaide 5000, SA
1 Jun 1996	First Consecration of a Bishop in Broome[19]	Broome 6725, WA
8 – 10 Jun 1996 •	Queensland Stamp and Coin Expo	Brisbane 4000, Qld
28 Sep 1996 •	Berri Stamp Festival	Berri 5343, SA
4 – 14 Oct 1996	150th Anniversary of European Settlement of the Tatiara District	Bordertown 5268, SA
5 – 7 Oct 1996	ASDA Centrepoint '96 Stamp and Coin Show	Sydney 2000, NSW
12 – 13 Oct 1996	St Peters Stamp and Coin Fair	Stepney 5069, SA
13 Oct 1996	Pets 'n' Vets in the Park	Glenelg 5045, SA
13 Oct 1996	50th Anniversary of TocH Children's Holiday Camp	Point Lonsdale 3225, Vic
17 – 20 Oct 1996	Melbourne '96 National Philatelic Exhibition	Caulfield South 3162, Vic
19 Oct 1996 •	Noarlunga Stamp Fair	Morphett Vale 5162, SA
25 – 27 Oct 1996	Queensland Stamp and Coin Expo	Brisbane 4000, Qld
26 – 27 Oct 1996	SWANPEX 96	Claremont 6010, WA
27 Oct 1996	Salisbury Stamp Fair	Salisbury 5108, SA
9 – 10 Nov 1996	LAUNPEX '96	Launceston 7250, Tas

1997

Date	Event	Location
2 Jan – 31 Dec 1997	Sesquicentenary of Maryborough	Maryborough 4650, Qld
6 Jan 1997	Lunar New Year – Year of the Ox	Haymarket 2000, NSW
6 Jan 1997	Lunar New Year – Year of the Ox	Cabramatta 2166, NSW
23 Jan 1997	Sir Donald Bradman – Australian Legend	Adelaide 5000, SA
25 – 29 Jan 1997	Fourth (Cricket) Test	Adelaide 5000, SA

---

19 Referenced in Australian Stamp Bulletin 235 as a permanent pictorial postmark.

17 Feb 1997	150th Anniversary of the City of Warrnambool	Warrnambool 3280, Vic
22 Feb 1997	First National Shell Show	Adelaide 5000, SA
27 Feb 1997	Australian Classic Cars	3 towns, SA
1 Mar 1997	150th Anniversary of the Settlement of Mildura	Mildura 3500, Vic
1 – 9 Mar 1997	Melbourne International Motor Show	Melbourne 3000, Vic
19 – 23 Mar 1997	Adelaide Motor Show	Plympton 5038, SA
21 – 23 Mar 1997	ANDA Coin, Note and Stamp Show	Sydney 2000, NSW
5 Apr 1997	Freemasons Grand Installation	Adelaide 5000, SA
17 Apr 1997	Birthday of Queen Elizabeth II	Elizabeth 5112, SA
1 – 3 May 1997	AGFEST Agricultural Festival	Carrick 7291, Tas
5 May 1997	75th Anniversary of Country Women's Association of NSW	Sydney 2000, NSW
10 – 19 May 1997	Kernewek Lowender (Cornish Festival)	Kadina 5554, SA
16 – 23 May 1997	Lions Australia 50th Anniversary Convention	Lismore 2480, NSW
2 Jun 1997	Centenary of East Fremantle Football Club	East Fremantle 6158, WA
7 – 9 Jun 1997 •	Brisbane Stamp and Coin Expo	Brisbane 4000, Qld
4 – 6 Jul 1997	Newcastle '97 Bicentennial Stamp Show	Newcastle 2300, NSW
19 – 26 Jul 1997 •	82nd Universal Conference of Esperanto	Adelaide 5000, SA
8 Aug 1997	Adelaide Rams Australia Post Match Day	Adelaide 5000, SA
22 – 24 Aug 1997	STAMPEX '97	Adelaide 5000, SA
16 – 18 Sep 1997	Yorke Peninsula Field Days	Kadina 5444, SA
27 Sep 1997 •	Adelaide Crows – AFL Premiers 1997	Adelaide 5000, SA
27 – 28 Sep 1997 •	Congress '97[20]	Goolwa 5214, SA
1 – 6 Oct 1997	50th Anniversary Reunion – Migrant Reception Centre	Bonegilla MILPO 3693, Vic
12 Oct 1997	Salisbury Stamp Fair	Salisbury 5108, SA
22 – 25 Oct 1997	Royal Hobart Show	Glenorchy 7010, Tas
23 – 26 Oct 1997 •	Stamp Show 97	Fremantle 6160, WA
24 – 26 Oct 1997	Stamp and Coin Expo	Brisbane 4000, Qld
25 – 26 Oct 1997	St Peters Stamp and Coin Fair	Stepney 5069, SA
23 Nov 1997	80th Anniversary of First Adelaide-Gawler Airmail	Adelaide 5000, SA
23 Nov 1997	80th Anniversary of First Gawler-Adelaide Airmail	Gawler 5118, SA

1998

1 – 11 Jan 1998	18th Australian Scout Jamboree	Springfield 4300, Qld
2 Jan 1998	150th Anniversary of Salisbury / 125th Anniversary of St Kilda	Salisbury 5108, SA
5 Jan 1998	Lunar New Year – Year of the Tiger	Haymarket 2000, NSW
5 Jan 1998	Lunar New Year – Year of the Tiger	Cabramatta 2166, NSW
5 Jan 1998	200th Anniversary of Voyage by George Bass	Bass 3991, Vic
5 Jan – 31 Dec 1998	150th Anniversary of St John the Evangelist Church[21]	Albany 6330, WA
8 – 18 Jan 1998 •	8th World Swimming Championships	Perth 6000, WA
27 Feb – 17 Mar 1998	Telstra Adelaide Festival of Arts	Adelaide 5000, SA
14 – 16 Mar 1998 •	NATSTAMP '98	Canberra 2600, ACT
29 Mar 1998	Licensed Post Office Conference	Caulfield East 3145, Vic
1 May 1998 •	150th Anniversary of Laying of Foundation Stone St Philip's on Church Hill	Sydney 2000, NSW
7 – 9 May 1998	AGFEST Agricultural Festival	Carrick 7291, Tas
12 – 15 May 1998	Lions International Multiple District 201 46th Convention	Canberra 2601, ACT

---

20   Congress '97 was the title of the annual South Australian Philatelic Council event.
21   Promoted in Australian Stamp Bulletin 243 as a permanent pictorial postmark.

8 Jun 1998	150th Anniversary of City of Salisbury	Salisbury 5108, SA
26 Jul 1998	Adelaide Rams Australia Post Match Day	Adelaide 5000, SA
3 – 31 Aug 1998	Back to Mt Isa Week	Mt Isa 4825, Qld
14 – 16 Aug 1998 •	ANDA Coin, Note and Stamp Show	Adelaide 5000, SA
29 Aug 1998	150th Anniversary of Cape Otway Lightstation	Apollo Bay 3233, Vic
26 Sep 1998	Adelaide Crows AFL Premiers 1998	Adelaide 5000, SA
29 Sep 1998	*Duyfken* 1606 Replica Project	Fremantle 6160, WA
2 – 4 Oct 1998	Queensland Stamp & Coin Expo	Brisbane 4000, Qld
10 – 11 Oct 1998	St Peters Stamp and Coin Fair	Stepney 5069, SA
18 Oct 1998	VPC Stamp Clubs' Open Day	Warragul 3820, Vic
24 – 25 Oct 1998	SWANPEX '98	East Perth 6004, WA
25 Oct 1998	Salisbury Stamp Fair	Salisbury 5108, SA
30 Oct – 1 Nov 1998	ANDA Coin, Note and Stamp Fair	Sydney 2000, NSW
2 Nov 1998	Frama Machine Last Day of Use	Perth 6000, WA
14 -15 Nov 1998	NOARPEX '98	Morphett Vale 5162, SA
3 – 6 Dec 1998 •	Holden Australian (Golf) Open	Adelaide 5000, SA
22 Dec 1998	50th Anniversary of Ukrainian Settlement in Australia / UCSPEX '98	Essendon 3040, Vic

1999

14 Jan 1999	Lunar New Year – Year of the Rabbit	Haymarket 2000, NSW
14 Jan 1999	Lunar New Year – Year of the Rabbit	Cabramatta 2166, NSW
1 Mar 1999	Tasmania Police -Celebrating Our Century	Hobart 7000, Tas
19 – 24 Mar 1999	Australia 99 World Stamp Expo	Melbourne 3000, Vic
21 Mar 1999	Nambour Stamp Fair	Nambour 4560, Qld
17 Apr 1999	125th Anniversary of Poowong	Poowong 3988, Vic
3 – 6 May 1999	Lions International Multiple District 201 47th Convention	Brisbane 4000, Qld
6 – 8 May 1999	AGFEST Agricultural Festival	Carrick 7291, Tas
14 – 16 May 1999	6th Sydney Pet & Animal Expo	Sydney 2000, NSW
15 – 17 May 1999	Kernewek Lowender (Cornish Festival)	Kadina 5554, SA
28 May 1999	Centenary of the United Grand Lodge of Mark Master Masons of Victoria	East Melbourne 3002, Tas
4 – 6 Jun 1999	ANDA Coin, Note and Stamp Show	Brisbane 4000, Qld
30 Jun 1999	150th Anniversary of Horsham	Horsham 3400, Vic
2 – 12 Jul 1999	Bicentenary of Matthew Flinders' Discovery of Shoal Bay	Yamba 2464, NSW
7 Aug 1999	80th Anniversary of First Adelaide-Minlaton Airmail	Adelaide 5000, SA
7 Aug 1999	80th Anniversary of First Minlaton- Adelaide Airmail	Minlaton 5575, SA
28 – 29 Aug 1999 •	Queensland Stampshow 99	Wynnum Plaza 4178, Qld
1 Sep 1999	7th Australian Masters Games	Adelaide 5000, SA
1 Sep 1999	Reopening of Sydney GPO	Sydney 2000, NSW
14 – 16 Sep 1999	70th Anniversary of the Country Women's Association in South Australia	Adelaide 5000, SA

29 Sep 1999	Centenary of Kalgoorlie Public Building	Kalgoorlie 6430, WA
2 Oct 1999	Re-enactment of the Last Mail Truck Run Birdsville-Birdwood	Birdsville 4482, Qld
2 Oct 1999	Congress 1999[22]	Mt Gambier 5290, SA
8 – 10 Oct 1999	APTA Sydney Centrepoint Stamp and Coin Show 99	Sydney 2000, NSW
11 Oct 1999	Salisbury Stamp Fair	Salisbury 5108, SA
16 – 17 Oct 1999	St Peters Stamp and Coin Fair	Stepney 5069, SA
23 – 24 Oct 1999	SWANPEX	East Perth 6004, WA
29 – 31 Oct 1999	APTA Queensland Stamp and Coin Fair	Fortitude Valley 4006, Qld
29 Oct – 3 Nov 1999	Rose Week '99 / Centenary of Rose Society of Victoria	Melbourne 3000, Vic
1 Nov – 31 Dec 1999	70th Anniversary of City to Bay Tram	Glenelg 5045, SA
1 Nov – 31 Dec 1999	70th Anniversary of City to Bay Tram	Adelaide 5000, SA
5 – 7 Nov 1999	STAMPEX 99	Adelaide 5000, SA
8 Nov 1999	1999 Rugby World Cup Winners	Sydney 2000, NSW
1 Dec 1999	Centenary of Fire and Rescue Service in Western Australia	Perth 6000, WA
31 Dec 1999 – 1 Jan 2000	Celebrate 2000	Sydney 2000, NSW

2000

2 – 9 Jan 2000	International Girl Guides Jamboree	Dakabin 4503, Qld
4 Jan 2000	150th Anniversary of Penola	Penola 5277, SA
13 Jan 2000	Lunar New Year – Year of the Dragon	Haymarket 2000, NSW
13 Jan 2000	Lunar New Year – Year of the Dragon	Cabramatta 2166, NSW
17 Jan 2000	'Barossa Glide' World Gliding Championships	Gawler 5118, SA
18 – 23 Jan 2000	'Tour Down Under' (Cycling)	6 towns, SA
25 Feb 2000	Centenary of the Grand Lodge of Western Australian Freemasons	East Perth 6004, WA
1 – 6 Mar 2000	Opening of First Tunnel on National Highway Adelaide-Crafers[23]	Adelaide 5000, SA
1 – 6 Mar 2000 •	Opening of First Tunnel on National Highway Adelaide-Crafers[24]	Stirling 5152, SA
9 Mar 2000	150th Anniversary of Naracoorte	Naracoorte 5271, SA
18 – 20 Mar 2000	Canberra Stampshow 2000	Canberra 2600, ACT
8 Apr 2000	South Australian Regional Masters Games	Port Pirie 5540, SA
13 Apr 2000 •	Birthday of Queen Elizabeth II	Elizabeth 5112, SA
28 Apr 2000	Heritage & Cane Festival 2000	Beenleigh 4207, Qld
4 – 6 May 2000	AGFEST Agricultural Festival	Carrick 7291, Tas
9 – 12 May 2000	Lions International Multiple District 201 48th Convention	Perth 6000, WA
8 Jun 2000	Olympic Torch Relay	Yulara 0872, NT
13 Jun 2000	Olympic Torch Relay	Brisbane 4000, Qld
29 Jun 2000	Olympic Torch Relay	Darwin 0800, NT
7 Jul 2000	Olympic Torch Relay	Perth 6000, WA
14 Jul 2000	Olympic Torch Relay	Adelaide 5000, SA
31 Jul 2000	Olympic Torch Relay	Melbourne 3000, Vic
2 Aug 2000	Olympic Torch Relay	Hobart 7000, Tas
4 Aug 2000	100th Birthday of HM Queen Elizabeth, the Queen Mother	Strathmore 3041, Vic
5 – 6 Aug 2000	Congress 2000 Philatelic Exhibition	Adelaide 5000, SA
11 – 13 Aug 2000	50th Anniversary of Brighton Philatelic Society	Brighton 3185, Vic
26 – 27 Aug 2000	Queensland Stampshow 2000	Wynnum Plaza 4178, Qld
2 Sep – 4 Oct 2000 •	Olympics 2000	Sydney 2000, NSW
5 Sep 2000	Olympic Torch Relay	Canberra 2600, ACT
12 Sep 2000	Olympic Torch Relay	Sydney 2000, NSW

---

22 Congress 1999 was the title of the annual South Australian Philatelic Council event.
23 Dates to be confirmed.
24 Dates to be confirmed.

12 Sep 2000	75 Years of Local Government Shire of Kondinin	Kondinin 6367, WA
13 Sep 2000	Preliminary Soccer Games for Sydney Olympics	Hindmarsh 5007, SA
13 – 15 Sep 2000	Olymphilex 2000[25]	Canberra 2600, ACT
15 Sep 2000	Olympic Family Hotel	Sydney 2000, NSW
15 Sep 2000	Olympic Games Opening Day	Sydney 2000, NSW
15 – 28 Sep 2000 •	Olymphilex 2000	Sydney 2000, NSW
15 Sep – 1 Oct 2000	Olympic Games 2000[26]	Sydney 2000, NSW
15 Sep – 1 Oct 2000	Centenary of Women in Olympic Games	Sydney 2000, NSW
17 Sep – 2 Oct 2000	Olympic Games Gold Medallists	12 cities / towns
1 Oct 2000	Olympic Games Closing Day	Sydney 2000, NSW
18 – 29 Oct 2000	Paralympic Village	Sydney 2000, NSW
20 – 22 Oct 2000	ANDA Coin & Banknote Fair	Melbourne 3000, Vic
21 – 22 Oct 2000	SWANPEX	Subiaco 6008, WA
22 Oct 2000	Salisbury Stamp Fair	Adelaide 5000, SA
17 – 19 Nov 2000 •	Launceston Stamp Show – LAUNPEX 2000	Launceston 7250, Tas
18 – 19 Nov 2000	St Peters Stamp and Coin Fair	Adelaide 5000, SA
23 – 24 Nov 2000	Navy League Centenary	Launceston 7250, Tas

2001

2 – 12 Jan 2001	22nd Asia-Pacific / 19th Australian Jamboree	Appin 2560, NSW
8 Jan 2001	Lunar New Year – Year of the Snake	Haymarket 2000, NSW
8 Jan 2001	Lunar New Year – Year of the Snake	Cabramatta 2166, NSW
8 – 26 Jan 2001 •	World Club Gliding Championships	Gawler 5118, SA
23 Apr & 7 Jun 2001	Arrival & Departure of Global Hawk Flight	Edinburgh RAAF DSTO[27] 5111, SA
7 – 10 May 2001	Lions International Multiple District 201 49th Convention	Wollongong 2500, NSW
25 – 27 May 2001	ANDA Coin, Note and Stamp Show	Brisbane 4000, Qld
9 – 10 Jun 2001	Centenary of Federation Mail Run	Gladstone 5473, SA
15 – 17 Jun 2001	APTA Stamp and Coin Show	Sydney 2000, NSW
4 – 13 Jul 2001	World Veterans' Athletic Championships	Brisbane 4000, Qld
24 Aug 2001	Historic Nightcap Track Mail Service Re-enactment	Lismore 2480, NSW
27 Aug 2001 •	Historic Nightcap Track Mail Service Re-enactment	Murwillumbah 2484, NSW
18 – 19 Sep 2001	Centenary of Federation	Morgan 5320, SA
25 Sep 2001 •	Re-enactment of RAAF First Overseas Deployment Flight	Werribee 3030, Vic
2 Oct 2001	Centenary of Commonwealth Naval Forces	Williamstown 3016, Vic
8 Oct 2001	Off to the Diggings – 150 Years of Gold in Victoria	Melbourne 3000, Vic
13 – 14 Oct 2001	St Peters Stamp and Coin Fair	Adelaide 5000, SA
14 Oct 2001	Salisbury Stamp Fair	Salisbury 5106, SA
24 Oct – 23 Nov 2001 •	Opening of Australian Prospectors and Miners Hall of Fame	Kalgoorlie 6430, WA
26 – 28 Oct 2001	2001 Centennial Stampshow	Brisbane 4000, Qld
10 – 11 Nov 2001	Congress 2001	Murray Bridge 5253, SA
17 – 18 Nov 2001	SWANPEX 2001	East Perth 6004, WA
5 Dec 2001	80th Anniversary of Airmail Services in Western Australia	Geraldton 6530, WA

---

25 Postmark inscribed "Royal Australian Mint" and ostensibly used only on the opening day; 15 September strikes have been sighted.
26 28 postmarks were produced, each depicting a game or sport.
27 DSTO = Defence Science and Technology Organisation.

2002

Date	Event	Location
8 Jan 2002	Lunar New Year – Year of the Horse	Haymarket 2000, NSW
8 Jan 2002 •	Lunar New Year – Year of the Horse	Cabramatta 2166, NSW
14 – 27 Jan 2002	Australian Open..	Melbourne 3000, Vic
16 Feb – 12 Apr 2002	Encounter 2002 – Tall Ships Re-enactment	17 towns, SA
6 – 9 Mar 2002	Lions International District 201 50th Convention[28]	Geelong 3220, Vic
12 Mar 2002 •	15th IALA[29]-AISM Conference.	Sydney 2000, NSW
14 Mar 2002 •	Australian Council of Stoma Associations (ACSA) 2002 Conference.	Canberra 2600, ACT
16 – 18 Mar 2002	Canberra Stamp Show.	Canberra 2600, ACT
6 – 7 Apr 2002	Flinders-Baudin Bicentenary	Victor Harbour 5211, SA
19 – 21 Apr 2002	ANDA Coin, Note and Stamp Show	Sydney 2000, NSW
6 – 9 May 2002	Lions International Multiple District 201 50th Convention	Geelong 3220, Vic
7 Jun 2002	Great Australian Outback Cattle Drive.	Marree 5733, SA
22 – 23 Jun 2002 •	St Peters Stamp and Coin Fair.	Adelaide 5000, SA
1 Jul – 31 Dec 2002	Centenary of Western Australian School of Mines.	Kalgoorlie 6430, WA
2 Jul 2002	125th Anniversary of Hermannsburg	Hermannsburg 0872, NT
11 Aug 2002	The Last Camel Train	Oodnadatta 5734, SA
31 Aug 2002	The Last Camel Train	Alice Springs 0870, NT
24 – 25 Aug 2002 •	Queensland Stamp Show 2002	Wynnum Plaza 4178, Qld
19 Sep 2002	Centenary of the Long Stamp in South Australia.	Para Hills 5096, SA
28 Sep 2002	Re-enactment of the Warook-Inneston Mail Run	Warooka 5577, SA
1 Oct 2002	Launch of RPSV[30] book Beating the Odds	Melbourne 3004, Vic
4 – 6 Oct 2002	Stampshow Melbourne 02	Melbourne 3000, Vic
12 – 13 Oct 2002	SWANPEX 2002	Crawley 6009, WA
13 Oct 2002	Salisbury Stamp Fair.	Salisbury 5108, SA
2 – 31 Dec 2002	Opening of New Western Australian Maritime Museum	Fremantle 6160, WA
14 Dec 2002	Cherry Harmony Festival	Manjimup 6258, WA
21 Dec 2002	30th Anniversary of Diplomatic Relations Australia / China	Sydney 2000, NSW

2003

Date	Event	Location
7 Jan 2003	Lunar New Year – Year of the Goat	Haymarket 2000, NSW
7 Jan 2003	Lunar New Year – Year of the Goat	Cabramatta 2166, NSW
8 Jan 2003	150th Anniversary of Victoria Police	Melbourne 3000, Vic
10 Jan 2003	Sterner (stamp vending machines) Last Day..	Corio 3214, Vic
13 – 26 Jan 2003	Australian Tennis Open..	Melbourne 3000, Vic

---

28 The March dateline is an error; see 6 – 9 May entry.
29 IALA = International Association of Marine Aids to Navigation and Lighthouse Authorities.
30 RPSV = Royal Philatelic Society of Victoria.

11 – 13 Apr 2003	Tasmania 2003 National Philatelic Exhibition	Hobart 7000, Tas
19 Apr 2003 •	150th Anniversary of Brighton PO	Brighton 3186, Vic
12 – 15 May 2003	Lions International Multiple District 201 51st Convention	Hobart 7000, Tas
31 May – 4 Jun 2003 •	Rotary International Convention	South Bank 4101, Qld
31 May 2003	15000 Motocross and Moto-Madness	Manjimup 6258, WA
30 Jun 2003	Frama Last Day	5 capital cities
23 – 24 Aug 2003	Queensland Stamp Show 2003	Wynnum Plaza 4178, Qld
30 – 31 Aug 2003	Congress 2003	Tanunda 5352, SA
3 – 6 Sep 2003	Spring Festival[31]	Mukinbudin 6479, WA
12 Sep 2003	Bicentenary of European Settlement of Tasmania	Rosny Park 7018, Tas
20 – 21 Sep 2003 •	St Peters Stamp and Coin Fair	Adelaide 5000, SA
3 – 5 Oct 2003	Newcastle Stamp Show	Newcastle 2300, NSW
11 – 12 Oct 2003 •	SWANPEX 2003	Crawley 6009, WA
12 Oct 2003	Salisbury Stamp Fair	Salisbury 5108, SA
15 – 16 Nov 2003	STAMPEX 2003	Morphettville 5043, SA
21 – 23 Nov 2003 •	ANDA and APTA Coin, Note and Stamp Fair	Sydney 2000, NSW
30 Nov 2003	75th Anniversary of Gulf Docking Company	Port Lincoln 5606, SA
1 Dec 2003	Easter Country Campout	Moora 6510, WA
17 – 18 Dec 2003	AEROPEX 03 – Aeroplane Centenary	Adelaide 5000, SA

2004

3 Jan – 31 Dec 2004	City of Mount Gambier – 50 and Loving It	Mount Gambier 5290, SA
5 – 15 Jan 2004	20th Australian Jamboree	Stirling 5152, SA
6 Jan 2004	Lunar New Year – Year of the Monkey	Haymarket 2000, NSW
6 Jan 2004	Lunar New Year – Year of the Monkey	Cabramatta 2166, NSW
15 – 17 Jan 2004	Freight Link Adelaide-Darwin	4 towns/cities, SA/NT
19 Jan – 1 Feb 2004	Australian Tennis Open	Melbourne 3000, Vic
1 – 3 Feb 2004	The Ghan Inaugural Journey	6 towns/cities, SA/NT
4 – 6 Feb 2004	The Ghan Inaugural Return Journey	4 cities/towns, SA/NT
13 – 15 Mar 2004	Canberra Stamp Show 2004	Canberra 2600, ACT
24 Mar – 31 Dec 2004	Bicentenary of Newcastle	Newcastle 2300, NSW
3 – 6 May 2004	Lions International Multiple District 201 52nd Convention	Cairns 4870, Qld
6 – 8 May 2004	AGFEST	Carrick 7291, Tas
18 May 2004	150th Anniversary of First Public Railway in Australia	3 towns, SA
4 Jun 2004	Olympic Flame	Sydney 2000, NSW
5 Jun 2004	Olympic Flame	Melbourne 3000, Vic
8 Jun 2004	Transit of Venus	Campbell Town 7210, Tas
9 Jun 2004	50th Anniversary of Hermes First Day Cover	Melbourne 3000, Vic
9 Jul 2004 •	150th Anniversary of Maryborough	Maryborough 3465, Vic
3 Aug 2004	150th Anniversary of Cobb & Co	Yuleba 4427, Qld
6 – 8 Aug 2004 •	ANDA and APTA Coin, Note and Stamp Show	Sydney 2000, NSW
9 Aug 2004	50th Anniversary of Meals on Wheels	Port Adelaide 5015, SA
21 – 22 Aug 2004	Queensland Stamp Show	Wynnum Plaza 4178, Qld
1 – 30 Sep 2004	150th Anniversary of Wingham	Wingham 2429, NSW
1 – 30 Sep 2004 •	Channel 9 – Celebrating 45 Years in Television	North Adelaide 5006, SA
4 – 5 Sep 2004	St Peters Stamp and Coin Fair	Adelaide 5000, SA
9 – 12 Sep 2004 •	Swan River 2004 Stamp Show	Fremantle 6160, WA
9 – 10 Oct 2004	Eureka Congress	Ballarat 3350, Vic
16 Oct 2004	Opening of Purves House	Ashburton 3147, Vic

---

31 Dates to be confirmed.

19 Oct 2004	150th Anniversary of Maryborough PO	Maryborough 3465, Vic
30 – 31 Oct 2004	Salisbury Philatelic Society Congress 2004	Salisbury 5108, SA
11 Dec 2004 •	Cherry Harmony Festival	Manjimup 6258, WA

2005

17 – 30 Jan 2005	Centenary of the Australian Tennis Open	Melbourne 3000, Vic
21 – 24 Apr 2005	Pacific Explorer 2005	Sydney 2000, NSW
21 – 24 Apr 2005	Centenary of First Special Postmarker	Sydney 2000, NSW
3 – 6 May 2005	Australian Lions Convention	Adelaide 5000, SA
5 – 7 May 2005	AGFEST	Carrick 7291, Tas
19 May 2005	Centenary of Prahran Philatelic Society	Prahran 3181, Vic
8 Aug 2005 •	XXII IUFRO[32] World Congress	Brisbane 4000, Qld
1 – 30 Sep 2005	150th Anniversary of Manly Wharf and The Corso	Manly 2095, NSW
15 – 25 Sep 2005	Royal Melbourne Show – 150 Years	Ascot Vale 3032, Vic
16 Sep 2005	Centenary of Chowey Bridge	Biggenden 4621, Qld
1 Oct 2005	150th Anniversary of Mangowine Homestead	Nungarin 6490, WA
1 – 2 Oct 2005 •	Sydney Stamp Expo 2005	Sydney 2000, NSW
1 – 2 Oct 2005 •	SAPC Philatelic Congress	Adelaide 5000, SA
10 – 15 Oct 2005	Denison Canal Centenary	Dunalley 7177, Tas
15 – 16 Oct 2005	Swan River 2005 Stamp Show	Crawley 6009, WA
21 Oct 2005 •	Bi-centennial Trafalgar Day Celebrations	Trafalgar 3824, Vic
28 Oct 2005	Melbourne 2006 Commonwealth Games	Melbourne 3000, Vic
29 Oct 2005	Salisbury Stamp Fair	Salisbury 5106, SA
19 – 20 Nov 2005 •	Defence Force Air Show	Bullsbrook 6084, WA
9 – 11 Dec 2005	Cherry Harmony Festival	Manjimup 6258, WA

2006

3 – 14 Jan 2006	13th Australian Scout Venture	Campbelltown 2560, NSW
5 Jan 2006	Lunar New Year – Year of the Dog	Haymarket 2000, NSW
5 Jan 2006	Lunar New Year – Year of the Dog	Cabramatta 2166, NSW
16 – 29 Jan 2006	Australian Tennis Open	Melbourne 3000, Vic
25 Jan – 14 Mar 2006	Melbourne 2006 Commonwealth Games – Queen's Baton Relay	22 cities/towns
28 Feb 2006	Melbourne 2006 Commonwealth Games – Games Village	Melbourne 3000, Vic
1 – 26 Mar 2006	Melbourne 2006 Commonwealth Games – Broadcasting Centre	Melbourne 3000, Vic
5 – 26 Mar 2006	Melbourne 2006 Commonwealth Games – Main Press Centre	Melbourne 3000, Vic

---

32 IUFRO = International Union of Forest Research Organizations.

15 – 26 Mar 2006	Melbourne 2006 Commonwealth Games – Snapshot!	Melbourne 3000, Vic
18 – 20 Mar 2006	Canberra Stampshow.	Canberra 2600, ACT
10 Apr – 31 Dec 2006	Southern Mallee Centenary.	3 towns, SA
1 – 31 May 2006	125th Anniversary of the Victorian College of Pharmacy	Melbourne 3000, Vic
4 – 6 May 2006	AGFEST.	Carrick 7291, Tas
6 – 7 May 2006	Mildura Philatelic Society Annual Stamp Fair	Mildura 3502, Vic
12 – 19 May 2006 •	150th Anniversary of Don.	Don 7310, Tas
15 May 2006	Lions International Multiple District 201 54th Convention	Broadbeach 4218, Qld
15 – 26 May 2006	Autism Awareness Week.	Sydney 2000, NSW
31 May 2006	150th Anniversary of the Arrival of HMCSS *Victoria*.	Williamstown 3016, Vic
4 Jun 2006 •	70th Anniversary of the Round the Houses Motor Event.	Albany 6330, WA
6 Jun 2006 •	90th Anniversary of the Returned & Services League of Australia	4 capital cities
23 Jun – 14 Jul 2006	100th Anniversary of GPO Clock and Chimes	Hobart 7000, Tas
30 Jun – 2 Jul 2006	V8 Supercars Championship	Darwin 0800, NT
11 – 15 Jul 2006	SCAR[33] / COMNAP[34] Conference	Hobart 7000, Tas
18 – 20 Aug 2006	STAMPEX 2006	Adelaide 5000, SA
21 – 22 Oct 2006	Swan River Stamp Show.	Crawley 6009, WA
23 Oct – 3 Nov 2006 •	25th Meeting of CCAMLR[35].	Hobart 7000, Tas
28 Oct 2006	Sutherland Philatelic Society Golden Jubilee.	Sutherland 2232, NSW
28 Oct 2006	Salisbury Stamp Fair.	Salisbury 5108, SA
11 – 18 Nov 2006 •	6th Golden Retriever National Championship Show.	Lenah Valley 7008, Tas

2007

2 – 13 Jan 2007	21st Australian Jamboree.	Elmore 3558, Vic
15 – 28 Jan 2007 •	Australian Tennis Open.	Melbourne 3000, Vic
1 Feb – 31 Dec 2007	Darwin Defenders 1942-1945.	Darwin 0800, NT
23 Feb 2007	World Paragliding Titles.	Manilla 2346, NSW
13 – 25 Mar 2007	World Police and Fire Games..	Adelaide 5000, SA
16 Mar 2007	Sesquicentenary of St Marys.	St Marys 7215, Tas
18 Apr 2007	50 Years of Guide Dogs.	Adelaide 5000, SA
3 – 5 May 2007	AGFEST.	Carrick 7291, Tas
5 – 6 May 2007	Mildura Philatelic Society Annual Stamp Fair	Mildura 3502, Vic
12 – 19 May 2007	Arafura Games 07.	Darwin 0800, NT
17 – 20 May 2007 •	Lions International Multiple District 201 55th Convention	Sydney 2000, NSW
15 – 17 Jun 2007	Sydney Stamp Expo.	Sydney 2000, NSW
22 – 24 Jun 2007 •	Celebration Year 10th Year Hosting V8 Supercars.	Darwin 0800, NT
2 Jul 2007	Centenary of Australian Naval Cadets.	Williamstown 3016, Vic
6 – 21 Jul 2007 •	Australian National Bridge Championships.	Fremantle 6160, WA
25 – 26 Aug 2007	Queensland Stampshow 2007	Wynnum Plaza 4178, Qld
1 Oct 2007	100th Anniversary of Australian Membership of the UPU.	Melbourne 3000, Vic
13 – 14 Oct 2007	SAPC Congress 2007.	Mount Gambier 5290, SA
21 – 22 Oct 2007	Swan River Stamp Show 2007	Crawley 6009, WA
22 Oct – 2 Dec 2007	Centenary of Women's Work Exhibition.	Castlemaine 3450, Vic
27 Oct 2007 •	Salisbury Stamp Fair.	Salisbury 5108, SA

---

33 SCAR = Scientific Committee for Antarctic Research.
34 COMNAP = Council of Managers of National Antarctic Programs.
35 CCAMLR = Commission for the Conservation of Antarctic Marine Living Resources.

2008

Date	Event	Location
8 Jan 2008	Lunar New Year – Year of the Rat	Haymarket 2000, NSW
8 Jan 2008 •	Lunar New Year – Year of the Rat	Cabramatta 2166, NSW
8 Jan 2008	Lunar New Year – Year of the Rat	Melbourne 3000, Vic
14 – 27 Jan 2008	Australian Tennis Open	Melbourne 3000, Vic
22 Feb 2008	Centenary of Australian Scouting	Elsternwick 3185, Vic
9 Mar 2008	Nairne Founders' Day	Nairne 5252, SA
14 – 16 Mar 2008 •	Canberra Stampshow 2008	Canberra 2600, ACT
24 Apr 2008	Beijing 2008 Olympic Torch Relay	Canberra 2600, ACT
1 – 3 May 2008	AGFEST	Carrick 7291, Tas
3 – 4 May 2008	Mildura Philatelic Society Annual Stamp Fair	Mildura 3500, Vic
16 – 19 May 2008	Lions International 56th National Convention	Darwin 0800, NT
30 Jun 2008	World Youth Day	Sydney 2000, NSW
15 – 20 Jul 2008 •	World Youth Day	Sydney 2000, NSW
22 – 24 Aug 2008	SUNSTAMP 2008	Wynnum Plaza 4178, Qld
29 Aug 2008	Centenary of the US Great White Fleet Visit	Port Melbourne 3207, Vic
1 Sep – 31 Dec 2008	Centenary of the Town Hall	Kalgoorlie 6430, WA
1 Sep – 31 Dec 2008	Centenary of the Town Hall	Boulder 6432, WA
3 – 6 Oct 2008	16th NSW Agoonoree[36]	Turramurra 2074, NSW
3 – 7 Oct 2008	STAMPEX 2008	Adelaide 5000, SA
18 – 19 Oct 2008	Swan River Stamp Show 2008	Crawley 6009, WA
20 Oct 2008	Re-opening of GPO Perth	Perth 6000, WA
20 Oct 2008	QANTAS A380 First Commercial Flight	Tullamarine 3043, Vic
25 Oct 2008	Salisbury Stamp Fair	Salisbury 5108, SA
3 & 11 Nov 2008	90th Anniversary of the End of World War I	Diggers Rest 3427, Vic
19 Nov 2008 •	Discovery of Wreck of HMAS *Sydney II*	Geraldton 6530, WA

2009

Date	Event	Location
4 – 10 Jan 2009	Yarra Brae Jamborette	Wonga Park 3115, Vic
4 – 15 Jan 2009	Scouts 14th Australian Venture	Pinjarra 6208, WA
8 Jan 2009	South Magnetic Pole Flight	Tullamarine 3043, Vic
19 Jan – 1 Feb 2009 •	Australian Tennis Open	Melbourne 3000, Vic
23 Apr 2009	Launch of Australian Postcard Society	Adelaide 5000, SA
1 – 3 May 2009	Lions International Multiple District 201 57th National Convention	Melbourne 3000, Vic
2 – 3 May 2009	Mildura Philatelic Society Annual Stamp Fair	Mildura 3502, Vic
4 May 2009	150th Anniversary of the Parish of Richmond	Richmond 2753, NSW
7 – 9 May 2009	AGFEST	Carrick 7291, Tas
25 Jun 2009 •	125th Anniversary of Arrival of Naval Vessels[37]	Williamstown 3016, Vic

---

36 Agoonoree is a scouting jamboree for young people with special needs.
37 The vessels in question were HMVS *Childers, Victoria II* and *Albert*.

26 – 28 Jun 2009	Australia Post Bicentennial.. … … … … … … … … … … … … … … … …	Sydney 2000, NSW
23 – 26 Jul 2009 •	Melbourne Stampshow . … … … … … … … … … … … … … … … … …	Melbourne 3000, Vic
27 Jul 2009	150th Anniversary of the Ballaarat[38] Mechanics Institute . … … … … … …	Ballarat 3350, Vic
6 Aug 2009	150th Anniversary of the Wreck of SS *Admella* . … … … … … … … … …	Mount Gambier 5290, SA
8 – 16 Aug 2009	Swan Hill Pioneers Week . … … … … … … … … … … … … … … … …	Swan Hill 3585, Vic
21 Aug 2009	100th Anniversary of the Shire of Moora . … … … … … … … … … … …	Moora 6510, WA
22 Aug 2009	Dawn to Dusk 2009 Flight. … … … … … … … … … … … … … … … …	Geraldton 6530, WA
22 – 23 Aug 2009	Queensland Stamp Show 2009 . … … … … … … … … … … … … … …	Wynnum Plaza 4178, Qld
1 Sep 2009	150th Anniversary of Brisbane . … … … … … … … … … … … … … …	Brisbane 4000, Qld
13 Sep 2009 •	25th Anniversary of SOUTHPEX. … … … … … … … … … … … … … …	Gosnells 6110, WA
1 Oct 2009	20th Anniversary of Tandanya National Indigenous Centre.. … … … … … …	Adelaide 5000, SA
3 – 4 Oct 2009	Swan River Stamp Show 2009 . … … … … … … … … … … … … … …	Crawley 6009, WA
17 Oct 2009	Salisbury Stamp Fair. … … … … … … … … … … … … … … … … …	Salisbury 5108, SA
23 Oct 2009	First National Philatelic Pub Crawl . … … … … … … … … … … … … …	Adelaide 5000, SA
24 Oct 2009	SA Philatelic Council Congress 2009 . … … … … … … … … … … … …	Adelaide 5000, SA
25 Oct 2009	50th Anniversary of the Community Philatelic Society . … … … … … … …	Adelaide 5000, SA
30 Oct – 2 Nov 2009	LAUNPEX 2009. … … … … … … … … … … … … … … … … … … …	Launceston 7250, Tas

2010

2 – 14 Jan 2010	22nd Australian Jamboree . … … … … … … … … … … … … … … …	Bargo 2574, NSW
4 – 8 Jan 2010 •	Girl Guides Australian Centenary Event . … … … … … … … … … … …	Grovedale 3216, Vic
4 Jan – 31 Dec 2010	150th Anniversary of Milton . … … … … … … … … … … … … … … …	Milton 2538, NSW
12 Jan 2010	Lunar New Year – Year of the Tiger . … … … … … … … … … … … …	Haymarket 2000, NSW
12 Jan 2010	Lunar New Year – Year of the Tiger . … … … … … … … … … … … …	Cabramatta 2166, NSW
17 – 24 Jan 2010	Tour Down Under.. … … … … … … … … … … … … … … … … … …	Adelaide 5000, SA
18 – 31 Jan 2010	Australian Tennis Open . … … … … … … … … … … … … … … … …	Melbourne 3000, Vic
8 Feb 2010	20th Anniversary of the South Australian Frama Group . … … … … … … …	Adelaide 5000, SA
12 – 14 Mar 2010	Canberra Stampshow.. … … … … … … … … … … … … … … … … …	Canberra 2600, ACT
17 Mar 2010	40th Anniversary of the Shepparton Philatelic Society . … … … … … … …	Shepparton 3630, Vic
26 Mar 2010	Lithgow Agricultural Show . … … … … … … … … … … … … … … …	Lithgow 2790, NSW
27 Mar 2010	Springwood Foundation Day . … … … … … … … … … … … … … …	Springwood 2777, NSW
27 Mar 2010	Yass Show . …	Yass 2582, NSW
1 Apr 2010 •	Royal Easter Show . … … … … … … … … … … … … … … … … …	Homebush South 2140, NSW
1 Apr 2010	100th Anniversary of the Ilfracombe-Isisford Motor Mail . … … … … … …	Isisford 4731, Qld
6 Apr 2010	150th Anniversary of Ipswich . … … … … … … … … … … … … … …	Ipswich 4305, Qld
30 Apr 2010	Australian Lions 58th Convention . … … … … … … … … … … … … …	Mildura 3500, Vic
1 – 2 May 2010	Mildura Philatelic Society Annual Stamp Fair . … … … … … … … … …	Mildura 3502, Vic
22 May 2010	Blacktown City Festival . … … … … … … … … … … … … … … … …	Blacktown 2148, NSW
23 May 2010	40th Anniversary of WA Stamp Mart . … … … … … … … … … … … …	Midland 6056, WA
11 Jun – 18 Oct 2010	120th Anniversary of Sacred Heart Church . … … … … … … … … … …	Kew 3101, Vic
28 Jun – 2 Jul 2010	Lions Club International Convention.. … … … … … … … … … … … …	Sydney 2000, NSW
10 – 11 Jul 2010	Congress . …	Murray Bridge 5253, SA
19 Jul 2010	Australia Remembers – Lost Soldiers of Fromelles. … … … … … … … …	Canberra 2600, ACT
5 Aug 2010	Royal Brisbane Show . … … … … … … … … … … … … … … … …	Brisbane 4000, Qld
6 Aug 2010 •	110th Anniversary of HMCS *Protector* . … … … … … … … … … … …	Port Adelaide 5015, SA
6 – 8 Aug 2010	60th Anniversary of the Brighton Philatelic Society . … … … … … … … …	Brighton 3186, Vic
20 – 22 Aug 2010	STAMPEX '10. … … … … … … … … … … … … … … … … … … …	Adelaide 5000, SA

---

38   "Ballaarat" is the correct original legal entry spelling.

21 – 22 Aug 2010	Queensland Stamp Show..	Wynnum Plaza 4178, Qld
3 Sep 2010	Royal Adelaide Show..	Goodwood 5034, SA
3 Sep 2010	St Marys Spring Festival...	St Marys 2760, NSW
10 Sep 2010	Orange Blossom Festival..	Castle Hill 2154, NSW
16 Sep 2010	Broken Hill Show..	Broken Hill 2880, NSW
17 Sep 2010	Cabramatta Moon Festival...	Cabramatta 2166, NSW
18 Sep 2010	Royal Melbourne Show...	Ascot Vale 3032, Vic
22 Sep 2010	150th Anniversary of the Swan Hill District Hospital.................	Swan Hill 3585, Vic
24 Sep 2010	UCI Road World Championships...	Geelong 3220, Vic
25 Sep 2010	Perth Royal Show..	Claremont 6010, WA
30 Sep 2010	Wagga Wagga Show...	Wagga Wagga 3232, Vic
2 Oct 2010	Griffith Show...	Griffith 2680, NSW
9 – 10 Oct 2010	Swan River Stamp Show...	Crawley 6009, WA
14 Oct 2010	Royal Geelong Show...	Geelong 3220, Vic
20 Oct 2010	Royal Hobart Show...	Glenorchy 7010, Tas
21 Oct 2010	North Coast National Exhibition...	Lismore 2480, NSW
23 Oct 2010	Salisbury Stamp Fair...	Salisbury 5108, SA
30 Oct 2010	The Gidge Show..	Gidgegannup 6083, WA
12 Nov 2010	Centenary of the Victorian Country Press Association[39]...........	Portland 3305, Vic
19 – 21 Nov 2010	Mandurah 2010 National Exhibition..	Mandurah 6210, WA
9 Dec 2010	Waverley Philatelic Society 400th Meeting................................	The Glen Retail 3150, Vic
10 Dec 2010 •	Centenary of the Arrival of River Class Destroyers[40].................	Williamstown 3016, Vic

2011

   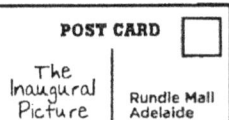 

3 Jan 2011	Centenary of Karoonda..	Karoonda 5307, SA
3 Jan 2011	Centenary of First Flight in Western Australia...........................	Perth 6000, WA
1 Mar 2011 •	Australian International Airshow...	Geelong 3220, Vic
31 Mar – 3 Apr 2011 •	Sydney Stamp Expo..	Sydney 2000, NSW
15 – 18 Apr 2011	Australian Lions International 59th Annual Convention............	Launceston 7250, Tas
7 – 8 May 2011	Mildura Philatelic Society Annual Stamp Fair............................	Mildura 3140, Vic
14 May 2011 •	Inaugural Picture Postcard Exhibition..	Adelaide 5000, SA
30 May 2011	Brisbane Arts Theatre – 75 Years of Theatre.............................	Springhill 4004, Qld
3 – 31 Jul 2011	150th Anniversary of the Discovery of Mount Bruce................	Tom Price 6751, NT
25 Jul 2011 •	150th Anniversary of All Hallows' School...................................	Fortitude Valley 4006, Qld
4 Aug 2011	Cadel Evans – Winner of Tour de France...................................	Barwon Heads 3227, Vic
5 – 7 Aug 2011	National One Frame Competition / 80th Anniversary of Geelong Philatelic Society.............	Geelong 3220, Vic
27 – 28 Aug 2011	Queensland Stampshow...	Wynnum Plaza 4178, Qld
1 Sep – 31 Dec 2011	150 Years of Postal Services – Warracknabeal...........................	Warracknabeal 3393, Vic
30 Sep 2011	175th Anniversary of the Foundation of the District of Port Phillip.................	Melbourne 3000, Vic
8 – 9 Oct 2011	Swan River Stamp Show...	Crawley 3009, WA
8 – 9 Oct 2011	Adelaide Congress..	Adelaide 5000, SA
18 Oct 2011	25th Anniversary of the Philatelic Society of Rockingham and Kwinana Districts.........	Rockingham 6168, WA
29 Oct 2011	Salisbury Stamp Fair...	Salisbury 5108, SA
29 Oct 2011	The Gidge Show..	Gidgegannup 6083, WA
28 Nov 2011	25th Anniversary of Visit of Pope John Paul II to St Leo's Church.................	Altona North 3025, Vic
2 Dec 2011	Centenary of Departure of Australasian Antarctic Expedition..	Hobart 7000, Tas

---

39 Reported in Stamp Bulletin 307 (p23) as a permanent postmark.
40 The vessels were *HMAS Parramatta* and *HMAS Yarra*.

2012

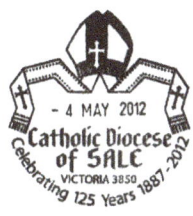    

Date	Event	Location
3 – 14 Jan 2012	15th Australian Scout Venture – Wild Days	Carrick 7291, Tas
16 – 29 Jan 2012	Australian Tennis Open and 100th Men's Championship	Melbourne 3000, Vic
16 Feb – 31 Dec 2012	40th Anniversary of the Blackburn Missionary Stamp Club	Forest Hill 3131, Vic
6 Mar 2012	150 Years of Community Spirit	Buderim 4556, Qld
16 – 18 Mar 2012 •	Canberra Stampshow	Canberra 2600, ACT
2 Apr – 31 Jul 2012	Centenary of Aramac PO	Aramac 4726, Qld
21 Apr 2012	Centenary of the First Powered Flight from Ham Common	Windsor 2756, NSW
4 May – 31 Dec 2012 •	125th Anniversary of the Catholic Diocese of Sale	Sale 3850, Vic
5 – 6 May 2012	Mildura Philatelic Society Annual Stamp Fair	Mildura 3500, Vic
17 – 20 May 2012	Philatelic Society of WA Centennial Exhibition	Claremont 6010, WA
6 Jun – 31 Dec 2012	Transit of Venus	Vermont South 3133, Vic
31 Jul – 31 Dec 2012	Trafalgar Railway Station Centenary	Trafalgar 3824, Vic
25 – 26 Aug 2012 •	Queensland Stampshow	Wynnum Plaza 4778, Qld
7 Sep 2012 •	200th Anniversary of the Birth of Dr Henry Backhaus	Bendigo 3550, Vic
6 – 7 Oct 2012	Congress 2012	Adelaide 5000, SA
20 – 21 Oct 2012	Swan River Stamp Show	Crawley 6009, WA
27 Oct 2012	Salisbury Stamp Fair[41]	Salisbury 5108, SA
29 Oct 2012	125th Anniversary of the Nhill PO	Nhill 3418, Vic
16 – 18 Nov 2012 •	Hobart Stamp Show	Hobart 7000, Tas
6 Dec 2012 – 6 Dec 2013	100th Anniversary of X-Ray Crystallography	University of Adelaide 5005, SA

2013

Date	Event	Location
2 – 12 Jan 2013	23rd Australian Scout Jamboree	Maryborough 4650, Qld
8 Jan 2013	Lunar New Year – Year of the Snake	Haymarket 2000, NSW
8 Jan 2013	Lunar New Year – Year of the Snake	Cabramatta 2166, NSW
8 Jan 2013	Lunar New Year – Year of the Snake	Melbourne 3000, Vic
26 – 29 Apr 2013 •	Australian Lions International 61st Annual Convention	Jamison Centre 2614, ACT
1 Mar – 31 Dec 2013	Centenary of the Royal Australian Naval College Osborne House	North Geelong 3215, Vic
6 – 10 May 2013	National Postcard Week	Adelaide 5000, SA
10 – 15 May 2013 •	Centenary of Commonwealth Postage Stamps	South Perth 6151, WA
17 May 2013 •	Philatelic Society of WA Stamp Mart	South Perth 6151, WA
14 Jun 2013	Official Opening of St Catherine's Church	Melton 3337, Vic
22 Jul 2013	Birth of a Prince[42]	St Marys 2760, NSW
6 Jul 2013	150th Anniversary of Oberon	Oberon 2787, NSW
17 – 18 Aug 2013	Perth Stamp and Coin Show	Crawley 6009, WA
31 Aug – 30 Dec 2013	Centenary of the Catholic Church	Currie 7256, Tas

---

41 The Australian Zoos FDI postmark was incorrectly used for the Salisbury Stamp Fair.
42 Prince George of Cambridge.

Date	Event	Location
1 Sep 2013	Centenary of Home Hill	Home Hill 4806, Qld
1 Sep 2013	150th Anniversary of Logan Village	Kingston 4114, Qld
21 – 23 Sep 2013	Queensland Stampshow	Wynnum Plaza 4178, Qld
3 Oct – 31 Dec 2013	Centenary of Midland PO	Midland 6056, WA
19 Oct 2013	Centenary of Quairading District High School	Quairading 6383, WA
19 – 20 Oct 2013	Swan River Stamp Show	Crawley 6009, WA
13 Nov 2013	Coutts Crossing School Centenary	Coutts Crossing 2460, NSW
30 Dec 2013 – 10 Jan 2014	19th Australian Rover Moot	Watleup 6166, WA

2014

Date	Event	Location
7 Jan 2014	Lunar New Year – Year of the Horse	Haymarket 2000, NSW
7 Jan 2014	Lunar New Year – Year of the Horse	Cabramatta 2166, NSW
7 Jan 2014	Lunar New Year – Year of the Horse	Melbourne 3000, Vic
26 Feb 2014 •	Centenary of Mawson's Return to Adelaide	Adelaide 5000, SA
3 Mar 2014	Centenary of Lock	Lock 5633, SA
5 Mar – Dec 2014 •	50th Anniversary of Caritas Australia	Adelaide 5000, SA
14 – 16 Mar 2014	Canberra Stampshow	Canberra 2600, ACT
15 Mar 2014	Opening of the Margaret Olley Art Centre	Murwillumbah 2014, NSW
24 – 25 May 2014	Mt Gambier Stamp Fair	Mt Gambier 5290, SA
1 Sep 2014 •	100 Years of Scouting	Mt Gambier 5290, SA
21 – 26 Sep 2014 •	Cuboree	Maryborough 4650, Qld
27 – 29 Sep 2014 •	Queensland Stampshow	Wynnum Plaza 4178, Qld
10 – 12 Oct 2014	STAMPEX	Adelaide 5000, SA
31 Oct – 30 Nov 2014	Troops Departing Commemoration	Albany 6330, WA
1 Nov 2014	40th Anniversary of the Salisbury Philatelic Society	Salisbury 5108, SA
1 Nov – 31 Dec 2014	50th Anniversary of the Glenorchy Philatelic Society	Glenorchy 7010, Tas

2015

Date	Event	Location
1 Jan 2015 •	50th Anniversary of Naming of Churchill	Churchill 3842, Vic
2 Feb 2015	The Borella Ride	Darwin 0800, NT
15 Mar 2015	Centenary of Toora	Toora 3962, Vic
16 – 19 Apr 2015 •	Sydney Stamp Expo	Sydney 2000, NSW
1 – 4 May 2015	Australian Lions International 63rd Annual Convention	Newcastle 2300, NSW
1 – 30 Jun 2015	Centenary of Palmwoods-Buderim Railway	Palmwoods 4555, Qld
1 – 30 Jun 2015	Centenary of Palmwoods-Buderim Railway	Buderim 4556, Qld
29 Jun – 31 Dec 2015	150th Anniversary of the Catholic Diocese of Bathurst	Bathurst 2795, NSW
1 Aug – 31 Dec 2015	100 Years of Community Service Toc H	Newcastle 2300, NSW

31 Aug – 6 Sep 2015 •	National Ballooning Championships	Northam 6401, WA
26 – 27 Sep 2015	Queensland Stampshow	Wynnum Plaza 4178, Qld
3 – 4 Oct 2015	Swan River Stamp Show	Crawley 6009, WA
9 Oct 2015 •	Centenary of Navy League – Victoria Division	Melbourne 3000, Vic
10 – 11 Oct 2015	SA Philatelic Council Congress	Adelaide 5000, SA
24 Oct 2015 •	Salisbury Stamp Fair	Salisbury 5108, SA
31 Oct – 1 Nov 2015	NORPEX	Newcastle 2300, NSW
2015	150th Anniversary of Willoughby City Council[43]	Chatswood 2067, NSW

2016

3 Feb 2016	Lunar New Year – Year of the Monkey	Haymarket 2000, NSW
3 Feb 2016	Lunar New Year – Year of the Monkey	Cabramatta 2166, NSW
3 Feb 2016	Lunar New Year – Year of the Monkey	Melbourne 3000, Vic
9 Feb 2016 •	80th Anniversary of CWA Tasmania	North Hobart 7000, Tas
18 – 20 Mar 2016 •	Canberra Stampshow	Canberra 2600, ACT
12 May 2016	Lions International Multiple District 201 64th Convention	Echuca 3564, Vic
16 Jul 2016 •	Howard Coalfest	Howard 4659, Qld
1 Sep 2016	Wangi Centenary	Wangi Wangi 2267, NSW
5 Sep 2016	Replica Duyfken-Hartog Re-enactment Voyage	Mandurah 6210, WA
13 Sep 2016	60th Anniversary of the Sutherland Philatelic Society	Sutherland 2232, NSW
18 – 23 Sep 2016 •	Cuboree	Maryborough 4650, Qld
24 – 25 Sep 2016 •	Queensland Stampshow	Wynnum Plaza 4178, Qld
20 Oct 2016	Swan River Stamp Show	North Perth 6006, WA
3 – 5 Nov 2016	Mandurah Stamp Show	Mandurah 6210, WA

2017

  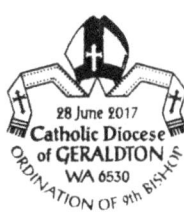  

10 Jan 2017	Lunar New Year – Year of the Rooster	Haymarket 2000, NSW
10 Jan 2017	Lunar New Year – Year of the Rooster	Cabramatta 2166, NSW
10 Jan 2017	Lunar New Year – Year of the Rooster	Melbourne 3000, Vic
15 Feb 2017	Basil Watson Airmail Centenary	Mt Gambier 5290, SA
30 Mar – 2 Apr 2017 •	Melbourne International Stamp Exhibition	Melbourne 3000, Vic
1 May 2017 •	175th Anniversary of St Mary's Primary School	Williamstown 3016, Vic
5 – 7 May 2017	Lions International Multiple District 201 65th Convention	Sandy Bay 7005, Tas
28 Jun 2017 •	Ordination of 9th Roman Catholic Bishop	Geraldton 6530, WA

---

43 Date(s) to be determined.

7 Jul 2017	120th Anniversary of Kalbar PO	Kalbar 4309, Qld
2 Sep 2017	National Ballooning Championships	Northam 6401, WA
15 Sep 2017	150th Anniversary of Cloncurry	Cloncurry 4824, Qld
6 – 8 Oct 2017 •	Stampex '17	Adelaide 5000, SA
14 – 15 Oct 2017	Queensland Stampshow 2017	Darling Heights 4350, Qld
22 Oct 2017	Centenary of the Trans-Australian Railway	Port Augusta 5700, SA
11 – 12 Nov 2017	Brisbane Stamp and Coin Show	Mansfield 4122, Qld
23 Nov 2017 •	Centenary of Adelaide-Gawler Airmail	Gawler 5118, SA
29 Nov 2017	50th Anniversary of WRESAT	Woomera 5720, SA

2018

8 Jan 2018	Lunar New Year – Year of the Dog	Haymarket 2000, NSW
8 Jan 2018	Lunar New Year – Year of the Dog	Cabramatta 2166, NSW
8 Jan 2018	Lunar New Year – Year of the Dog	Melbourne 3000, Vic
25 Jan 2018 •	Queen's Baton Relay	Canberra 2600, ACT
3 Feb 2018	Queen's Baton Relay	Sydney 2000, NSW
9 Feb 2018	Queen's Baton Relay	Hobart 7000, Tas
10 Feb 2018	Queen's Baton Relay	Melbourne 3000, Vic
18 Feb 2018	Queen's Baton Relay	Adelaide 5000, SA
24 Feb 2018	Queen's Baton Relay	Perth 6000, WA
1 Mar 2018	150th Anniversary of Cunnamulla PO	Cunnamulla 4490, Qld
2 Mar 2018	Queen's Baton Relay	Darwin 0800, NT
16 – 18 Mar 2018	Canberra Stampshow	Canberra 2600, ACT
30 Mar 2018	Queen's Baton Relay	Brisbane 4000, Qld
4 – 7 May 2018	Lions International Multiple District 201 66th Convention	Townsville 4810, Qld
25 – 27 May 2018	Newcastle Philatelic Society 100th Anniversary Stamp and Coin Expo	Newcastle 2300, NSW
6 – 8 Jul 2018	Perth Stamp and Coin Show	Perth 6000, WA
16 Jul 2018	90th Anniversary of St Mary's School	Altona 3018, Vic
1 Oct – 30 Nov 2018 •	100 Years of Poland Regaining Independence[44]	Jamison 2614, ACT
20 – 21 Oct 2018	Swan River Stamp Show	North Perth 6006, WA
27 Oct 2018	W.S. Cox Plate	Moonee Ponds 3039, Vic
17 Nov 2018 •	Orange East Stamp and Coin Fair	Orange East 2800, NSW
10 Dec 2018	Home of Australian Philately	Adelaide 5000, SA

2019

8 Jan 2019	Lunar New Year – Year of the Pig	Haymarket 2000, NSW
8 Jan 2019	Lunar New Year – Year of the Pig	Cabramatta 2166, NSW
8 Jan 2019	Lunar New Year – Year of the Pig	Melbourne 3000, Vic

---

44   Dates to be confirmed.

4 May 2019 •	Lions Clubs International 67th Convention	Geelong 3220, Vic
28 Jun 2019	Maryborough Festival	Maryborough 4650, Qld
19 – 20 Jul 2019	Bunbury Stamp, Coin, Banknote and Postcard Show	East Bunbury 6230, WA
4 Aug 2019	First Airmail Flight Centenary Adelaide to Minlaton	Adelaide 5000, SA
4 Aug 2019	First Airmail Flight Centenary Adelaide to Minlaton	Minlaton 5575, SA
24 Aug 2019 •	70 Years of Ukrainian Settlement	Woodville 5011, SA
7 Sep 2019 •	Post Office Centenary, Beelbangera	Beelbangera 2680, NSW
19 Oct 2019	70th Anniversary of Latrobe Valley Philatelic Society	Traralgon 3844, Vic
1 – 3 Nov 2019 •	Perth Stamp and Coin Show	Perth 6000, WA

2020

1 Jan 2020 •	150 Years Heart of Prom Country	Foster 3959, Vic
8 Jan 2020	Lunar New Year – Year of the Rat	Haymarket 2000, NSW
8 Jan 2020 •	Lunar New Year – Year of the Rat	Cabramatta 2166, NSW
8 Jan 2020	Lunar New Year – Year of the Rat	Melbourne 3000, Vic
13 – 15 Mar 2020 •	Canberra Stampshow	Canberra 2601, ACT
30 Sep – 2 Oct 2020	Perth Stamp and Coin Show	Perth 6000, WA
16 Oct 2020 •	Sunraysia Daily Centenary	Mildura 3500, Vic
17 – 18 Oct 2020	Swan River Stamp Show	Cannington 6107, WA
9 Dec 2020 •	Shoalhaven Philatelic Society Centenary	Nowra 2541, NSW

2021

8 Jan 2021	Lunar New Year – Year of the Ox	Haymarket 2000, NSW
8 Jan 2021	Lunar New Year – Year of the Ox	Cabramatta 2166, NSW
8 Jan 2021	Lunar New Year – Year of the Ox	Melbourne 3000, Vic
12 – 14 Mar 2021	Perth Stamp and Coin Show	Perth 6000, WA
21 Mar 2021 •	Philatelic Society of Queensland Centenary	Wynnum West 4178, Qld
29 May 2021	Dandenong Philatelic Society 50th Anniversary	Melbourne 3000, Vic
1 Aug 2021	Ballaarat Engine 150 Years	Busselton 6280, WA
28 Aug – 6 Sep 2021 •	National Ballooning Championships	Northam 6401, WA
9 – 10 Oct 2021 •	Toowoomba One Frame Exhibition	Clifford Gardens 4350, Qld
22 – 24 Oct 2021	Newcastle Stamp and Coin Expo	Newcastle 2300, NSW
25 Oct 2021	150th Anniversary of Establishment of Robertstown	Robertstown 5381, SA
29 – 31 Oct 2021 •	Perth Stamp and Coin Show	Perth 6000, WA
13 – 14 Nov 2021 •	Brisbane Stamp and Coin Show	Mansfield 4122, Qld

2022

Date		Event	Location
6 Jan 2022	•	Lunar New Year – Year of the Tiger	Haymarket 2000, NSW
6 Jan 2022		Lunar New Year – Year of the Tiger	Cabramatta 2166, NSW
6 Jan 2022		Lunar New Year – Year of the Tiger	Melbourne 3000, Vic
1 Mar 2022		150 Years – Maitland – Heart of the Yorke Peninsular	Maitland 5573, SA
27 – 29 May 2022		Newcastle Stamp and Coin Expo	Newcastle 2300, NSW
24 Jun 2022	•	St John the Apostle – Celebrating 50 Years	Holt 2615, ACT
23 – 24 Jul 2022		Melbourne Money Expo	Melbourne 3000, Vic
26 – 28 Aug 2022	•	Antarctic Stamp and Postcard Exhibition	Hobart 7000, TAS
30 Sep – 2 Oct 2022		Perth Stamp and Coin Show	Perth 6000, WA
22 Oct 2022	•	Killarney Co-operative Centenary	Killarney 4373, Qld
22 Oct 2022		W.S. Cox Plate	Moonee Ponds 3039, Vic
2 Nov 2022	•	First Commercial Flight Charleville to Cloncurry Centenary	Charleville 4470, Qld

2023

Date		Event	Location
17 Jan 2023		Lunar New Year – Year of the Rabbit	Haymarket 2000, NSW
17 Jan 2023		Lunar New Year – Year of the Rabbit	Cabramatta 2166, NSW
17 Jan 2023		Lunar New Year – Year of the Rabbit	Melbourne 3000, Vic
19 Mar 2023	•	Urunga Rail Centenary	Urunga 2455, NSW
12 Apr 2023	•	40th Anniversary – Canberra GPO	Canberra 2601, ACT
24 – 26 Mar 2023		Perth Stamp and Coin Show	Perth 6000, WA
8 – 13 May 2023	•	23rd Australian National Ballooning Championships	Northam 6401, WA
27 – 31 May 2023		Rotary International Convention	Melbourne 3000, Vic
10 Jun 2023	•	175th Anniversary of Nanango	Nanango 4615, Qld
1 Jul 2023	•	Post Office Centenary, Kahiba	Kahiba 2290, NSW
1 Jul 2023	•	Maryborough Highland Gathering	Maryborough 3465, Vic

OUTRO

The main aim of this publication is to provide collectors with a detailed guide to the commemorative postmarks from the very first, in 1879, to the end of 1980. The Introduction explains why this arbitrary cut-off point was selected. Still, to reiterate, it is because, from 1981, the output of postmarks by Australia Post far exceeded what most collectors would consider acceptable or desirable. Substantial determination is required for anyone to aim at completion of these later years. Happily, more recently, that voluminous production rate has been reduced somewhat, so even this jaded collector has considered taking up 'new issues' again.

The first edition of Australian Commemorative Postmarks ignored postmarks from 1981. The 1981 to 2023 list presented here provides a starting point for those seeking a guide to modern issues. The notes preceding the post-1980 list indicate that it is subject to further work and may be expanded for a future edition.

Again, I invite readers to advise of errors and omissions by snail-mailing me at the address below.

Peter Bond
Editor

PO Box 964
ROSNY PARK   TAS   7018
Australia

BIBLIOGRAPHY

The editor gratefully acknowledges the following resources:

Australian Commemorative Hand Postmarks 1905-1984	Hans Sorge, 1985
Australian Air Mail Catalogue	Nelson Eustis, 1984, 1997
Australian PictorMarks	Janet S. Eury & Colleen A. Woolley, 2001, 2013
Australian Postmarks & Slogans 1917-1979	D&M Wallen, 1982
Australian Special & Commemorative Handstamps	H. Lealman, c1981
Australian Stamp Bulletin	Australia Post, 1980-1999
Catalogue of Australian Pre-stamped Envelopes	Colin R. Parker, 1981
Illustrated Catalogue of Pre-Stamped Envelopes	J.E. Koch, 1980
Philatelic Bulletin	Australia Post, 1970-1979
"Pictor Marks" Australian Pictorial Postmarks 1970-1984	Clarrie Peck, c1986
Stamp Bulletin	Australia Post, 1999-2023
Unstamped Pictorial Covers (Other Than First Day Covers) of the Australian Post Office	Noel G. Almeida, 1982
Wikipedia.com	

ALSO PUBLISHED BY PETER JAMES BOND

The Postage Stamps of Aden 1937–1968

The Postage Stamps of Aden 1937-1968 is a detailed guide to the stamps of Aden. It includes the issues of the Federation of South Arabia and the protectorate states. Also provided are a brief history of Aden and an introduction to the postal history of Aden. All issues are illustrated in colour and given a retail value. Where practicable, individual stamps are also assigned a value.

ISBN 978-0-6487713-4-0

Available from most online book retailers.

www.ingramcontent.com/pod-product-compliance
Lightning Source LLC
Chambersburg PA
CBHW040728020526
44107CB00085B/2915